Mike Oakley was born and brought up in Dorset before moving to Bristol in the mid 1960s, where he worked in town and country planning until retiring in 1996. In recent years he has developed a keen interest in the history and role of railway stations and halts, particularly in the West Country. As a result, he has built up a substantial library of photographs of Devon's stations and halts, a selection of which are reproduced in this book. He is also the author of 'Discover Dorset' *Railway Stations* (2001), *Somerset Railway Stations* (2002), *Gloucestershire Railway Stations* (2003), *Wiltshire Railway Stations* (2004), and *Bristol's Railway Stations* (2006).

Tipton St Johns.
Looking north from the footbridge in 1958. The main building, which
survives today, is on the up (towards Sidmouth Junction) platform. A train
enters the down platform on which stands a brick shelter.

DEVON
RAILWAY STATIONS
Mike Oakley

THE DOVECOTE PRESS

Okehampton. Staff pose on the down platform before it received
its canopy in the rebuilding of the late 1920s.

First published in 2007 by The Dovecote Press Ltd
Stanbridge, Wimborne, Dorset BH21 4JD

ISBN 978-1-904-34955-6

© Mike Oakley 2007

Mike Oakley has asserted his rights under the Copyright, Designs
and Patent Act 1988 to be identified as author of this work

Printed and bound by KHL Printing, Singapore

All papers used by The Dovecote Press are natural, recyclable products made
from wood grown in sustainable, well-managed forests.

A CIP catalogue record for this book is available
from the British Library

CONTENTS

Barnstaple Junction. An engraving of the arrival of the
first train from Crediton for the ceremonial opening on
12th July 1854. The train has just passed through a
ceremonial arch (right). Another arch can be seen
behind the station.

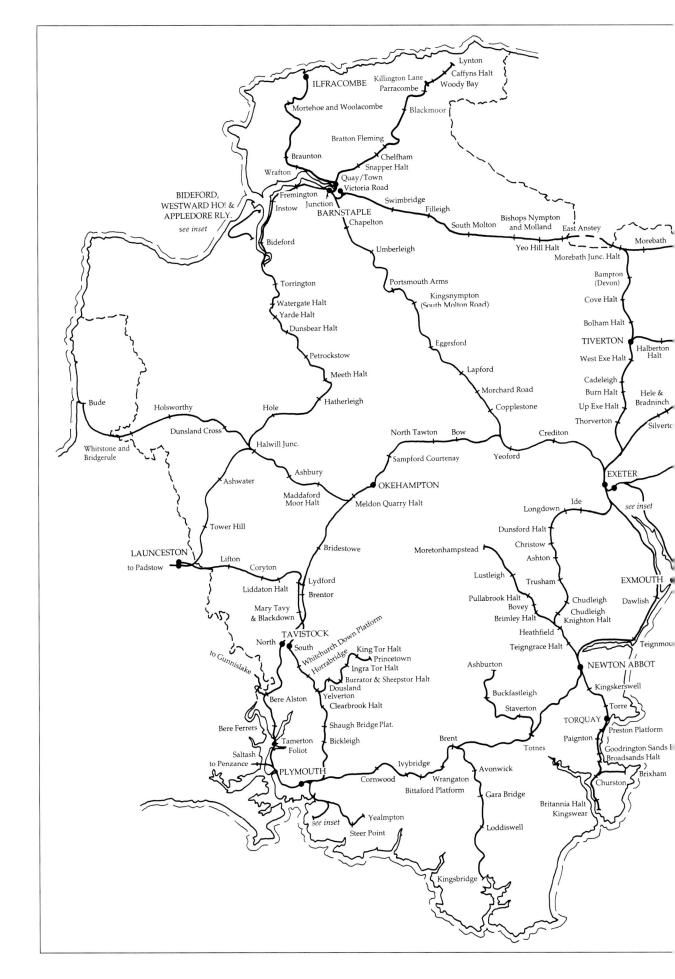

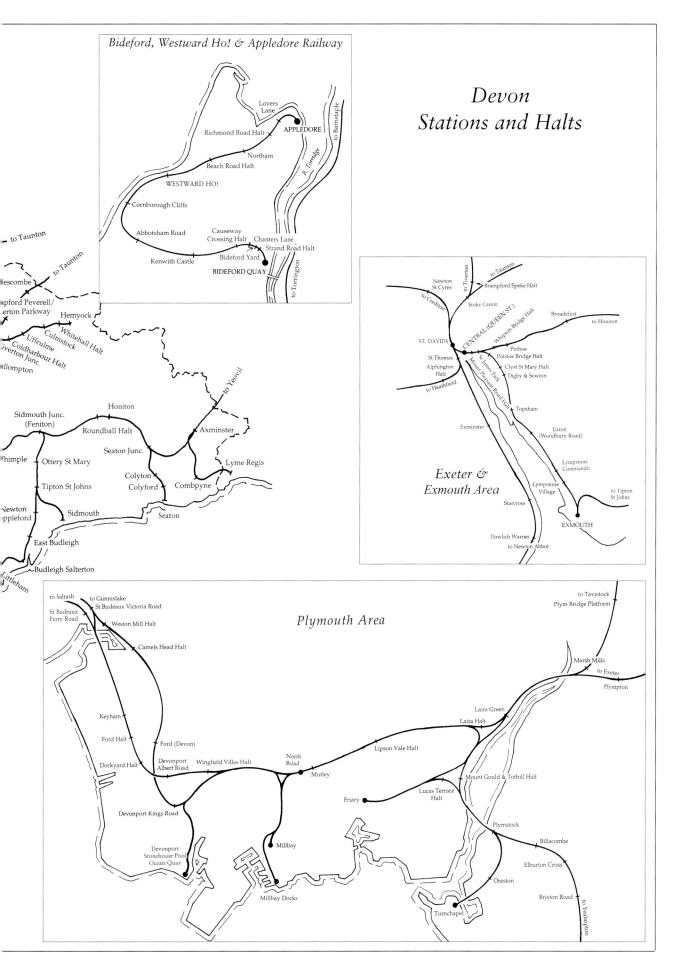

Devon
Stations and Halts

Bideford, Westward Ho! & Appledore Railway

Lovers Lane
Richmond Road Halt
APPLEDORE
Northam
Beach Road Halt
WESTWARD HO!
Cornborough Cliffs
Abbotsham Road
Causeway Crossing Halt
Chanters Lane
Strand Road Halt
Kenwith Castle
Bideford Yard
BIDEFORD QUAY
R. Torridge
to Barnstaple
to Torrington

to Taunton
to Taunton
...escombe
...pford Peverell/...erton Parkway
to Taunton
Hemyock
Whitehall Halt
Culmstock
Uffculme
Coldharbour Halt
...iverton Junc.
...llompton

Sidmouth Junc. (Feniton)
Honiton
Roundball Halt
to Yeovil
Axminster
Seaton Junc.
Lyme Regis
...himple
Ottery St Mary
Colyton
Colyford
Combpyne
Tipton St Johns
Newton ...ppleford
Sidmouth
Seaton
East Budleigh
Budleigh Salterton
Littleham

Exeter & Exmouth Area

Newton St Cyres
to Tiverton
to Taunton
Brampford Speke Halt
to Crediton
Stoke Canon
ST. DAVIDS
CENTRAL (QUEEN ST.)
Whipton Bridge Halt
Broadclyst
to Honiton
St Thomas
Alphington Halt
St James Park
Pinhoe
Polsloe Bridge Halt
Clyst St Mary Halt
Digby & Sowton
Mount Pleasant Road Halt
to Heathfield
Topsham
Exminster
Exton (Woodbury Road)
Lympstone Commando
to Tipton St Johns
Lympstone Village
Starcross
EXMOUTH
Dawlish Warren
to Newton Abbot

Plymouth Area

to Saltash
to Gunnislake
St Budeaux Victoria Road
to Tavistock
Plym Bridge Platform
St Budeaux Ferry Road
Weston Mill Halt
Camels Head Halt
Marsh Mills
to Exeter
Plympton
Keyham
Laira Green
Laira Halt
Ford Halt
Lipson Vale Halt
Ford (Devon)
Dockyard Halt
Devonport Albert Road
Wingfield Villas Halt
North Road
Mutley
Mount Gould & Tothill Halt
Friary
Lucas Terrace Halt
Devonport Kings Road
Plymstock
Billacombe
Devonport Stonehouse Pool Ocean Quay
Millbay
Elburton Cross
Oreston
Brixton Road
to Yealmpton
Millbay Docks
Turnchapel

INTRODUCTION

The arrival of the railway in Devon revolutionised its economic and social life. New commercial possibilities opened up for the larger cities and towns, such as Exeter and Plymouth, but one of the greatest impacts came along the coasts. Railway companies developed services to resorts such as Seaton, Sidmouth, Exmouth and Torquay in the south and Ilfracombe in the north. Further lines ran through the county to the north Cornwall resorts of Bude and Padstow. In parallel a network of lines was opened across the heart of Devon serving the many market towns and villages, bringing new opportunities for the county's agriculture. Although many lines were developed and opened by small local companies, these were usually operated from the outset, or soon absorbed, by the Great Western Railway or the London & South Western Railway, whose rivalry was a feature in the evolution of Devon's railway system.

The development of the rail network and the services carried is well covered in publications (see Further Reading section) but often only passing reference is made to the over 230 stations and halts that, at one time, served Devon's residents and holiday makers. This book seeks to fill this gap, setting out in alphabetical order their history, architectural features and roles. Each station and halt has been researched, mainly from published sources, and sites have been visited during 2006 and 2007 where no recent information has been available regarding their current use. In three instances (Barnstaple, Exeter and Plymouth), a short section is also included where the history of the local network is particularly complicated. Where the term 'Halt' is included in the name it can be assumed that normally no facilities for the handling of freight were ever provided. Where the terms 'up' and 'down' platforms are used they normally refer to the platform used for travel towards or away from London respectively. Where this is not clear, further indication is provided by reference to the nearest station along the line.

The photographs reproduced are drawn from a large collection assembled in recent years. They have been selected primarily to illustrate significant and interesting features of the station or halt; thus only a few include engines or trains as their presence can obscure details of the station or halt buildings!

DEVON'S PASSENGER RAIL NETWORK 1840-2006

Passenger services came to Devon in the early 1840s, when the Bristol & Exeter Railway opened on 1st May 1844 from Beam Bridge, just west of Wellington in Somerset, terminating at the first Exeter St Davids station. Engineered by Isambard Kingdom Brunel to the broad gauge of 7ft ¼ inch, other stations in Devon opening along the line at this time were Tiverton Road (later Junction), Cullompton and Hele.

Extensions of the line through the county soon followed, promoted this time by the South Devon Railway, the broad gauge line opening in 1846 as far as Teignmouth in May and Newton Abbot at the end of December. The section of line between Starcross and Teignmouth, closely following the coast, was difficult and expensive to construct and even today is vulnerable to damage by rough seas. Initially locomotive haulage was used but for a short time, 1847-1848, passengers were propelled by an atmospheric system; this was abandoned in the autumn of 1848 in favour of steam locomotives once more. An atmospheric pumping station building survives today, close to Starcross station, now in use by a fishing and cruising club.

The year 1848 saw the further extension of the South Devon Railway through Totnes to a temporary Plymouth terminus east of the city at Laira Green. This extension again provided constructional and operational challenges including severe inclines (eg Dainton Bank) and the crossing of deep valleys, the latter achieved by a number of spectacular wooden viaducts, later replaced by stone. Also in 1848 broad

South Molton. This is a rare view of a broad gauge train leaving the station towards Barnstaple, probably at the opening in 1873. Note particularly the original signal box, a wooden elevated structure alongside the goods shed.

gauge branches were opened from Tiverton Junction to Tiverton and from Newton Abbot to the initial Torquay station at Torre.

Significant developments followed in the Plymouth area. From Laira Green the main line was extended west and south in 1849 to the first main city station, Millbay. During the late 1850s further extension of the main line continued, the Cornwall Railway opening from Plymouth Millbay over the Royal Albert Bridge via Devonport. The line and the famous Bridge opened on 4th May 1859. In the following month a branch line opened north from the main line east of Plymouth to Tavistock, principal stations at that time were Bickleigh and Horrabridge. Yelverton station was added later in 1885. The line to Tavistock was subsequently extended north and west via Lydford to Launceston in east Cornwall in 1865.

During the 1850s action was also undertaken to bring passenger services to north Devon, in particular linking to Exeter. Following a number of disputes between the Bristol & Exeter Railway and the London & South Western Railway, a broad gauge line opened in May 1851 from the Bristol & Exeter main line at Cowley Bridge, just east of Exeter, to Crediton. The North Devon Railway extended this line through to Barnstaple in the summer of 1854. The Bideford Extension Railway continued the line to Bideford in 1855; this included passenger services on the previously freight only line from Fremington to Barnstaple.

By the mid 19th century all the early passenger lines had good levels of passenger services, particularly on the main line through Exeter to

Plymouth. Indeed, by the mid 1850s many of the original single track lines had been doubled.

Also in the mid 19th century, action was being planned and implemented to develop a second route from London into Devon and the South West on a more southerly alignment rather than via Bristol. In the 1840s railway companies were opening lines in Dorset, Somerset and Wiltshire leading west from London. After the failure of an earlier scheme an Act was passed authorising the construction of a line between Salisbury and Exeter. At Salisbury the new line was planned to connect with a route already carrying passengers to and from London. The whole line from Exeter to Waterloo opened in 1860. The London & South Western Railway (LSWR) provided its own terminus much closer to Exeter city centre than the original Bristol & Exeter Railway, Exeter St Davids. Known for over 70 years as Queen Street, it was renamed Exeter Central following major rebuilding in the 1930s. The connection between the St Davids and Queen Street stations, involving a sharp curve, a short tunnel and a gradient of 1 in 37, opened in 1862. During the early 1860s the LSWR took over the operation of the lines north from Exeter to Barnstaple and Bideford.

The opening of the southern route into Devon opened up possibilities for rail links to a number of resorts in east Devon. The Exeter to Exmouth branch opened in 1861; this was followed by the branch lines south from the LSWR main line to Seaton in 1868 and Sidmouth in 1874. Over 20 years later a line opened from Tipton St Johns on the Sidmouth branch, first to Budleigh Salterton (1897) and then to Exmouth (1903). In the far south-east of Devon the branch line from Axminster to Lyme Regis (Dorset) opened in 1903. Finally in the east of Devon a further development linking to the Bristol & Exeter Railway was the Culm Valley line east from Tiverton Junction to Hemyock, opening in 1876.

South Devon was well served for passengers from early days with the opening of the through line to Plymouth and Torquay (Torre) by 1848. Many towns and villages in this part of the county actively sought links to these early lines. In particular there was pressure for an extension of the Torre branch to serve the rest of the Torbay coast and the mouth of the Dart. In 1857 the Dartmouth & Torbay Railway gained approval for a significant extension, Paignton being reached in 1859 and Churston (then known as Brixham Road) in 1861. A further extension to serve Dartmouth was problematical as the town was sited on the west bank of the Dart. A terminus at Kingswear on the east bank of the Dart was the compromise solution, opening in 1864. A ferry across the river mouth to the rail-less Dartmouth station provided the final link.

Further branch lines from the Exeter to Plymouth main line opened from Newton Abbot to Moretonhampstead in 1866, Totnes to Ashburton in 1872 and Brent to Kingsbridge in 1893. North-east of Plymouth, the Princetown branch opened in 1883 from the Plymouth to Tavistock line opened nearly 25 years earlier. Short branches opened south-east from Plymouth to Turnchapel in 1897 and Yealmpton in 1898. Finally the Teign Valley line, from Heathfield on the Moretonhampstead branch to the Exeter – Plymouth line just south of Exeter, opened in two stages in 1882 and 1903.

An early rail link to North Devon had come in 1854 with the line from Exeter to Barnstaple and in 1855 on to Bideford. Barnstaple gained a further link with the Devon & Somerset Railway from the Taunton to Exeter line at Norton Fitzwarren which opened to Wiveliscombe (Somerset) in 1871 and through to Barnstaple in 1873. The line on to Ilfracombe opened in 1874. Twenty four years later, in 1898, came the narrow gauge Barnstaple to Lynton line. The Taunton to Barnstaple line was subsequently linked via the Exe Valley route to the Taunton to Exeter line at Stoke Canon in two stages in 1884 and 1885. This line passed through Bampton and Tiverton.

Further developments took place in mid Devon. A line opened west from Coleford Junction on the Exeter to Barnstaple line in a number of stages, reaching Okehampton in 1871; an extension opened to Lydford by 1874. Two years later LSWR trains reached the Plymouth area using running rights over the earlier 1865 Lydford – Tavistock – Plymouth line. This arrangement lasted until 1890 when the Plymouth, Devonport & South Western Junction Railway opened from Lydford south-west to the Tamar Valley, entering the west side of Plymouth, via Bere Alston to Devonport, and then on to the new Plymouth Friary station in 1891.

A number of routes serving west Devon were developed in the late 19th century. In 1879 a line opened north-west from between Lydford and Okehampton through Halwill to Holsworthy; it was further extended on to Bude (Cornwall) in 1898. A further new line ran south-west from Halwill to reach Launceston (Cornwall) in 1886, some 21 years after the Cornish town had welcomed its first line from Tavistock.

Bideford had been linked to the rail network way back in 1855 and a southerly extension was opened as far as Torrington in 1872. After a period of 53 years the North Devon & Cornwall Junction Light Railway linked Torrington to Halwill in 1925. Finally the isolated Bideford, Westward Ho! & Appledore Railway opened in two stages to Northam from Bideford in 1901 and on to Appledore in 1908. The term isolated is appropriate as this short line was not connected to the other line in Bideford, being separated by the River Torridge.

Having reached its maximum extent in the mid 1920s there followed, as in all parts of the West Country, a retraction of Devon's passenger rail network, at first slow and then, after the Second World War, rapid. Even before the 1925 Torrington to Halwill services had begun, closure had come in 1917 to the Bideford, Westward Ho! & Appledore Railway, the War Department requisitioning the under used infrastructure and locomotives for wartime uses. With car travel becoming more popular further early casualties were the picturesque Lynton to Barnstaple Railway in the north of the county (1935) and the Yealmpton branch from Plymouth (1930). In the latter case passenger services were resumed on the, by then freight only, line for the period 1941-1947 to serve the many residents who had left the war ravaged city of Plymouth for nearby rural areas. The nearby Turnchapel branch closed in

1951.

Even before the often blamed Beeching Report of 1963 a number of further closures took place. The Princetown branch lost its passenger services in 1956 and two years later, in 1958, came the end of passenger services on the Teign Valley line south-west from Exeter. The Dart Valley line from Totnes to Buckfastleigh and Ashburton closed to passengers in 1958; reopening as far as Buckfastleigh as a private venture in 1969, and today the branch operates as a major tourist attraction as the South Devon Railway. The Moretonhampstead branch closed to passengers in 1959; in this case however, after initial work, plans to reopen faltered, efforts being transferred to the reopening of the Dart Valley line.

Into the 1960s closures continued, accelerating after publication of the Beeching Report. The lines north from Plymouth to Tavistock, Lydford and Launceston closed at the end of 1962, and a year later passenger services ceased on the Kingsbridge branch. East of Exeter, on the Taunton line, all stations except Tiverton Junction had closed by October 1964, passenger services to Tiverton also ceased. Tiverton Junction remained open until 1986 when it was replaced by Tiverton Parkway, sited close to the east end of the North Devon Link Road. The Culm Valley line east from Tiverton Junction closed to passenger services in 1963. Also in 1963 passenger services ceased on the Exe Valley line north from Stoke Canon through Tiverton to Morebath Junction on the Taunton to Barnstaple line, which itself closed to passengers three years later in 1966.

During the 1960s passenger facilities on the southern route into the county were much reduced; the line was singled for much of its length between Axminster and Exeter and a number of intermediate stations closed. However, the two stations of Feniton (Sidmouth Junction) and Pinhoe reopened in 1971 and 1983. Other closures included the branch lines to Lyme Regis (1965), Seaton (1966) and Sidmouth (1967). Also in 1967 the line from Tipt\on St Johns to Exmouth via Budleigh Salterton closed. A large section of the former Seaton branch has seen new life as the route of the Seaton Tramway. The Exmouth branch survived and today a frequent service operates to Exeter with through trains both to Paignton and Barnstaple.

In south Devon the passenger services on the main Exeter to Plymouth line were severely curtailed with all stations being closed between Totnes and Plymouth. In the case of Ivybridge a station reopened on a different site in 1994. Passenger services on the line beyond Paignton to Kingswear were withdrawn in 1973 but almost immediately reinstated with the opening of what is now the private Paignton & Dartmouth Railway. There was however no resumption of passenger services on the short Brixham branch which had closed in 1963.

The 1960s and early 1970s finally saw the almost complete withdrawal of passenger services in west and north Devon. The line from Meldon Junction west of Okehampton to Halwill and the continuing lines on to Holsworthy/Bude and to Launceston/Padstow closed in October 1966. The route from Okehampton west and south to Tavistock and Bere Alston closed from May 1968. The section from Bere Alston into Plymouth via the Tamar Valley survived as far as St Budeaux, together with the spur line to Calstock and Gunnislake in Cornwall. The line on to Devonport closed, services transferring to the Cornwall main line. East of Okehampton passenger services were withdrawn in June 1972 from the line to Coleford Junction and Crediton. This last section is now again in use particularly on summer Sundays for passenger services run by the Dartmoor Railway taking tourists on to Dartmoor. The line from Barnstaple to Bideford and south to Torrington closed to passengers in late 1965. The further southward extension on to Halwill had closed earlier in the year. The final closure in the far north of the county came with the withdrawal of passenger services on the Barnstaple to Ilfracombe line in 1970. Spared from all these closures was the Exeter to Barnstaple line, along which a local passenger service continues to run with many of the stations designated as request stops.

THE STATIONS AND HALTS

ABBOTSHAM ROAD

OPENED: 18th May 1901 (with the opening of the Bideford Quay – Northam section of the Bideford, Westward Ho! & Appledore Railway). (see text)

CLOSED: 28th March 1917.

At a point where an east-west section of the Bideford, Westward Ho! & Appledore Railway crossed the north to south road from Westward Ho! to Abbotsham, the station opened at, or shortly after, the commencement of services on the line between Bideford and Northam in May 1901. Immediately east of the level crossing on a short passing loop, the original name of the site was Mudcott Loop but it was renamed Abbotsham Road when the two short (30 ft) and low (6 inches) platforms came into use. Abbotsham village was about three quarters of a mile south of the station. No shelters were provided but photographs indicate there were nameboards and wooden seats on the platforms. The level crossing was originally protected by gates but these were removed in 1905, the line then being protected by cattle guards. A small signal cabin stood on the up side of the line adjacent to the level crossing. Abbotsham Road was once identified as a possible junction between a main line from Bideford to Clovelly and a branch to Appledore. Kenwith Castle was also identified as another possible junction site. The station closed after 16 years in 1917 (see Bideford Quay text).

ALBERT ROAD HALT

OPENED: 1st October 1906 (on the Lydford – Devonport line originally opened through this site in 1890).

CLOSED: 13th January 1947.

The catalyst for this halt was the commencement of LSWR steam rail motor services between Plymouth Friary and St Budeaux in 1906. Although records indicate that the halt opened on 1st October, the rail

Abbotsham Road. An indistinct view in about 1912 towards Westward Ho!. To the left is the down platform with its wooden seat and nameboard. Note the small signal at the end of the platform.

motor services did not actually commence until 1st November, the rail cars not being available until then. It is thought that the halt had been completed even earlier in 1905.

Albert Road Halt. Looking south in July 1939. A Callington branch train emerges from the Devonport Park Tunnel.

Sited in a deep cutting between Devonport Park Tunnel to the south and Ford Tunnel to the north, two short platforms served passengers, the only shelter being a pagoda style hut on the down (east) platform. After just over 40 years the halt closed in January 1947 and today there is no sign in the cutting which is almost totally overgrown.

Alphington Halt. In the 1960s, looking south towards Christow on the Teign Valley line. Note the slats to avoid slipping on the wooden end ramp.

lasted until closure of the halt in June 1958, when passenger services were withdrawn on the line. Today there is no trace of Alphington Halt.

ALPHINGTON HALT

OPENED: 2nd April 1928 (on the Exeter – Heathfield line originally opened through this site in 1903).
CLOSED: 9th June 1958.

Sited north of the then growing village of Alphington on the southern outskirts of Exeter, the halt opened in April 1928 and was mainly used by steam rail motors, which had been introduced on the Exeter to Heathfield line in 1923. A corrugated iron shelter with a backward sloping roof, similar to that at Dunsford Halt, stood on the wooden 100 ft long platform on the east side of the single line. This timber structure, unlike at many halts in Devon,

APPLEDORE

OPENED: 1st May 1908 (with the opening of the Northam – Appledore section of the Bideford – Westward Ho! & Appledore Railway).
CLOSED: Passengers and Goods – 28th March 1917.

The arrival of the railway in Appledore in May 1908 prompted much celebration. Following the arrival of the first train, guests were entertained at the nearby

Appledore. An end balcony carriage of the Bideford, Westward Ho! & Appledore Railway stands at the low platform. In the distance the engine is about to use the run round loop (right).

Ashburton. A view from the approach road in about 1912 showing the main station building with road side canopy under which stands a horse drawn carriage.

public hall in Irsha Street. Speakers optimistically referred to the 'expected huge influx of visitors bringing wealth to the town'.

The track layout comprised a main running line with a run-round loop on the up (towards Bideford) side. A long dead end siding, branching from the main line at the station throat, ran parallel to the running line and loop. The running line extended beyond the end of the 300 ft long 1 ft high platform, terminating in a single road engine shed. The shed contained a water crane fed from a nearby water tower. A small coaling stage stood beyond the shed. The long siding was primarily used for importing locomotive coal; it was also used for storing the Company's nine goods wagons. A store/lock up with a sliding door on the rail side was next to the siding.

The main station building, very similar to that at Westward Ho!, was a small red brick structure with two chimneys and a hipped slate roof. Contrasting yellow and white bricks gave a decorative effect around the windows and doors and at the corners. Internally there were three rooms: a central waiting room with an office/mess room to the left (viewed from the platform) and the ladies' room/toilets to the right. The gent's toilet was at the far right of the building with an entrance from the platform. Fireplaces were in the rear walls of the waiting room and office but not in the ladies' room. Two separate doors from the platform gave access to the waiting room and office. There were no doors or windows in the rear wall of the building. Lighting at the station was provided by gas. Also on the down platform north of the main building was a small single storey ten lever signal cabin. The stone wall at the rear of

the platform was topped by iron railings supported on brick pillars. Appledore had a station master and limited staff; accommodation for these was provided in two railway cottages at right angles to the station with a gable end facing the track. An unusual feature at Appledore was a footbridge across the site carrying a footpath from Irsha Street to nearby allotments.

Following early closure of the line in 1917, the railway's infrastructure being required for war-time purposes (see Bideford Quay text), the station building was partially demolished leaving the platform and rear wall in situ beside Torridge Road, which was built along the former track bed between Appledore and Richmond Road Halt. Until the mid 1990s the raised platform was still in situ beside the road but, following road improvements, a normal kerb was installed and a grassy bank extended back to a footpath beside the surviving station rear wall. In May 2007 the site of the station was readily identified by a mural on the surviving wall proclaiming 'Appledore Station' in raised lettering. This had been provided by the Appledore Residents Association in 2005 and also gave a short history of the line. Two fireplace alcoves are still detectable in the wall, though now brick filled. The two railway cottages survive in residential use.

ASHBURTON

OPENED: 1st May 1872 (with the opening of the Buckfastleigh, Totnes & South Devon Railway, Totnes – Ashburton).
CLOSED: Passengers – 3rd November 1958.
Goods – 10th September 1962.

Sited south of, and close to, the town centre, Ashburton station opened as the terminus of the branch line from Totnes. The first train was met by local dignitaries who then marched in a procession to the Market Hall, led by the Ashburton Rifle Band. In North Street, and its approaches, fir trees were planted and triumphal arches erected. Flags and banners spanned the streets.

The main building comprised limestone walls, a pitched slate roof, two chimney stacks and a small road side canopy over the entrance. Facing north-west at the end of St Lawrence Lane, it housed a booking office, station master's office, waiting room and toilets for ladies and gents. The entrance to the last, at the north end, was shielded by a screen. Behind the building was an overall train shed

Ashburton. On 3rd March 1956 a branch line train to Totnes hauled by 0-4-2T 1470 stands at the platform. Note the overall wooden roof, large stone goods shed (left) and cattle pens (right).

covering sections of both the up and down platforms; the shed was of a style seen at a number of west country stations and particularly at nearby Moretonhampstead. The shed roof was supported on the up (east) side by five timber posts set into the platform; the west wall of the train shed was the rear of the main building, the roof rafters being held by seven support brackets. The wooden roof was of diagonal timbers, the whole structure being strengthened by a series of struts and tie bars. Louvres close to the roof apex allowed the escape of steam and smoke. In the early days the gap between the timber support posts on the up platform were filled in by planking from roof to platform level; this was later reduced to only the top third thus giving much needed extra light under the train shed. The original oil lamps at the station were later partly replaced by electric lighting but only under the roof.

Both platforms were constructed of earth and hardcore infill, the up platform being faced with bricks and the down platform by stone. Both were edged with round edge stone slabs. Underneath the train shed the platforms were paved but beyond the roof they were surfaced with tar and chippings. The two tracks under the train shed continued through the station to end loading docks behind a long section of iron railings with a gate. In 1903 24,688 passenger tickets were issued; in 1913 there was a similar figure of 23,367 but in 1923 and 1933 there were significant falls to 13,851 and 4,843. Five staff were based at Ashburton prior to the Second World War.

Ashburton was also a busy station for freight movements associated particularly with the local agriculture; the four cattle fairs held per annum generated traffic for up to 90 trucks per fair. Coal imports were also significant for the adjacent gas works, though these closed just prior to the Second World War. The large goods shed with a road side canopy stood on the down side, alongside the open section of the platform. Two square windows overlooked the platform and a large brick lined arch spanned the sidings which ran through the shed to a loading dock. Within was a two ton capacity crane, the only crane in the yard. A lean-to goods office was at the south end replacing earlier sliding doors; the office was originally constructed of wood but was later replaced in brick. Ashburton engine shed, stone built with a slate roof, a water tower fed from a well, and a turntable in use until 1900, were sited south of the station on the up side.

Passenger services ceased in November 1958 and goods facilities followed in September 1962. The closure prompted moves to preserve the branch and re-start services, the Dart Valley Light Railway Company being inaugurated in June 1965, followed by the Dart Valley Railway Association (DVRA) formed on 14th October 1967. The Totnes to Buckfastleigh section of the branch was purchased but the further section north to Ashburton was only leased, as the Ministry of Transport had identified that part for inclusion in a major improvement of the A38 trunk road. Having lain derelict for some years and despite the uncertain future, renovation work took place at Ashburton, including the re-erection of signs. Although special trains, particularly for DVRA members, ran to Ashburton, public services were never resumed and the station was last used on 2nd October 1971, the site being vacated on the 21st.

Ashbury. A view in 1965 looking north-west towards Halwill. The main building is on the down side (left) with an open shelter and small signal box on the up. The goods yard is behind the main building.

These events at least ensured that most of the station buildings were not demolished and today they remain in various uses within the Chuley Road industrial estate. The station building is now Station Garage, the road side entrance canopy has gone but the wooden roof is intact, complete with tie bars. The goods shed, in this case with the canopy, is used as part of the Chuley Road garage complex whilst the former engine shed, now Engine House, was in 2006 used by a dog and cat grooming salon and by 'Devon Holistics'. The nearby Railway Cottages remain but the former Railway Hotel has appropriately been renamed 'the Silent Whistle'.

ASHBURY

OPENED: 20th January 1879 (with the opening of the Meldon Junction – Holsworthy section of the Devon & Cornwall Railway).
CLOSED: Passengers – 3rd October 1966.
Goods – 7th September 1964.

Opening with the line at the beginning of 1879, the station, at some 850 ft above sea level, was named after the small hamlet of Ashbury, some two miles to the north. It also served the village of Northlew, a half mile beyond. Ashbury station was sited on a passing loop between Meldon Junction and Halwill Junction; after 1921 when the Maddaford Moor loop was taken out this was the only crossing place for trains on this section of line. The Ashbury loop was lengthened in 1936 to accommodate long

holiday trains en route to Bude or Padstow.

The main single storey stone building, rendered in cement, was on the down (towards Halwill) side of the line. There was no platform canopy. It incorporated staff accommodation at the west end with a small porch on the road side. The platform had a good display of flowers and shrubs. A small open stone shelter with a slate roof served passengers on the up platform at the north end of which was a small 12 lever signal box. Inter-platform movements were either via a flight of steps and the road overbridge at the east end of the station or via a rail level board crossing at the west end of the platforms. Passenger numbers were generally low at Ashbury. In 1928 6,141 tickets were issued and 6,424 collected; by 1936 the figures had fallen greatly to 2,363 and 3,774.

To the west of, and behind the main building, was a small goods yard. The one long siding ran alongside a goods shed which had small canopies on both the road and rail sides. The yard also included cattle pens and a dock close to the west end of the down platform. Also in the yard were two stores for animal feed. The 1879 wooden signal box (10 levers) stood on the west end of the up platform. Late in its life it was extended at its east end to accommodate a small ticket office. This made it easier for one man to operate the station, which, by that time, had lost virtually all staff including the station master.

Goods facilities ceased in September 1964 but the station remained open for passengers until October 1966 when services were withdrawn on the line. Following closure the station building was converted to a house. When seen in 2005 a small porch had been added on the platform side at the east end. The platforms were still in place, the track bed between now converted to a lawn. The former goods shed was still there.

ASHTON

OPENED: 9th October 1882 (with the opening of the
  Teign Valley Railway, Heathfield – Ashton).
CLOSED: Passengers – 9th June 1958.
  Goods – 1st May 1961.

Sited in the settlement of Lower Ashton in the valley
of the River Teign, Ashton opened in October 1882
as the northern terminus of the Teign Valley Railway
from Heathfield. Beyond this, the line operated
initially as a goods siding to Teign House, later
known as Christow. The terminus status ceased in
1903 with the opening of the Exeter Railway from
Ashton to Exeter via Christow. On the west side of
the line, the station was a low brick built structure
with one chimney but no canopy. Immediately north
of the station was a level crossing, carrying a minor
road towards Higher Ashton.

South of the station was a run round loop with two
sidings, one on the down and one on the up side; the
former ran through Ashton engine shed (56 ft x 17
ft), a brick structure with a gable style slate roof. The
shed function ceased in 1903, thereafter it was used
as a store before demolition in 1960. Also on the
down side was a water tower (removed in 1928), a
coal platform and a small signal box (17 levers), in
use until May 1920. From the goods loop a short
spur led into a loading bay behind the south end of
the station platform. From 1934 to 1939 a camping
coach stood in this spur. Finally a brick building,
with a slate roof and chimney, stood close to the level
crossing on the up (east) side. It contained a porters'
room, coal store and lamp room.

Close to the station on the B3193, three cottages
were built by Lord Exmouth in 1882 for railway
employees. They still bear the name, Exmouth
Cottages. A station master and porter were based at
Ashton until 1929; thereafter two porters in shifts
were in charge. In 1903 6,192 passenger tickets were
issued, figures for 1913, 1923 and 1933 were 6,872,
7,261 and 5,695.

The sidings were lifted in September 1957 and
passenger services ceased in June 1958. Goods
services stopped on 30th September 1960, after
serious flooding washed away an embankment on
the line near Ashton. Formal withdrawal of the
facilities came in May 1961. The former station
building, with extensions, is now in residential use,
Station Cottage, a plaque indicating the previous
station use. Parts of the level crossing and an old
railway notice on an adjacent gate are also remnants
of the railway age at Ashton.

ASHWATER

OPENED: 21st July 1886 (with the opening of the
  Halwill Junction – Launceston (Cornwall) section of
  the North Cornwall Railway).
CLOSED: Passengers – 3rd October 1966.
  Goods – 7th September 1964.

The North Cornwall Railway (NCR), which left the
line to Holsworthy and Bude just to the west of Halwill
Junction, opened first to Launceston in July 1886 and
then to Padstow in March 1899. It became a major
route with holiday trains running through to the
Cornish coast from London, sometimes crossing at the
Ashwater loop. South-west of Halwill the NCR
followed the valley of the River Carey to the hamlet of
Ashmill, where the station opened with the line serving
the village of Ashwater, a half mile to the west.

Ashton. Looking north in 1958. The station building (left) is
now in residential use with a plaque stating that it was once
a station.

Ashwater. In about 1963 a BR delivery van stands in the
station forecourt.

Ashwater. Looking south-west in 1939. The dark stone main building stands on the up (towards Halwill) side of the line.

The impressive main building on the up (west) side of the line was in two sections built of dark stone. A two storey section at the south end incorporating the station master's house had a steeply pitched roof at right angles to the line. A single storey section with an apex roof incorporating the station facilities was at the north end. A feature of the building was the tall arched gable windows. At the south end of the platform was a short dock siding.

On the down side was a small shelter and a signal box, the latter controlling the station loop and access to a small goods yard behind the up side building. The yard included a goods shed with both road and rail side canopies over the loading bays. The passing loop was extended by 88 ft from 18th October 1936 to accommodate the long holiday trains. In 1928 4,733 passenger tickets were issued and 5,149 collected. By 1936 the figures had fallen to 2,728 and 3,014.

The passing loop and signal box were closed as from 7th November 1965. Ashwater had become unstaffed from 6th September. Goods facilities were withdrawn in September 1964 but the station remained open until early October 1966 when passenger services were withdrawn on the line. In 2005 the station building was a dwelling with a coal merchant occupying the site of the former goods yard.

AVONWICK

OPENED: 19th December 1893 (with the opening of the Kingsbridge & South Devon Railway, Brent – Kingsbridge).

CLOSED: Passengers – 16th September 1963
Goods – 11th June 1956.

Sited between Avonwick to the north and Diptford to the south, at a location known as Beneknowle, the station opened with the commencement of services on the Kingsbridge & South Devon Railway. The single platform was on the down (east) side of the

Avonwick. Looking south in about 1954 showing the William Clarke design main station building with its wide platform canopy and the matching goods shed (foreground).

line. On the platform stood the main stone building with three tall chimneys stacks and a wide platform canopy. The architect for Avonwick station and all other stations on the Kingsbridge line was William Clarke, who was also responsible for the similar design of stations on other west country lines (eg Bristol and North Somerset). The Avonwick building incorporated, from north to south, the station master's office, the waiting room and booking office and toilets. Access to the platform, and the building itself, was via a gate at the south end of the building. A small matching stone goods shed stood behind the north end of the platform.

A siding with access controlled by a ground frame left the line north of the station on the down side; it served cattle pens and a number of small stores. In later years it was occupied by a camping coach; the siding was lifted on 5th December 1956. In the Second World War Avonwick had a station mistress and later a porter was in charge. Demotion to halt status and unstaffing came from 11th June 1956, the day goods facilities were withdrawn. In its last days passenger use was very limited; passenger services ceased when the line closed in September 1963. All track was removed in May 1964. The station buildings were renovated and extended for use as a guest house.

AXMINSTER

OPENED: 19th July 1860 (with the opening of the
    Yeovil Junction – Exeter section of the London &
    South Western Railway).
CLOSED: Passengers – remains open for services on the
    London (Waterloo) – Salisbury – Exeter line.
    Goods – 18th April 1966.

In the south-west of the town, Axminster station opened in July 1860 as an important rail head for East Devon on the last section of the London & South Western Railway (LSWR) route from London to Exeter. It became a junction station on 24th August 1903 with the opening of the Axminster & Lyme Regis Light Railway, a branch to the Dorset resort worked by the LSWR from the start and absorbed by it from 1907.

On the down (towards Exeter) platform stood the large and impressive main station building with its tall chimneys, steeply pitched roofs and prominent gables. The building incorporated the station master's house and the principal station facilities. It was, when built and still today, a fine example of a William Tite station building found at many

Axminster. A view in late Victorian times of the impressive Sir William Tite building with its steeply pitched roofs and tall chimneys. It survives today in a good condition but with shortened chimneys.

locations on the LSWR. Also on the down platform, at the north end, was a small building used at various times as a parcels office and staff premises. A large hipped roof waiting shelter with two gabled roofs at right angles to the line served passengers on the up platform. The two platforms varied in length through the station's history. At one time the up was much shorter with the down platform extending north through a road over bridge that crossed the station site. Both platforms were lengthened in the 1930s in order that they could accommodate eight carriage trains. A further extension was added in the late 1980s. A covered footbridge connected the two platforms immediately to the south of the main building and shelter.

The arrival of branch line trains at Axminster from 1903 brought a number of changes to the track layout. The line from Lyme Regis crossed the main line south of the station on a girder bridge and then descended a 1 in 80 gradient to a bay line created behind the south end of the up platform. A run round loop was provided parallel to the bay line. Beside the buffers of this Lyme Regis bay was Axminster water tank on a tall brick base and with a tall brick chimney for the stationery steam engine that pumped water from the nearby River Axe. The tank supplied water cranes on both platforms. Also close to the tower was

Axminster. A general view looking south-west in 1958 showing the main building with its wide platform canopy (left), the hipped roof waiting shelter (right) and the covered footbridge.

a coaling stage for branch line engines.

Axminster's large goods yard was behind the main station building on the down side. The goods shed incorporated a 40 cwt capacity crane. The yard also included a five ton capacity crane, cattle pens and a number of stores owned by local businesses. A particular source of business was that arising from the nearby Axminster carpet factory. A small engine shed, believed to have been constructed of corrugated iron and dating from the 1860s, was sited for some years at the south end of the goods yard. This shed housed a locomotive for banking engines ascending the Honiton bank. However, earthworks related to the construction of a steeply graded link on the down side between the goods yard and the Lyme Regis branch required the demolition of the engine shed. Use of this link was, however, abandoned in 1915. Movements at Axminster were controlled by a 30 lever signal box at the Exeter end of the down platform. The box closed on 5th March 1967.

The Lyme Regis branch closed on 29th March 1965 and goods facilities were withdrawn at Axminster from April 1966. The main line through the station was singled from 11th June 1967; surprisingly no passing loop was retained at Axminster. The up platform was abandoned and the waiting shelter, footbridge and water tower were demolished. In the 1990s there were plans also to demolish the main station building and replace it with a chalet type building. A 1,000 signature petition was submitted to save the original structure and a cheaper plan for renovation was eventually adopted.

Today all trains stop at the former down platform. Axminster serves as a rail head for a wide area of west Dorset and east Devon. There is considerable commuting traffic to and from Exeter and a number of services start and terminate at Axminster. The former up platform remains in a derelict state but the main building, following recent renovation, is in good condition though the tall chimneys were shortened in the 1960s. The ground floor is used for railway business while the upper floors, when seen in mid 2006, were in use for commercial and residential purposes. At the north end of the down platform the former parcels office is used as a station café. The far north end of the platform beyond the railway bridge is now coned off. The goods yard, in 2006, was occupied by several businesses including two building supplies firms.

BAMPTON (DEVON)

OPENED: 1st August 1884 (with the opening of the Tiverton & North Devon Railway, Tiverton – Dulverton).
CLOSED: Passengers and Goods – 7th October 1963.

In a cutting on the west side of the town, the station opened at the beginning of August 1884. South of a road over bridge carrying the Bampton to South Molton road (A361), the station had a passing loop with two platforms. As from June 1911, the station was renamed Bampton (Devon) to avoid confusion with Bampton (Oxon).

The main building on the east (down) side of the line was a stone structure with two parallel wings at right angles to the line. Each wing had an apex slate roof with gabled ends and ornate ridge tiles, topped by a chimney. An enclosed porch between the wings

Bampton (Devon). Looking south in about 1963 showing the main building on the down platform (left), the wooden waiting shelter and the stone goods shed (centre background).

Bampton (Devon). Crowds on the up platform after attendance at the October Pony Fair in about 1910.

on the platform side served as a waiting area; behind this porch was the booking hall and booking office. The northern wing housed the ladies' waiting room and ladies' toilet, the former with a door in the northern elevation. In the south wing was the station master's office at the rear and the gent's toilet in the front, both having doors in the southern elevation. There was no door in the rear of the building on the road side, passengers accessing the platform and building via a wooden gate alongside the southern end. A wooden shelter with a backward sloping roof and small fretted canopy served passengers on the up (west) platform. Attractive gardens were a feature of Bampton station and at one time a greenhouse stood to the south of the main building. Passenger numbers were never particularly high: in the 1930s 60-70 passengers were handled daily, by the 1950s the number had risen to some 200, an unusual trend in Devon.

Freight traffic was of equal, and often of greater, importance at Bampton, activity being concentrated in the fair sized goods yard to the south of the station, principally on the east side of the line. Facilities included a stone goods shed, with a siding running through, and an office annex at the north end. Also in the yard was a loading dock and crane. A 22 lever signal box was sited on the west side of the line, alongside cattle pens.

For many years the despatch of stone, quarried in the area, was a major generator of traffic at Bampton, a network of tramways leading into the yard for transfer of stone to rail wagons. By 1950 this traffic ceased, with the local quarries being worked out or transport of stone lost to road

haulage. Another generator of traffic of both passengers and freight was the annual October Pony Fair. Much of this traffic was also lost to road transport in 1947. Coal/coke and general merchandise also brought business to Bampton goods yard, which closed in October 1963, on the same day that passenger services ceased.

Following closure, all the station buildings were demolished and the cutting was largely filled. The former station site is now used as a car park and children's playground, whilst the former goods yard is now occupied by industrial units. The adjoining Station Road is a reminder of Bampton's railway era.

BARNSTAPLE

The following sets out a résumé of the history of Barnstaple's railway network. This should be read in conjunction with the diagram on the following page.

The North Devon Railway opened from Crediton to Barnstaple (later Junction) station in August 1854, thus completing the through route from Exeter. Full passenger services on to Bideford commenced in November 1855 although it is possible that they started as far as Fremington in August 1854 (see Fremington text). The line on to Torrington opened in July 1872. This first Barnstaple station was on the west bank of the River Taw estuary. Passenger services began across a new railway bridge over the Taw to the river side Barnstaple Quay in July 1874 with the commencement of services on the Ilfracombe line. This station (from 1866 known as Barnstaple Town) closed in May 1898 being replaced by a new Town station some 250 yards to the north-west. This new structure was built to also

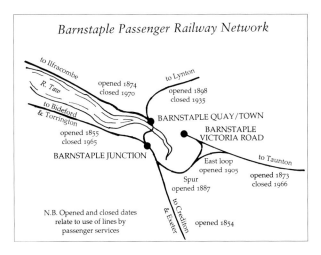

Barnstaple Passenger Railway Network

to Ilfracombe
R. Taw
opened 1874
closed 1970
to Lynton
opened 1898
closed 1935
to Bideford
& Torrington
opened 1855
closed 1965
BARNSTAPLE QUAY/TOWN
BARNSTAPLE
VICTORIA ROAD
BARNSTAPLE JUNCTION
East loop
opened 1905
to Taunton
Spur
opened 1887
opened 1873
closed 1966
N.B. Opened and closed dates
relate to use of lines by
passenger services
to Crediton
& Exeter
opened 1854

accommodate the narrow gauge Barnstaple to Lynton trains.

Another line serving Barnstaple came with the Devon & Somerset Railway whose second section from Wiveliscombe to Barnstaple Victoria Road station opened in November 1873, completing a through route from Taunton. Initially isolated from earlier rail lines at Barnstaple, a spur was opened linking to the North Devon Railway in 1887. The alignment of the spur however, required trains on the Taunton line to other north Devon destinations beyond Barnstaple to reverse at Victoria Road station. This was eliminated from 1905 with the opening of the East loop allowing trains to bypass Victoria Road station, a factor in its relatively early closure to passengers in 1960.

All the above lines in the Barnstaple area apart from the 1854 route to Crediton and Exeter are now closed, that to Lynton very early in 1935, to Bideford and Torrington in 1965, to Taunton in 1966 and finally to Ilfracombe in 1970.

BARNSTAPLE JUNCTION

OPENED: 1st August 1854 (with the opening of the North Devon Railway, Crediton – Barnstaple).

CLOSED: Passengers – remains open for services on the Exmouth – Exeter – Barnstaple lines).
Goods – 5th March 1970.

Sited on the western edge of the town on the west side of the River Taw estuary, the station, known then simply as Barnstaple, opened to the public at the beginning of August 1854 as the terminus of the North Devon Railway from Crediton. For the previous six years freight trains had been running to the west, from Barnstaple to Fremington. The

terminus status only lasted until November 1855, when passenger services began through Fremington to Bideford. (Some sources suggest that a limited passenger service was run on the freight line to Fremington from August 1854 – see Fremington text.) From 20th July 1874 it became a junction station with the opening of the Barnstaple & Ilfracombe Railway via a new bridge over the Taw. At that point the suffix 'Junction' was added to avoid confusion with the new Barnstaple Quay, later Town, station, which opened on the Ilfracombe line, on the north side of the estuary.

Barnstaple was ceremonially opened on 12th July 1854, over a fortnight before public services began. Following the arrival of the first train at 11.30 hrs, a procession, led by the North Devon Mounted Rifles marched over the bridge and through decorated streets to a dinner held at the new Corn Market for some 760 people (*see illustration on the Contents page*).

Until 1874, when Barnstaple became a junction, there was only one platform on the up (north-east) side; on this platform stood a fine stone building in the North Devon Railway style. A single storey section incorporated the main facilities, including booking, waiting and toilet facilities, and also the station master's office. At the west end accommodation for the station master was provided in a two storey house. A wide canopy, with an arc shaped roof, and a number of other extensions were later added, this reflecting the developing importance of Barnstaple in the north Devon rail network. In 1874 a down platform was constructed, there then being three tracks, one alongside each platform and a central track. Further developments came in 1924 when, following some excavation of the hillside, a down loop track was added behind the down platform, which became an island with two faces. On this island was a building with waiting and refreshment facilities and a horizontal canopy protecting passengers on both sides. A covered footbridge, originally erected in 1878 to link the up and down platforms, was extended on to steps in the hillside which, via a path, gave direct access to the station for residents south of the station.

In 1928 64,346 passenger tickets were issued and 114,417 collected; by 1936 the number issued had halved to 32,070 and the number collected had fallen to 76,865. A census held on 7th May 1963 showed that 618 passengers joined and left trains at Barnstaple Junction on that day. Surveys held during a 1976 winter week and a 1977 summer week showed that, in relation to trains on the Exeter line,

1,738 and 4,903 passengers used the station in those two weeks.

In addition to being a busy passenger station, Barnstaple Junction also had extensive goods facilities, the yard being behind and to the north-east of the station, with sidings running north towards the river and Barnstaple bridge. The main wooden goods shed, with a siding running through, was behind the south-east end of the up platform. The yard had many different uses through the years including numerous cattle pens, a slaughter house at the far end, a large timber works complex and a number of facilities for individual local traders. The yard contained a 7.5 ton capacity crane. From 1948 only complete wagon loads were handled at Barnstaple Junction, all parcels traffic being concentrated at Barnstaple Victoria Road.

At the south-east end of the yard was Barnstaple locomotive shed, the largest such facility in north Devon; a two track wooden structure, it remained largely unchanged throughout its life until closure on 6th September 1964. The shed was particularly busy after closure of the GWR depot at Barnstaple Victoria Road in 1952 and the shed at Torrington in 1959. Nearby was a 50 ft turntable which had replaced a 35 ft version in the 1890s. Two signal boxes controlled movements at Barnstaple Junction over the years. In the V between the Bideford and Ilfracombe lines north-west of the station, stood the West (from 2nd October 1949 B) box. The 1874 tall box was replaced in 1924 by a shorter 40 lever box which finally closed on 21st May 1971 in conjunction with extensive track rationalisation. The

Barnstaple Junction. A view south in about 1910 showing the station building, the covered footbridge and the goods yard behind the building.

Barnstaple Junction. Looking north-west in 1945. The hill side (left) had been cut back in 1924 to allow an extra loop to be inserted, turning the down platform into an island (left centre). The wooden goods shed stands behind the south-east end of the up platform.

East (from 2nd October 1949 A) box (also 40 levers), close to the goods yard entrance, remained in use until 1st November 1987. Following closure, it was moved to Ropley on the Mid Hants Railway.

From the mid 1960s activities began to decline, the first withdrawal being passenger services to Bideford and Torrington in October 1965. Services continued to Ilfracombe until October 1970. In March that year general goods services had been withdrawn, though wagon loads continued to be handled until 1987. In April/May 1971 extensive track rationalisation was undertaken including the singling of the Exeter line south-east towards Umberleigh.

Barnstaple Quay. A view looking south-east at the original 1874 station with a large horizontal canopy. To the right is the River Taw railway bridge.

The former up platform became the main terminal point and the far side of the island platform (no 3) was taken out of use. The footbridge was demolished in 1977. The building on the former island was demolished in about 1980. In August 1990 a new run round loop was laid south of the station, the former down track alongside the island was taken up and the platform closed. The sole remaining track alongside the remaining former up platform was cut short at the north end. Also in 1990 the remaining sidings in the goods yard were lifted. In contrast to all reductions however, a new travel centre was opened on the surviving platform on 11th November 1981. In the mid 1990s the station's name reverted to its original Barnstaple.

Today Barnstaple is the terminus for trains on the lines from Exeter, services often starting from Exmouth. The trains are well used by students travelling to and from North Devon College. The station building, with the canopy still in place, is primarily in use for railway related functions including an information centre, the booking office and toilets. There is also an office, open in the summer for cycle hire for cyclists on the Tarka Trail which uses much of the trackbed west of Barnstaple to Bideford and Torrington. The former island platform is in a derelict state, though the former large shrub and flower containers are still there.

A large part of the former goods yard is occupied by a retail park and a large B&Q store. The goods shed was demolished in the mid 1990s in the course of this redevelopment. Beyond the north end of the station site the scene in early 2007 was dominated by construction work associated with the Barnstaple western by-pass.

BARNSTAPLE QUAY/TOWN

FIRST STATION
OPENED: 20th July 1874 (with the opening of the Barnstaple – Ilfracombe Railway).
CLOSED: 16th May 1898 (replaced by second station 250 yards to the north-west).

SECOND STATION
OPENED: 16th May 1898 (replacing the first station at the opening of the Lynton & Barnstaple Railway)
CLOSED: Passenger – 5th October 1970.
  Goods – No facilities provided.

With the opening of the Barnstaple to Ilfracombe line in July 1874 and the commencement of services across the River Taw rail bridge, a new station was opened close to the north end of the bridge. A stone building with a large horizontal canopy, the new station, initially known as Barnstaple Quay, was much more convenient for the majority of Barnstaple residents and businesses than the Barnstaple Junction station, south of the river. From July 1886 the name was changed to Barnstaple Town. A decade later construction of the narrow gauge Lynton & Barnstaple Railway (L&BR) was under way. The site of the 1874 station was too restricted for adaptation as a junction and it was decided to construct a second Barnstaple Town station, some 250 yards further north-west along the quay. This opened on 16th May 1898 on the day services commenced on the Lynton & Barnstaple line. The new site was provided by Barnstaple Corporation in exchange for the site of the old, on which a bus station was opened in 1922. The second station cost some £6,000 with £2,000 being contributed by the L&BR.

The principal feature of the second station was a 500 ft long platform, parallel to the quay alongside the north-east side of the single track Ifracombe line. There was insufficient room for a loop line. The north-east face of the platform was used by the narrow gauge trains of the L&BR. There were plans for a second platform for L&BR trains but this was never built. The main station building, with a frontage of 114 ft and facing north-east, was at the south-east end of the platform. Constructed of stone and gas lit, it incorporated the main station facilities including the booking office, waiting room and station master's office. A long glazed canopy, supported by cast iron pillars, extended 150 ft north-west along the platform, away from the building, providing shelter for passengers on both the Ilfracombe and Lynton trains. After closure of the L&BR in 1935, the long canopy was replaced by a much shorter Southern Railway style version with a fretted valence. The narrow gauge L&BR track was lifted at the station in 1937. In 1928 79,496 passenger tickets were issued and 149,034 collected at Barnstaple Town. By 1936 the total had reduced dramatically to 32,745 and 74,269. By the latter date there were no services on the Lynton line.

There were no freight facilities at Barnstaple Town, these being provided for the town at both Barnstaple Junction and Barnstaple Victoria Road stations. To the north-west of the Town station there were limited 'exchange' sidings including a timber platform between the standard and narrow gauge tracks, where transfer of goods could take place between the two systems. These sidings were lifted in April 1948. The main London & South Western Railway brick signal box stood south-east of the station on the up side; this box contained a wheel controlling the gates of a level crossing which carried a road to Castle Quay. There was also, before 1935, a L&BR box to the north-west of the station, in the V between the Ilfracombe and Lynton lines.

Passenger services ceased at Barnstaple Town with the withdrawal of services on the Ilfracombe line from October 1970. Many Barnstaple residents and businesses felt that it should have been retained, being much closer to the town centre than the surviving Barnstaple Junction station (the GWR Victoria Road station had closed to passengers ten years earlier in 1960). The retention of the Town station would have meant, however, the continued use of the Taw railway bridge, with its maintenance costs.

The main building and the former main signal box survive today. For some years the building was derelict and then served as a restaurant, with the area beneath the retained canopy filled in, giving extra accommodation. Today the building is a special

Barnstaple Town. Looking south-east in about 1910. A mixed Lynton and Barnstaple train hauled by L&BR 2-6-2T stands in the bay platform. Note the original long glazed canopy.

school (Pathfield School) with the canopy still surviving. The old signal box was leased for some years to the Lynton & Barnstaple Railway Association for a museum. It has now been absorbed into the adjoining school with the museum moved to Woody Bay. Nearby a plaque on the adjoining housing to the west (Castle Quay Court) records the previous existence of the L&BR terminus. The former Ilfracombe trackbed is now a pleasant river side walk and the former trackbed of the L&BR is now covered by part of the Civic Centre car park. The site of the first 1874 station is now an open area beside the quay, alongside The Strand.

Barnstaple Town. A view in 1969 looking north-west under the post 1935 canopy which is today incorporated within the Pathfield School that occupies the station building.

BARNSTAPLE VICTORIA ROAD

OPENED: 1st November 1873 (with the opening of the Wiveliscombe – Barnstaple section of the Devon & Somerset Railway).

CLOSED: Passengers – 13th June 1960.
Goods – 5th March 1970.

Victoria Road station opened in November 1873 as the terminus of the second section of the broad gauge Devon & Somerset Railway from Wiveliscombe (Somerset). The first section from Norton Junction, west of Taunton to Wiveliscombe, had opened two years earlier. A spur line to Barnstaple Junction station opened on 1st June 1887 (see diagram), thus permitting through workings from the Taunton line to other destinations in north Devon such as Ilfracombe. Through working at this stage involved reversal of trains at Victoria Road. From 1873 to 1887 links between the Victoria Road and Junction stations at Barnstaple had been provided by a horse bus service. A further development came from 1st July 1905 when the East loop opened allowing through workings from the Taunton line to Barnstaple Junction eliminating Victoria Road. The suffix Victoria Road only came late in the station's life from 26th September 1949.

The single long platform was on the north side of the line, the southern face principally handling arrivals and a bay line behind the east end of the platform handled departures. The long wooden single storey building, sited behind the west end of the platform, contained all the main station facilities. In 1876 this had replaced an early temporary structure. A horizontal canopy attached to the platform face of the building provided shelter for passengers; a long arc roof canopy, east of the building, was a later addition, sheltering passengers both on the main and bay platforms. A slim canopy on the road side gave limited shelter over the main station entrance at the east end of the building. In 1903 32,987 passenger tickets were issued at Victoria Road; by 1933 the figure had more than halved to 15,715. Over this period the number of staff remained constant, however, with 35 based there in 1903 and 37 in 1933, the total hardly varying over the thirty years.

Opposite the platform was a run-round loop and a number of sidings in the goods yard. These sidings served an end loading dock and cattle pens at the west end of the station site. The yard contained a six ton capacity crane. On the southern side of the yard was the large stone built goods shed, through which ran a siding. A long canopy ran along the northern side of the goods shed, sheltering deliveries by road vehicles. Barnstaple Victoria Road was, for many years, particularly important for handling goods traffic. In 1948 all parcels traffic in Barnstaple was concentrated here and the station remained open for freight traffic for nearly ten years after passenger services ceased. At the eastern end of the goods yard was a two road timber engine shed. To the south of the shed was a 42 ft turntable, originally transferred from Wiveliscombe, when this ceased to be a terminus in 1873. Movements, both at the station itself and in the yard, were controlled from the brick and wood signal box sited beyond the east end of the platform on the up side.

Passenger services ceased at Victoria Road in January 1960, services from Taunton being transferred to Barnstaple Junction until this line closed in October 1966. For a while the former station building was used as a store with the long platform canopy enclosed. The former station site was subsequently partly used in the construction of

Barnstaple Victoria Road. A view east from the buffer stops in the 1960s showing the single platform, wooden station building and a glimpse of the substantial goods shed (extreme right), the last surviving today as a church.

the new Eastern Avenue. The site of the station building itself is now within the large Western Power Company depot. The goods yard is now mostly covered by the appropriately named Great Western Industrial Estate, with access from Old Station Road. The former goods shed was converted into the Grosvenor Church and continues in this use today.

BEACH ROAD HALT

OPENED: 18th May 1901 (with the opening of the Bideford Quay – Northam section of the Bideford, Westward Ho! & Appledore Railway).
CLOSED: 28th March 1917.

The halt was a request stop adjacent to a level crossing carrying Beach Road in Westward Ho! north-south across the line between Westward Ho! station and Northam. It was aimed to serve residents in the Beach Road and Eastbourne Terrace area. The crossing gates were removed in 1905. Closure came after only 16 years (see Bideford Quay text). There is no record of any facilities at the halt, passengers accessing the trains by steps on the carriages.

BERE ALSTON

OPENED: 1st June 1890 (with the opening of the Plymouth, Devonport & South Western Junction Railway, Lydford – Devonport).
CLOSED: Passengers – remains open for services on the Plymouth – Gunnislake (Cornwall) branch.
Goods – 28th February 1966.

To the north of the village, Bere Alston opened in June 1890 with the start of services on the Lydford to Devonport line. Sited on a curve, as the area's topography did not permit any significant straight stretch of line, Bere Alston became a junction station on 2nd March 1908 with the opening of the Callington branch, which veered north-west from the main line immediately west of the station.

The main building, including accommodation for the station master, was sited on the down side (see Footnote under St Budeaux Victoria Road text). An apex style canopy covered the central section of the platform and a toilet block, originally with a large roof ventilator, stood at the south end of the building. The up platform became an island after 1908, Callington branch trains normally using the northern outer face. A waiting shelter with an unusual open canopy section at the east end stood on

Bere Alston. An early view of the station through the initial wooden footbridge. The platform on the left is not yet an island.

the island platform. A footbridge connected the two platforms at the Plymouth end; originally constructed of wood, it was later replaced by a metal and stone structure.

Bere Alston goods yard, with a goods shed, was sited beyond the branch line track on the northern up side of the station. Large quantities of fruit and flowers were once despatched from the yard, in particular strawberries grown in the Tamar Valley. An average of 250 tons of strawberries were despatched per anum before the Second World War. Goods facilities were withdrawn at the end of February 1966.

The Callington branch was truncated at Gunnislake in 1966. Two years later, on 6th May 1968, the main line beyond Bere Alston to Tavistock and Lydford closed, the track terminating at buffers approximately 100 yds past the station. The continuation of this line south to St Budeaux and Devonport was singled on 7th September 1970. The 30 lever signal box at the east end of the island platform also closed on that date. All tracks at Bere Alston were taken out of use apart from the former down side track; a new junction was laid from the now Gunnislake branch to this down track. Thus from 1970, trains on the Plymouth/Gunnislake service reversed at Bere Alston. There are currently aspirations for reopening the line to Tavistock

Today the station building with canopy remains in use as a private house. The former island platform shelter also still stands, appearing to be derelict when seen in late 2006. Also still standing is the former goods shed, within an area on the far side of the island platform now used for the storage of old cars. The old signal box, now derelict, also remains but the footbridge has gone. Nearby, to the north-west, the former railway cottages continue in residential use.

BERE FERRERS

OPENED: 1st June 1890 (with the opening of the
   Plymouth, Devonport & South Western Junction
   Railway Lydford – Devonport).
CLOSED: Passengers – remains open for services on the
   Plymouth – Gunnislake (Cornwall) branch.
   Goods – 8th October 1962.

Sited towards the south end of a long peninsula
between the Rivers Tamar and Tavy, the village of
Bere Ferrers was (and is still today) ill served by road
links to the Plymouth area. The rail service, which
commenced in June 1890 with the opening of the
line between Lydford and Devonport, was well
placed to serve the villagers and other residents of
the peninsula, the rail route to Plymouth being some
8 miles compared to the road route of 23 miles. No
doubt reflecting the potential for high traffic levels
the station, known as Beer Ferris until the 18th
November 1897, was an impressive structure serving
a relatively large number of passengers: in 1928
16,259 passenger tickets were issued and 36,130
collected, in 1936 the returns remained high with
15,812 issued and 34,394 collected.

The principal building, with a large apex canopy
and incorporating the station master's
accommodation, was on the down (towards
Plymouth) side (see Footnote under St Budeaux
Victoria Road text). A small stone shelter stood on
the up platform. An open metal footbridge
connected the platforms at the south end. A goods
yard with a small goods shed was sited south of the
station on the down side with a siding terminating

Bere Ferrers. A view south from the road bridge in 1962
showing the main building (left), stone shelter(right) and
open footbridge. Note the small decorative flower beds
edged with white stones.

behind the main building. The yard closed in
October 1962 and the tracks lifted in 1965. The
original signal box at the south end of the down
platform closed on 27th October 1968.

Bere Ferrers was unfortunately the scene of a bad
accident on 24th September 1917. A contingent of
New Zealand troops on a train from Plymouth to
Bulford Camp in Wiltshire was told that a meal
would be provided at the first stop. When the train
was halted by signals at the up platform, a number
of the hungry troops jumped from the train on the
non-platform side and ten were killed by a fast
Exeter to Plymouth train.

Only the former down platform is now used on the
single track Tamar Valley line to Gunnislake, a small
concrete shelter providing cover. The station building
and yard are now privately owned as a residence.
North of the building the former Pinhoe signal box
was re-erected in the early 1990s bearing the original
spelling Beer Ferris. Track has been relaid in the
former yard and a number of carriages and engines
stand there including an ex LMS sleeper. The former
goods shed has been converted into a house.

BICKLEIGH

OPENED: Passengers – 22nd June 1859 (with the
   opening of the South Devon & Tavistock Railway,
   Tavistock Junction – Tavistock).
   Goods – 1st February 1860.
CLOSED: Passengers and Goods 31st December 1962.

A classic Devon country station, Bickleigh was sited
half a mile east of the village at a passing place on the
line between Tavistock and Plymouth. The station
opened for passenger services with the
commencement of services on the line. Goods
facilities became available about seven months later.

There were two platforms, the down (towards
Tavistock) on the main running line and the up on
the loop. The down platform, constructed of earth
infill faced with stone, had a surface of blue
Staffordshire brick with edges of concrete slabs. The
principal station building, of South Devon Railway
design, on this platform, was built of stone covered
with concrete rendering. The apex slate roof with
gable ends and topped by a single chimney stack was
parallel to the line. On the platform side was a single
door, three windows and a canopy which gave
shelter over two platform seats. On the road side of
the building was a square flat roof extension with a
door and three windows. This building incorporated

Bickleigh. A view north in about 1906 showing the main building on the down (towards Tavistock) platform, the original signal box and the water tower in the distance.

the main station waiting room, booking office and toilets. The southern end of this down platform was backed by a wooden fence while the northern end had shrubs and flower beds. Lighting was by gas lamps on cast iron posts.

The up platform was of similar basic construction, with a chipping surface. A rail level board crossing linked the two platforms at the southern end. At the centre of this up platform was a stone built open building with a slate roof, its doorway and window frames lined with granite. For its whole length the platform was backed by black spiked iron railings. The two different designs of the buildings suggest that the up side shelter was built at a slightly later date in the 1860s. In 1903 10,331 passenger tickets were issued at Bickleigh, the figure rose to 12,994 in 1913 but then fell to 12,304 in 1923 and 9,685 in 1933.

A water tower stood at the north end of the down platform, behind which a siding ran to a loading dock and nearby cattle pens. There were three signal boxes over the years. A two storey hipped roof brick box was the first, standing at the south end of the down platform. At an early date this was replaced by a GWR box at the south end of the up side, the original box becoming a goods shed, though changing very little in appearance. The second box was demolished in 1913 and replaced by a third, this time a 23 lever box on the south end of the up platform. This replacement was needed to allow a southern extension of the loop.

Running parallel to the line to the west was the road from Bickleigh to Shaugh Prior and Plympton. From this, a short spur formed the station entrance and access also to the station master's house, which remains in residential use. Both passenger and goods services ceased at the end of December 1962. The station buildings were subsequently demolished.

BIDEFORD

FIRST STATION
OPENED: 2nd November 1855 (with the opening of the Bideford Extension Railway, Fremington – Bideford).
CLOSED: 9th June 1872.

SECOND STATION
OPENED: 10th June 1872 (on the Torrington Extension Railway, Bideford – Torrington).
CLOSED: Passengers – 4th October 1965.
Goods – 6th September 1965 (principally at site of first station).

Contemporary accounts suggest that, in addition to local residents, some 4,000 visitors came to Bideford to mark the ceremonial opening of the broad gauge Bideford Extension Railway on 29th October 1855. Church bells pealed, cannons boomed and the town was decorated with flags and banners. The Mayor of Bideford hosted a dinner at the Guildhall and a ball followed. Public services commenced three days later.

The first station, known as Bideford Cross Parks, was sited on the east bank of the River Torridge in an area of the town appropriately known as East-the-Water. About a half mile north of the road bridge across the river, it was inconvenient for the main town on the other side of the Torridge. The siting was dictated by the need for proximity to Bideford Quay which would generate freight traffic for the railway. A turnpike road connected the station to the east end of the long Bideford bridge. Descriptions indicate that not only was the station poor and inadequate, reflecting the financial problems of the railway company, but it was also incomplete when services started. Such a state of affairs seemed to have caused little concern as the businesses and residents of the town were desperate for Bideford to join the Devon railway network. It was built as a terminus with one platform, one waiting room, a goods shed, a turntable and a small engine shed. Standard gauge passenger trains using a third rail on the original broad gauge line arrived at Bideford from 2nd March 1863. Broad gauge goods and local passenger trains continued to use the station until its closure.

There were no regrets in the town when the Cross Parks station closed on 9th June 1872 with the opening, on the following day, of the second station, half a mile to the south. Following its closure the Cross Parks site was developed as Bideford's main goods yard and continued to serve the town in this

Bideford. Looking north through the second station in 1939. Houses in Springfield Terrace rise above the north end of the down platform on which stands the main building. Note the evidence of canopy extensions on both platforms.

role until its closure in September 1965. However the river side wharf had been closed much earlier by the Southern Railway, operations for the area being concentrated at Fremington. In the 1950s 13 men were employed at the yard. After closure the tracks remained in place for some years but in the 1980s the whole site was redeveloped for housing, now Ethelwynne Brown Close.

The impetus for the construction of the second station, close to the east end of Bideford bridge, was the development of the standard gauge Torrington Extension Railway which opened from Cross Parks to the new station on 10th June 1872 and on to Torrington some five weeks later on 18th July. The short section of line between Bideford's first and second stations was difficult to construct, squeezed between the hillside to the east and the river to the west. Some demolition of property was involved with the line running through the former rear gardens of some properties in Barnstaple Street.

The station site itself was also confined. So steep was the hillside that at the northern Barnstaple end of the station the down platform was overlooked by houses in Springfield Terrace, whilst the up platform overlooked properties below in Barnstaple Street. The main buildings on the down (towards Torrington) platform incorporated all the principal

station facilities but not accommodation for the station master, whose house was close to the line a few yards from the end of the up platform. The spacious station forecourt in front of the down side building was used by road vehicles providing transport to a number of north Devon resorts. Buildings on the up side were smaller, with a waiting room being the main facility. This platform was accessed by steps up from the road below. No footbridge was provided; a rail level board crossing at the north end provided the inter-platform link. In the early days a small canopy was erected on both platforms; at a later date the London & South Western Railway extended the canopies including cover to the up platform steps. The Royal Hotel on Barnstaple Street used its proximity to the station to its advantage, an entrance being provided from the north end of the up platform direct into the hotel's second floor. For some years the Hotel ran a refreshment room for the station, making Bideford the only station on the Torrington line to have a bookstall and refreshment facilities. Goods facilities were very limited at the station itself, one short dock siding terminating at the south end of the down platform and another short siding with a stub beyond the south end of the up platform. Bideford signal box (12 levers), sited at the south end of the up platform, was constructed of wood on a stone base.

Although the second station continued to be badly located for the main part of the town, passenger volumes were high. In 1928 60,117 passenger tickets

Bideford Quay. A Bideford, Westward Ho! & Appledore Railway train stands at the quay terminus in about 1910. An employee walks towards the camera with a detachable lever to work the loop line points. The River Torridge is to the right.

were issued and 106,762 collected. By 1936 the number issued had fallen greatly to 33,292 but the number collected had held up well at 92,618. A detailed breakdown indicated that, on average, the passenger volume was three times greater in July than in February. The numbers continued to be good into the 1950s when the station master was supported by 12 men.

The station closed in October 1965 and some buildings were demolished including the up side shelter. The station signal box closed on 26th February 1967, with the up side line being taken out of use, and then demolished. The station was reopened briefly for some days between 10th and 22nd January 1968 to assist the local transport system thrown into chaos by damage to the Bideford road bridge. The down side building survived, being used for some years by the Midland Bank and then as a restaurant. The station site is now owned by Devon County Council, the building being used as a centre for its Northern Devon Coast and Countryside Service. The Tarka Trail cycleway passes through the site. A plaque on the building records that the Trail was opened by the Prince of

Wales on 28th May 1992. Renovation work has been undertaken, including the rebuilding of the signal box on its original site. This work was originally undertaken by the Bideford Railway Station Group. This Group in January 1992 merged with the Instow Signal Box Group (see Instow text) to undertake work at both station sites. Track has been relaid between the platforms and a Mark 1 carriage, beside the former up platform, acts as a museum, café and information centre. Picnic tables and a large Tarka Trail information board stand beside the signal box.

BIDEFORD QUAY

OPENED: 18th May 1901 (with the opening of the Bideford Quay – Northam section of the Bideford, Westward Ho! & Appledore Railway).
CLOSED: Passengers and Goods – 28th March 1917.

The ceremonial opening of the first section of the Bideford, Westward Ho! & Appledore Railway (BWH&AR) took place on 24th April 1901. Two hundred invited guests travelled on a special train to Westward Ho! and Northam with a break at Westward Ho! for refreshments. The engine was decked with Union Jacks and Herr Groop's German band played and travelled on the train! Public services began over three weeks later on 18th May.

The southern terminus of the BWH&AR was on

the quay at Bideford some 200 yards north of the Bideford road bridge over the River Torridge. The site was between today's High Street and Cooper Street. The basic layout was a single track with a run-round loop in the centre of the wide road. The run-round loop was only finally installed in 1903 after a lengthy dispute with the Town Council. As the line terminated in the middle of a public highway 'The Quay' it was impractical to install a buffer stop. There was also a short quay side siding used both for coal deliveries and also, on occasions, for storing the railway's nine goods wagons. Use of the siding was not encouraged by the Council and the wagons were normally kept at Appledore after the extension to the town opened in 1908. No signals or levers were installed, this part of the line being regarded as a street tramway. When engines ran round points were changed with a detachable lever as on a tram line.

The booking office and waiting room were in the ground floor of a building to the west of the line at 20, The Quay. There was no station master at Bideford Quay, the Railway's General Manager being in charge of operations on the quayside. The Manager's office was to the left of the entrance to 20, The Quay with the waiting room/office to the right. In sunny weather potential passengers waited for the trains seated on benches beside the quay.

Clearly a major problem for the railway was the proximity of horses and noisy steam engines on the quay. This conflict was one of the reasons behind the strained relations between the BWH&AR and the Town Council. To minimise the problem railway timetables were organised so that locomotives spent as little time as possible at the quay terminus. Most workings departed as soon as the engine had run round.

In 1916 the Government decided that locomotives and track and other railway equipment were needed for the war effort in France. To meet this need a number of minor railways were earmarked for closure and requisition, including the BWH&AR. The last train ran on 28th March 1917 and three locomotives were moved two days later across specially laid tracks over Bideford Bridge to the goods yard at Bideford East-the Water for overhaul before leaving the area. The lines on the quay were taken up and subsequently the line of the railway was used for the layout of what is now Kingsley Road. In early 2007 a modern office block stood at 20 The Quay, occupied by the Portman Building Society.

BIDEFORD STRAND ROAD HALT

OPENED: 18th May 1901 (with the opening of the Bideford Quay – Northam section of the Bideford, Westward Ho! & Appledore Railway).
CLOSED: 28th March 1917.

This halt was a request stop some 650 yards from Bideford Quay. Also known as 'The Strand', it was close to the present road of this name. Today Kingsley Road closely follows the alignment of the railway. No platform was provided and passengers accessed the trains by steps on the carriages. Closure came after only 16 years (see Bideford Quay text).

BIDEFORD YARD

OPENED: 18th May 1901 (with the opening of the Bideford Quay – Northam section of the Bideford, Westward Ho! & Appledore Railway).
CLOSED: 28th March 1917.

With a passing loop, this halt was sited at the main locomotive and carriage sheds of the Bideford, Westward Ho! & Appledore Railway. Bideford Yard was not shown in the public timetable as an official stopping place, with trains calling principally to pick up and set down railway staff. The general public did however also use the halt but there is no record of any platform. After the early closure of the railway in 1917 (see Bideford Quay text), the spacious carriage shed was used as a bus garage and the engine shed as a dairy. The carriage shed was later used by a firm of agricultural merchants. It survives today.

BILLACOMBE

OPENED: 17th January 1898 (with the opening of the GWR branch Plymstock – Yealmpton).
CLOSED: Passengers and Goods 7th July 1930.
REOPENED: 3rd November 1941 (for use by Plymouth residents evacuated during the Second World War).
CLOSED: Passengers – 6th October 1947
Goods – 29th February 1960.

Billacombe opened with the commencement of services from Plymouth Millbay on the Yealmpton branch, known in its early days as the South Hams Railway. Standing on the south side of the line with a loop line to the north, the station building of a then standard GWR design, was stone built with a blue

Billacombe. A general view east in about 1939 of the small station building which had closed nine years earlier. It was soon to reopen between 1941 and 1947. The siding in the foreground (right) is leading to the small goods yard.

grey slate roof and two chimneys. Over the platform was a canopy supported by three large girders imbedded in the front wall of the building. The canopy included glass roof panels and a vertical plank valence. The small building incorporated a booking office and waiting room, a ladies' waiting room and a gent's toilet. The platform was 300 ft long and at its western end was the station entrance through two large steel gates. In 1903 5,901 passenger tickets were issued at Billacombe; in 1913 and 1923 the figures were 7,412 and 3,613. Only one member of staff was based there after 1913.

Two matching stone structures stood in the small goods yard at the Plymstock (west) end of the station site on the up (south) side: a goods shed and a small goods office. A ground frame with 5 levers controlled movements at the station and in the yard. Goods handled included a daily coal service, milk, farm produce, quarry stone and lime from Moore's quarry, north of the station.

After closure to passengers in 1930, the building was leased to one of the company employees as a dwelling; such an arrangement continued until the early 1960s. Extra accommodation was provided by a wooden structure on the platform beneath the canopy which provided a sheltered way between the doors on the platform side. During the 1941/1947 period when passenger services were resumed on the branch (see Yealmpton text) a section of the platform were sealed off by concrete posts and wire to protect the privacy of the building's occupants. Unlike at Yealmpton, no booking facilities were provided for the 1941/1947 opening, passengers obtaining tickets on the train or at their destination.

Following closure to goods in February 1960, the site was sold to English China Clays, the station building being initially used as a laboratory before falling into disrepair. A private road to an English China Clay quarry was built along the former trackbed. Over the period April 1987 to January 1991 the station building was carefully dismantled by members of the Plym Valley Railway for re-erection at Marsh Mills. The station goods yard has now been covered by the widened Elburton Road, east of Billacombe roundabout.

BISHOPS NYMPTON AND MOLLAND

OPENED: 1st November 1873 (with the opening of the Wiveliscombe – Barnstaple section of the Devon & Somerset Railway).
CLOSED: Passengers – 3rd October 1966.
Goods – 3rd August 1964.

The station, on a then single track section of the Devon & Somerset Railway, opened in November 1873 with the name of Molland. A crossing loop and up side platform were added in 1876 and the name changed to Bishops Nympton and Molland from 1st March that year. The station was not, however, very close to either settlement, Molland being two miles to the north-east and Bishops Nympton three miles to the south-west.

The main building, on the down side, was a single storey stone structure including a central section with an apex slate roof at right angles to the line and two wings with low roofs parallel to the line. Two tall chimney stacks rose from the roofs. The booking, waiting and ladies' room were in the building, with a flat roof annex at the west end housing the gent's toilet. An hotel adjoined the rear of the building. On the up platform was an open front wooden waiting shelter, with a roof sloping towards the line. Both

33

Bishops Nympton and Molland. A view east in 1955 showing the single storey stone building on the down (towards Barnstaple) platform. The 1937 signal box is at the east end of the platform.

platforms were some 300 ft long. No footbridge was ever provided, inter-platform movement being via a rail level board crossing at the east end of the platforms. In 1903 7,790 passenger tickets were issued but by 1933 the figure had fallen to 4,875. Staff numbers remained at three over this 30 year period.

The goods yard was behind, and to the west of, the down platform, the goods shed with a through siding being immediately behind the platform. At the west end of the goods shed another siding terminated close to cattle pens.

Signal box facilities changed over the years. An original box stood at the east end of the down

platform adjacent to the main buildings. Track layout alterations to the down side sidings in about 1902, and extension of the platforms and loop, necessitated a new box, this time at the Barnstaple end of the down platform. In 1937 the crossing loop was lengthened again and a new refuge up siding was added. Another new 30 lever signal box was erected on the east end of the down platform, close to the site of the original pre 1902 box.

Goods facilities closed in August 1964 and passenger services ceased in October 1966, with the withdrawal of services on the line. Both the station building and goods shed were converted into dwellings and it is still possible to stand on the surviving up platform within the garden. Only part of the down platform survives.

BITTAFORD PLATFORM

OPENED: 18th November 1907 (on the Totnes – Plymouth GWR line originally opened through this site in 1848).
CLOSED: 2nd March 1959.

Opening in November 1907, the platform served a small community at Bittaford Bridge and a large mental hospital a half mile to the north. Sited just to the east of a double track viaduct (132 yds long) over the River Lud, two wooden platforms were originally provided but were later replaced with stone structures. Passengers were protected by pagoda style huts on both platforms. About 12,000 tickets were issued annually at Bittaford in the 1930s; one member of staff was based at Bittaford for much of its life. Parcels traffic was also handled. Today no trace remains following closure nearly 50 years ago in 1959.

Bittaford Platform. An up express train towards Newton Abbot passes through. Note the wooden platforms and two classic pagoda huts.

BLACKMOOR

OPENED: 16th May 1898 (with the opening of the
  Lynton & Barnstaple Railway).
CLOSED: Passengers and Goods – 30th September 1935.

Sited at Blackmoor Gate, a cross roads on Exmoor at
a height of some 900 ft above sea level, the buildings
were quite extensive, reflecting the fact that
Blackmoor (as it was always known), was intended
to be the principal intermediate station on the
narrow gauge Lynton & Barnstaple Railway.
Although the station site was isolated, four
converging roads meant that it was accessible from
surrounding villages or hamlets including
Parracombe to the north-east. In the very early days
the nameboard stated 'Blackmoor for Parracombe'.

Two low platforms, on the principal passing loop
on the line, served passengers; that on the down side
(towards Lynton) had no shelter. On the up side a
large chalet building in what was called a
'Nuremberg' style was very similar to that at Lynton.
The building incorporated both the station facilities
and accommodation for the station master. As at
Lynton, this accommodation comprised two
bedrooms on the first floor with the living room
(parlour) and kitchen on the ground. The ground
floor also included the general waiting room,
refreshment room and ticket office. The ladies'
toilets were in the main part of the building with the
gent's toilets at the south end in a low annex. Unlike
at Lynton, the layout of the building interior
remained unaltered at Blackmoor. In 1928 6,515
passenger tickets were issued and 8,571 collected; by
1934 the figures were 4,025 and 4,654.

A small goods yard, including a goods shed, was
on the up side behind the south end of the platform.
Also in the yard in the early days were stables for the
horses pulling a bus service to Ilfracombe. A further
small goods hut stood alongside the south end of the
main building. There was also a short siding on the
down side to the south of the platform; this was
removed in 1930. A water tower stood at the north
end of the down platform; from this tower water was
piped to a water crane on the up platform. After
closure the metal tank on top of a stone base was
removed but the base survived, adapted now as a
store. Also surviving is a concrete signal post.

Closure of Blackmoor to passengers and goods
came at the end of September 1935. Following a
period of dereliction the main building was sold in
1938 for £700. It has been renovated and extended

Blackmoor. In about 1925 the engine Exe with a train for
Barnstaple is alongside the up platform on which stands the
large Nuremberg style building. Note the large water crane.

and now is part of a large public house, the 'Old
Station House Inn'. An earlier function, as illustrated
on a photo in the current building, was as the station
café and guest house. There are also many other
photographs of the L&B Railway and copies of the
timetable schedules. Over one of the bar counters is
a notice General Waiting Room.

BOLHAM HALT

OPENED: 23rd April 1928 (on the Tiverton – Bampton
  line originally opened through this site in 1884).
CLOSED: 7th October 1963.

Bolham Halt opened in April 1928 on the east side
of an embankment which carried the Tiverton to
Bampton line south-north high above the village
centre. The 109 ft long platform was a sectionalised
concrete structure from the outset. It was backed by
a six strand wire fence with concrete posts with the
lamp and nameboard posts doubling up as fence

Bolham Halt. Looking north in 1963 shortly before the halt
closed. The platform was constructed of concrete
components from its opening in 1928.

Bovey. A typical 0-6-0 saddle tank locomotive pulling a north bound train into the down platform in about 1900. The station building on the up platform as yet has no canopy. Today it houses the Bovey Tracey Heritage Centre.

posts. A basic open front corrugated iron shelter with a backward sloping roof provided limited protection in this exposed position. A wooden bench was provided along the back wall of the shelter. A zig-zag sloping path, including steps, led down to the road close to the north side of a stone rail over bridge. Bolham was only a small village but the halt's central location meant that it was well used, particularly for market day and Saturday trips to Tiverton and Bampton. Today there is no trace of the halt itself but the sloping path (now with brambles!) and a wooden gate by the road side survive. A picnic table and seat stand on top of the embankment.

BOVEY

OPENED: 4th July 1866 (with the opening of the Moretonhampstead & South Devon Railway, Newton Abbot – Moretonhampstead).
CLOSED: Passengers – 2nd March 1959.
Goods – 4th December 1967.

Bovey station, on the western edge of the town of Bovey Tracey (the suffix Tracey was never applied to the station) opened in July 1866. Sited about mid way between Newton Abbot and Moretonhampstead, there was a crossing loop and two platforms. At the opening the up (towards Newton Abbot) platform of 300 ft was much the longer; in about 1894 the down platform was extended to the same length from its original 190 ft. Both platforms were originally built with a stone face and a metalled surface. The north end extension of the down, although having a metalled surface, was faced with brick. On the up platform the small section in front of the main building was later paved. No footbridge was provided, inter-platform movements being via a rail level board crossing at the southern end of the station.

The main station building, at the south end of the up platform, was principally constructed of granite blocks with a pitched grey slate roof, plain ridge tiles and two cylindrical squat chimneys, the main chimney having two flues and the other, at the south end, only one. At either end of the building were small wings with flat roofs. On the platform side were arched window recesses, an arched doorway and, a later addition, a wide timber canopy supported by six ornamental wall brackets. At the rear of the building part of the roof extended down to form a small canopy over two of the five windows and the double door entrance. These doors led into the booking hall and general waiting room. On the north side of this room was the ladies' room and, beyond this, in the flat roof wing and only accessible from the platform, was the gent's toilet. To the south of the central waiting room was the station office/booking office and, in the wing, the parcels office. To the south of the main building was an iron building, with an arc shape roof, originally used as a shelter for passengers waiting to board the buses based at the station for trips on to Dartmoor. This building was later used as a store.

On the down platform stood an open front brick waiting shelter, equipped with seating. This shelter was added when the platform was lengthened in about 1894. The grey slate pitched roof, with plain ridge tiles and one chimney, extended forward towards the line, giving some protection to passengers. A flat roof extension at the northern end once housed a gent's toilet but this use ceased in the

1930s. In 1903 38,297 tickets were issued, other figures were: 1913 (34,646), 1923 (28,754), 1933 (14,546) and 1943 (20,052). By 1953 the figure had fallen to 10,521.

Bovey goods yard, sited north of the main building, included a substantial stone goods shed (50 ft x 39 ft), adjacent to the rear of the up platform. With walls matching the station building, the roof was of corrugated iron, topped by one chimney. Three large openings, one at each end and one in the eastern side, had large sliding doors. Three large windows gave light, particularly needed when the doors were closed. Two were in arched recesses on the platform side and one at the southern end giving light to the internal goods office. Inside the shed facilities included a full length loading platform served by a through goods siding, which terminated at a loading bay close to the station building. The shed also incorporated a two ton capacity crane. A further long siding served the yard east of the goods shed, both sidings leaving the line north of the station, linking to the main line and loop.

A seventeen lever signal box stood on the up platform towards the northern end. Just beyond the goods shed, it was built mainly of timber under a slate pitched roof with ridge tiles. The rear wall was of brick; all round visibility was good through sliding wood framed windows. To the south of the

station, in the forecourt and approach road, was the area where the many connecting bus and coach services started and terminated, passengers using the iron shed noted earlier.

Closure to passengers came in March 1959, goods facilities lasted a further eight years until December 1967. Following closure both platforms and the down shelter were removed and the track bed was used as part of a new alignment of the A382 by-passing Bovey Tracey centre to the west. The area to the south of the station and the former approach road has been redeveloped for housing. The station building, after periods of both short re-use and dereliction, has now been completely renovated and on 10th April 2004 was opened as the Bovey Tracey Heritage Centre, incorporating historic details of the town and railway. The goods shed also survives as a depot for the Dartmoor National Park Authority.

BOW

OPENED: 1st November 1865 (with the opening of the Coleford Junction (west of Crediton) – North Tawton section of the Devon & Cornwall Railway).
CLOSED: Passengers – 5th June 1972.
Goods – 1st May 1961.

The Devon & Cornwall Railway from Coleford Junction, on the Exeter to Barnstaple line, to Okehampton and Holsworthy opened in stages, the first of which ran to North Tawton, opening at the beginning of November 1865. This station, the only intermediate facility on the first stage, opened as Nymet Tracey, a hamlet to the north-east but the

Bovey. A general view from the south in about 1910 showing the main station building, now with a canopy, the down side shelter and the substantial goods shed (beyond the station). In the foreground are GWR Motor Buses bound for Haytor Rocks, Becky Falls and Mannaton.

37

Bow. Battle of Britain 4-6-2 No 34056 Croydon, hauling a Torrington to Waterloo train, runs past the up platform towards Crediton on 3rd August 1955.

Bow. The fine station building, including the two storey station master's accommodation, viewed from the forecourt on 3rd August 1955.

name soon changed to Bow, a village over a mile to the north. Records suggest that for some years the suffix 'Devon' was also used.

The substantial local stone main building stood on the down (towards Okehampton) side. It included a two storey station master's house and a single storey section incorporating the principal station facilities. Both the house and the lower section had steeply pitched roofs at right angles to the line. Other features of the building included tall round headed windows in pointed arches, a small platform canopy and a variety of chimneys. The gent's toilet was in an annex at the extreme west end. On the up platform was a wooden shelter also with a wide canopy. There was no footbridge, inter-platform connection was via a rail level board crossing at the east end of the platform. In this very isolated position passenger volumes were generally low. In 1928 8,600 tickets were issued and 9,746 collected; by 1936 the totals had more than halved to 3,723 and 4,784.

Bow's small goods yard with three sidings and a stone goods shed was to the rear of the down platform. A cattle dock siding terminating close to the west end of the main building ran between the goods shed and the west end of the platform on which stood the signal box.

Goods facilities were an early casualty in May 1961 followed by closure of the signal box on 21st January 1964. Bow remained open to passengers until June 1972 when the local service between Okehampton and Exeter was withdrawn. The through service to Plymouth via Bere Alston had ceased in 1968. The station building was subsequently converted into a house, fenced off on the platform side from the down side track. This remains in use both by freight traffic from Meldon Quarry, west of Okehampton, and also by the weekend passenger services, run by the Dartmoor Railway, between Exeter and Okehampton but which do not call at Bow. The former up platform remains, but in a derelict state. The former goods yard and shed were, in 2007, occupied by a company specialising in building materials.

BRAMPFORD SPEKE HALT

OPENED: 1st May 1885 (with the opening of the Exe Valley line Stoke Canon – Tiverton).
CLOSED: 7th October 1963.

A footpath down a wooded slope and across the River Exe meadows, including an iron lattice footbridge over the river, connected the village of Brampford Speke to the station, just to the east. At the centre of the 300 ft platform, on the west side of the single track line, stood the station building, of local stone with twin gables and decorative barge boards. All the facilities, including the waiting room, booking office and station master's office, were in this building. At the opening two porters/signalmen and the station master comprised the staff, accommodation for the station master being provided in a detached two storey stone building,

Brampford Speke Halt. A general view north in about 1900 illustrating the foliage covered two storey station master's house, the twin gabled station building and the small signal box, the last being demolished in 1907.

behind the south end of the platform. Brampford Speke handled passenger and parcels traffic but no significant freight, there being no goods yard or shed. A small eight lever signal box was a short lived structure on the platform north of the building, being demolished in 1907.

The station was threatened with early closure when the GWR announced that it was to construct a new junction station at the point, some one mile south of Brampford Speke, where the Exe Valley line joins the main GWR Taunton to Exeter line. The GWR felt that as passengers on the Exe Valley trains could then use the new Stoke Canon station, Brampford Speke would be redundant. The passenger levels did not, however, fall greatly and the station won a reprieve. Closure did come as a war-time measure from 1st January 1917 to 1st January 1919, the only station on the Exe Valley line so affected. From 1st October 1923 staffing ceased and the station was re-designated a halt. The station building was no longer used and a small corrugated hut with a bench seat was the sole facility. The station building was later converted into a house.

Today both the former station building and station master's house continue in residential use. The station access path, including the iron bridge, is still in use, with a section of the path forming part of the Exe Valley Way. Alongside the path is a gate with the nameboard, Station House.

BRATTON FLEMING

OPENED: 16th May 1898 (with the opening of the Lynton & Barnstaple Railway).
CLOSED: Passengers and Goods – 30th September 1935.

Opening as Bratton, the name changed in the timetable to Bratton Fleming as from October 1899. At the opening of the line to Lynton in May 1898 the first train was greeted by a triumphal arch.

Sited on a hillside some 185 ft below the village, the station was on a passing loop. Two low platforms served passengers but no shelter was provided on the down (towards Lynton) side. On the up platform, cut into the hillside, was the small stone built main building with a hipped roof. It contained the waiting room and booking office. A small glazed entrance porch was at the Barnstaple end of the building; a rear entrance as at Chelfham was not possible because of the site topography. Access to the platform was via a steeply inclined path behind the main building. The ivy covered waiting room and mossy roof enhanced this attractive building, the

station also being renowned for its display of roses. In August 1899 Sir George Newnes, the Chairman of the Lynton & Barnstaple Railway, awarded £5 to Bratton Fleming for its attractive flower beds.

A small goods yard on the down side north-west of the platform was accessed by a siding which bisected the low platform close to its north end. The siding terminated in front of a small goods shed. In 1932 this siding and the station loop were removed. Rail movements at the station were controlled from a frame inside a small box on the up platform south of the main building. A water tank, which was seldom used being hand pumped, stood south of the station on the up side.

Following closure of the line in September 1935, the station site was sold for £100. The building was subsequently incorporated into a private house with a conservatory added on the platform side and an extension at the Lynton end. The goods shed was demolished, and the yard converted into a private garden. Station Road runs from the village centre.

BRAUNTON

OPENED: 20th July 1874 (with the opening of the Barnstaple & Ilfracombe Railway).
CLOSED: Passengers – 5th October 1970.
    Goods – 7th September 1964.

Conveniently sited in the centre of the village, immediately south of a level crossing carrying the road west to Croyde Bay, Braunton opened in late July 1874. Until the doubling of the tracks in 1890 it acted as a passing point on the Barnstaple to Ilfracombe line. The principal building, comprising a two storey station master's house with a single storey section on its north side, stood on the shorter down (towards Ilfracombe) platform. The booking and

Bratton Fleming. A general view in about 1900 of this attractive north Devon station showing the main building on the down (towards Barnstaple) side. Note the small glazed entrance porch on the end wall. The building is now incorporated into a house.

waiting facilities and parcels office were within the single storey section. The ladies' toilets were in the ground floor of the station house section, the gent's in an annex on the south side of the whole building. At the north end of the platform was a store with doors on to the platform. A wooden shelter with a canopy served passengers on the up platform. Water cranes, supplied by a water tank which drew water from the adjacent River Caen, stood on both platforms, that on the down at the north end and that on the up at the south end.

In 1928 40,213 passenger tickets were issued and 49,227 collected at Braunton. By 1936 the figures had fallen to 22,175 and 31,835. Many of the passengers coming to Braunton were heading for the nearby Saunton Sands and Croyde Bay and the station nameboard referred to these two attractions.

South of the station on the up (towards Barnstaple) side was the goods yard incorporating a goods shed, cattle dock and pens and five sidings. Two short sidings opposite the yard on the down side were used by waiting banking engines. These were principally used on summer Saturdays to assist long trains up the 1 in 74 and then 1 in 40 inclines on the six mile climb to Mortehoe. A further short siding beyond the north end of the down platform and the level crossing was used by oil tank wagons. Braunton signal box, at the north end of the down platform, had 24 levers and controlled the adjacent level crossing gates with a gate wheel. It became only a ground frame when the Ilfracombe line was singled on 17th December 1967.

Braunton. Looking south at both the main building on the down platform (right) and the wooden shelter on the up. Note the fine water crane at the north end of the down platform.

Goods facilities were withdrawn in September 1964 and the station closed to passengers in October 1970 with the withdrawal of services on the Ilfracombe line. Following closure, much of the station site was cleared and has now been redeveloped. The former station master's house is in use as a newsagents; the single storey section has gone. The former goods shed is used as a youth club. Other new buildings on the station site include the Caen Medical Centre. Nearby is a new house, The Sidings, and to the south rails remain in the road at the north end of Station Road.

Brent. A general view looking west on 14th June 1958 showing, from left to right, the large goods shed with an office at the east end, the island platform at which stands a Kingsbridge branch train, the signal box, the covered footbridge and the main building with three chimneys on the later up platform.

BRENT

OPENED: 15th June 1848 (on the Totnes – Plymouth (Laira Green) section of the South Devon Railway opened 6 weeks earlier on 5th May).
CLOSED: Passengers – 5th October 1964.
  Goods – 6th April 1964.

Located on the northern edge of the village beneath Brent Hill, the station opened in 1848 on the Totnes to Plymouth (Laira Green) extension of the South Devon Railway. Records indicate that, although services commenced on the single track broad gauge line on 5th May, Brent station did not open for passengers until 15th June (see also Ivybridge and Plympton). Between two road over bridges, from both of which access was later provided to both station and goods yard, the original 1848 building and platform were on the down (towards Plymouth) side of the single track. It is believed that an up side loop line was added in about 1865.

Major changes came in 1893 with the doubling of the main line to Plymouth through Brent and the

opening of the branch line south to Kingsbridge. An island platform was created on the down side, the outer face of which was used by the Kingsbridge trains; a run-round loop ran parallel to the platform loop. The main building on the new up platform was built of red and blue bricks with a slate roof and three chimneys; it incorporated a ladies' room, a combined booking hall/waiting room, a booking office, the station master's office and a gent's toilet all entered from under a platform canopy. There were no doors at the rear of the building, access to the platform being through a gate under a roof between the west end of the building and the steps of a covered footbridge. Beyond the footbridge was a collection of huts for lamps, cycles and other stores; the ramp at this Plymouth end of the up platform led down to a rail level board crossing used by porters conveying trolleys to the down island platform. A feature of the up platform was the attractive gardens including palm trees and climbing roses.

The footbridge steps on the island platform led, under cover, to the former broad gauge era building which, with canopies sheltering passengers on both platform faces, incorporated toilets, a waiting room and staff room. In 1903 30,204 passenger tickets were issued at Brent; this figure rose to 31,013 in 1913 but fell to 30,880 in 1923 and 20,561 in 1933. There was a relatively high staffing for a rural station, 14 being based here in 1903 and 18 in 1929. In the 1958-1960 period staff comprised a station master, two booking clerks, four porters, three signalmen and one shunter.

Over the years the staff were employed both at the station itself and in the goods yard, behind the down platform beyond the run round loop. A large goods shed, constructed of red/blue bricks with a slate roof and a two storey office block at the east end, included a 30 cwt capacity crane for unloading both road vehicles and wagons on the through loop siding. At the Plymouth end of the yard were end and side loading facilities, also a water tank on top of a stores building. Brent station was important for livestock movements and a number of cattle pens stood at the Totnes end of the yard.

Rail operations at Brent were controlled from a signal box on the Totnes end of the down island platform. An original 1893 wood and brick box, provided with the opening of the Kingsbridge branch, was replaced in 1921 by a large standard GWR brick box with 66 levers. This closed on 17th December 1973. Passenger services ceased in October 1964, goods facilities having been

withdrawn in April. The main station buildings were demolished soon after closure. Today the signal box is still there on the remnant of the island platform; in recent years it was used by permanent way staff but, when viewed in late 2006, appeared derelict. The former goods shed also remains used for commercial purposes, Primrose Junction. The former goods yard is a car park.

BRENTOR

OPENED: 1st June 1890 (with the opening of the Plymouth, Devonport & South Western Junction Railway, Lydford – Devonport).
CLOSED: Passengers – 6th May 1968.
    Goods – 4th April 1960.

In the valley of the River Burn, that runs approximately north-south from Lydford to Tavistock, the Launceston & South Devon Railway (L&SDR) opened its line to Lydford and Launceston in 1865. When the Plymouth, Devonport & South Western Junction Railway (PD&SWJR) decided to construct its line to Devonport, it chose the Burn valley south from Lydford for the first section of its route to Tavistock before it continued south and west to the Tamar Valley. Between Lydford and Tavistock the L&SDR opened Mary Tavy and Blackdown station some three miles north of Tavistock. The PD&SWJR line opening in June 1890, ran almost parallel to the earlier line through the valley and in this instance it was decided to site a station further north just to the south-east of North Brentor, named after the nearby Tor.

Like all stations on the PD&SWJR, the local stone

Brentor. The station building, now renovated as a splendid house, seen from the road-side on 7th August 1958, the signal box can be seen to the left.

built main building, with a large apex style canopy, was constructed on the down (towards Tavistock) side of the double track line. All station facilities and accommodation for the station master were incorporated in the impressive structure. A stone shelter served passengers on the up platform behind which ran the single track Launceston line. No footbridge was ever provided at Brentor. For some 30 years inter-platform movement was via rail level board crossings at both ends of the platforms. From the 1920s, however, steps were added from the platforms at the north end to a road over bridge, thus giving a safer route. In 1928 6,192 passenger tickets were issued and 7,388 collected; figures for 1936 were 5,541 and 7,112. Staffing ceased on 4th September 1967.

Provision for goods traffic was not extensive. There was no goods yard or goods shed though, for a limited period, a small building on the south end of the down platform acted as a store. Behind the south end of the down platform a siding served a loading bay and cattle pens. Much of the freight business generated by the surrounding rural area was handled at the Tavistock stations. The limited goods facilities at Brentor ceased to operate in April 1960. Brentor signal box, a stone base structure with a slate roof and a large expanse of timber framed windows stood beyond the south end of the down platform. It closed from the 10th June 1961 and was demolished. In its latter years it was only open for short periods.

The station closed in May 1968 with the withdrawal of passenger services. The station building was later restored and is now a splendid house with the canopy in place. The extensive garden, with the area between the platforms filled, also includes the adjacent trackbed of the former Launceston line. The former waiting shelter on the up platform survives.

BRIDESTOWE

OPENED: 12th October 1874 (with the opening of the London & South Western Railway line, Okehampton – Lydford).
CLOSED: Passengers – 6th May 1968.
Goods – 5th June 1961.

Sited about a mile and a half south-east of, and high above the village of Bridestowe, the station was to the north-east of a road bridge carrying the old B3278 from the village towards Lydford. Opened in mid October 1874, the station was a typical London & South Western Railway (LSWR) design. The main stone building, comprising a two storey station master's house and single storey section incorporating the main facilities at the southern end, was on the up (towards Okehampton) side of the line. A stone open front shelter with a slate roof served passengers on the down platform. An open footbridge connected the two platforms at the south end; the original bridge was replaced by a concrete Southern Railway structure in the 1930s.

The rather remote location and the distance up a steep hill from the village did not encourage large passenger volumes at Bridestowe. In 1928 5,712 passenger tickets were issued and 7,466 collected; by 1936 the figures had fallen to 3,342 and 4,623. During the Second World War passenger numbers were boosted both by a nearby American Army camp and also by a number of evacuees from

Plymouth. As well as the station master's house on the platform, railway cottages were built to the west and east of the station site.

Bridestowe's goods yard, on the up side principally behind the main station building, included a stone goods shed with a dock at the north end and a small canopy over a siding that ran along the west side. Also in the yard were cattle pens. From 1935 a camping coach was sited in the yard. A siding on the down side north of the station was added in 1880. This coincided with the opening of a mineral line linked to peat extraction works on the moor east of the station at Nodden Gate. This steeply graded line on which motive power for some years was provided by horses, terminated end on to the down siding. The two lines were separated by a boundary gate across which traffic was exchanged. Operated by the West of England Peat Company, the line was known as the Rattlebrook Peat Railway. The line ceased to carry traffic by 1925. The track was removed in 1932, buffer stops being erected on the main railway side of the gate at the end of the siding.

The signal box at Bridestowe was just beyond the Okehampton (north) end of the up platform. The original 1874 box had only nine levers but this number was increased in 1903. The box closed on 14th July 1964, some three years after goods facilities were withdrawn at the station. The station remained open for passengers until early May 1968 when services ceased on the line between Okehampton and Bere Alston on the Exeter to Plymouth line.

Following closure very little demolition took place and subsequently the station buildings were developed into an impressive large residence including the station building with extensions, the waiting shelter and footbridge. Between the surviving platforms infilling created a large lawn.

Bridestowe. Looking south-west towards Lydford on 3rd October 1964, the main building standing on the up (towards Okehampton) platform. A 1930s concrete footbridge connects the two platforms at the south end close to a road bridge.

BRIMLEY HALT

OPENED: 21st May 1928 (on the Newton Abbot – Moretonhampstead branch originally opened through this site in 1866).
CLOSED: 2nd March 1959.

On the southern outskirts of Bovey Tracey, and with its name taken from the two hamlets of Higher and Lower Brimley, about a mile to the west, the halt opened in May 1928. Like many other halts opened around this time in Devon, it was an attempt by the GWR to compete with the ever growing threat of road travel competition. On the up (east) side of the Newton Abbot – Moretonhampstead branch, the platform was faced with stone blocks with a surface of rolled stone chippings, edged with concrete slabs

Brimley Halt. A view south from a road overbridge on 3rd September 1956. A wooden shelter and two wooden benches serve passengers.

along the 72 ft (110 ft with the ramps) length. Passengers were protected by an open fronted, centrally positioned, waiting shelter (12 ft x 8 ft), constructed of horizontal timber planks on a shallow concrete plinth. There was a backward sloping corrugated iron roof. Inside the shelter was a simple wooden bench; two further benches, one at each end of the platform, two posts (originally concrete but later metal) from which hurricane lamps were hung and the nameboard completed the fixtures. A sloping cinder path from the east end of a road bridge beyond the north end of the platform provided the sole access. No staff were ever based at Brimley. In its final years new housing to the south of Bovey Tracey brought more passengers than at any time in the halt's history. Closure came, however, in March 1959 with the withdrawal of services on the branch. The site of the halt is now covered by a section of the Bovey Tracey western by-pass; the former branch trackbed being used for much of the road alignment.

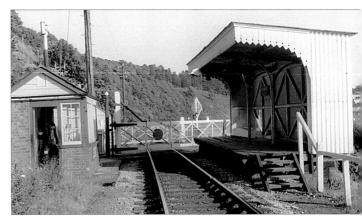

Britannia Halt. The wooden shelter and level crossing gates in a photograph of 1966, looking south towards Kingswear.

BRITANNIA HALT

OPENED: 1877 (on the Churston – Kingswear line
 originally opened through this site in 1864).
CLOSED: See text.

H.M.S. *Britannia* was withdrawn from active service in 1863 and moored in the River Dart to serve as a training base for naval officers. On 18th October 1877 the Prince of Wales, Prince Albert Edward, brought his two sons, Prince Albert Victor and Prince George Frederick to enter H.M.S. Britannia as naval cadets. North of Kingswear a platform was erected on the up side at a level crossing leading to the Floating Bridge. The royal train from Paddington stopped at this platform which was decorated with flags and covered with a maroon carpet. It is recorded that between five and six thousand spectators were present, with 300 boats moored in the river. The day concluded with bonfires, illuminations and a torchlight procession.

The GWR retained the platform for many years for special visitors to H.M.S.Britannia. It was originally called Kingswear Crossing Halt, then Steam Ferry Halt and finally, Britannia Halt. The platform was provided with a shelter in 1894 and new crossing gates were erected in 1897, the crossing keeper being provided with a cottage. Over the years the halt never appeared in a public timetable but was used by naval personnel and also by workers at the shipyard across the river at Noss. In 1988 the level crossing

gates were replaced by lifting barriers on the now A379 as it approaches the Higher Ferry slipway. The halt, declared unsafe, was removed in 1988, no formal closing date being recorded. In 1990 a new electronic control panel for the whole Paignton & Dartmouth Railway was installed at Britannia Crossing. The crossing keeper's cottage remains.

BRIXHAM

OPENED: Passengers – 28th February 1868, Goods –
 1st May 1868 (with the opening of the Torbay &
 Brixham Railway).
CLOSED: Passengers and Goods – 13th May 1963.

The Brixham branch, some two miles long, was one of the shortest in the country. Was it not for the large fishing industry, it is doubtful whether Brixham would have had a railway, as there is little doubt that many other towns of this size, two miles from an existing line, would have had a greater claim for a branch. The formal opening of the Torbay & Brixham branch and Brixham station took place on 1st January 1868: shops and businesses were closed, flags and triumphal arches were erected and the special train arrived at Brixham to the strains of 'See the conquering hero comes', played by the band of the Brixham Artillery Volunteers. A Wolston Testimonial dinner was held at the Assembly Rooms in honour of Richard Wolston, who had been campaigning for many years to bring the railway to Brixham. Public services did not commence for another two months as the branch line and the station facilities at Churston and Brixham had not met the requirements of the Board of Trade inspectors. Eventually the branch and Brixham

Brixham. A view towards the terminal buffers after 1905, the year in which the large steel and wooden canopy was added in front of the building. An 0-6-0-ST stands at the platform. The goods shed is seen beyond the goods trucks (right).

station opened for passenger services on 28th February 1868; goods facilities were available on 1st May.

Brixham station was sited on the hillside some 120 ft above the town centre and harbour, a location which, though preventing major engineering works and property demolition, and thus keeping the costs down, was, without doubt, to the detriment of the station's prosperity, particularly in its latter days with road transport competition. The single platform, with the principal wooden building, was on the down (north) side of the line. Following extensions in both 1894 and 1918, the main platform was 203 ft long with a 132 ft long extension, with a canopy at the east end used for the extensive fish traffic. At the rear of this 'fish platform' was a dedicated fish shed. Trains of fish trucks left Brixham almost daily up to its closure. A large and rather out of scale steel and wood glazed canopy some 66 ft long was added by the GWR in 1905 along the full length of the main building. This replaced an earlier structure which was only fixed to the building for half its length. In 1910 the building incorporated from west to east: a booking clerk's office with station master's office behind, the booking office hall and waiting room, a ladies' room with toilets behind, a refreshment room with scullery and attendants room behind and a smoking room. To the west of the building was a coal store and a stone gentlemen's toilet, erected in 1905, separate from the main wooden building. Between the main building and the fish shed was a separate brick built

porters' room. The buildings were, throughout their life, lit by gas supplied by works in the town below. In 1903 68,765 passenger tickets were issued at Brixham; comparable figures for 1913, 1923 and 1933 were 83,603, 58,521 and 52,735. A staff of 15 were based at Brixham in 1913.

Nearest to the platform line was a run-round loop; beyond this were two sidings holding 13 and 12 wagons and beyond this again was an 11 wagon siding passing through the goods shed. The shed incorporated a two ton capacity crane. Beyond this again was a short coal siding (7 trucks long), all the sidings terminating in buffers high above large retaining walls. A six ton capacity crane was sited for some years west of the station site on the down side.

A small engine shed stood on the down side at the west end of the platform. An original wooden structure, with slate roof, opened in February 1868 and was demolished in 1896, being replaced the following year by a corrugated iron shed. The second shed closed on 22nd July 1929 but the track was retained as a siding. Adjacent to the engine shed was a water tower. Operations at Brixham were controlled by an 1894 signal box (17 levers), sited at the west end of the station site on the up side, high above the southern retaining wall. The box closed in September 1958 being replaced by two ground frames.

A short term suspension of services occurred from 12th February to 9th April 1951 at the time of the national fuel crisis. Brixham station closed to passengers and goods traffic in May 1963 and the buildings were demolished in December 1966 after vandalism and storm damage. Today the Brixham station site is covered by housing, principally Harbourview Close, off Ropewalk Hill. The high stone retaining wall along the south side towers above South Furzeham Road, on the north side of which a small section of track rail forms a fence alongside a footway down from the houses above. At the west end of the station site the 10 ft headroom road bridge remains connecting Station Hill and North Furzeham Road.

BRIXTON ROAD

OPENED: 17th January 1898 (with the opening of the GWR branch Plymstock – Yealmpton).
CLOSED: Passengers and Goods – 7th July 1930.
REOPENED: 3rd November 1941 (for use by Plymouth residents evacuated during the Second World War).
CLOSED: Passengers – 6th October 1947
    Goods – 29th February 1960.

Sited south of, and adjacent to, the bridge where the road to Modbury and Kingsbridge crosses the Yealmpton branch line, Brixton Road opened in 1898 when services began between Plymouth Millbay and Yealmpton on what was sometimes then known as the South Hams Railway. Named after the village, the suffix 'Road' was justified as Brixton was over a half mile further east along what is now the A379. The station building, of a then typical GWR design, was stone built with a blue grey tiled roof and two chimneys. Over the platform was a canopy supported by three large girders imbedded in the building's front wall. The canopy incorporated glass roof panels and a vertical plank valence. The building contained a booking office, waiting room and toilets for ladies and gentlemen. The north-south platform was some 300 ft long. The station entrance was via double gates at the foot of Brixton Hill on the A379. In 1903 10,430 passenger tickets were issued; in 1913 the figure was 10,720 but by 1923 it had fallen to 8,712.

South of the station two trailing sidings left the branch line in a north-east direction, serving a small goods yard in which there were two stone buildings matching the main station building. These were a goods shed at a 45 degree angle to the building with a small canopy on the siding side and a small goods office parallel to, and behind, the station building. A small signal box with 19 levers originally stood at the south end of the platform and this was replaced in about 1926 by two ground frames.

After closure to passengers in 1930, the building was leased to one of the company employees as a dwelling and this arrangement continued until the early 1960s. Extra accommodation was provided by a wooden structure on the platform beneath the

Brixton Road. Looking north in about 1910. The bridge beyond the station carries the road to Yealmpton and Kingsbridge. The station closed initially in 1930 but reopened 1941-1947 though the building remained a private house.

canopy which, in particular, provided sheltered access between the doors on the platform side. During the 1941/1947 period, when passenger services were resumed on the Yealmpton branch (see Yealmpton text), sections of the platform were sealed off by concrete posts and wire to protect the privacy of the building's occupants. Unlike at Yealmpton, no booking facilities were ever provided, passengers obtaining tickets on the train or at their destination.

In May 1962 the goods shed was demolished. A United Dairies refrigeration and distribution depot had been established in the yard even before goods facilities were withdrawn in February 1960. In November 1971 the whole station site was sold by British Rail to Devon County Council for a long term road improvement scheme, which was not implemented. In October 1978 the site was sold again, Devon County Council retaining only a small section at the north end adjacent to the road bridge. The remainder was bought by a builder who demolished much of the original station building but utilised the resulting material to create a house reflecting the character of the original station. It remains today.

BROADCLYST

OPENED: 19th July 1860 (with the opening of the Yeovil Junction – Exeter section of the London & South Western Railway).
CLOSED: Passengers – 7th March 1966.
    Goods – 6th September 1965.

Sited approximately one mile south of the village of Broadclyst, the station opened in July 1860 with the start of services on the last section of the London & South Western Railway (LSWR) from London to

Broadclyst. Looking west from the signal box steps on 12th September 1964. The main buildings on the down side are now incorporated within the 'Old Broadclyst Station' development. Note the four railway cottages on arches just visible on the extreme right.

Exeter. The station name varied in the timetables over the years from the single word to the two words Broad Clyst.

The large and impressive William Tite design main building stood on the down (towards Exeter) platform. It included the two storey station master's house at the west end and the station facilities in a lower single storey section. Features of the building included tall chimneys, steeply pitched roofs and a horizontal platform canopy. A standard LSWR hipped roofed waiting shelter served passengers on the up side. An open lattice type footbridge linked the platforms at the west end close to a road over bridge. The platforms were shorter than at other stations between Axminster and Exeter, the up platform accommodating four carriages and the down only three. No extensions were added during the station's life. Lighting was by oil

Broadclyst goods shed, in a small yard, was to the east of the station on the down side. An end dock was sited close to the east end of the down platform. The yard was principally used by local traders, in particular large quantities of sugar beet were despatched. In the early 1960s there was also the export of three wheeled invalid carriages manufactured locally. On the up side, east of the station, was a further set of sidings originally occupied by railway civil engineers from 1896 but greatly expanded in 1929. Until the closure of the depot in 1964 the depot held stocks of sleepers, rails and other construction materials. Movements at Broadclyst were controlled from a 14 lever signal box at the east end of the up platform. The box closed as from 12th December 1965; in its final year it was only open on a 'when required' basis. In the vicinity of the station were two sets of railway cottages, four on the up side, behind the platform, and two close to the east end of the goods yard. The four cottage set was built on large brick arches due to poor ground conditions and as protection against flooding.

General goods facilities were withdrawn at Broadclyst in September 1965 and closure to passengers came in the following March when local services were withdrawn between Honiton and Exeter. The line was singled through the station in June 1967, the down track being retained. Unlike two other stations on the line within Devon, Broadclyst was not reopened. Today the up platform survives without the waiting shelter, though mostly covered in vegetation, and remnants of the down can also be seen. The buildings on the down side remain largely intact however, within the overall development 'Old Broadclyst Station'. The station building itself, with a long west extension, and the goods shed are both in commercial use. Between the building and the shed, industrial units have been inserted. The former permanent way depot on the upside is now used by large retail premises. The railway cottages survive.

Buckfastleigh. The main building on the down (towards Ashburton) platform with 517 class 0-4-2T No 1466 entering the station in about 1912. The large goods shed is to the left of the train.

BROADSANDS HALT

OPENED: 9th July 1928 (on the Paignton – Kingswear line originally opened through this site in 1861).

CLOSED: 23rd September 1929.

The details of this very short lived halt are sketchy. A single platform, two miles south of Paignton on the Kingswear branch, was authorised on 24th April 1928. In the estimated cost of £657 were steps to the road, lighting and a footpath. Close to Broadsands viaduct, its use is recorded as being only for excursion traffic between 9th July 1928 and 23rd September 1929; the halt never appeared in the public timetable. No record of expenditure has been found and no photograph is known.

BUCKFASTLEIGH

OPENED: 1st May 1872 (with the opening of the Buckfastleigh, Totnes & South Devon Railway, Totnes – Ashburton).

CLOSED: Passengers – 3rd November 1958.
Goods – 10th September 1962.

RE-OPENED: 5th April 1969 (on the Dart Valley, now South Devon Railway).

Buckfastleigh opened at the beginning of May 1872 with the commencement of services on the then broad gauge Buckfastleigh, Totnes & South Devon Railway. The line was converted to standard gauge in 1892. A typical GWR branch line station, sited in the River Dart Valley, it was east of Buckfastleigh village and south-west of Buckfast Abbey, constructed between 1907 and 1932. The latter generated considerable traffic reflected in the station board 'Buckfastleigh for Buckfast Abbey'. At the opening of the line there was considerable rivalry between Buckfastleigh and Ashburton regarding the scale and form of celebrations. The opening special train halted for 1½ hours at Buckfastleigh for toasts to be made at the Kings Arms Hotel. Some 1,500 poor people of the area were given an 'ample tea'; there was a procession through the decorated streets and festivities concluded with a bonfire and fireworks. (See also Ashburton text.)

The main platform and building were on the down (towards Ashburton) side of the line. The building, constructed of limestone with yellow brick edges, had ten windows and five doors. Two of the doors were on the platform side and three on the road side. The windows were constructed of wood, with an apex top and slate sills. The doors were of a similar design. The slate roof ran parallel to the platform. There were three chimney stacks, two on top of the ridge in the original building and one in the road side roof of a later northern extension of the building. A typical GWR wooden canopy with a saw tooth edge, covering the platform, was supported by seven ornamental brackets and timber beams. From north to south the building incorporated the station master's office, a parcels office, a gentlemen's waiting room, a ladies' waiting room and gent's toilet.

Towards the south end of the main platform was a large corrugated iron pagoda style hut with three sets of double doors. This was principally used as a general store. Beyond the far end of the platform was the station master's house. A second short platform was added on the up side alongside a loop line, which was itself lengthened in 1906. This second

Buckfastleigh. The main station building in its new role as the northern terminus of the South Devon Railway on 22nd June 2006.

platform, on which no shelter was erected, was used particularly for the loading and unloading of horses competing at the Buckfast races. Both platforms were filled with earth and hardcore behind a limestone face; they were topped with chippings and edged with stone slabs. The platforms were linked at the southern end by a rail level board crossing. In 1903 28,687 passenger tickets were issued at Buckfastleigh; in 1913 the total fell to 26,397; figures for 1923 and 1933 were 19,700 and 10,269. At its peak the station staff comprised the station master, two signalmen, one clerk, three porters and two lads.

Served by two main trailing sidings, the goods yard was sited to the north-west of the station. Reflecting the importance of freight traffic at Buckfastleigh, a substantial goods shed stood north of the main building behind the platform, its apex slate roof ending in wood planks over the track entrances. A southern steel extension was later added to the shed. The west road side of the shed was equipped with heavy sliding wooden doors under a canopy, giving access to a timber loading bay. By these doors stood a brick building used as a goods office. At the north end of the station on the down side was the 27 lever signal box built of wood on a brick base. Goods despatched from the yard included wood, stone, timber and agricultural/horticultural produce. Coal was the principal import. Alongside the shed were two further sidings terminating at loading docks. A five ton crane stood close to the north end of the shed.

Passenger services ceased in November 1958 and goods facilities were withdrawn in September 1962. After closure the building itself was used by Caladec, suppliers of underfloor heating and electronic components. Moves were soon afoot for the

preservation and reopening of the line with the formation of the Dart Valley Light Railway Company and the Dart Valley Railway Association (see Ashburton text). The station re-opened for passenger services on 5th April 1969 and was formally opened by Dr Beeching on 21st May 1969 (the line had already closed before his report was published!).

The station building has been beautifully restored for use by passengers on the now South Devon Railway. The goods shed, with some modern cladding is, in part, a museum, while a large new cafeteria and shop have been built west of the goods shed. The pagoda hut remains on the down platform which has been extended at the southern end. The original signal box is still in place but disused; in 2006 a new box was under construction at the south end of the station. A water tank has been re-erected, obtained from the GWR goods depot at South Lambeth; another import is the open footbridge at the south end obtained from Keynsham between Bristol and Bath. The former station master's house remains in residential use. The former trackbed north of the station is lost under the new A38 carriageway. To the north-east of the station extensive workshops have been developed in recent years. In May 2006 it was reported that the South Devon Railway had obtained planning permission for further development of the station site including a steam locomotive shed, turntable, carriage and wagon workshop, diesel shed and a building for the storage of long term projects.

BUDLEIGH SALTERTON

OPENED: 1st May 1897 (with the opening of the Budleigh Salterton Railway, Tipton St Johns – Budleigh Salterton).
CLOSED: Passengers – 6th March 1967.
Goods – 27th January 1964.

Opened as Salterton in May 1897, the station was renamed Budleigh Salterton just over a year later on 27th April 1898. For six years it was the terminus of the line from Tipton St Johns on the Sidmouth branch. As from 1st June 1903 Budleigh Salterton became a passing place with the opening of the extension on to Exmouth via Littleham.

The inaugural train was greeted by local dignitaries and the Sidmouth Volunteers Band, playing 'See the conquering hero comes'. Mrs Drummond, the wife of the Budleigh Salterton

Railway Chairman, declared the line open and then her husband formally handed the line over to the London & South Western Railway. The day was declared a public holiday in the town, the streets and houses being suitably decorated. A 'sumptuous free tea' was served to children aged under 14.

The 1897 station, in the north-west of the town, was a half mile from the seafront. It comprised a 316 ft long platform on the down (south) side of the line on which stood a single storey brick building with three tall chimneys and a wide horizontal canopy with a fretted valence. A flat roof extension was on the east end. With the opening of the line on to Exmouth, a second up platform of equal length was added, on which a small wooden shelter with a backward sloping roof was provided. An open metal footbridge linked the platforms, the base of the steps being close to the east ends of the building and shelter. The first train from the expanded station was apparently so full that a duplicate train had to be laid on (More flexible arrangements than today?).

Records reflect the fact that many more passengers travelled to the resort than those who left. In 1928 37,088 passenger tickets were issued and 55,420 collected. By 1936 the figures had fallen greatly to 12,424 and 19,217. Records also show that the proportion of passengers to and from Budleigh Salterton travelling first class was higher than average. In the early 1920s the station master was supported by six staff. In 1965 the last station master left the station and in 1966 there were only three staff. Over the years the staff made great endeavours to make the station attractive and it won 15 prizes in 'Best Kept Station' competitions. A special feature from 1952 was the display in white washed stones on the up side garden, 'A spot of glorious Devon – Budleigh Salterton'.

The station goods yard was on the down side west of the station. A goods loop ran through a brick goods shed which had a goods office annex at the east end. A siding trailed back behind the west end of the down platform to a dock and cattle pens. A two ton capacity crane was provided in the yard. Goods traffic was generally fairly light, fish and stone from a local quarry being the main exports. A small wooden engine shed stood from the early days at the west end of the yard serving branch line engines. It remained in use for some years after the opening of the line to Exmouth but was then closed and demolished. A low ground level 20 lever signal box off the west end of the down platform opened in June 1903 with the Exmouth extension. The box

Budleigh Salterton. Looking north-west in 1962 with the main building (left) on the down (towards Exmouth) side of the line. Note the unusual open metal footbridge. The station site is now redeveloped for housing.

controlled the signals, passing loop and access to the goods yard.

Goods facilities ceased in January 1964 followed by passenger services three years later with the closure of the line. The station buildings and platforms were demolished with the east of the site being redeveloped for housing. The western part was initially used for a Normans Cash and Carry Warehouse, the former goods shed being incorporated in the development. This western half has now also been developed for housing including the appropriately named, Norman Close.

BURLESCOMBE

OPENED: 1st May 1867 (on the GWR Taunton – Exeter line originally opened through this site in 1844).
CLOSED: Passengers – 5th October 1964.
Goods – 17th February 1964.

A short distance north-west of the centre of Burlescombe, and sited in a cutting, the station opened in May 1867. At 350 ft above sea level, Burlescombe was at the highest point of the line between Taunton and Exeter. The main single storey building incorporating all the main facilities, with a lower annex on its northern end, was on the up (towards Taunton) side of the line. Also on the up platform, north of the building, was a metal hut used as a store. A terrace of railway staff cottages stood behind the main building on top of the cutting. A wooden shelter served passengers on the down platform; adjoining its south end was a wooden hut.

No footbridge was provided, inter-platform movements being available either via a rail level

Burlescombe. A view north towards Taunton on 7th June 1921. The main single storey building is on the up platform together with a metal store hut. A wooden shelter and a small hut stand on the down platform.

board crossing at the northern end of the platforms or by using a road bridge which crossed the station site at the southern end. Steps linked the bridge to the platforms. In 1903 8,612 passenger tickets were issued at Burlescombe, the figure rose to 8,756 in 1913 and 10,638 in 1923 but then fell to 9,455 in 1933. A staff of eleven men were based there in the 1930s.

On the up side south of the road bridge was a small goods yard served by a goods loop. The Westleigh Mineral Railway, a mile long line, ran into the yard from the west. Opened in 1875 it was of a 3 ft gauge until 1899 when the gauge was standardised, which allowed direct connection to the loop. Goods facilities at Burlescombe were

Burn Halt (for Butterleigh). Looking north in 1960 towards Tiverton with the small wooden shelter on the stone platform. The halt was a late-comer on the Stoke Canon to Tiverton line in 1929.

withdrawn in February 1964.

Burlescombe signal box, on the southern end of the up platform beyond the road bridge, closed on 17th February 1964. In October that year, passenger services ceased and the buildings were subsequently demolished. Today there is no lineside trace but the railway cottages above the cutting remain. Housing has been developed on the up side, south of the road bridge covering part of the former goods yard.

BURN HALT (FOR BUTTERLEIGH)

OPENED: 26th January 1929 (on the Stoke Canon – Tiverton line originally opened through this site in 1885).

CLOSED: 7th October 1963.

Burn Halt (for Butterleigh) was a late addition to passenger facilities on the southern section of the Exe Valley line, opening some 44 years after passenger services commenced. Burn itself consisted of one farmstead, whilst Butterleigh was an ecclesiastical parish, a collection of scattered farmsteads. A footbridge over the River Exe, adjacent to the halt, also provided access to a few farms on the right (west) bank of the river. The halt was sited on the east (down) side of the single track line and was accessed by a short fenced footpath from the main Tiverton road (A396), which ran above the site, immediately to the east. The 109 ft long platform, faced with reconstituted stone blocks, had thick edging slabs. On and behind the centre of the platform was a small waiting shelter, built of horizontal wood planks and covered by a backward sloping corrugated iron roof. Traffic was occasional rather than regular, mainly comprising school children to and from Tiverton and shoppers to and from Tiverton and Exeter. Overall control was exercised from Cadeleigh, the next station to the north. The halt closed in October 1963 and no trace remains today.

BURRATOR AND SHEEPSTOR HALT

OPENED: 18th May 1925 (on the Yelverton – Princetown branch previously opened through this site in 1883) (see text).
CLOSED: 5th March 1956.

Opening as an unadvertised workman's platform on 14th February 1924, it was initially called Burrator Platform. Workmen travelled to and from the platform working at the Plymouth Corporation's large Burrator reservoir whose southern end was close by to the north-east. The siting of what was renamed Burrator Halt in 1929 gave a fine view over the reservoir, which was originally constructed between 1893 and 1898. A further change came with the addition of the suffix 'and Sheepstor' the name of a nearby tor and village.

The halt opened to the general public in May 1925. It was a basic heavy timber platform supported on wooden trestle legs with cross members. Along the back of the platform there was originally a wooden fence; this was later replaced by concrete posts with a steel rail and several wires. Behind the ramp at the south end of the platform was the timber waiting shelter on a concrete base with two small windows on the line side and a door in the southern wall. Two lamp standards provided lighting at the halt which closed to passengers in March 1956 with the withdrawal of services on the Princetown branch.

CADELEIGH

OPENED: 1st May 1885 (with the opening of the Exe Valley line Stoke Canon – Tiverton).
CLOSED: Passengers and Goods – 7th October 1963.

Opening at the beginning of May 1885, the station was then known as Cadeleigh and Bickleigh, the former being about 1¾ miles to the west and 300 ft higher, and the latter three quarters of a mile to the south-east. This double name was retained until 1st May 1906, from which date the station was known simply as Cadeleigh. The name Bickleigh was not used to avoid confusion with the station of that name on the Plym Valley line.

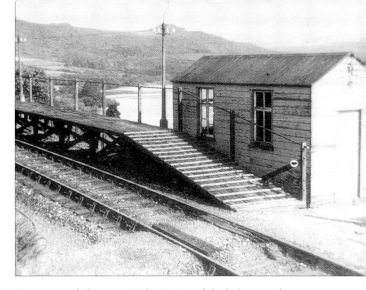

Burrator and Sheepstor Halt. A view of the halt on 26th September 1951. Behind the wooden waiting shelter can be seen the waters of Plymouth Corporation's Burrator reservoir.

The layout was basically up and down platform tracks, a goods loop behind the up (west) platform and a short stub siding running south from the south end of the loop serving cattle pens. The goods loop was lengthened at the north end in November 1929; the short cattle dock stub was removed a few years later. The original platforms were 322 ft long and faced with stone. Re-modelling of points at the southern end of the station in the early 1930s led to a rebuilding of the platform faces and edges, using blocks of reconstituted stone for the faces and concrete slabs for the edges. The platforms were slightly shortened at the south end. Inter-platform movements were via a rail level board crossing at the south end.

The main station building on the down (east) side was very typical of the southern section of the Exe Valley line with two stone built wings at right angles to the line. These wings had hipped roofs with gables and decorative barge boards and were topped by ornate ridge tiles. Between the two wings was a lower section in the front of which was a porch forming a waiting area. Behind the porch was a lamp room, the porters' room and a coal store. There was no entrance to the building from the rear, all passengers passing through a gate at the northern end of the building and then entering the building itself through a door into the central porch. The north wing of the building housed the general waiting room at the front and the ladies' waiting room and toilets to the rear. A lean-to annex on the northern end of the building formed the gent's

Cadeleigh. Looking north towards Dulverton in the early 1960s showing the main building on the down platform (with the roof of the station master's house behind), the signal box and waiting shelter on the up platform and the large goods shed. The station site is now the Devon Railway Centre.

toilets. At the front of the southern wing was the ticket office behind which was the station master's office. Accommodation for the station master was provided in a two storey house behind the north end of this down platform. On the up platform stood a small wooden waiting shelter with a backward sloping roof and a small fretted edged canopy.

In 1903 10,084 passenger tickets were issued at Cadeleigh; the figure fell subsequently to 8,892 in 1913, 6,560 in 1923 and 6,756 in 1933. Being adjacent to the main A396 road from Exeter to Tiverton, bus competition was severe and by 1957 it was recorded that only about 20 passengers a day regularly boarded trains at Cadeleigh. In the 1920s and 1930s three staff were based at the station.

For long periods freight traffic was more important at Cadeleigh, responsible for up to 80% of the station receipts. Sugar beet, timber and livestock were important exports. Coal and coke were the principal imports, together with general merchandise. The annual autumn cattle market generated considerable traffic but even this was lost to road haulage after the Second World War. The principal goods facilities behind the up platform included a goods shed, through which ran the goods loop. The shed incorporated only a 30 cwt crane but a larger crane was available in the yard, originally of five ton capacity but later replaced by a stronger structure to deal with the lifting of timber. Movements at the station were controlled by a signal box on the up platform, close to the waiting shelter.

Both passenger and goods services ceased at Cadeleigh in October 1963. For some years

subsequently the station site was used as a road depot by Devon County Council. The buildings remained largely intact with the main building used as a store. In 1997 the site was bought and developed in the following years as the Devon Railway Centre. Mark 1 railway carriages housing model railway layouts stand on track re-laid between the platforms. The station building, well restored after lying virtually derelict for nearly 20 years, is now used for a café, shop, exhibition and offices. The adjoining former station master's house, with extensions, was, in 2006, occupied by the Railway Centre Manager. The former goods shed also remains, containing a number of items including locomotives and old rolling stock. A section of the former rail track bed is now a road leading to an overflow car park used both by the Railway Centre and the adjoining Bickleigh Mill, another tourist attraction.

CAFFYNS HALT

OPENED: December 1906. (on the Barnstaple – Lynton line originally opened through this site in 1898) (see text).
CLOSED: 30th September 1935.

Records indicate that this halt, with a low level platform on the up (towards Barnstaple) side of the line, opened as New Mill Halt in December 1906. Initially it was used only by players at the nearby golf course. Indications are that public use of the halt came in about 1916 but it first appeared in the public timetables as Caffyns Halt in July 1924. A small shelter stood in the centre of the platform; the nameboard stating Caffyns Halt (for Golf Links). The halt closed in September 1935 and the site was cleared in the 1980s.

Caffyns Halt. The small shelter standing on the up (towards Barnstaple) side of the Lynton & Barnstaple Railway.

Camels Head Halt. A view south-east in about 1939 from the south end of the up platform towards the staggered down side platform with a pagoda hut.

CAMELS HEAD HALT

OPENED: 1st November 1906 (on the Lydford –
  Devonport line originally opened through this site in
  1890).
CLOSED: 4th May 1942.

The halt opened with the commencement of LSWR steam motor rail services between Plymouth Friary and St Budeaux. Named after a nearby public house, two short staggered platforms (the down/east side being slightly closer to Ford station) served passengers in this developing residential area. The platforms, originally of wood, were later constructed of concrete components. Photographic evidence indicates that a pagoda type shelter stood on the down platform but provision of a shelter on the up (west) side is uncertain. Following closure in 1942 the remains of the halt were left for many years but today there is no trace at the former site alongside Ferndale Road.

CAUSEWAY CROSSING HALT

OPENED: 18th May 1901 (see text) (with the opening
  of the Bideford Quay – Northam section of the
  Bideford, Westward Ho! & Appledore Railway).
CLOSED: 28th March 1917.

Sited about three quarters of a mile along the line from Bideford Quay the halt, sometimes known as 'The Causeway', was at a point where the first section of the Bideford, Westward Ho! & Appledore Railway (BWH&AR) crossed the south to north road from Bideford to Northam. It is possible that it did not open with the line in May 1901, as no entry appears in the Bradshaw timetable until March 1902. The Board of Trade insisted that full blown

Causeway Crossing Halt. A train on the Bideford, Westward Ho! & Appledore Railway stands at the halt. Beside the tall signal box is the crossing keeper's lodge in which a small window can just be seen, possibly used for the issue of tickets.

level crossing gates be installed; at first these were hand operated but they were soon replaced by gates worked from a tall (2½ storey) signal box erected on the down side of the line adjacent to the crossing. The box, the largest on the BWH&AR, was timber built with glazed window panels. Beside the box was the crossing keeper's cottage and beyond this again a short (30 ft), low (6 inches) platform. It is possible that, at busy times, tickets were sold from a hatch in the cottage wall. The halt was an important stop for trains, being sited on the northern edge of Bideford, close to housing development. It closed after only 16 years in 1917 (see Bideford Quay text). When seen, early in 2007, the cottage appeared derelict and two level crossing gate posts stood at the entrance to a house on the west side of Northam Road.

CHANTERS LANE

OPENED: 18th May 1901 (with the opening of the
Bideford Quay – Northam section of the Bideford,
Westward Ho! & Appledore Railway).
CLOSED: 28th March 1917.

The halt, sometimes known simply as 'The Lane',
was in Bideford, just to the north of the main
Bideford Yard, which included the Railway's carriage
and locomotive sheds. At this point the first section
of the Bideford, Westward Ho! & Appledore
Railway crossed Chanters Lane over a level crossing
busy enough to warrant a gate and signals. There
was a gate-keeper's cottage to the east of the crossing
but no record of a platform, passengers accessing the
train by means of steps on the carriages. The halt
closed after only 16 years in 1917. (see Bideford
Quay text).

CHAPELTON

OPENED: 8th June 1857 (on the North Devon Railway,
Crediton – Barnstaple, originally opened through
this site in 1854).
CLOSED: 19th April 1860.
REOPENED: 1st March 1875.
CLOSED: Passengers – remains open as a request stop
for services on the Exeter – Barnstaple line.
Goods – 4th January 1965.

From the opening of the line from Crediton to
Barnstaple in 1854, a siding was available at

Chapelton. The main station building stands at the north-
west end of the up (towards Exeter) platform. In the
foreground is the rail level board crossing connecting the
platforms. Across it runs a siding into the goods yard behind
the down platform.

Chapelton. Records indicate that a wooden
passenger platform was added on the up side,
opening in June 1857, with an initial service on all
days, including Sundays. In April 1858 the service
reduced to Tuesdays and Fridays only but, for a short
period at the end of May and early June of that year,
a daily service resumed with the Bath & West Show
held at Barnstaple. In October 1858 it is recorded
that there was only a service on Fridays and in April
1860 this first basic station closed. The station
reopened in March 1875 with a full daily service.
Throughout its life the name of the station in
timetables has varied: Chappletown, Chapleton and
today's Chapelton.

With its reopening the original wooden platform
was replaced by a stone structure, again on the up
(towards Exeter) side, on which stood, at the
Barnstaple end, a London & South Western Railway
style building, incorporating the station master's two
storey accommodation. Booking and waiting
facilities were in a single storey section with a very
tall chimney. A gent's toilet was added, at a later
date, in a separate flat roof block at the Exeter end.
When the line was doubled through the site from
19th October 1890, a down platform was added, on
which stood a waiting shelter in the centre and a 23
lever wooden signal box towards the Exeter end. No

footbridge was provided and inter-platform movement was via a rail level board crossing at the Barnstaple end. Chapelton station, over many years received awards in best kept garden competitions.

In 1928 8,437 passenger tickets were issued and 9,070 collected, in 1936 the figures were 5,250 and 5,960. A census held on 7th May 1963 indicated that 22 passengers joined and left the station. Further surveys over a winter week in 1976 and a summer week in 1977 showed that only five and thirteen passengers used the station in those weeks.

Behind the down platform two sidings formed the goods yard. From its opening in 1930 a large saw mill, adjacent to the yard, kept the ten ton capacity yard crane very busy moving pit props and other timber products. The yard closed in January 1965, followed by the signal box on 20th January 1966. The up line and platform were taken out of use on 21st May 1971. It was unusual on this line that, in this case, the platform with the original main building was not retained for further use.

Today Chapelton is a request stop for Exeter to Barnstaple services, trains using the 1890 former down platform, on which stands the original waiting shelter. The former station building remains in good condition on the unused, fenced off, former up platform, a small canopy and other extensions added. A Southern Railway style nameboard has been restored.

Chelfham. In about 1910 much foliage covers the small stone building on the up (towards Barnstaple) platform. At the far end of this platform is the open gent's toilet. The down platform has no shelter but a siding bisects the platform (left foreground).

CHELFHAM

OPENED: 16th May 1898 (with the opening of the
  Lynton & Barnstaple Railway).
CLOSED: Passengers and Goods – 30th September
  1935.

Sited immediately to the north of Chelfham viaduct, the principal engineering structure on the narrow gauge Lynton & Barnstaple Railway, the station, in a wooded setting, was named after a large farmstead, half a mile away to the south-east. The population in the immediate locality of the station was minimal but it served the villages of Stoke Rivers to the east, Shirwell to the north-east and Loxhore to the north.

Two very low platforms served passengers on a passing loop but there was no shelter on the down (towards Lynton) side. At the south end of the up platform was a picturesque small stone building, with an apex roof, containing a waiting room and booking office. At the rear the entrance was protected by a small porch. In the 1920s a small

wooden extension was added to the building at the south end providing more shelter. Also on the up platform at the north end was an open roof gent's toilet and a centrally sited wooden shed containing a seven lever ground frame. This frame controlled the loop and access to a short siding, trailing from the down line, that bisected the down platform at the south end. The siding was rarely used except by a single coal wagon.

In 1928 3,387 passenger tickets were issued and 7,581 collected. The figures had reduced to 2,490 and 2,552 in 1934. Following closure of the station at the end of September 1935 the building was derelict for a short while. It was withdrawn at auction in 1938 when the bidding stopped at £275. It was later sold and became a private residence with an extension on to the former platform. Today it is owned by the Lynton & Barnstaple Railway Association and available for self catering accommodation for its members.

CHRISTOW

OPENED: 1st July 1903 (with the opening of the Exeter
  Railway, Exeter – Ashton).
CLOSED: Passengers – 9th June 1958.
  Goods – 1st May 1961.

Sited just to the north of a bridge carrying a road to Doddiscombsleigh, a village one mile to the east and also a mile north of the village of Christow, the station opened at the beginning of July 1903 with the commencement of services on the Exeter Railway between Exeter and Ashton. A through line to

Christow. In this view looking north in 1958 the main red brick building stands on the up (towards Exeter) platform. Above the building can be seen the tall water tank. The main buildings survive today within a splendid house and garden.

Heathfield and Newton Abbot was thus completed, some 21 years after the southern section as far as Ashton opened. During these 21 years a line, operated as a siding, was used by freight traffic from Ashton as far north as Teign House, just south of Christow station.

Christow was unique on the line in that a loop, which allowed passing trains, was available from the outset. Indeed, it was the only passing place on the Exeter to Heathfield line until the whole line was upgraded in 1943 as a war-time expediency, the route being seen as an alternative to the vulnerable sea coast route from Exeter to Newton Abbot. The main red brick building with a slate roof and one chimney stood on the up (towards Exeter) side of the line. Close to its northern end was a tall brick goods shed, higher than the station building. A later extension to the station building virtually closed the gap between it and the goods shed. On the down (towards Heathfield) platform was a brick waiting shelter with one chimney. A rail level board crossing at the northern end of the platforms was available for inter-platform access for passengers and goods. Another late addition was a flight of steps from the east side of the road bridge to the south end of the down platform. This allowed the road bridge to be used as a safer route for inter-platform movements. Passenger figures were consistently higher at Christow than at other stations on the line. In 1913 14,480 tickets were issued; the total rose to 16,115 in 1923 but fell to 11,592 in 1933.

North of the station were several sidings including those in the Christow goods yard on the up side. Here were cattle pens and a tall water tank, which supplied water to water cranes at the south end of the down platform and north end of the up. The sidings at Christow were particularly busy with stone from a nearby quarry. Just north of the station on the down side was the 1925 loading plant of Scatter Rock Macadams Ltd. An aerial ropeway at one time crossed the tracks north of the station to the goods yard. In 1943 the loop line was extended northwards by about 370 yards as part of the war-time upgrading.

Christow signal box (30 levers), at the north end of the down platform, continued in use until passenger trains ceased on the line in June 1958. In September 1960 freight services also stopped from Ashton northwards, following serious flooding, but the formal date of freight services withdrawal was not until the beginning of May 1961. After all services ceased, the main buildings at Christow survived and today the former station, with extensions, is a splendid house. The down platform and waiting shelter also survive in the extensive garden.

CHUDLEIGH

OPENED: 9th October 1882 (with the opening of the Teign Valley Railway, Heathfield – Ashton).
CLOSED: Passengers – 9th June 1958.
   Goods – 4th December 1967 (coal depot only from 14th June 1965).

South-west of the market town of Chudleigh, and immediately south of a road bridge carrying the original alignment of the A38 over the line, the station opened in October 1882. Sited on the down (east) side of the line, the wooden station building

with an apex slate roof, a small platform canopy, one chimney, a small porch on the road side and two wings with apex slate roofs, was very similar to that at Heathfield.

Close to this main building, on its south side, was a wooden goods shed with an apex slate roof and sliding doors in the front and rear walls. Behind this shed, at the south end of the platform, ran a short siding, on which was stabled a camping coach from 1934 to 1939. The approach road to Chudleigh station was prone to flooding and in the 1920s a supplementary platform was added to the north of the station, reached by a raised gangway from an adjacent lane. Over the period 1913 to 1933, the number of passenger tickets issued at Chudleigh fell greatly from 19,895 to 2,695.

To the south of the station itself was a goods siding on the down (east) side of the line. For a period this was used for the transfer of oil from rail to road tankers. Rail movements were, for a period between 1893 and 1910, controlled from a small box acting as a ground frame on the up (west) side of the line, south of the station. The box was dismantled in about 1930. Passenger services ceased on the line in June 1958; goods facilities continued until December 1967, though, from June 1965, Chudleigh was only a coal depot. The site of the station is now lost under a major junction of the re-aligned up-graded A38.

Chudleigh. A Teign Valley train enters the station travelling towards Ashton and Exeter in about 1910. The main building with a small canopy stands on the down (east) side of the line. Alongside is the wooden goods shed.

Chudleigh Knighton Halt. A view of about 1960 showing the pagoda hut standing behind the replacement stone faced platform.

CHUDLEIGH KNIGHTON HALT

OPENED: 9th June 1924 (on the Heathfield – Exeter line originally opened through this site in 1882).
CLOSED: 9th June 1958.

Sited south of the village of Chudleigh Knighton, the halt opened in June 1924, forty two years after the Heathfield to Ashton line opened. This late addition to passenger facilities on the north-west (up) side was originally a timber structure, with a pagoda style

Churston. This south facing view of about 1910 shows the up and down (towards Kingswear) platforms (right), the main station building and the Brixham branch platform and shelter (left). Churston is now busy on the Paignton & Dartmouth Railway.

corrugated iron shelter, provided at a cost of £300. After the Second World War a stone faced platform was introduced, replacing the original structure. Trains of four to five carriages were once filled at the halt, providing enough traffic to justify its own additional train to Newton Abbot several times a week. The halt closed after 34 years in June 1958 with the withdrawal of passenger services on the line. The site of the halt is now under the alignment of the up-graded A38 that by-passes the village.

CHURSTON

OPENED: Passengers – 14th March 1861, Goods - 1st April 1861 (with the opening of the Paignton – Brixham Road (Churston) section of the Torbay & Dartmouth Railway).

CLOSED: Passengers – remains open for services on the Paignton & Dartmouth Railway (see text). Goods – 4th December 1967 (coal depot only from 14th June 1965).

The early history of Churston needs to be set in the context of the evolving local railway network. The station, then called Brixham Road, opened in March 1861 with the completion of the latest section of the broad gauge Torbay & Dartmouth Railway (T&DR) south from Paignton. Goods facilities became available two weeks later. The terminus role lasted for just over three years until the opening of the last section of the T&DR to Kingswear on 16th August 1864. For these three years transport from Churston was by horse bus to Kingswear at which a ferry service linked to Dartmouth across the River Dart

(see Kingswear text). Renamed Churston, the station finally took on the role of a junction with the commencement of services on the Brixham branch from 28th February 1868.

The station facilities evolved over this period of changing roles from 1861 to 1868. Sited immediately south of an over bridge carrying the road to Kingswear and Brixham (now A3022), the original platform and building were on the down (towards Kingswear) side. A second platform with shelter opened on the up side in 1865, together with a siding for iron ore traffic. The new service to Brixham in 1868 brought an additional separate bay platform with a shelter beyond the north end of the down platform. Following limited platform lengthening in 1892, in conjunction with the reduction in track gauge from broad to standard, more significant changes came in 1911/1912 including the lengthening of the crossing loop and the extension of the main platforms at the south end to a total length of 700 ft, accommodating the long holiday trains to Kingswear. Passenger traffic was at a reasonable level with 48,516 tickets issued in 1903. Comparable figures for 1913, 1923 and 1933 were 52,802, 40,969 and 15,774.

The opening of the Brixham branch necessitated the relocation of the small goods yard and goods shed to a site alongside the branch north-east of the station beyond the road bridge. The yard included a three ton capacity crane. A short dock siding behind the up platform was used both for horse boxes and storage of fish trucks. The fishing industry based at Brixham was the source of much freight traffic at Churston over the years. As from 9th February 1913 operations at Churston were controlled by a brick signal box (48 levers) on the down platform between the principal building and the covered footbridge. This box had replaced an 1892 box (39 levers) that had stood in the V between the main line from Paignton and the Brixham branch.

Churston's junction role continued until the closure of the Brixham branch on 13th May 1963, though the bay line was not taken out of use until 14th June 1968. General freight facilities were withdrawn in June 1965, the remaining coal depot closing in December 1967. Passenger services declined in the 1960s and the station was unstaffed, except on summer Saturdays, from 20th May 1968. The station loop and signal box were taken out of use on 20th October 1968 and the unstaffed building boarded up in 1971.

Following the take over of services on the Paignton

– Kingswear line by the Dart Valley Railway from 1st November 1972, Churston's fortunes revived. In 1979 the passing loop was restored and a signal box opened. The Brixham bay line was re-laid in November 1980 and a turntable, formerly at Goodrington, was installed in 1984 at the former entrance to the Brixham bay. The signal box closed again in 1991, when control of operations on the whole line was taken over by a new Panel near the former Britannia Halt, north of Kingswear. In the 1990s Churston, because of available space, became the engineering centre for the line, a new locomotive depot opening on the site of the former up bay line in 1993. A carriage painting workshop followed on the down side adjacent to the main building in 1996. The station building itself was renovated and reopened to the public in 1993; the covered footbridge has also been renovated. Churston is now playing a key role in the operation of the new Paignton & Dartmouth Railway. The former Railway Hotel is renamed the White Horse Hotel. The former goods yard is now a housing development.

CLEARBROOK HALT

OPENED: 29th October 1928 (on the Plymouth – Yelverton – Tavistock line originally opened through this site in 1859).
CLOSED: 31st December 1962.

A late addition to passenger facilities on the Plymouth to Tavistock line south of Yelverton, the halt served the adjacent small community of Clearbrook. It was also built to attract potential day trippers to the surrounding woodland, although in 1928 it came too late for that summer season. Described by one railway historian as 'one of the most austere efforts of the GWR', the halt was on the west side of the single track line. The platform was constructed of earth infill behind old railway sleepers, the rear of the platform being unfenced but backed by a grass bank and shrubs. At the northern end of the platform was an arc roofed corrugated iron shelter, beside which, alongside its southern end, was a solitary seat. The halt's nameboard was a large wooden structure mounted on old rails with cast iron letters. Access to the nearby road was via a path and steps. It was reported that on occasions cakes were taken by a barrow from the halt to a local shop. Following closure at the end of December 1962, the site was purchased by a local resident and turned into a garden.

Clearbrook Halt. Looking north in about 1960 towards Tavistock, this basic halt opened in 1928 for potential day trippers to nearby woodland.

CLYST ST MARY AND DIGBY HALT

OPENED: 1st June 1908 (on the Exeter – Exmouth line originally opened through this site in 1861).
CLOSED: 27th September 1948.

Sited on the Exmouth branch immediately to the north of a rail bridge over the Exeter to Sidmouth road (originally A35, now A3052), the impetus for the provision of this halt was the introduction of a steam rail-motor service in June 1908 between Exeter and Topsham. The halt served the village of Clyst St Mary, a mile to the south-east and the Digby Mental Hospital, half a mile to the south. Two wooden sleeper platforms, 120 ft long, were provided, with rear fencing but no shelters. In need of reconstruction after the Second World War the halt was closed in September 1948 and dismantled soon after. Today there is no trace and no photograph is known. Forty seven years later Digby and Sowton station was opened about 300 yards to the south.

COLDHARBOUR HALT

OPENED: 23rd February 1929 (on the Culm Valley line, Tiverton Junction – Hemyock originally opened through this site in 1876).
CLOSED: 9th September 1963.

About half a mile west of the village of Uffculme was Coldharbour Mill, a large worsted woollen mill which, from June 1877, was served by a nine wagon capacity siding on the north side of the Culm Valley

Coldharbour Halt. A view in about 1960 looking east towards Hemyock. The wooden shelter stands on the sleeper face platform. The level crossing gates (right) are controlled from the adjacent cabin.

appearance of a small signal cabin.

As at Whitehall Halt, further east along the line, operations at Coldharbour were informal, including the practice of the train guard leaving London newspapers in the shelter for collection by the local residents. Payment for the papers was made in a tobacco tin stored in the shelter.

The halt closed in September 1963 when passenger services ceased on the line. Freight trains continued to pass through until the end of 1975, serving the dairy factory at Hemyock. Coldharbour Mill closed in 1981 and became a working wool museum. The site of Coldharbour Halt is now a part of the Mill car park. To the east a footpath follows the trackbed to Uffculme.

COLYFORD

OPENED: 16th March 1868 (with the opening of the
Seaton & Beer Railway, Seaton Junction – Seaton).
CLOSED: Passengers – 7th March 1966.
Goods – Facilities never provided.
REOPENED: 9th April 1971 (as the then northern
terminus of the Seaton Tramway).

line. The principal traffic handled at the siding was coal for the mill. A short distance to the east, Coldharbour Halt opened in February 1929, at a cost of £111. The sleeper face tarmac surface platform, surmounted by a wooden horizontal plank shelter, with a backward sloping roof, stood on the down (towards Hemyock) side of the line. Wooden fencing ran along the back of the platform.

The halt was west of, and adjacent to, a level crossing which carried a minor road north to south from Coldharbour to Smithincott. The level crossing was controlled from a hut, also on the north side of the line, which doubled as a small ticket office. A small ticket window, sheltered by a canopy, was provided at the rear of the hut, which had the

The smallest station on the Seaton branch, opened in March 1868, Colyford served the village immediately to the west over the River Axe. The platform, on the west side of the single line, was immediately to the south of a level crossing carrying the main Lyme Regis to Exeter road. A crossing keeper's cottage, built in 1867 at a cost of £625, stood by the level crossing at the north end of the platform. It included the station booking office. The cottage was later demolished and replaced by a concrete shelter. Also in the centre of the platform was a wooden waiting shelter, with a small chimney, that, following the demolition of the crossing cottage, also became the booking office. There was also a cast iron gent's urinal, sited on the platform south of the wooden shelter.

In 1928 4,968 passenger tickets were issued and 4,271 collected; figures for 1936 about halved to 2,385 and 2,414. The maximum staffing at Colyford was one porter. No specific goods facilities were provided but Colyford did handle parcels and boxes of fish.

By 1959 the wooden shelter/booking office had gone but the concrete shelter survived. The station closed with the withdrawal of passenger services on the branch in March 1966. Some five years later Colyford became the northern terminus of the

Colyford. Looking south from the level crossing gates in 1958 showing the wooden shelter and the concrete shelter (right), the latter replacing the crossing keeper's cottage. At the far end of the platform, beyond the shelter, is the cast iron gent's urinal which is today's sole surviving structure.

Seaton Tramway (*see Seaton text*). The old platform and shelter were demolished but the gent's urinal was not and is still there today. A crossing loop has been laid on the station site and passengers board and leave the trams at rail level. From 1980, when the tramway was extended north to a new terminus at Colyton, lifting barriers, operated by the tram driver, were installed at the level crossing.

COLYTON

OPENED: 16th March 1868 (with the opening of the Seaton & Beer Railway, Seaton Junction – Seaton).
CLOSED: Passengers – 7th March 1966.
Goods – 3rd February 1964.
REOPENED: 8th April 1980 (as the final northern terminus of the Seaton Tramway).

Opening in March 1868 as Colyton Town (the suffix was dropped in September 1890), the single platform station was on an embankment just east of the River Coly and about a half mile east of the village. The large red brick building, which included two storey accommodation for the station master at the southern end, stood on the down (towards Seaton) east side of the line. Features included round headed windows, a steeply pitched roof and double sliding doors from the platform to the booking office. The main station facilities were within this building.

At the north end of the platform was a detached flat roof brick shed, with stone quoins and sliding doors on the platform side. This was principally used as a store for parcels conveyed on passenger trains. The main goods facilities were in a two siding yard opposite the platform on the west side of the line. A brick goods shed with an apex roof, a canopy on the track side, and a small lean-to office at the north end

Colyton. The view south in 1958 with the main building, including the two storey accommodation for the station master, on the down (towards Seaton) side of the line. The water tank is beyond the south end of the platform. The goods shed is seen over the two wagons in the siding.

stood beside the main siding. The outer siding ran alongside a store belonging to Messrs Bradford & Sons.

A water tank, provided from 1873, was sited just beyond the south end of the platform. It stood on long legs and a roof was later added. Colyton signal box, at the far north end of the platform on the east side of the line, dated from 5th March 1899. The box controlled access to the goods yard. It was reduced to a ground frame as early as 4th April 1922 and finally closed on 11th November 1958. It was then demolished, being replaced by a two lever ground frame.

In 1928 19,814 tickets were issued at Colyton and 27,331 collected. By 1936 the figures had fallen to 13,431 and 15,398. A station master was based at Colyton until 1928 when the station came under the control of the Seaton station master. Colyton was unstaffed from 3rd February 1964, the same day that the goods yard closed. Passenger services continued for another two years until March 1966 when services were withdrawn on the Seaton branch.

Trackwork was lifted in the goods yard by May 1964 but the goods shed was spared and survives today. Likewise the station building was not demolished and received a new lease of life when Colyton became the northern terminus of the Seaton Tramway when it opened to Colyton on 8th March 1980 (see Seaton text). The old platform is not used directly by tram passengers who enter and leave trams at rail level just north of the station. The

63

station building, with additions, is used as a booking office, shop and café, with railings along the platform edge. A fine new canopy protects café customers taking refreshments at tables on the platform. The former parcels store survives at the north end of the platform as does the station master's accommodation.

COMBPYNE

OPENED: 24th August 1903 (with the opening of the Axminster & Lyme Regis Light Railway).
CLOSED: Passengers – 29th November 1965.
   Goods – 5th December 1960.

Combpyne, the only intermediate station on the branch line from Axminster to Lyme Regis, opened in August 1903. At nearly 500 ft above sea level, it was above and east of the settlement after which it was named. The single north-west – south-east platform was originally served by one track on the down side but an up loop on the south-west side was added in 1906. Beyond this up loop was a further loop siding off which were two short stubs, one to the north-west and one to the south-east, the latter serving a small loading dock.

As from 12th August 1921, the up loop was taken out and converted to a siding linking to the remaining through line at the Lyme Regis end of the station site. This siding was later used for some years to house a camping coach. A new platform face constructed of concrete slabs was built alongside the through line whilst the original up loop face was

Combpyne. Looking north in 1958 at the isolated platform which by that time was single faced. At the far end of the siding is a camping coach. The station master's house and single storey station building stand at right angles to the platform (left).

converted to a grass bank. A 14 lever signal box originally stood off the Lyme Regis end of the platform, though only four levers were ever used. The box also closed on 12th August 1921, all signalling being removed from the site. The box continued to be used as only a ground frame until 17th June 1930, when it was replaced by a small two lever ground frame. The box itself was removed to nearby Hook Farm where it was used to store grain.

Combpyne was unusual in that the main brick station building, containing the ticket office, a waiting room, toilets for ladies and gents and the station master's house were sited away from the platform to the south-west at right angles to the line. The post of station master was abolished in 1930, a leading porter at Combpyne coming under the supervision of the Lyme Regis station master.

Being relatively remote from settlements little traffic was generated locally. However, nearby spectacles brought some business, in particular the 1839 cliff landslip some two miles to the south. A boost came in 1908 when a further slip was followed by a ground fire that lasted eight months. The nameboard at the station proclaimed 'Combpyne for Landslip'!

Closure to goods came in December 1960. The siding was retained to stable the camping coach until all passenger facilities ceased with the withdrawal of passenger services from the Lyme Regis branch in November 1965. The former station building and station master's house remain in residential use and the site of the old platform is now a lawn.

COPPLESTONE

OPENED: 1st August 1854 (with the opening of the North Devon Railway, Crediton – Barnstaple).
CLOSED: Passengers – remains open as a request stop for services on the Exeter – Barnstaple line.
   Goods – 6th September 1965.

At the summit (350 ft) of the line between Crediton and Barnstaple, and a half mile north of the village of Copplestone, the station opened at the beginning of August 1854. The section of the line from Coleford Junction, north of Yeoford to Copplestone, was doubled in 1883 but northwards to Umberleigh it always remained single.

The main station building on the down (towards Barnstaple) platform was typical of the substantial structures developed from the outset by the North Devon Railway (NDR). Similar to that at five other stations on the line, it incorporated the booking

office, waiting room, toilets and the station master's office. It also included the two storey station master's house. There was no platform canopy. A wooden shelter with a backward sloping roof provided additional waiting facilities beyond the Barnstaple end of the building. On the up platform there was only a stone waiting shelter, again without a canopy. Inter platform movement was via a rail level board crossing at the north end of the platforms, no footbridge being provided. At the Crediton end of the up platform was, for many years, a water tower with a long hose. This tower, with a plaque 'L&SWR Wimbledon Works 1887', replaced an earlier NDR water crane. A water crane also stood at the Barnstaple end of the down platform.

Statistics indicate that Copplestone was the least patronised of all the stations between Crediton and Barnstaple. In 1928 4,224 passenger tickets were issued and 5,226 collected; comparable figures for 1936 were 2,377 and 3,710. A census of 7th May 1963 showed only ten passengers joining and leaving trains on that day at Copplestone. Further surveys over a winter week in 1976 and a summer week in 1977 give figures of only three for the former and one for the latter!

Copplestone goods yard, on the down side beyond the north end of the station, included a goods loop, a loading dock with a five ton capacity crane, cattle pens and a wooden goods shed through which ran a siding. The shed included a loading platform, a two ton crane and goods office. The yard's two main sidings terminated at buffer stops, one adjacent to a slaughterhouse. Around the yard were a number of buildings housing local firms. The yard closed in September 1965. The 1873 10 lever signal box was on the up side at the north end of the up platform, opposite the goods yard. Built of wood on a stone

base, the box closed on 17th October 1971 and was subsequently demolished.

Today Copplestone is a request stop for Exeter to Barnstaple services, trains using the former down platform on which stands a modern glass shelter at the Crediton end. The former station house, fenced off from the platform, is in private residential use; remnants of the former up platform are still evident. New housing has been developed to the rear of the station and, when seen early in 2007, development was also under way on the former goods yard.

CORNBOROUGH CLIFFS

OPENED: October 1911 (on the Bideford Quay – Northam section of the Bideford, Westward Ho! & Appledore Railway originally opened through this site in 1901).
CLOSED: 28th March 1917.

Cornborough Cliffs was a late addition to the facilities on the Bideford, Westward Ho! & Appledore Railway, just over three miles from Bideford Quay. Sited where the line ran south-west to north-east along the cliffs, it first appeared in the public timetables in October 1911. The most remote stopping place on the line, it was popular in the summer months for walkers who walked along the cliffs from Westward Ho! and returned by train. A short (30 ft), low (6 inches) platform on the up

(towards Bideford) side, it was accessed via a footpath on the seaward side of the line. The halt closed less than six years after opening when services ceased on the line. (see Bideford Quay text).

CORNWOOD

OPENED: Late August 1852 (on the Totnes – Plymouth (Laira Green) line originally opened through this site in 1848).

CLOSED: Passengers and Goods – 2nd March 1959.

Sited in the upper valley of the River Yealm, records indicate that the station opened in late August or on 1st September 1852, some four years after the single track broad gauge line opened from Totnes to Plymouth. It was originally, realistically, called Cornwood Road, being one mile south of the village, but was renamed Cornwood in April 1864. The station facilities were, without doubt, elaborate for the low level of traffic generated. The original 1852 building and platform were on the up (towards Brent) side; a down platform and waiting shelter were added when the line through Cornwood was doubled in 1893. Both the main building and waiting shelter had small chimneys and canopies. The platforms were linked by a covered footbridge towards the east end, the wide steps on both sides being also covered. By the mid 1950s the footbridge roof had been removed. A metal parcels shed was sited towards the east (Brent) end of the up platform beyond which was the 17 lever signal box, which closed on 26th February 1963. In 1921 seven men were based at Cornwood, including a station master, whose house was behind the up platform. Today all line side trace of the station has gone but the former station master's house remains in residential use.

Cornwood. A view east in about 1910 showing the original 1852 main building on the up (towards Brent) platform (left), the 1893 down platform and waiting shelter and the covered footbridge.

Coryton. Looking east in about 1960 at the local stone building on the up (towards Lydford) side of the line. Note the fire buckets beside the metal goods lock up.

CORYTON

OPENED: 1st July 1865 (with the opening of the Launceston & South Devon Railway), Tavistock – Launceston (Cornwall).

CLOSED: Passengers and Goods – 31st December 1962.

Sited one mile west of the village of Coryton, this picturesque country station stood on the up (north) side of the line, the 300 ft long platform being stone faced and slab edged with a paving and chipping surface. A wood slatted fence ran along the back. A local stone building with a slate roof and stone chimneys stood on the east end of the platform housing the waiting room and booking office. An extension at the west end incorporated the toilets. West of the building was a corrugated iron goods lock up with an arc roof. In 1903 7,469 passenger tickets were issued at Coryton; the figure rose to 7,527 in 1913 but fell to 6,867 in 1923 and 3,508 in 1933.

There were very limited facilities for goods traffic, with one goods siding terminating at the west end of the platform at a loading dock, and a further siding to the west, reached at first by a cross over, serving cattle pens. The station, in the early days dealt with large quantities of manganese; by 1872 4,000 tons were handled per annum. No signal box was ever provided at Coryton, access to the sidings being provided by a ground frame, the frame being taken out on 31st March 1965.

Although it was one of the smallest stations on the line, Coryton at one time had its own station master, a large double gable house being provided behind the station. The station became unstaffed and reduced to halt status as from 14th September 1959. Both passenger and goods facilities were withdrawn at the end of December 1962. The station building was not demolished and following renovation and extension, it was incorporated within a fine dwelling. The station master's house also survives as a residence.

Cove Halt. A GWR pagoda style hut serves passengers on the east side of the Tiverton to Bampton line. To the left are the crossing keeper's cottage and signal cabin which both survive today together with remnants of the platform. In the distance are quarry buildings.

COVE HALT

OPENED: 9th June 1924 (on the Tiverton – Bampton line originally opened through this site in 1884).
CLOSED: 7th October 1963.

A siding was laid in the village of Cove during the early days of the line which opened in 1884. The siding was sited to the south of a level crossing carrying a minor road west from the village. Records show that, in March 1923, a low, ballast level, wooden platform was installed at Cove siding, on the east side of the line. However, the halt did not apparently open until early June 1924. Soon after its opening, and by 1926, the volume of passenger traffic led to the construction of a more substantial halt, with a 109 ft long stone platform. Access to the halt was via a wicket gate, adjacent to the level crossing. Shelter was provided in a corrugated iron GWR pagoda style hut, the only one of its type on the whole Exe Valley line. At the rear of the platform were concrete posts and wire. To the north of the level crossing, on the west side, was the crossing keeper's cottage and a small 13 lever signal cabin, which was reduced to a ground frame only in 1923. Use of the siding ceased in 1954 and the halt itself closed in October 1963 with the withdrawal of passenger services on the line. Today the crossing keeper's cottage and signal cabin survive in residential use. A copse has grown over the site of the halt but remnants of the platform can be seen in the undergrowth.

CREDITON

OPENED: 12th May 1851 (with the opening of the Exeter & Crediton Railway, Cowley Junction – Crediton).
CLOSED: Passengers – remains open for services on the Exeter – Barnstaple line.
Goods – 4th December 1967.

The initial history of Crediton station, at the south-eastern end of the town, was complex and was one of the worst examples of early railway company rivalry. Crediton was originally the terminus of the broad gauge Exeter & Crediton Railway, a company closely allied with the Bristol & Exeter Railway. As such, it should subsequently have come under the auspices of the Great Western Railway. The London & South Western Railway (LSWR), however, had other ideas seeing Crediton as a potential jumping off point for other lines in mid and north Devon. This came about from 1876 when the LSWR gained control of the Exeter to Crediton line.

Although the line to Crediton was completed by 1847, it did not open for broad gauge services until May 1851, the delay being entirely due to the prolonged disputes over ownership and gauge. A

Crediton. A general view east from the footbridge on 3rd August 1955 showing the main building with a shelter beyond on the up platform (left) and a smaller building and a waiting shelter on the down. All these except the smaller building on the down side survive today. The brick goods shed is seen beyond the buildings on the up side.

compromise had been reached, in that one line was laid at broad gauge and one at standard, though the latter was unused, with standard gauge trains not reaching Exeter until 1860! The terminus status of Crediton only lasted three years as, from 1st August 1854, services began on the broad gauge line from Crediton north to Barnstaple. Mixed gauge trains operated to Exeter from 1st February 1862 and to Bideford from 2nd March 1863. Further services through Crediton came with the opening of the standard gauge line to North Tawton in 1865 and subsequently in stages through to Plymouth via Okehampton. Broad gauge services to Barnstaple and Bideford ceased on 30th April 1877 and to Exeter on 20th May 1892, Crediton being one of the last outposts of the broad gauge in Devon.

Ceremonial opening took place on Monday 12th May 1851; at 1.0 p.m. a five coach train arrived from Exeter St Davids carrying directors of the Exeter & Crediton and Bristol & Exeter Railways. A half hour later a second train of nine coaches arrived conveying several hundred more passengers. The trains were met by a deputation of local residents and a procession, led by the band of the Royal East Devon Yeomanry, walked through the streets, decorated with flowers, trees and triumphal arches, to the Market House for a banquet held for 230 people.

An initial 1851 terminus building was replaced by a new structure on the present site, with the opening of the extension to Barnstaple in August 1854. The structures at Crediton generally date from this time. The main building, sited on the up (towards Exeter) side was of brick, originally with three tall chimneys and what was described as a veranda around the building, at the junction of the walls and roof. It incorporated the station master's office, the booking office and other facilities. The veranda was removed in later years and a platform canopy added when the platforms were widened, following the abolition of the broad gauge. A small canopy over the road side entrance protected passengers. South of the main building, a wooden weather board shelter, also with a platform canopy, was added in LSWR times. On the down platform was a smaller building similar to that on the main also initially with an all round veranda. This incorporated cloakrooms and facilities for porters. On its north side was another later wooden waiting shelter with a small canopy. A footbridge was constructed in 1878 adjacent to, and east of, the level crossing at the Barnstaple end of the station. It was a double bridge with one side for pedestrians, for use when the crossing gates were closed, and the second linking the two platforms. The two sections were separated by a barrier; in early days there was a roof but this was later removed. Crediton was a relatively busy station; in 1928 19,788 passenger tickets were issued; this figure subsequently fell to 8,724 in 1936. Equivalent figures for the number of tickets collected in the two years were 22,448 and 12,898. A later survey showed that, in a winter week in 1976, 62 passengers used the station. The equivalent figure for a summer week in 1977 was 218. During the Second World War Crediton station handled many children evacuated from major urban areas threatened with bombing.

Freight facilities were quite extensive at Crediton. At the west end of the station there was originally a siding with a wagon turntable from which four short sidings radiated. These and cattle pens at the west end of the platform were removed when the platform was lengthened in about 1875. The main goods yard was on the up side to the east of, and behind, the up platform. An early wooden goods shed with a curved roof was used for transferring goods between broad and standard gauge trains. A subsequent brick shed was again replaced by a steel framed structure in the late 1950s. The yard also contained cattle pens, a five ton capacity crane, an end loading dock, a wagon turntable and also a number of buildings relating to local firms. There were also sidings on the down side, including one serving more cattle pens. These sidings were often used for carriage storage. The yard itself closed for general goods traffic in December 1967.

Traffic movements were principally controlled by the 22 lever Crediton West signal box, sited west of the level crossing on the up side, the gates of which it controlled. Lifting barriers replaced the gates from 27th January 1974. When the Exeter to Crediton line was singled in 1984, the box controlled the crossing loop at Crediton. The box remains today, the last of its design and vintage, now only acting as a base for the exchange of line tokens. An 1875 East signal box (16 levers) east of the station goods yard and on the up side, was reduced to a ground frame in about 1916, taken out of use in 1970 and subsequently demolished.

Today the main building on the up platform remains with many of its original features still in place, but lacking the tall chimneys. The building houses the excellent Crediton Station Tea Rooms and also an exhibition on the history of the Exeter to

Crediton. An archive view of about 1915 showing First World War recruits assembled on the platform 'off to join the 6th Devons – Crediton's total over 300'.

Crediton A detailed look at the down side building, a single chimney stack replacing the original three tall chimneys, and the later wooden waiting shelter. Today the building incorporates the excellent Crediton Station Tea Rooms and an exhibition on local railway history.

Barnstaple line. A metal plaque at the north end of the up platform records the celebrations held on 12th May 2001, marking the 150th anniversary of the opening of the Exeter & Crediton Railway. The up side wooden shelter remains as does the wooden shelter on the down. The original building on the down platform has, however, gone. The goods shed, fenced off from the running lines, was re-used within a small industrial estate but in 1993 it was damaged in a fire and subsequently demolished.

CULLOMPTON

OPENED: 1st May 1844 (with the opening of the Beam Bridge (south of Wellington, Somerset) – Exeter section of the Bristol & Exeter Railway).
CLOSED: Passengers – 5th October 1964.
   Goods – 8th May 1967.

Opening at the beginning of May 1844, the station principally served the busy market and wool town of Cullompton, half a mile to the west. From its opening until December 1867, it was named Collumpton in the timetables. The principal building, incorporating the main booking and waiting facilities, was on the up (west) side of the line, that closest to the town itself. A smaller matching building stood on the shorter down platform. Both buildings had small horizontal canopies. The platforms were linked by a covered footbridge at the southern end of the buildings, originally of wood but later replaced by a steel structure. The goods yard with a goods shed was on

Cullompton. In about 1890 mixed gauge is still in place at the then two track station. This view looking north shows the short down platform, the original wooden footbridge and, in the distance, the original goods shed.

Cullompton. By the 1960s the station had been rebuilt for some thirty years with four tracks running through. This view looking south shows the up side building with a conventional canopy and the long open footbridge.

the down side behind, and to the north of, the station.

As at Tiverton Junction, the station was rebuilt in the early 1930s to accommodate four tracks through the station, two through and two platform loops. The down loop and a 49 lever signal box on the north end of the up platform came into operation on 25th October 1931, the up loop following six weeks later. The up and down side buildings now had conventional canopies with a wooden fretted valence. A long open footbridge connected the platforms across the four tracks. In 1903 27,235 passenger tickets were issued at Cullompton; the total then gradually fell over the years to 24,651 in 1913, 23,564 in 1923 and 23,768 in 1933. A staff of 12 men were based at Cullompton in 1903; this rose to 21 in 1938.

In the 1930s rebuild the goods facilities were also expanded, now served by a goods loop behind the down platform. The 1931 brick goods shed was much larger than its predecessor. In the yard was a six ton capacity cane.

Passenger services ceased in October 1964 but goods facilities continued for nearly three years to May 1967. The loops were taken out of use in 1969. The station buildings and footbridge were demolished in 1978 but the buildings in the goods yard remained for some years, for a period used by a road transport firm. Today a motorway service station covers the sites of the former goods yard and down side structures. Remnants of the up side platform can, however, still be seen.

CULMSTOCK

OPENED: 29th May 1876 (with the opening of the Culm Valley Light Railway, Tiverton Junction – Hemyock).
CLOSED: Passengers and Goods – 9th September 1963.

Sited close to the village centre, the station on the down (towards Hemyock) side of the Culm Valley line opened at the end of May 1876. Ceremonies were held on this opening day at Culmstock, in contrast to those at Hemyock, which were held three days later. The first train was greeted by a procession led by the Holcombe Regis Brass Band playing 'See the conquering hero comes'. The assembled crowd of several hundred cheered and, as the train left the station, the band played 'God save the Queen'.

The red brick station building, with external timber framing, red roof tiles and one chimney, standing on a brick face platform, housed the booking and waiting facilities. The wooden framing was later removed. At the east end was a low wooden annex housing the gent's toilets. In 1903 5,603 passenger tickets were issued, the figure fell to 5,375 in 1913 and 4,403 in 1923 and then rose a little to 4,511 in 1933. Two staff was the normal level at Culmstock.

The small goods yard was opposite the station building. Its original layout comprised a loop siding through a wooden goods shed, with a one ton capacity crane. In this position road vehicles needed

Culmstock. The red brick building and goods lock up on the north side of the Culm Valley Railway on 7th September 1963, two days before the station closed.

to cross the main running line to reach the shed. Two sidings, trailing back in a westerly direction, served a cattle dock and loading platform. The goods shed was demolished in 1932 to allow a longer loop to be introduced. The shed was replaced by a standard GWR corrugated iron lock up on the platform, east of the station building. This replacement shed had a sliding door on the platform side and an apex style roof. The cattle dock and loading platform remained in the same position, each served by a trailing siding from the longer loop. In 1877 the goods yard had a 1½ ton capacity crane but by 1904 the crane capacity was only one ton. By 1938 a three ton crane was provided but this was removed by 1956.

Staffing ceased at Culmstock on 2nd May 1960 and both passenger and goods services ceased in September 1963. Traffic continued through the site until late 1975 associated with the dairy factory at Hemyock.

Today all station structures have gone. The former Railway Hotel behind and west of the station, which contains a number of photographs of the railway era (and serves a good lunch!) is now the Culm Valley Inn. Its car park covers most of the west end of the former station site. The inn sign features a small engine. Part of the loading platform wall forms the southern boundary of the car park and on the loading platform site are picnic tables.

To the east of the station is a large modern residence, 'Station House', and other housing units. West from the former station site a footpath follows the track bed towards Uffculme.

DARTMOUTH

OPENED: 16th August 1864 (with the commencement of the Kingswear – Dartmouth ferry service following the opening of the Brixton Road – Kingswear section of the Torbay & Dartmouth Railway).

CLOSED: See text.

As its name implies, the original aim of the Torbay & Dartmouth Railway was a rail terminus at Dartmouth. However, due to construction and associated cost problems, the line terminated at Kingswear on the east bank of the River Dart, with a link ferry service to a pontoon at Dartmouth (see also Kingswear text). Despite the lack of tracks it was decided to provide station facilities on the quay at Dartmouth. After early structures on the pontoon itself, a station building (65 ft x 21 ft) was opened in 1889, at a cost of £4,680. It included a booking office, waiting room and facilities for handling parcels. At a later date an office was incorporated, controlling the movement of cars to and from the cross river ferry. The 'station' had a fine cast iron crest on the ridge above the slate roof and also a canopy, with a glazed roof and valence on the road side. The pontoons beside the building were roofed with corrugated iron.

For many years the GWR claimed it was the only railway company with a station to which no rails were laid! Despite the lack of trains, the station master at Dartmouth was of a higher grade than his colleague at Kingswear because of the large scale of important traffic to and from the Royal Naval

Dartmouth. A view of the 'station with no trains'. A solid tyred GWR parcels delivery van stands in front of the station in about 1920. To the right is the entrance to the covered way down to the ferry pontoon. Note the sign 'To the Ferry Steamer'.

Dawlish. Passengers wait on the up platform in about 1912.
A steam rail motor approaches from the Newton Abbot
direction.

College. From 1901 to 1954 the GWR operated the
ferry itself; the ferry rights before 1901 and up to
1972 were held by the railway but leased out. In
1972 the rights were sold to Dartmouth Council and
today the ferry is operated by the Paignton &
Dartmouth Railway. The fine 1889 building remains
in use as the Station Restaurant, leased from South
Hams District Council. The ferry pontoon is
uncovered.

DAWLISH

OPENED: 30th May 1846 (with the opening of the
   Exeter – Teignmouth section of the South Devon
   Railway).
CLOSED: Passengers – remains open for services on the
   Exeter – Newton Abbot line.
   Goods – 17th May 1965.

There can be little doubt that the station at Dawlish
has no rival in being closest to the sea. It was,
however, of some regret to many that this old
established resort lost much of its sea front thanks to
Brunel's determination to run the South Devon
Railway along the coast rather than go inland. The
station siting gave little scope for the development of
passenger and goods facilities of any size and also,
over the years, has led to considerable problems of
damage by stormy seas.

The original 1846 station, opening with the single
track South Devon Railway (SDR) from Exeter to
Teignmouth, comprised a small timber building on
the up (towards Exeter) side with a timber train shed
covering the single platform and track. A second
down platform with wooden shelter was added,
alongside a loop line, in May 1858. North of the
station on the up side, was a pumping station for the
atmospheric railway that operated through the
station in 1848/1849; this building was demolished
in 1868. The up side station building and train shed
were destroyed by fire in August 1873.

Fortunately a new station was already planned for
Dawlish, associated with the doubling of the track
from Starcross to Dawlish in February 1874.
Subsequent doubling of the line on to Teignmouth in
1905 reduced the curvature south of the station; in
1901/1902 a new sea wall had been constructed in
readiness for this doubling, further reducing the
width of the beach at Dawlish. The principal two
storey building of the new station, completed in
April 1875, was on the up side; a waiting room was
provided on the down platform. Elaborate vaulted
canopies with valances covered the southern sections
of both platforms, which were lengthened in 1875
and again in 1934. The impressive canopies, very
difficult to maintain in the salty atmosphere, were
replaced in 1961 by concrete brackets and wired
glass. The glass did not stand up to the stormy
conditions that included storms thrown up by the sea
and it was subsequently replaced by strengthened
perspex. Water columns stood on both platforms.
The footbridge at the south end of the station was

originally fully enclosed but its 1937 replacement was only partially enclosed. A staff of 14 were based at Dawlish between the two World Wars.

The Dawlish goods yard, sited behind the up platform at the north end, incorporated a small goods shed and a six ton capacity crane. Of limited capacity and principally used by coal trucks and occasionally by horse boxes, the yard closed in May 1965, the goods shed being demolished five years later. The former yard is now the station car park.

A tall signal box, towards the north end of the up platform, opened on 9th September 1920, replacing an earlier box on the down platform. The box was last used on 27th September 1986, though it had only been used on summer Saturdays since 1970. Operations at Dawlish are now controlled by the Exeter Panel, the up line being signalled for by-directional movements because of the occasional storm damage to the down track.

Today Dawlish is served by both local and main line services. When visited in mid-2006, the 1961 canopies and 1937 footbridge were still in place, though somewhat rusty. The tall signal box was derelict and boarded up. In the ground floor frontage of the main building a take away food shop was operating.

Dawlish Warren. Crowds alight from rail motor no. 72 on to the down (towards Newton Abbot) platform of the original station in late 1911. Although the photo is titled Dawlish Warren Halt, the nameboard on the up platform is Warren Platform.

DAWLISH WARREN

FIRST STATION
OPENED: c 1st August 1905.
CLOSED: 23rd September 1912
SECOND STATION
OPENED: Passengers – 23rd September 1912.
　Goods – 10th June 1912.
CLOSED: Passengers – remains open for local services
　on the Exeter – Newton Abbot line.
　Goods – 5th August 1967.

Sited on the Exeter to Newton Abbot line on the section which had been doubled between Starcross and Dawlish in February 1874, the first station, known as Warren Halt, opened for passenger services on about 1st August 1905. The up and down platforms each had two timber framed pagoda style huts, one larger than the other. The name changed first to Warren Platform on 1st July 1907 when staffing was introduced and then to Dawlish Warren on 1st October 1911.

The first station closed on 23rd September 1912, being replaced by the second, 17 chains to the north, on the same day, this time sited on two loop lines from the up and down main lines. This new station had wooden buildings on the southern end of the platforms, the principal building being on the up side behind which was the main approach road. The original down side building was replaced after a fire destroyed it on 9th January 1924. An open footbridge connected the two platforms a short distance beyond the south end of the station; this was replaced in 1964 but removed in 1977. Dawlish

Devonport Albert Road. Looking west, probably in the early 1900s, at the early building with horizontal canopies and tall chimneys. A covered footbridge is at the west end.

Warren closed as a war-time staff saving measure from 1st January 1917 to 5th April 1919. In the 1930s five to six staff were based at Dawlish Warren; staffing ceased on 3rd May 1971.

A small goods yard, with a 30 cwt capacity crane, an end loading dock and cattle pens, opened on 10th June 1912 beyond the south end of the station on the up side. A small pagoda style goods shed also stood behind the up platform north of the main building. This was adapted as a waiting room in 1956 but later removed. Rail traffic at Dawlish Warren was controlled by a 58 lever signal box at the north end of the down platform. Opening on 12th October 1911, it finally closed 75 years later on 14th November 1986. The building was retained for possible conversion into a holiday flat but the project failed and the box was demolished in May 1990.

The prime purpose of Dawlish Warren station was to serve holiday makers using the amusement facilities sited to the east of the line. Over the years these have been both varied and extensive and many facilities remain today. This role encouraged the introduction of camping coaches from 1935 behind the up platform when a ten berth coach was available for £5 per person per week. They were reintroduced after the Second World War and by 1959 nine coaches were in position. After its closure in August 1963, the goods yard was used exclusively by the camping coaches. After 1964, when British Railways dropped the camping coach business, the Dawlish Warren coaches passed to the Staff Association and were renewed in 1982, though no longer rail connected.

Today Dawlish Warren is used by local services between Newton Abbot and Exeter; the loop lines operate as refuges for local trains permitting fast through trains to overtake both up and down. Concrete huts stand on both platforms; that on the down platform replaced the 1924 building in 1980. The original wooden building on the up platform, having been used for holiday accommodation for some years, was destroyed in a 2003 fire. In spring 2007 its replacement, in the style of a two storey brick signal box, was nearing completion.

DEVONPORT ALBERT ROAD

OPENED: 4th May 1859 (with the opening of the Plymouth – Truro section of the Cornwall Railway).
CLOSED: Passengers – remains open for local services on the main line to Cornwall and the Tamar Valley branch to Gunnislake.
    Goods – 15th April 1967.

Sited in a cutting to the south of Albert Road in Devonport, the station opened in 1859 just to the east of the 125 yd Devonport tunnel. The suffix Albert Road was only added from 26th September 1949 but dropped from 6th May 1968. The main entrance, facing on to an approach road off Portland

Road, was on the down (south) side. In the early years buildings with horizontal canopies and tall chimneys were provided on both platforms with a covered footbridge at the west end. These were subsequently replaced by substantial buildings with large apex style canopies on both of the curved platforms which extended east almost to the Havelock Terrace road bridge. A replacement GWR style covered footbridge now connected the platforms at the east end and at one stage a metal covered stairway ran from the up side of the footbridge linking with a footpath east to Havelock Terrace.

In 1903 109,507 passenger tickets were issued at Devonport; this figure rose to 302,186 in 1913 but the latter figure also included returns from Dockyard and Ford Halts that had opened in 1905 and 1906. Because of space limitations, only a single siding was provided, adjacent to the station, sited between the west end of the down platform and the tunnel entrance; a small goods shed once stood close to the tunnel mouth. The main Devonport goods yard was a little way to the east of the station. Known as Valletort Road Yard, it was sited between Valletort Road and Collingwood Road and incorporated a goods depot, crane and cattle pens. At the station itself a small 1899 signal box stood at the west end of the down platform. This closed on 27th November 1960.

Goods facilities at Devonport Albert Road were withdrawn in 1967 and the station became unstaffed

Devonport Kings Road. Looking east on 30th August 1961. Rebuilt West Country Class no.34104 Bere Alston hauls the 1425 hrs Plymouth Friary to Waterloo train west out of the station.

as from 19th May 1969. Today it remains open with a local service both on the main line into Cornwall and on the Tamar Valley line to Gunnislake. The main station buildings have gone and, when visited in late 2006, the only facilities were a modern metal shelter on the down platform and an open footbridge (dated 1935) at the east end linking the platforms. There were no seats on either platform, even in the shelter. Artwork and an associated plaque that had been erected a few years earlier were not to be seen. In summary, Devonport station was not in good condition.

DEVONPORT KINGS ROAD

OPENED: 17th May 1876 (with the opening of the London & South Western Railway line Plymouth – Devonport).
CLOSED: Passengers – 7th September 1964
Goods -7th March 1971.

Initially called Devonport and Stonehouse, the station opened in mid May 1876 as the western terminus of the London & South Western Railway (LSWR) line from London and Exeter. At this time the LSWR services entered Plymouth from the east

75

from Lydford using a third rail on the broad gauge GWR Tavistock branch via Marsh Mills. LSWR trains then used the main east-west GWR line through the city and a new LSWR spur into the Devonport LSWR station. The opening was a time of great celebration. A large delegation led by the Mayor of Plymouth met the LSWR directors who arrived on a special train. Following speeches 750 guests attended a banquet laid out in the spacious new goods shed.

The scale and grandeur of the new LSWR station reflected the significance of Devonport in the commercial life of the Plymouth area, with much activity focusing on the important dockyard. The north facing façade of the stone built French gothic style building was dominated by a tall tower and two parallel structures with apex roofs at right angles to the approach road. A horizontal canopy over the main entrance provided shelter for arriving and departing passengers. Behind the impressive front building two platforms were covered by twin parallel train sheds with glazed arches at the western ends. There were four parallel tracks, two serving the platforms and the central tracks terminating at buffers at the western end of the station building.

The terminal role of the station ceased with the opening in 1890 of the Plymouth, Devonport & South Western Junction Railway from Lydford to Devonport via the Tamar Valley west of the city. LSWR trains used this new route and now entered Devonport station (the suffix Stonehouse had been dropped). from the west These services passed through the station, initially to Plymouth North Road or to Mutley, but then from 1891 to the new LSWR Friary terminus east of Plymouth city centre. Some historical accounts indicate that the Devonport station was designed from the outset for such through services but others suggest that the 1876 western walls had to be pierced in 1890.

For many years, and particularly in and between the two World Wars, Devonport (the suffix Kings Road was only added from 26th September 1949) was a very busy station being used particularly by naval personnel based at the dockyard. In 1928 63,067 passenger tickets were issued and 100,563 collected. Comparable figures for 1936 were 47,101 and 84,531. The passengers were served by a large refreshment room on the south side platform, which had become the main departure platform for London bound LSWR trains after the opening of the 1890 route. Unfortunately the fine train shed roofs and end arches were virtually destroyed in the Second

Devonport Kings Road. Looking east at the impressive main building on the north side of the through lines. To the right is the glazed west end of one of the twin train sheds.

World War, all that remained being cleared in the 1950s. From this time standard Southern Railway platform canopies were erected and a long covered footbridge over the four tracks connected the platforms.

Freight facilities at Devonport Kings Road were concentrated in the goods yard and large goods shed south of the station, the yard incorporating a large 10 ton capacity crane. The single line to Stonehouse Pool passed under the shed. Operations at the station and in the yard were controlled from a signal box at the east end of the station and yard; this box closed on 14th February 1963.

Devonport Kings Road closed in September 1964 as part of a major rationalisation of lines in the Devonport area. The former LSWR route through the station and north as far as just short of St Budeaux Victoria Road closed, with all passenger services being diverted to the GWR route via Devonport Albert Road and Keyham. Freight facilities survived at Kings Road until March 1971, the former station building also being used to handle some goods traffic. The whole station site was subsequently redeveloped for the new Plymouth College of Further Education.

Today the only remnants are the old retaining wall and ornamental fence on the northern edge of the College complex and the former bridge under Paradise Road, with soot stains on one arch. The trackbed north of the bridge is used as a car park with access from the college underneath the bridge itself.

DEVONPORT STONEHOUSE POOL OCEAN QUAY

OPENED: 9th April 1904 (when transatlantic liners started to call at Stonehouse Pool Ocean Quay).
CLOSED: 28th May 1910.

In the autumn of 1903 the America Line announced that all its ships travelling across the Atlantic would, from 1904, call at Plymouth before terminating at Southampton Docks. The London & South Western Railway (LSWR) saw the potential for possible passenger traffic and decided to invest in facilities at Plymouth. A covered 350 ft long platform with waiting and refreshment rooms, together with ticket, enquiry and telegraph offices, were constructed together with a customs/luggage hall. Floors were covered with a cork carpet and the refreshment room lit by gas and electricity.

Sited at Stonehouse Pool Ocean Quay, to the west of the GWR Millbay Docks, the aim of the LSWR was to provide facilities equal to those of the GWR. Sited on a curve, which somewhat handicapped operations, the station building bore bold lettering on the roof, 'London South Western Railway', the 'and' being apparently omitted, it was rumoured, to impress American passengers who appreciated brevity! A steam crane lifted luggage, on specially constructed wheeled crates, from the deck of tenders to the railway platform.

The first American line boat 'St Louis' berthed on 9th April 1904 and rivalry commenced between the LSWR and GWR. In 1907 the platforms were extended to permit two boat trains to be handled simultaneously. Business for the LSWR did not, however, come up to expectations and an agreement of 13th May 1910 between the LSWR and GWR led to cessation of boat trains from Stonehouse Pool as from 28th May 1910. The rail disaster at Salisbury involving a LSWR boat train from Plymouth on 1st July 1906 had not assisted patronage on LSWR trains.

In 1912 the platform roofing was removed from the station and the Stonehouse Pool line from Devonport station saw no further passenger traffic apart from a very occasional special naval train. All freight movement to Ocean Quay ceased in June 1966 and the line closed officially on 30th May 1970.

Devonport Stonehouse Pool Ocean Quay. A view across Stonehouse Pool of the short lived station.

DIGBY AND SOWTON

OPENED: 29th May 1995 (on the Exeter – Exmouth line originally opened through this site in 1861).
CLOSED: Remains open for passenger services on the Exeter – Exmouth line.

On the Exmouth branch about 380 yards south of the site of Clyst St Mary and Digby Halt, which closed in 1948, the incentives for the opening of this station were the development of the Sowton Industrial Estate to the east of the line and the redevelopment of the former Digby Mental Hospital site, west of the line, for housing. The single platform on the east side of the single line was built on the site of the former down track. Constructed of concrete beams supported by breeze block pillars, the platform is surfaced with paving bricks. A metal and

Digby & Sowton. The 10.28 hrs to Exmouth at the 1995 station on 7th March 2006. The covered bridge carries segregated pedestrian and cycleways towards a park and ride facility.

Dockyard. Looking south, the nameboard indicating the name as Dockyard Halt. The suffix halt was dropped in May 1969 at this facility in Devonport.

glass shelter serves passengers. A metal bridge with segregated cycle and pedestrian paths (the former covered and the latter open) links the platform to the west side of the line. Close by is a large car park designated for use as 'park and ride' both for the station and the Devon and Exeter Hospital at Wonford to which there is a bus link. The car park sign indicates that it is also a Devon County Council 'Park and Share' facility. At the west end of the bridge is a bus turning circle and a semi-circular shelter. Nearby is Clyst Halt Lane.

DOCKYARD

OPENED: 1st June 1905 (on the Plymouth - Saltash - Truro line originally opened through this site in 1859).
CLOSED: Remains open for local passenger services on the main line to Cornwall and the Tamar Valley branch to Gunnislake.

As in many instances in the Plymouth area, the catalyst for the opening of Dockyard Halt, on the main GWR Cornwall line between Devonport and Keyham, was the commencement of steam rail motor services through the city. In this case records indicate that the halt opened exactly one year after the services commenced through the site to Saltash on 1st June 1904. The up (260 ft) and down (315 ft) platforms had slightly unusual shelters, an unfamiliar pagoda style. They were of the usual corrugated iron construction up to gutter level but the roof design was not of the normal pagoda style but of a more conventional apex shape. Originally

provided at an estimated cost of £557, Dockyard survives today, the suffix halt being dropped from 5th May 1969. A modern metal shelter now stands on the down platform but not on the up (towards Plymouth).

DOUSLAND

OPENED: 11th August 1883 (with the opening of the Princetown Railway, Yelverton – Princetown).
CLOSED: Passenger and Goods – 5th March 1956.

Sited on a curve, and to the west of a level crossing with the minor road from Dousland to Meavy, the station opened with the start of services on the Princetown branch. For some years Dousland was the only intermediate station on the branch until the introduction of three intermediate moorland halts. The platform (500 ft) on the down (north) side of the line was constructed of stone filling faced with brick. The surface was of loose stone chippings edged with concrete slabs with rounded shoulders on the line side. In later years a short timber extension was added to the platform at the west end. Separating the platform from the road behind was a high granite wall. At the east end of the platform stood the station building constructed of brick with cement rendering. There were three windows on the road side and one at the east end and on the road side two chimneys rose from the slate roof. On the platform side the roof extended forward to form a small canopy over a single door and two windows, one smaller than the other. This door gave access into the main room off which were the ticket office, parcels office, waiting room and ladies' toilet. The gent's toilet was at the rear of the west end of the building with access from the platform. In 1903 6,641 passenger tickets were issued at Dousland, this rose to 6,946 in 1913 and then fell to 6,158 in 1923 and 4,201 in 1933. Five staff were based there in 1913. The station master's house, 'Station Cottage', was sited north of the level crossing. Now modernised and extended, it survives today as 'Crossings Cottage'.

Immediately to the west of the main building was Dousland signal box, which opened in 1915 and replaced an earlier box which had stood close to the level crossing. From this time the crossing was controlled by a brick built, concrete rendered covered ground frame. The small station platform box was built of granite, its rear wall being part of the rear platform wall, this resulted in the box being

Dousland. No. 4402 hauling a train from Princetown towards Yelverton in about 1939. The signal box partly hides the brick station building. In the foreground is the timber west extension of the platform and beyond the signal is the goods shed.

only 10 ft high to the roof from the platform level. The apex timber and slate roof was topped with a zinc sheet ridge. With a 14 lever frame, there was good all round vision from eight timber frame windows. The box controlled movements at the station and in the small goods yard to the east on the down side.

There was no loop at the station itself but a goods loop on the north side of the line ran alongside the goods shed (47 ft long) built also of brick with cement rendering. On the line side was a small goods platform along the whole length of the building. A small wedge shape canopy constructed of wood planks protected the opening on to the platform through heavy wooden doors. At the western end of the shed was a goods loading bay for rail traffic also protected by a small wood canopy. Against the east end of the shed was a small metal lean-to hut. From the goods loop there were two short sidings, one ran behind the east end of the platform.

Passenger and goods services were withdrawn in March 1956. The main station building has been converted into a house. The letters from the former nameboard are fixed to the surviving brick face of the old platform. The former small goods yard was used by a coal merchant form 1957-1971 after which it was used for gardens of new houses.

Dunsbear Halt. Seen in 1962, the halt was on the down (east) side of the North Devon & Cornwall Junction Light Railway. The provision of two huts, one wooden (in distance) and one stone built, was because of the extensive use by workmen at the nearby Marland Clay Works.

DUNSBEAR HALT

OPENED: 27th July 1925 (with the opening of the
    North Devon & Cornwall Junction Light Railway,
    Torrington – Halwill Junction).
CLOSED: Passengers – 1st March 1965.
    Goods – 2nd May 1960.

Unlike the halts at Watergate and Yarde, Dunsbear Halt opened with the commencement of services on the line at the end of July 1925. The potential use of the halt by workers at the nearby Marland Clay Works was clearly a decisive factor in its early provision. The Works were about a mile's walk away to the south-east and some 50 to 70 workers used the

Dunsford Halt. A view east shortly before the halt closed in 1958. A bicycle leans against the sole platform seat beside the corrugated iron shelter.

track bed of the former Torrington and Marland Mineral Railway which diverged from the 1925 line just south of the halt.

Sited on the down (east) side of the line just to the north of an ungated level crossing, the platform was built of local stone capped with brick. Originally only a small wooden waiting shelter was provided at the north end of the platform but it was later supplemented by a second shelter at the south end, this time stone built. A short siding opposite the platform was occasionally used by local farmers and also by clay works traffic. The siding closed on 2nd May 1960 and passenger closure came five years later in March 1965. After closure the shelters were removed but the platform was left and still existed in spring 2007, grass covered beside the Tarka Trail cycleway.

Dunsland Cross. Looking south in 1939 at the station on a crossing loop between Halwill and Holsworthy. The main building is on the down (towards Holsworthy) platform. An open shelter and small signal box are on the up side.

DUNSFORD HALT

OPENED: 16th January 1928 (on the Exeter – Heathfield line originally opened through this site in 1903).
CLOSED: 9th June 1958.

Nearly two miles east of the village of Dunsford, the halt opened in January 1928 some 25 years after the line was completed between Exeter and Heathfield. An early proposed name was Farrents Corner Halt. Sited just east of the point where the south-north alignment of the line changes to west-east, the halt was close to the proposed junction with a branch line to Chagford, a line that was never built. The halt's original timber edged platform (100 ft long) on the south side of the line was replaced by concrete components, with stone facing, soon after the Second World War. On the platform was a corrugated iron shelter with a backward sloping roof. The halt closed in June 1958 with the withdrawal of passenger services on the line; the site is now completely overgrown and no trace can be seen.

DUNSLAND CROSS

OPENED: 20th January 1879 (with the opening of the Meldon Junction – Holsworthy section of the Devon & Cornwall Railway).
CLOSED: Passengers – 3rd October 1966.
Goods – 7th September 1964.

At about 600 ft above sea level, Dunsland Cross station was sited in an isolated position half a mile south of a cross roads of the same name. Few lived close to the station apart from those in a terrace of railway houses just to the west. The station, at a

East Anstey. A view east in 1955 towards Wiveliscombe. On the down platform (right) are the main buildings and the 1902 signal box. A small wooden shelter stands on the up platform.

crossing loop on a south to north section of the line between Halwill Junction and Holsworthy, opened in January 1879. Timings meant, however, that relatively few trains crossed at this point.

The main single storey building, stone built with cement rendering, was on the down side. With no platform canopy the building incorporated the principal station facilities with staff accommodation at the south end. A small open stone shelter with a slate roof served passengers on the up platform. Inter-platform movements were via a rail level board crossing at the south end. Passenger numbers were generally low at Dunsland Cross. In 1928 4,478 tickets were issued and 4,550 collected; by 1936 the figures had more than halved to 1,844 and 2,091. Passenger numbers were at certain times boosted by pupils travelling to and from Shebbear College, a boys' school, some five miles to the north-east. The station nameboard advised 'Alight here for Shebbear College'.

The small goods yard, behind the down platform mainly comprised a long siding running alongside a stone goods shed with sliding doors on the road side and a small canopy over the track. Goods inwards included road stone and sea sand from Bude Wharf, which was used for local land improvement. In the 1930s an animal feed store was erected next to the goods shed. A small wooden 11 lever signal box, with a slate roof, at the south end of the up platform, controlled the loop and entry to the goods yard. The box closed on 2nd January 1966 when all track was taken out of use apart from the down loop.

Goods facilities were withdrawn in September 1964 but the station remained open for passengers until October 1966 when passenger services ceased

on the line. Following closure the main building was converted into a house. In 2005 the down platform was there but the up platform had gone, the former track bed being a lawn. The former goods shed was in use as self catering holiday accommodation. Nearby is Lynne Acres, an archery centre just to the west of the goods yard.

EAST ANSTEY

OPENED: 1st November 1873 (with the opening of the Wiveliscombe (Somerset) – Barnstaple section of the Devon & Somerset Railway).
CLOSED: Passengers – 3rd October 1966.
　　　Goods – 30th September 1963.

About a half mile south of the village of East Anstey, the station opened at the beginning of November 1873, on the down side of a then single track section of the Devon & Somerset Railway. A passing loop was introduced in 1876, being lengthened in 1910 and 1937. With the addition of the loop came the provision of an up platform which, together with the original down, was lengthened at the time of loop extensions. At nearly 800 ft above sea level, East Anstey station was at the highest point on the Taunton to Barnstaple line.

The main building, on the down side, was a single storey stone structure including a central section with an apex roof at right angles to the line and two wings, with roofs parallel to the line. Two tall chimney stacks rose above the roof of the west wing. The station booking, waiting and toilet facilities were within this building. At the centre of the up platform was a small open front wooden shelter. There was no footbridge, a rail level board crossing at the west end provided inter-platform access. In 1903 6,807 passenger tickets were issued at East Anstey, the figure fell to 4,949 in 1933. The latter figure included passengers using Yeo Mill Halt. In 1903 seven staff were based at East Anstey but by 1933 this had reduced to four.

The goods yard, with a stone goods shed, was sited behind, and to the west of, the down platform. At the west end of the shed were cattle pens. Unlike many rural stations in Devon, coal traffic was apparently light, as much local wood was used for fuel. A monthly market held next to the station generated a fair volume of traffic, as did the despatch of rabbits!

East Anstey signal box, a brick structure with a slate roof and multi pane wooden windows, stood on the west end of the down platform. It opened in 1902. Goods traffic ceased at East Anstey in September 1963 but passenger traffic lasted for just over another three years, until October 1966, when services were withdrawn on the line. The station house and goods shed were subsequently converted into houses.

East Budleigh. Looking south towards Budleigh Salterton in 1958. The single storey building, now part of a large residence, stands on the up (west) side of the line. Beyond the platform is the small goods loop.

EAST BUDLEIGH

OPENED: 15th May 1897 (with the opening of the Budleigh Salterton Railway, Tipton St Johns – Budleigh Salterton).
CLOSED: Passengers – 6th March 1967.
Goods – 27th January 1964.

The station opened in May 1897 as Budleigh, the prefix 'East' being added from 27th April 1898. In the valley of the River Otter, it was sited just west of the village of Otterton, south of a bridge which carried the road from Otterton to Woodbury over the single track line from Tipton St Johns to Budleigh Salterton. The village of East Budleigh was approximately one mile to the south-west. The name of East Budleigh was probably used to avoid confusion with Ottery St Mary or even Otterham, a station in north Cornwall.

The brick single storey building, with three tall chimneys and a wide horizontal canopy with a fretted valence, stood on the 297 ft long platform on the up (west) side of the line. At the northern end of the building was an annex with a slightly backward sloping roof. Towards the south end of the platform was a small brick goods shed. Only a single track passed through the station itself but to the south was a small goods loop with two short spurs, one leading north to cattle pens and a cattle loading dock behind the south end of the platform. The loop also served a concrete cattle food store. Access to the loop was controlled by a ground frame, no signal box being provided at East Budleigh.

Camping coaches were for some years stabled on the southern spur from the goods loop. When the coaches were there the spur was isolated from the loop so that there was no possibility of damage to the coaches during shunting operations. Apparently when the coaches needed to be moved away for maintenance a small section of track had to be slewed to re-connect the spur to the loop!

In 1928 12,993 passenger tickets were issued and 18,082 collected. Records indicate a drastic fall by 1936, the comparable figures being 2,170 and 3,230. East Budleigh was the station for two local attractions of Ladram Bay and Bicton Gardens and the station nameboard stated this for some years. By 1936 however, it appears that road competition in conveying visitors to these two places had bitten hard. The original staffing was by a station master and porter but East Budleigh became unstaffed on 25th April 1966. Goods facilities had been

Eggesford. On a long curve in the Crediton to Barnstaple line, this view north in 1965 shows the station before the major damage to the down platform in November 1967. The 1873 signal box stands opposite the Barnstaple end of the up platform.

withdrawn in January 1964. The station closed in March 1967 when passenger services ceased on the line.

Today the station buildings virtually all survive as a large residence. An extension has been added to the northern end of the building and the platform, goods shed and concrete store all remain. The trackbed and goods yard are now covered by the large garden. The road bridge to the north survives. The gate to the private drive states 'The Old Station'.

EGGESFORD

OPENED: 1st August 1854 (with the opening of the North Devon Railway, Crediton – Barnstaple).

CLOSED: Passengers – remains open for services on the Exeter – Barnstaple line.
Goods – 4th January 1965.

Named after Eggesford House, the nearby seat of the Earl of Portsmouth, who, in Victorian times, was a great supporter of the North Devon and London & South Western Railways, the station was in an isolated position in the River Taw valley. Villages principally served by the station were Chawleigh, some two miles to the east and Chulmleigh, two miles to the north. Sited on a long curve in the line between the main Barnstaple road (A377) and the river, Eggesford, which opened at the beginning of August 1854, had a passing loop and two platforms.

The main station building, an impressive multi-gabled North Devon Railway (NDR) structure, was on the up (towards Exeter) platform; it incorporated all the main station facilities and also accommodation for the station master. A number of other buildings also stood on the platform, including an open fronted waiting shelter. A short dock siding led into the Barnstaple end of the platform. Not quite opposite, but staggered in the Barnstaple direction, was the down platform, with a wooden waiting shelter opposite the main building and an 1873 wood framed signal box opposite the Barnstaple end of the up platform. The wooden shelter was later replaced by a concrete structure. No footbridge was provided, inter-platform movements being via a rail level board crossing at the Barnstaple end of the up platform. At the Exeter end of the down platform was a short siding which lasted until 1936. Also at the Exeter end of the up platform was a level crossing carrying a minor road to Wendworthy.

A mill leat ran from the River Taw behind the down platform and under the tracks at the Barnstaple end of the station. The 1873 signal box was perched above this leat, its front supported by the platform and its rear on two cast iron posts. All was well for over 90 years until 21st November 1967 when flooding caused the down platform to partly subside. The down loop, down platform and signal box were closed for two years. The down platform was repaired in concrete with small extensions to the undamaged section but it did not regain its original full length. A new flat roofed signal box, relocated from a site in Buckinghamshire, was erected on the down side adjacent to the level crossing. It opened on 28th September 1969, closing some 18 years later on 1st December 1987. The level crossing gates were locked and unlocked from the box but operated by

Elburton Cross. Looking north-west on 16th September 1942, ten months after the station reopened during the Second World War. The building itself is not in use. A train approaches from the Plymouth direction.

hand, lifting barriers were introduced on 30th November 1969.

In 1928 9,040 passenger tickets were issued at Eggesford and 10,176 collected; by 1936 the figures had halved to 4,304 and 5,480. A census on 7th May 1963 indicated that 40½ passengers (1 child = ½ passenger) joined and left trains that day. Surveys in a winter week in 1976 and a summer week in 1977 indicated that 95 and 160 passengers used Eggesford in those weeks. At the maximum the station master was supported by two signalmen and six other staff.

A medium sized goods yard was sited on the up side beyond the Barnstaple end of the station. The yard was equipped with a 7½ ton capacity crane (replacing a five ton crane), a goods shed (with a two ton crane) behind the platform, cattle pens and also other stores. A long siding led on from the goods yard towards the Fox and Hounds Hotel. Some 365 ft long, it incorporated a loop, alongside which was a slaughter house and loading dock. At the far end of the siding were more cattle pens. These pens were sometimes used in association with a cattle auction held adjacent to the Hotel. The goods yard closed in January 1965. Today various users operate in the former yard.

Today Eggesford is the only passing station on the Crediton to Barnstaple line, with small metal shelters on each platform, both at the Exeter end. The station building, now privately owned in residential use, retains its fine features.

ELBURTON CROSS

OPENED: 17th January 1898 (with the opening of the GWR branch, Plymstock – Yealmpton).
CLOSED: 7th July 1930.
REOPENED: 3rd November 1941 (for use by Plymouth residents evacuated during the Second World War).
CLOSED: 6th October 1947.

Opening in January 1898, with the commencement of services from Plymouth Millbay on the Yealmpton branch (then sometimes known on the South Hams Railway), Elburton Cross was a small passenger only facility catering for the village after which it was named. Sited on the single line with no loop, it had a long (223 ft) stone edged platform on the up (towards Plymouth side) on which stood a wooden building with a backward sloping roof. This served as a common waiting room/ticket office. No ladies' room was provided, the sole toilet facility being a cast iron gent's urinal to the east of the building. The main entrance was by a gate in Station Road; another access was via a kissing gate in Sherford Road, at the southern end of the bridge which crossed the line at this point. Records indicate that in 1903 11,355 tickets were issued at Elburton Cross, comparable figures for 1913 and 1923 were 20,831 and 17,836.

When the Yealmpton branch reopened from 1941-1947, the station was opened but the building was not re-used due to the small amount of traffic expected. Today, because of housing development, the alignment of the former trackbed is hard to trace. A dwelling has been built on the site of the former station. The old kissing gate on Sherford Road survives.

EXETER

The following gives a résumé of the history of the passenger railway network in the Exeter area. This should be read in conjunction with the diagram.

Passenger services came to Exeter at the beginning of May 1844 with the opening of the final stage of the Bristol & Exeter Railway from Beam Bridge, west of Wellington in Somerset, to Exeter St Davids station. The South Devon Railway opened its line on from St Davids to Teignmouth in May 1846, Newton Abbot in December 1846 and to the eastern edge of Plymouth in May 1848. From the Bristol & Exeter Railway north of the city a branch was opened from Cowley Bridge to Crediton in May 1851; the line on to Barnstaple opened in August 1854. To the east of Cowley Bridge a further branch opened 30 years later north from Stoke Canon to Tiverton, the Exe Valley line. To the south-west of St Davids the Exeter Railway opened, in July 1903, to Ashton linking with the earlier (1882) Teign Valley line completing an inland route to Newton Abbot via Heathfield.

The second major route into Exeter was that of the London & South Western Railway which opened from Yeovil Junction to the second Exeter terminus at Queen Street (later Central), in July 1860. The link line down a steep gradient to Exeter St Davids opened in February 1862. Ten months earlier, in May 1861, the Exmouth branch had opened south from the LSWR main line in the east of the city.

Most of the above lines remain open today for passenger traffic, the only closures being the Heathfield and Newton Abbot route in 1958 and that from Stoke Canon to Tiverton in 1963.

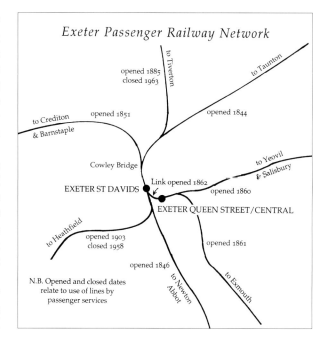

Exeter Passenger Railway Network

EXETER CENTRAL (QUEEN STREET)

OPENED: 19th July 1860 (with the opening of the Yeovil Junction – Exeter section of the London & South Western Railway).

CLOSED: Passengers – remains open for services to London (Waterloo) and for local services to Exmouth and other stations in Devon.
Goods – 4th December 1967.

The 18th July 1860 was a day of celebrations in Exeter with the ceremonial opening of the Yeovil Junction to Exeter section of the London & South Western Railway (LSWR), thus completing the through route to the city from London (Waterloo) via Salisbury. However, contemporary accounts of these celebrations indicate that, though enthusiastic, they were not on the scale of those for the arrival of the first Bristol & Exeter Railway train at Exeter St Davids, sixteen years earlier. Public services commenced at Queen Street the next day.

A further contrast with the 1844 opening was that the first train arrived at a station sited adjacent to the city centre. This time the City Council had not raised objections to the siting of the station or the laying of tracks within the city boundary (see Exeter St Davids text). Abutting on to Queen Street (hence the name), the new station was a terminus for some 18 months

Exeter Queen Street. Looking west in about 1910 at the twin train shed station. Part of the original B signal box, demolished in 1927, is in the left foreground. Queen Street goods yard is on the extreme right.

until 1st February 1862, when the link line, under Queen Street and down a steep incline (1 in 37), opened to St Davids station. Queen Street station also became the terminus for Exmouth branch line trains from 1st May 1861.

The new LSWR station was constructed in the Longbrook valley in a section of the adjacent old Rougemont Castle moat. The two storey domestic style building was of wood construction with a pantilled roof. This initial 1860 station had only one main platform and a bay line, both on the city side; the tracks and platform were covered by a wooden train shed. An up platform and bay were added in 1874, together with two through lines. A second shed with wrought iron trusses, supported on cast iron columns was added. There was separate road access to the up and down station buildings. With the wooden roofs and smoke from the stationery engines, the atmosphere for passengers and staff at Queen Street was far from ideal and unfavourable comments were made by Exeter businesses and citizens, contrasting the situation with that at Exeter St Davids where major rebuilding in 1862-1864 had produced an impressive station.

Despite these concerns, no significant moves were made for over 60 years regarding the replacement of the inadequate facilities. In 1925 one major improvement was the lengthening of the up platform by 600 ft to the exceptional length of 1,210 ft; the bay platform was also lengthened on the up side by 300 ft. Records also indicate frequent maintenance work on the deteriorating wooden buildings. In June 1927 fire badly damaged the timber buildings on the down side. In the early 1930s traffic was overwhelming the facilities. Queen Street was the station where long LSWR trains to and from the South West were joined or split. The two central tracks were used for carriage storage, while the bay lines were used by the frequent Exmouth trains. A major new station was clearly urgently required but, although initial plans had been drawn up in the mid 1920s, it was not until 1931 there was real action. Early in that year one possible scheme was rejected by the City Council, the proposed single storey structure opposite the elegant Rougemont Hotel being considered inappropriate. There was also concern at a scheme which appeared similar to that proposed for Exmouth! Eventually a more ambitious proposal by the LSWR was approved by the City Council.

Work commenced on the new station in mid 1931; this involved the demolition of virtually all the wooden LSWR buildings including the train sheds, the basic platforms remained however. Work was particularly difficult with services being largely maintained throughout. The new station comprised two principal elements: a three storey building in red brick and reinforced concrete on the down side and a generally two storey crescent shaped building, also on the down side, at a higher level at right angles to the tracks and facing on to Queen Street. This crescent, 259 ft long, included a higher 77 ft wide central block topped by a small tower. A horizontal canopy sheltered passengers entering and leaving the station. The ground floor of both wings was used by shops and offices while the upper floor was occupied by railway offices. These included a bomb proof control room supervising operations west of Salisbury. The main booking hall, at the base of the central block, was some 45 ft square, approached from the street by one of three sets of swing doors. The ground floor also incorporated cloakrooms and station offices. Two bridges behind the crescent building spanned the four tracks, one for passengers and one for luggage. The down platform was lengthened at the east end to 950 ft bringing it comparable to the earlier extended up platform; both were widened and covered with extensive umbrella style canopies and provided with excellent waiting and refreshment rooms. A 120 ft long covered concrete footbridge was opened on 17th April 1932 at the east end of the platform adjacent to New North Road to which a link was provided, together with a booking office. The new access replaced that from Northernhay. The new station was ceremonially opened on 1st July 1933 and given the new name of Exeter Central, the name Queen Street now being considered inappropriate with a second entrance at New North Road.

During the Second World War business was particularly heavy at the new Central station. The New North Road entrance was closed during the War and again in 1966, the latter because of staff shortages. The designation of Exeter Central as an open station from 19th March 1984 led to reopening of this entrance on 2nd July 1984.

Post war, Exeter Central continued to be well used and in 1959 it was recorded that more than two million passengers passed through the booking hall. Today the station remains basically the structure completed in 1933. Although in many ways a shadow of its former self, business remains brisk with commuters, shoppers and students using the conveniently sited station and benefiting from the

Exeter Queen Street. A general view in the mid 1930s from the east of the redeveloped station. Note the very long platforms and umbrella style wide canopies. The 1888 goods shed is seen to the right.

many local services still operating in the Exeter area. The two through lines have been out of use for some years: the up side from November 1969 and the down from 1984. They were lifted soon after disuse.

The majority of the crescent building on Queen Street is now in non-railway use with access to the station through an entrance in the north-west segment leading to the small booking office, pedestrian bridge and platforms (two main and one down bay). The former fine booking hall is in non-railway commercial use. The original waiting facilities have gone, only a shelter under the canopy on the up side is provided. Refreshment facilities were closed on 5th September 1971. In 1983 the canopy on the down side was shortened. The 1930s concrete footbridge at the north-east end has been replaced in recent years by a modern metal structure with ramps to the platforms. Over the access way to the bridge from New North Road is a fine metal arch, proclaiming 'Exeter Central Station'.

In parallel with the evolving passenger facilities, extensive goods facilities have been provided over the years. An original small goods station north of and behind the station on the up side was replaced in 1888 by a large brick structure (135 x 30 ft) covering two tracks. A further eight sidings were in the yard. There were also extensive sidings west of the station beyond Queen Street bridge on the down side above the incline to St Davids. On the up side, also above the incline line, was another smaller goods yard. A three road brick engine shed (170 ft) long was originally sited on the down side, north-east of New North Road bridge. It was extended in 1872 and 1877. The principal locomotive facilities were transferred to Exmouth Junction in 1887 and the Queen Street shed was then used for stabling and servicing. In 1930 the site of this shed was used for

the construction of carriage sidings whose use continued to 1970. The goods yard north of the station closed to general use on 4th December 1967. Blue Circle cement continued to use sidings until January 1980. By 1993 all sidings in the former yard were lifted, except one line adjacent to the bay platform. The goods yard has now been redeveloped for a large housing development 'Isca Place'. Adjacent to this on New North Road the former station master's house is now in use as offices.

Signalling at Queen Street/Central changed a number of times over the years. Early A and B boxes controlled movements east of the station and in 1875 a C box was erected at the west end of the station blocking the down through line, turning it into a siding. All down trains then had to use the down platform line. This 1875 box was replaced as from 13th September 1925 by a new 35 lever box at the west end of the up platform, thus permitting the down through line to reopen. The original A and B boxes were replaced on 15th June 1927 by a large 90 lever box at the east end of the up platform. This was designated A and the 1875 box was re-designated B; this latter was taken out of use on 23rd February 1970 and remains in place today in a derelict state. A box was renamed Exeter Central and remained in use until 6th May 1985. Operations were taken over by the new Exeter Power Box from 6th May 1985; the Central box was later demolished after use for some years by permanent way staff.

EXETER ST DAVIDS

OPENED: 1st May 1844

CLOSED: Passengers – remains open for services to
London (Paddington and Waterloo), Bristol, the
Midlands and North and to stations in Devon and
Cornwall.
Goods: See text

The 1st May was a day of much celebration in Exeter
with the opening of St Davids station. The Illustrated
London News reported that, with most businesses
closed, thousands, dressed in holiday clothes,
gathered at 12.30 p.m. to greet the arrival of the first
train on the completed Bristol & Exeter (B&E)
Railway. Celebrations included a 'great' dinner in the
goods shed and a dinner dance held in an adjoining
marquee.

The City Council had refused permission for the
B&E to construct either the station itself or any of its
line within the then city boundaries. A site was thus
selected north-west of the city centre just outside the
boundary at Red Cow village in the parish of St
David. This location lent itself naturally to the
provision of a Brunel style one side station (as at

Exeter St Davids. The second station completed in 1864 is
seen from the east. To the right is the station master's house.
A tramcar can be seen in front of the building, dating the
photo as after 1905 and before 1912 when the train shed
was demolished.

Taunton) with both up and down
platforms/buildings built on the city side of the line
overcoming the need for passengers and luggage to
cross the tracks. The track layout included
appropriate cross-overs to allow maximum use of
the unusual siting of the platforms. The up building,
in the form of a parallelogram 144 ft long and with
a slate and zinc roof was to the north. The down
building, at the south end of the site, was of similar
construction but with fewer rooms. Canopies
covered the platforms themselves, attached to the
two buildings. To the north of St Davids was a ticket

Exeter St Davids. A close up view of the fine road side
frontage in about 1912. Features include the high façade,
with 26 ornamental urns, rising above the single storey
railway offices with a number of tall chimney stacks and the
very wide canopy (porte cochere) protecting passengers at
the main entrance. This canopy was removed in 1939.

Within a decade the facilities of this one side station were proving inadequate for the needs of the B&E and South Devon Railway (SDR) operations. The prospect of trains of the London & South Western Railway also using St Davids prompted proposals for a new station. Work commenced in 1862 and at a cost of £48,200 (including £29,760 for the station itself) the new St Davids station opened in July 1864. Some 360 ft long, faced with Westleigh stone and with cornices, parapets, dressings and arches in Bath freestone, a major feature was the large overall train shed. Also about 360 ft long and 132 ft wide, it was 60 ft high and supported by 23 iron trusses 15 ft apart on masonry walls 32 ft high. At either end of the train shed impressive screens of glazed, ornamental ironwork on columns provided further weather protection. Along the roof was a continuous skylight extending about 12 ft either side of the ridge, the remaining roof covering being slate. An additional feature that helped illumination under the shed was a double row of windows in the up side wall. At night a triple row of incandescent gas lamps provided illumination. A further striking feature of St Davids was the imposing high façade on the down side facing the approach road; surmounted by 26 massive classical ornamental urns, it rose above a single storey set of railway offices with a number of tall chimneys. Attached to these offices two distinctive canopies protected passengers; in front of the main entrance was a very wide canopy, or porte cochère, designed to protect passengers arriving and departing by road whilst to the north of this was a narrower conventional canopy.

Beneath the train shed of this 1864 structure were three platforms: the GWR down Platform (640 ft long), the central island (510 ft) used by up and

Exeter St Davids. A view south along the platforms in the 1960s of the remodelled station featuring the canopies and the tall lift shafts. It remains basically the same today.

down LSWR trains and the western island (750 ft) used by LSWR down and GWR up trains. Unfortunately there was only one track between the two island platforms which hindered operations. The scale of traffic at the end of the nineteenth century is shown by the number of passengers handled at St Davids in January 1895 (12,574) and July 1895 (22,077).

Following a number of minor improvements including a 1905 extension of the booking and parcels facilities and a 1909 extension of the down platform, major rebuilding of St Davids took place over the period 1912–1914. The track layout remained fairly similar to that which it replaced but included two additional running lines through the station: an extra through line between the down and the middle island platforms for use by through non-stop trains and also an additional platform track between the middle and up island platforms. Space was available because of the removal of broad gauge tracks in the 1890s. A bay platform line was also added on the down side at the north end. There were now six through lines, five through platform faces and one bay line/platform. In the course of the rebuilding the two island platforms were reconstructed on slightly different sites; the major work was, however, the removal of the overall train shed and replacement by extensive platform canopies. New buildings of standard GWR design were erected on the island platforms. Also provided was a new passenger footbridge, incorporating some part of an earlier structure, at the southern end and a new luggage bridge at the north end. A particular feature of this 1912-1914 rebuild was the retention of the down side high façade overlooking the station approach.

Exeter St Davids. The frontage of Exeter St Davids on 19th April 2007 showing the central widened down side section together with the additional first storey offices (left centre). The ornamental urns have gone from the top of the façade.

The new buildings were designed to blend in well with the architectural style of the 1862 station. During the 1912-1914 period St Davids continued to function with the use of temporary portable buildings, which were moved around the station complex as work progressed. The total cost of this rebuild was £33,325. In July 1914, coinciding with the completion of work, 28,755 passengers were handled.

The period 1938-1940 saw yet more changes: in particular the down side building in front of the 1862 high façade was remodelled, being widened by some 11 ft for a length of 170 ft, an additional first floor storey being added to house divisional offices. The 1862 canopies were replaced by a 350 ft long canopy along the face of the down side building. Also completed was the removal of steps direct from the down platform to the footbridge, being replaced by a new staircase lined with brown and white tiles behind the platform wall in space created by the widening of the down side building. The direct access by steps from the outside of the building to the footbridge remained. This was later blocked up in the 1960s. Also in the 1938/1940 rebuild, the main refreshment rooms were moved to the current site, the original rooms south of the footbridge being converted to cloakrooms. In 1938 a hostel for refreshment room staff was built at the foot of St Davids Hill opposite the station; this was very similar to the earlier station master's house behind the north end of the down platform.

St Davids station today has changed relatively little since the 1938-1940 rebuild. The third non platform through track between the down and middle island platform has gone. The old GWR waiting room on the down platform retains many of its original features; the principal extra facility is a modern glass waiting room on the central island.

In parallel with developments of the passenger facilities was the evolution of those for goods. The original goods shed, sited to the north of the 1848 up passenger building, was of timber with a slate roof; it incorporated two through and one terminal track. It was later replaced by a larger timber shed again on the up side at the north end of the up platform. This larger facility could accommodate 20 wagons and contained 15 hand cranes with a capacity of 1½ - 2 tons to transfer goods from road to rail haulage and vice versa. Following the end of rail use it was taken over by National Carriers; it was damaged in a fire on 8th November 2001. Together with a brick built goods shed, it remains today. Also still there, but derelict, is the large brick built former transfer shed used when both broad and standard gauge wagons were in use at St Davids. The varied size of the end rail apertures gives a clue to the use of the building sited north of the level crossing on the up side.

At one time the complex passenger and freight operations at St Davids were controlled by eight busy signal boxes over a two mile stretch south from Cowley Bridge Junction. Detailed description of the development and changes in the signalling at Exeter is beyond the scope of this book but the boxes included the large Exeter West box, which in 1958 had 131 levers. All boxes were superseded from 5th May 1985 by the Exeter MAS powerbox which today stands to the south of the station on the up side.

EXETER ST THOMAS

OPENED: 30th May 1846 (with the opening of the
Exeter - Teignmouth section of the South Devon
Railway).

CLOSED: Passengers – remains open for local services
on the Exeter – Newton Abbot line.

Goods – no facilities ever provided.

The initial basic 1846 structure, on the down side of
the single track South Devon Railway to
Teignmouth, was improved in 1847 with the
addition of a ground level wooden building and a
wooden train shed over part of the platform.
Development was problematical as the station,
initially called St Thomas (Exeter) and from April
1853 St Thomas, was sited on a viaduct. Trains using
the atmospheric system ran through the station from
13th September 1847 until 6th September 1848.
Unlike other stations on the route, it had no gap in
the pipe and apparently trains often overshot the
platforms, as they had to brake against the
propulsion force!

Its status as the headquarters of the South Devon
Railway (SDR) was the impetus for the development
of an impressive station constructed with the
doubling of the track between Exeter and Exminster
in 1861. The principal two storey Italianate style
building, incorporating the SDR offices, stood on the
down side. The platform level facilities included a
general waiting room, a ladies' waiting room, the
station master's office and toilet facilities. An up side
platform was added and both platforms were
covered by an imposing stone and wooden train
shed. A two storey up side building was also
constructed; the limited facilities included a waiting
room and toilets. Access to both platforms was via
steps from ground level within the buildings. There
was no footbridge, inter-platform movements being
under the line at the north end of the station.

In this 1861 development, the platforms were

Exeter St Thomas. Looking north towards Exeter St Davids
in about 1910. The up side building (left) and the overall
roof lasted until 1970/1971. The two storey main building is
on the down side.

Exeter St Thomas. A detailed view of the up side platform
under the train shed in the 1960s. Note the fire buckets.

staggered with the up side platform outside the
overall roof extending towards Exeter and the down
side open section towards Exminster. This stagger
was eliminated in 1929/1930. In 1929 the up
platform was lengthened by 220 ft (at a cost of £835)
in a narrow section at the Exminster end; in 1930 the
down platform was extended from 400 ft to 620 ft
at the Exeter end (at a cost of £712). A small signal
box stood on the down side at the north end of the
down platform from 1867 to 1959. Adjacent to it
was a small siding added in 1905 for use by local
terminating steam rail cars. This siding was lifted in
1949.

As a war-time measure Exeter St Thomas, as it had
finally been named in May 1897, closed to release
staff for war-time duties from 2nd April 1917 to 3rd
March 1919. Non railway uses began in the
principal down side building and in the viaduct
arches from about 1959. The up side building and

Exeter St Thomas. A view on 30th June 2006 of the former down side two storey building, now the Imperial China Restaurant.

OPENED: Late August 1852 (on the Exeter –
Teignmouth section of the South Devon Railway
originally opened through this site in 1846).
CLOSED: Passenger – 30th March 1964
Goods – 4th December 1967 (coal depot only since
6th September 1965).

Opening six years after South Devon Railway services commenced through the site on the single track, the original platform and building were on the up side of the line. The latter incorporated accommodation for the station master and other station facilities. A down platform was added with the doubling of the track from Exeter to Exminster in 1861, a stone shelter being erected eight years later. Also in 1869 a road bridge was erected immediately to the north of the station; this provided inter-platform access via steps linked to the platforms. A gents' urinal was added south of the down platform shelter at the time of gauge conversion in 1892. A siding behind the up platform led to a coal shed, alongside were cattle pens.

The first major change came in June 1924 with the laying of a down loop behind a now down island platform. Further extensive alterations came in 1931 with the quadrupling of the tracks through Exminster, as part of the GWR improvements of the line between Taunton and Newton Abbot to cater for the growing holiday traffic. A new up line was constructed behind the up platform and immediately in front of the station building, which ceased to serve passengers. A 1911 extension to the front of the building was thus only used for twenty years. There were now four platform faces with two new shelters on the island platforms. Two extra spans were added to the road bridge and a small booking office was constructed at its western end, access to both island platforms being via steps from the bridge. A larger water tower was also constructed on the up

overall roof were demolished in 1970/1971, though glass had been removed from the roof in the 1950s. Partial staffing was introduced from 23rd May 1971 and today the station is completely unstaffed.

The imposing down side building has been renovated and in mid 2006, with a fine glass road side canopy, was the 'Imperial China' Chinese restaurant. Concrete shelters provide cover on the two platforms which are, once again, slightly staggered, the up platform being longer at the Exeter end and the down towards Exminster. Access to the up side platform is via a metal staircase and to the down via steps in the north end of the surviving building.

Exminster. A general view north on 23rd June 1963 of the two island platform station and tall 1924 signal box. The building on the up side (left) no longer serves passengers. Wooden shelters stand on the island platforms and the larger replacement water tower is on the up. The main building, including accommodation for the station master, is beyond the water tower

platform, replacing a smaller version.

The 1893 signal box with 14 levers, at the south end of the down platform, was replaced by a box east of the loop on 9th June 1924 when the new down loop came into use. A further line was added behind the box in 1941, which led to three sidings which were extended further in 1942 for extensive use during the Second World War. After the war these sidings were used for carriage storage. An extension to the box was added in 1941 for operating the new sidings; this increased the number of levers from 56 to 80. The box finally closed on 17th October 1986 and was subsequently used for a variety of purposes over the years including bird watching. The box was dismantled in late 2006 by the Gloucestershire Warwickshire Railway with a view to restoration for future location on the northern extension of the railway at Broadway in Worcestershire. A number of uses are being considered but the aim is for it to be mainly a working box controlling movements at the station.

The trackwork at Exminster gradually reduced after 1962, the station itself closing to passengers in March 1964. All freight facilities were withdrawn in December 1967, only the handling of coal being undertaken since September 1965. Today all trace of the platforms has gone; the station building remains in situ, the site being used by an architectural salvage business.

EXMOUTH

OPENED: 1st May 1861 (with the opening of the Exeter & Exmouth Railway).

CLOSED: Passengers – remains open for services on the Exeter – Exmouth line.

Goods – 4th December 1967 (coal depot only from 6th September 1965).

Exmouth station, sited adjacent to the town centre but a little way from the sea front, opened at the beginning of May 1861. There were great celebrations in the town with flags and triumphal arches over the streets. A banquet was held at the Globe Hotel. The first train of 11 carriages, carrying 150 passengers, was also decorated with flags. A second long train of 19 carriages, pulled by two engines, conveyed 500 passengers whilst a third comprised 16 carriages. It was reported that in the first five days of the service to Exeter, 2000 passengers were carried daily and that, in the first six months, 159,416 used the service.

Exmouth. The first station (1861) in about 1905. The domestic style of the building reflects that it was basically two converted houses. From the building a single island platform ran south to north.

Exmouth. The 1924 terminus photographed four years later in 1928. This was constructed behind the 1861 building which was demolished giving space for a large forecourt for the new station.

The first station, the terminus of the line from Exeter, was basically two converted houses sited on Imperial Road (later Station Parade) from which a single island platform ran south to north. The line along the east face had an engine run-round loop but the other face did not. An overall canopy covered the sections of the platform closest to the building, which itself had a narrow road side canopy. The early goods facilities comprised a goods shed, loading dock with crane and three sidings to the west of the station. From this goods yard a line continued west to Exmouth Docks; this line was completed in 1864 and the Docks opened in 1868. To the east of the station was a wooden engine shed and a turntable, the latter installed in 1862 and removed in 1927. Full signalling was not installed until about 1875 when a 24 lever signal box was erected close to the junction of the engine shed line and platform

Exmouth. The 1976 Exmouth station adjoins the bus station in this photograph of 7th March 2006. This third station building is set back some 80 yards behind the site of the 1924 structure.

run-round loop.

The opening of the line from Tipton St Johns and Budleigh Salterton in 1903 brought a greater influx of passengers to the already congested station. New traffic included, from 1914, through carriages from London Waterloo via Sidmouth Junction and Tipton St Johns. Limited improvements were undertaken including alterations to the track layout, an extension of the bay platform and an increase in number of levers in the signal box to 30.

Plans were prepared by the London & South Western Railway (LSWR) in 1916 for a new station to be constructed in the goods yard area but the First World War halted any action. Eight years later however, the Southern Railway, at a cost of £70,000, undertook a major redevelopment. The new second Exmouth station came into operation on 20th July 1924. A two storey red brick building flanked by two single storey wings was constructed behind the 1861 station which, on completion of the new station, was demolished, its site being used as the new forecourt. The main booking hall and waiting room were on the ground floor of the building with accommodation for the station master above. The parcels office was in the west wing and the booking office in the east. Behind this building was a large glazed concourse from which, through lattice sliding metal gates, two long island platforms ran north each covered with long apex style canopies on pillars. All four platform faces could accommodate long trains though only the two outer platform lines had engine run round loops. Trains normally arrived at these outer platform faces after which the engines were able to run round and shunt the trains to the inner faces ready for departures. Some

commentators likened the 1924 station to London Waterloo, noting in particular the practice of the lattice gates to the platforms only opening ten minutes before train departures! In the 1930s there was a station master and 22 staff based at the station and goods yard, 12 working in the yard.

Other developments at Exmouth in the 1920s included expansion of the goods yard, partly on land reclaimed from the River Exe estuary. A large new goods shed was erected. Other facilities in the larger yard included a loading dock, cattle pens, extra sidings and a five ton capacity crane. Traffic generated by the docks was particularly important, coal being a major import, the majority of the town's coal arriving by sea. Other imports included wood pulp and cider apples, the latter being destined for the Whiteways factory at Whimple. Incoming traffic dominated use of Exmouth goods yard through the years.

Associated with all these developments, came the erection of a new 70 lever signal box in the V between the Exeter and Tipton St Johns lines. The box had two balconies from which the signalmen could receive or hand over tokens relating to operations on the two single track lines. The original engine shed was also replaced in 1927 by a concrete structure with a large water tank at the southern end.

Between the Wars passenger volumes were high, but declining at Exmouth. In 1928 181,024 passenger tickets were issued and 434,362 collected. By 1936 the figures had fallen to 116,418 and 294,690. After the Second World War it is recorded that numbers rose again; in the early 1960s an average of 225,000 tickets were issued at Exmouth per annum and 400,000 collected.

Despite the high figures decline had set in at Exmouth by the mid 1960s. The engine shed closed on 8th November 1963 with the introduction of diesel multiple units on the line; the shed was demolished in 1967. Traffic volumes were hit by the closure of the line from Tipton St Johns and Budleigh Salterton on 6th March 1967. In December of that year the line to Exmouth Docks closed and freight facilities ceased, though the yard had only operated as a coal depot since September 1965. In 1968 the signal box closed on 3rd March and two months later on 6th May the station became partially unstaffed. Early in 1969 much of the track was lifted, only a single line surviving serving the no.4 platform on the east side of the station. The booking hall and office closed, tickets being issued from a kiosk adjacent to the one platform. The station frontage was let for shops. In summary, by the late 1960s Exmouth station was in a poor state.

A revival came however in the mid 1970s with the traffic on the Exmouth line to Exeter continuing at a good level. A transport interchange was built on the station site, the fine 1924 building being demolished. A new single storey brick building was opened on 2nd May 1976 set back from the 1924 station by some 80 yards. The new building abuts the former no.2 platform which was re-instated but shortened at its southern end to give a total length of 481 ft. The remaining single line was slewed west away from the no.4 platform to serve this re-instated platform. To the west of the station itself was Exmouth bus station, the whole development costing some £100,000. Some of the former goods yard has been developed for car parking whilst the surviving goods shed is now incorporated within the Exmouth Leisure Centre. To the east of the new station a new road, Marine Way, was opened on 10th December 1981 covering the former site of platforms 3 and 4 and that of the engine shed. Today Exmouth station continues to be busy with a good service to Exeter.

EXTON (WOODBURY ROAD)

OPENED: 1st May 1861 (with the opening of the
 Exeter & Exmouth Railway).
CLOSED: Passengers – remains open as a request stop
 on the Exeter – Exmouth line.
 Goods – 6th March 1961.

On a single track section of the Exmouth branch, the station stood alongside the east bank of the River Exe estuary. Opening in May 1861 as Woodbury Road, referring to a village two miles to the east, the name changed to Exton from 15th September 1958, now relating to the nearer settlement. On the east side of the line, the original platform was later extended in concrete at the north end to give a total length of 429 ft. Behind the platform was a two storey station master's house, adjoined at its southern end by a single storey stone booking office and waiting room. These buildings were once slate hung. No platform canopy was provided.

In 1928 15,652 passenger tickets were issued and 21,522 collected. By 1936 the figures had more than halved to 7,594 and 8,340. At the maximum the station was staffed by the station master, two signalmen and two porters. Staffing ceased from 28th February 1965 at which point Exton was re-designated as a halt. This designation ceased on 5th

Exton. Looking north at the single platform station in about 1910. The name changed from Woodbury Road to Exton in September 1958. Beyond the two storey station master's house is the signal box replaced by a ground frame in 1918.

May 1969 when it became just Exton.

Two sidings ran behind the building leaving the line beyond the north end of the platform. These sidings were particularly used by a local coal merchant. Access to the sidings was originally controlled by a small signal box behind the north end of the platform but this box was replaced by a ground frame as from 25th June 1918. During the Second World War the sidings were busy with supplies being brought to the new Royal Marines Camp that had been developed a little way to the south. Camping coaches were also berthed here on occasions between 1935 and 1964. Freight facilities were withdrawn from 6th March 1961 and the sidings were lifted on 19th February 1965.

In 1965 there was also some boarding up of the buildings but in 1975 Exton was one of the stations on the Exmouth line to be improved, the old buildings being replaced by a modern shelter. Improved lighting was also installed. The former station house with extensions is now in residential use after a brief period as a restaurant. A modern chalet bungalow has been built alongside to the south and houses now cover the former goods yard. Today Exmouth branch trains stop at Exton only on request.

FILLEIGH

Filleigh. A fine picture looking east at the main building with station staff in about 1910. The location of the first signal box is shown by the rodding tunnel under the platform. The signalman is standing in the doorway.

OPENED: 1st November 1873 (with the opening of the
Wiveliscombe – Barnstaple section of the Devon &
Somerset Railway).
CLOSED: Passengers – 3rd October 1966.
    Goods – 3rd August 1964.

The station, when opened in November 1873, was known as Castle Hill, after a nearby mansion belonging to Lord Fortescue. It was renamed Filleigh, a village about one mile to the south-west, as from 1st January 1881, to overcome confusion with a London suburban station, itself now renamed West Ealing.

For much of its life, the main facility at Filleigh was a platform and stone building on the up (north) side of the line. This building comprised a central section with an apex style slate roof at right angles to the line, together with two wings, each with an apex roof parallel to the line. The main booking, waiting and toilet facilities were within this building. Two further buildings stood on the platform west of the building, used for goods and other storage. Beyond this again, at the west end of the platform, was Filleigh signal box. A 42 lever box, it opened on 20th June 1937, coincidental with the provision, opposite the platform, of the station's first loop line, alongside which a down platform was added. There is no record of a waiting shelter ever being provided on this second platform. The 1937 box replaced an earlier small facility within the main building. The loop, down platform and signal box were closed on 6th September 1964. In 1903 8,200 passenger tickets were issued at Filleigh; by 1933 the total had nearly halved to 4,555. Over these thirty years the total staff based at Filleigh varied between two and four. The station was used particularly by pupils and staff of West Buckland School.

Filleigh goods yard was to the west of the station, on the up side. As from 15th December 1937, an extra goods loop was provided. This loop was in use until 20th December 1961. The yard was involved with the delivery of goods for places to the north such as Parracombe and Lynton, as the Lynton and Barnstaple Railway, opening in 1898 and closing in 1935, did not deliver goods from its stations. An additional facility, from west of the goods yard, was a private siding to stores on the Fortescue Estate. This link lasted up to about 1960. Goods services were withdrawn at Filleigh in August 1964.

Following withdrawal of passenger services on the line, and station closure in October 1966, the station building was used as a house for some years. Demolition came with the use of the station site by the North Devon Link Road (A361).

FORD (DEVON)

OPENED: 1st June 1890 (with the opening of the
Plymouth, Devonport & South Western Junction
Railway, Lydford – Devonport).

CLOSED: Passengers – 7th September 1964.
Goods – 1st September 1952.

Opening in June 1890 with the commencement of
services on the Lydford to Devonport line, via the
Tamar Valley, Ford station (the suffix Devon was
added from 9th July 1923) was sited partially in a
cutting, a short distance north-east of Ford viaduct.
The principal building, with a large apex style
canopy and incorporating the main offices, stood on
the down (south-east) side of the line. The forecourt
was approached from the south by Alexandra Place
and from the south-east by Railway Terrace. On the
up (north-west) side passengers were served by a
waiting shelter. The platforms were linked by a
footbridge at the south end; originally of wood
construction it was later replaced by a standard
Southern Railway concrete component bridge.
Access to the up side of the station was via an
inclined footpath linking the east end of Station
Road to the platform between the footbridge steps
and the waiting shelter. In 1928 21,950 passenger
tickets were issued at Ford and 32,135 collected;
comparable figures for 1936 were 19,898 and
40,848. A signal box at the south end of the up
platform operated until 2nd March 1947.

A short siding was sited south of the station on the
up side; the limited freight facilities ceased at the
beginning of September 1952. Passenger services
lasted a further 12 years until September 1964. The
station buildings were demolished in the 1970s and
the large cutting filled in during the 1980s. A public
park and housing now cover the former station site,
though the remains of the up side entrance at the top
of the inclined footpath can still be seen at the east
end of Station Road. To the south-east of the new

Ford (Devon). A general view south of the station in about
1939 showing its location north-east of Ford viaduct. The
original wooden footbridge has been replaced by a standard
Southern Railway concrete structure.

housing, adjacent to the former down side of the
station site, is Railway Terrace, including Railway
Cottages. To the north of the former station is the
inappropriately named Brunel Terrace.

FORD HALT

OPENED: 1st June 1904 (on the Plymouth – Saltash –
Truro line originally opened through this site in
1859).

CLOSED: 6th October 1941.

On the main GWR Plymouth to Cornwall line
between Devonport and Keyham, Ford Halt opened
in June 1904 as an unadvertised stopping place for
workmen only. In January 1906 authorisation was
given for conversion to public use: the platforms
were widened and lengthened to about 400 ft, a
small booking office was constructed on the down
platform and pagoda style waiting rooms provided

Ford Halt. Looking south towards Devonport showing the
pagoda hut on the up platform. The photograph is before
1922 as the suffix 'Platform' is on the nameboard.

Fremington. A general view north-east in 1963 showing the main building on the down side (right), the elevated signal box on the up platform, with a waiting shelter alongside, and tall cranes in the extensive quay yard.

Fremington. A close up of the main wooden building on the down (towards Bideford) platform with the gent's toilet in an annex at the west end. Also illustrated are the wooden hut at the west end and the metal shelter with an arc roof east of the building.

on both platforms. Public services commenced at what became Ford Platform in May 1906. The suffix platform was dropped from 10th July 1922, halt being re-introduced. Due to work on the nearby Keyham viaduct all trains used the up (towards Plymouth) platform from March 1936 to 2nd May 1937. Staffing continued until 1937 but, following heavy bombing in the area, Ford Halt closed in October 1941 and never reopened. Today some remnants of the brick platform faces can still be seen. The brick replaced earlier wooden structures.

FREMINGTON

OPENED: 1st August 1854 or 2nd November 1855 (see text).

CLOSED: Passengers – 4th October 1965.
Goods – 6th September 1965.

The development and fortunes of the railway and adjacent quay were closely linked at Fremington. In the early nineteenth century coastal trading ships were able to reach Bideford but not Barnstaple, because of navigation problems on the River Taw. By an Act of 1838 the Taw Vale Railway and Dock Company was authorised to construct a dock at Fremington and a horse drawn railway from there to the southern end of the River Taw bridge at Barnstaple. Freight only operations started on this line on 25th April 1848. Passenger services subsequently commenced on the line from Crediton to Barnstaple on 1st August 1854.

Commentators on the railway history of the area do not agree on the date upon which passenger services actually commenced at Fremington. There is newspaper evidence that the station opened for passengers when services on the Bideford Extension Railway started at the beginning of November 1855. However, some sources suggest that it opened as a terminus in August 1854 when services commenced on the Crediton to Barnstaple line. A possible answer is that a very limited passenger service started on the generally freight only line but the more comprehensive service started in 1855. Whatever the specific date, the facilities at the outset were limited with one platform on the down (towards Bideford) side on which stood a wooden building incorporating the station facilities. A further wooden hut at right angles to the line at the west end, and a small metal shelter with an arc shaped roof at the east end, were later added on this platform. By 1869 a passing loop had been laid together with an up platform behind which was a further loop line. A brick waiting shelter served passengers close to the signal box on this platform.

The outstanding feature of the layout at Fremington was the siding complex on the up side alongside the quay, reflecting the fact that the main business here was the transfer of freight from ships to the railway, in particular the import of coal and the export of clay. The London & South Western Railway (LSWR) and the Southern Railway (SR) imported much of their coal for use at their Devon depots through Fremington and the SR concentrated its trade here after closure of its quay facilities at Bideford. In 1928 16,015 tons of coal were imported through Fremington and by 1936 the figure had risen to 28,602. Exports of clay brought to the quay by rail from the quarries at Meeth and Marland, south of Torrington, were also of great importance, 20,000 tons being recorded in 1929. To cope with the large tonnage of coal and clay three large six ton capacity steam cranes operated at the quay. Rail movements at the station were controlled from the elevated signal box on the up platform. A wooden cabin on tall brick columns with windows on all sides, it was designed to give a good overall view over the station and quay sidings.

In contrast to this extensive freight traffic passenger volumes were low. The siting of the station three quarters of a mile north of the village on the east side of a creek was a major deterrent. The shortest route for pedestrians to and from the village was via a footway alongside the track on the railway bridge over the creek. By road the distance was some two miles. The bus service to Barnstaple was much more convenient for Fremington residents. In 1928 3,102 tickets were issued at the station and 3,026 collected; by 1936 the figures had fallen to 1,879 and 1,836. As early as 1930 it was reported that only ten

per day were issued and ten collected. In both the LSWR and SR days, many express trains did not stop at Fremington.

Goods facilities were withdrawn in September 1965 and passenger services ceased a month later. The signal box remained open until 3rd November 1968 when the loop was taken out of use. The quay closed entirely at the end of 1969. The station buildings were demolished, though both platforms survived for some years in a derelict state. In 2007 the grassed over up platform survives. The Tarka Trail cycleway passes through the site and Fremington Heritage Centre is on the site of the original down side building. The rail bridge over the creek remains carrying the Tarka Trail.

GARA BRIDGE

OPENED: 19th December 1893 (with the opening of the Kingsbridge & South Devon Railway, Brent – Kingsbridge).

CLOSED: Passengers and Goods – 16th September 1963.

Gara Bridge (the word Gara is Celtic, meaning rough), picturesquely sited in a woodland valley, opened in December 1893. It was the most important intermediate station on the line between Brent and Kingsbridge, being the only passing station. The down (towards Kingsbridge) platform was on the east side and the up platform to the west.

Gara Bridge. Looking north in about 1910 at the only passing station on the Kingsbridge branch. The main William Clarke design building with a decorative wide canopy is on the down (towards Kingsbridge) platform, together with a stone goods shed (right). On the up platform (left) is a stone waiting shelter with canopy and a small signal box with a wheel controlling the level crossing gates.

Gara Bridge. In August 1934 a camping coach is in use behind the down platform sited on a short siding that served an original loading dock. The coach is an 1891 clerestory composite.

The station's main stone building, designed by William Clarke (see Avonwick text), featured three tall chimneys and a wide horizontal wooden canopy. The building incorporated the station master's office, a general waiting room, booking office and toilets. Access to the platform and the building (via platform doors) was through a gate at the south end of the building. A matching stone goods shed stood on the platform, south of the main building. A stone waiting shelter with a small wooden canopy served passengers on the up platform. A station master's house was provided on the down side of the line south of, and behind, the platform.

Behind the down platform at the south end, was a short siding initially serving a loading dock; it was later used for two camping coaches. Attractive gardens, including stone setts from Plymouth, gave a pleasant setting for the coaches, whose toilet facilities were in the station building. South of the station, also on the down side, were sidings serving cattle pens. A small signal box stood at the north end of the up platform; with 24 levers, it incorporated a wheel controlling the adjacent level crossing gates.

Both passenger and goods services ceased at Gara Bridge in September 1963. The station buildings were subsequently converted into a private residence. The station master's house also survives.

OPENED: 9th July 1928 (on the Paignton – Kingswear line originally opened through this site in 1861).

CLOSED: Remains open for services on the Paignton & Dartmouth Railway (see text).

In the mid 1920s the GWR decided that the holiday trade in the Torbay area justified the provision of a halt to serve Goodrington Sands, south of Paignton. At a cost of £630, Goodrington Halt opened on the single track line in July 1928, 'Sands' was added two months later. At this time the double track south from Paignton terminated just north of Tanners Lane level crossing, from which a path led south to the halt on the up side of the line. Train tickets were available from a window in the crossing keeper's cottage. The double track was later extended a short way south of the level crossing and a down platform came into use on 4th July 1930. The line south from Goodrington has remained basically single track apart from occasional loops. The two platforms at Goodrington Sands were extended to a length of 600 ft and concrete shelters were provided in 1933. These developments coincided with major development of goods facilities between Goodrington and Paignton on the up side including a large goods shed in 1931.

During the early years the beach facilities at Goodrington were fairly basic but the halt came into its own in 1936 when Paignton U.D.C. opened a new park, boating lake and children's playground on the beach side of the line. Some services that had terminated at Paignton were extended south to Goodrington Sands Halt, which normally was open from May to September each year. During the Second World War, the halt was open throughout the

Goodrington Sands Halt. Looking north in the late 1950s towards Paignton. In the distance is the covered footbridge which replaced the Tanners Lane level crossing in June 1957. To the left carriages stand in the sidings behind the up platform.

year, residents and visitors being encouraged to use the train rather than cars, because of fuel shortages. In June 1957 the Tanners Lane level crossing was replaced by a covered footbridge on which a small booking office was erected. The abutments of the bridge were in place before the Second World War, one of the few features of the 1937 major rail expansion plans in the Paignton area that was completed before the war started (see Paignton text). In 1957 a large complex of carriage sidings, with a turntable, was developed behind the halt's up platform.

Following the take-over of the Paignton – Kingswear line by the Dart Valley Railway, only the down track and platform were used for the new services through Goodrington. The suffix halt was dropped. Since 1988 the halt has been dominated by the large water chute of the Quay West complex, built partly on the site of the original halt car park behind the down platform. To serve this leisure complex a large car park has been laid out west of the line; visitors to the complex cross the line by the covered footbridge which remains with steps to the halt's down platform. The original steps to the former up platform have been fenced off. This car park is used extensively by visitors to the now Paignton & Dartmouth Railway. The halt's notice board states, 'Goodrington Sands for Quay West Water Park'. The down platform serves the trains but there is no shelter; the former up platform remains but unused. In autumn 2006 the former loop and a siding were laid at Goodrington not for re-use of the up platform but for stock storage.

Halberton Halt. A view of the halt in about 1960. The shelter and a bicycle are under the road bridge.

HALBERTON HALT

OPENED: 5th December 1927 (on the Bristol & Exeter Railway Tiverton branch, Tiverton Junction – Tiverton, originally opened through this site in 1848).
CLOSED: 5th October 1964.

When the Bristol & Exeter Railway single track branch line from Tiverton Junction to Tiverton was built, it was of broad gauge. Allowance was also made for the possible later addition of a second track. Thus the track formation and the bridge spans were particularly wide. In 1884 the gauge of the single track was reduced to standard. In December 1927 the GWR opened a halt about mid-way along the branch to serve the village of Halberton, about half a mile to the north. Sited on the south side of the single track in the space originally left vacant for the second track, the platform was 109 ft long overall, including the ramps. It was constructed of infill behind a wooden sleeper face; the tarmac surface was edged with wood. A corrugated iron shelter with a backward sloping roof provided shelter; protection was also enhanced by the unusual siting of the halt underneath a road bridge carrying a minor road from Halberton towards Butterleigh. Oil lamps lit the platform and the approach path.

It is recorded that a further feature of Halberton was that bicycles used by local residents to access the halt were often parked at the halt, the favourite parking space being under the bridge span! Another unusual feature on the branch was that along the spare formation for one mile either side of the halt a single row of apple trees was planted and bore fruit.

The halt closed when passenger services ceased on the branch in October 1964. Today the formation of the track has been assimilated into the fields but the bridge remains. When visited in mid 2006 no trace of the halt could be seen in the undergrowth now flourishing beneath the span.

HALWILL

OPENED: 20th January 1879 (with the opening of the Meldon Junction – Holsworthy section of the Devon & Cornwall Railway).
CLOSED: Passengers – 3rd October 1966.
Goods – 7th September 1964.

The station opened in January 1869 with the commencement of services on the Okehampton to Holsworthy section of the Devon & Cornwall Railway, a line that was extended to Bude in November 1898. Most records indicate that at its opening the name was Halwill and Beaworthy,

Halwill. Looking north in 1962, the main building on the down platform (left) and a stone shelter and tall signal box on the up. The nameboard at this time states: 'Halwill for Beaworthy – junction for Bude, North Cornwall and Torrington'. The goods shed is seen beyond the main building.

villages about a mile to the south-west and south-east. One source suggests however, that the name was only Beaworthy. The name changed to Halwill Junction in March 1877, some eight months after the opening of the North Cornwall Railway to Launceston, which veered west, then south, from the Holsworthy line just to the north of the station. This line was extended to Padstow in 1892. The 'junction' suffix was officially dropped from 1st January 1923. This was clearly rather inappropriate as, from 27th July 1925, its junction role was enhanced further with the arrival of the North Devon & Cornwall Junction Light Railway from Torrington, which joined the Bude line about a mile north of the station. Halwill was now truly the railway crossroads of west Devon. In the 1960s the nameboard stated Halwill for Beaworthy.

The main single storey stone building on the down platform had no canopy and incorporated all the booking, waiting and toilet facilities. A stone shelter served passengers on the up (towards Okehampton) platform. A separate short bay platform, accommodating only three carriages, was added behind the down platform for use by local trains towards Bude. Most through trains had carriages for Bude but local trains were sometimes run to take passengers leaving through trains with carriages only for Padstow. An entirely separate bay platform was also added in 1925 on the up side north of the station to serve trains to and from Torrington. This

platform had no shelter and was reached by a path from the north end of the up platform. The bay line had its own run-round loop north of the platform, illustrating the principle that movements on this line were not permitted to interfere with traffic on what was regarded as the two main lines to Bude and Padstow. No footbridge was ever provided at the station.

Passenger figures for Halwill do not accurately represent the true volume at the station as much exchange between trains took place here. In 1928 11,016 tickets were issued and 11,483 collected; by 1936 the figures had more than halved to 5,753 and 5,706. Staffing was relatively high with a spacious house being provided for the station master and a row of cottages for rail workers.

A moderate sized goods yard developed over the years behind the down platform. The yard included a goods shed, cattle pens and a number of stores linking local agriculture to freight traffic (eg fertilizers and cattle feed). There was no engine shed but a 50 ft turntable was sited in the yard. A slaughter house, developed by the London & South Western Railway, stood at the north end of the yard. In 1932 it dealt with some 48,000 animals and thus cattle products formed an important export from Halwill. This abattoir was later taken over by the Ministry of Food before being sold off. The yard also acted as a marshalling yard for wagons converging at Halwill from the four lines.

To the south of the station on the up side beyond a level crossing, a large marshalling yard was constructed in 1943 capable of holding some 26 ammunition wagons. This was in preparation for the D Day Landings and the influx of American soldiers. The yard sidings were gradually lifted over the period 1958-1963 having been used for wagon storage after the War. Rail movements at Halwill were controlled from a tall wooden signal box at the north end of the up platform. This contained apparatus for the holding of tokens used for the passage of trains on the single line tracks radiating from Halwill.

Goods facilities were withdrawn at Halwill in September 1964 and passenger services ceased in October 1966 with the withdrawal of services on the Bude and Padstow lines. Passenger services had ceased on the Torrington line in March 1965. Over the years a small settlement known as Halwill Junction had developed around the station. This has now expanded considerably with the former station site now redeveloped for housing, including such names as Stationfields and Beeching Close. A recreation ground covers the former large marshalling yard.

HATHERLEIGH

OPENED: 27th July 1925 (with the opening of the
    North Devon & Cornwall Junction Light Railway,
    Torrington – Halwill).
CLOSED: Passengers – 1st March 1965.
    Goods – 7th September 1964.

The town of Hatherleigh was the largest on the route of the North Devon & Cornwall Junction Light Railway (ND&CJR). Unfortunately the town was not well served by the railway, the station being some mile and a half north-west of the town centre. Four days before opening to the public a special train, with Col Stephens, the Engineer and Managing Director of the line on board, stopped for lunch at Hatherleigh, the meal being set out on trestle tables along the platform. On the opening day there was little interest with only a small crowd on the platform and a nearby house decorated with flags. Sited on the east bank of the River Lew, close to its confluence with the River Torridge, Hatherleigh was one of the three passing loops on the line between Torrington and Halwill. The loop could accommodate a locomotive and 21 wagons. The attractive stone building stood on the stone built up platform; the wooden platform canopy being a forward extension of the roof. No shelter was provided on the down platform and inter-platform access was via a rail level board crossing at the south end.

Passenger traffic was very low at Hatherleigh. Without doubt, the decision to link the ND&CJR with the LSWR line at Halwill and not Okehampton was a serious error. Residents of Hatherleigh who wished to visit Okehampton, the nearest large town, faced a 20 mile journey by rail with a change at Halwill against a seven mile journey by road. In 1928 only 1,708 tickets were issued and 2,027 collected; by 1936 the figures had fallen to 565 and 684.

The limited goods facilities comprised two sidings behind the up platform with access from north of the station. Cattle pens were sited beside the outer siding

Hatherleigh. In the early 1960s a class 2MT No. 41298 with a ball clay train for Halwill takes on water from the down platform water crane. The attractive stone building stands on the up (towards Torrington) platform. Note the rail level board crossing.

Heathfield. Looking north in about 1910. A 44xx class
2-6-2T hauls a Newton Abbot bound train from Moretonhampstead into Heathfield. At this time there is no down
platform, which was not provided until 1927. The 1882
Teign Valley Company signal box stands beyond the
platform goods shed. The scene is dominated by Candy's
Brick & Tile Works to which there is a siding (bottom left).

HEATHFIELD

OPENED: 1st July 1874 (on the Newton Abbot –
  Moretonhampstead line originally opened through
  this site in 1866).
CLOSED: Passengers – 2nd March 1959.
  Goods – 4th December 1967 (coal depot only from
  June 1965).

and also two stores but there was no specific goods
shed. Cattle and sheep movements were the main
generators of freight traffic at Hatherleigh, this
traffic creating much greater receipts than
passengers. Rail movements were controlled by a
seven lever frame at the north end of the up
platform. Water cranes, the only ones on the line
between Torrington and Halwill, were on the north
end of the up platform and the south end of the
down. These were supplied from a water tank that
drew water from the River Lew.

Goods facilities ceased in September 1964 and the
station closed for passengers six months later, at the
beginning of March 1965, with the withdrawal of
services on the line. Today the station survives as a
private house with an extension under the canopy,
The Old Station House. Both platforms survive with
the space between a sunken lawn.

More than the majority of stations in Devon,
Heathfield evolved over the years with its ever
changing roles. Opening as Chudleigh Road in July
1874, the original station was a basic 200 ft long
platform on the up (east) side of the broad gauge
Newton Abbot & South Devon Railway, which had
opened from Newton Abbot to Moretonhampstead
some eight years earlier. The station building, at the
southern end of the platform, close to a road bridge,
was constructed of wood on a masonry base; it had
a platform side horizontal canopy, a hipped grey
slate roof and a brick chimney at either end. This
main structure (24 ft x 15 ft) housed, from south to
north, the station master's office, a booking
hall/general waiting room and a ladies' waiting
room. Two wings (each 12 ft long and 13 ft wide)
contained a parcels room/store at the southern end
and the gent's toilet to the north. The platform itself

had a chipping surface, except for a paved section in front of the building. The station was dominated by a large brick and tile factory on the down side, served, from 1887, by a siding, which left the single track line opposite the station building.

The opening of the first section of the standard gauge Teign Valley line from Heathfield to Ashton on 9th October 1882 brought the first major change to Heathfield station. The name had changed from Chudleigh Road eight days earlier, necessary because the new Teign Valley line had a station named Chudleigh. Heathfield did not become, at this point, a junction station, rather an interchange, handling trains running on two different gauges. To serve the Teign Valley trains a bay platform, some 270 ft long, was constructed adjoining the original 1874 platform on its east side. It stopped short of the station building at the southern end but extended further than the original platform at the northern end, creating an island platform in a staggered form. No new structure was erected, passengers sharing the original branch line building. Where the two platforms were adjacent, the width was some 25 ft. A signal box, with 25 levers, was erected on this wide section by the Teign Valley Company. Beyond the north end of the station, where the two different gauge lines entered the site, two parallel exchange sidings enabled freight to be exchanged.

The need for this exchange ceased in 1892, when the Moretonhampstead branch was converted to standard gauge. A connection was made between the branch line and the Teign Valley line, though not at this time direct but via a siding. The Teign Valley line was completed north of Ashton through to Exeter in 1903 and traffic increased. This merited a further change and, at last, from October 1916, further track re-modelling created a direct connection. A new GWR 43 lever (increased to 58 in 1927) signal box with a hipped grey slate roof was provided at the far north end of the 1882 bay platform. The box ceased to be used after October 1965, the number of levers being reduced from 53 to 44 in 1943.

Further major changes came at Heathfield in 1927, when the GWR installed a loop line on the down side of the Moretonhampstead line, alongside a 320 ft long 12 ft wide platform with an arc top corrugated iron shelter. The platform was shorter than the up island because of the siding to the brick and tile works at the south end. At the same time, in order to accommodate the loop, the original 1874 platform on the up side was both narrowed but also lengthened at the north end to a length of 413 ft,

terminating at the same point as the 1882 bay platform, thus eliminating the stagger. The down and island platforms were linked by a rail level board crossing at the northern end, no footbridge ever being provided.

During the Second World War, facilities on the Teign Valley line were enhanced, it being designated on a diversionary route between Exeter and Newton Abbot away from the vulnerable coast route (would still be useful today!). At Heathfield a double track junction was installed in 1943, two through tracks running between the down and island platforms with the Teign Valley only trains terminating in the bay. The loop line was also lengthened.

Passenger traffic was always at a reasonable level. In 1903 12,744 passenger tickets were issued at Heathfield. Further figures were 1913 (11,575), 1923 (13,346), 1933 (20,719), 1943 (18,181) and 1953 (9,905). Figures from 1933 on include Chudleigh Knighton Halt; also Teigngrace Halt from 1943.

At no stage was there a major goods yard or shed at Heathfield, the principal facility being a goods lock up on the platform north of the main building. The scale of this building, always of a similar wood construction to the main building, but with no windows or chimneys, varied with the changes at the station. From an original small scale, it was enlarged following the arrival of the Teign Valley services but then, when the platform was narrowed in 1927, it resumed its original smaller size and also its position adjacent at the north end of the building. Sliding doors were provided both on the platform and road sides. Despite the lack of facilities at the station itself, the line was busy for freight, in particular generated by ball clay works in the area.

Passenger services ceased at Heathfield in March 1959 but general goods continued to be handled until June 1965, the coal depot closing later in December 1967. The sidings to the brick and tile works were disused from 1966. New traffic came to the line through the station from October 1966 with the opening of an oil terminal a half mile north-west of the station, to which trains ran until January 1996. A large Geest factory north east of the station was also rail served from April 1963 to December 1975, using a siding laid in 1961. The station building was demolished in the 1970s and, when viewed from the A38 bridge in late 2006, the platforms were derelict and weed covered with rusting tracks alongside.

Hele & Bradninch. Looking north towards Taunton in the 1960s. The main building with its slender horizontal canopy stands on the down platform. The 1925 signal box controls the level crossing gates.

HELE & BRADNINCH

OPENED: 1st May 1844 (with the opening of the Beam Bridge (south of Wellington, Somerset) – Exeter section of the Bristol & Exeter Railway.

CLOSED: Passengers – 5th October 1964.

  Goods – 17th May 1965.

In the village of Hele, the station opened at the beginning of May 1844. The suffix '& Bradninch', referring to a settlement a mile to the north, was added in 1867. The main building, housing the station facilities at the north end of the down (towards Exeter) platform, was similar to other small stations on this line. A slender horizontal canopy extended to the platform edge, supported by four pillars. Passengers on the up platform were served by a waiting shelter with a roof that extended forwards over the platform giving limited protection. A small chimney rose above the shelter roof. Unlike some other stations on this line (eg Tiverton Junction), the station was not redeveloped in the 1930s. In 1903 17,474 passenger tickets were issued; this figure rose to 17,789 in 1913 but then fell to 13,201 in 1923 and 13,511 in 1933. Between the First and Second World Wars eight or nine staff were employed at the station.

The up side shelter backed on to a large goods shed with a goods loop running through. At the north end of the shed was a substantial goods office. Other goods facilities included cattle pens north of the shed, on the up side beyond a level crossing. South of the goods shed, also on the up side, was a coal platform and a four ton capacity crane. A number of additions were made to the sidings in the 1890s. To the west of the station was the factory of the Hele Paper Company, which later became part of Wiggins Teape. A siding was laid to it in 1919 and the factory was rail connected until the early 1980s. During the Second World War a long up side loop was brought into use.

The station signal box stood at the north end of the down platform; the original 1874 box was replaced by a new box in 1925. This box was extended at the south end in 1943 to accommodate extra levers (total now 43) required to control the extra goods facilities added as a war-time measure. The box originally contained a wheel to operate the gates of a level crossing immediately to the north of the station. Full lifting barriers replaced the gates in 1970. Operations continued at the box until closure on 9th December 1985 when control came under the Exeter MAS panel. The level crossing had changed to automatic half barriers before the box closed.

Passenger services ceased at Hele & Bradninch in October 1964; goods facilities were provided for a further seven months until May 1965. Today both the main building, minus the canopy and fenced off from the line, and the goods shed survive. The building itself appeared to be disused when seen in 2007. The goods shed is used by a car repair firm. The nearby former Railway Hotel is now the Crossways Tavern.

HEMYOCK

OPENED: 29th May 1876 (with the opening of the Culm Valley Light Railway, Tiverton Junction – Hemyock).

CLOSED: Passengers – 9th September 1963.

  Goods – 6th September 1965 (except private siding).

Sited in the settlement of Millhayes about half a mile north of Hemyock, passenger services commenced on the Culm Valley Light Railway on 29th May 1876. Celebrations at Hemyock were delayed until 1st June. As reported in the Tiverton Gazette 'there were rejoicings which will be long remembered in the history of this quiet little village'. The terminus itself was decorated and in the village there were arches and flags. When the train conveying representatives from other settlements on the line arrived, the band of the Devon Rifle Volunteers struck up 'See the conquering hero comes'. Lunch was held in a large marquee near the station while a dinner was given to about 250 'working people' of the neighbourhood in Hemyock Square. Rural sports were staged and, in the evening, a ball was held in the lunch marquee.

The station itself was on a rather cramped site north of the River Culm and west of a minor road. The short platform and station building on the north side of a single track was just to the east of a very short run round loop. From this loop a short siding trailed back into a timber engine shed with a slate roof. A further siding led from the loop to the timber goods shed behind the station building, the siding running through the shed which contained a 30 cwt capacity crane. Trailing back from this siding was a further siding to the carriage shed, also built of timber. Between the carriage and engine sheds was an open coal stage and a water tower. The station building itself, of red brick with external timber framing, red roof tiles and one chimney, housed booking and parcels facilities. A flat roofed concrete block extension, used as a waiting room, was added at the east end in about 1930. At the west end of the building was a small wooden signal box. Behind the box was a lean-to housing the gent's toilet. In the north side of the building itself was a sliding door to facilitate transfer of light goods from road vehicles. In 1878 a refreshment room was built north of the station outside railway property. Designed to accommodate some 120-130 people, it was built to serve the large number of visitors expected at Hemyock visiting local attractions such as the Wellington Monument and the Blackdown Hills. These visitors failed to materialise and the room soon closed, the building being used to accommodate animals.

Soon after opening a cattle dock was erected south and east of the platform track; another change was that the goods shed siding was extended over an ungated road crossing to serve Millhayes Mill. Being ungated no engines were permitted to cross the road. In 1920 the platform track was extended beyond the cattle dock over the road to serve, via a gated crossing, what had now become a dairy factory. The mill had been taken over by the Culm Valley Dairy Company and then this became a United Dairies Factory from 1915. The import of coal to the factory and despatch of milk products was a feature of Hemyock for many years. In extending the platform track a short dead end spur was added at the east end of the platform which was slightly re-aligned and shortened.

Major changes came at Hemyock early in the 1930s when the layout west of the station was modified. The engine shed had closed on 21st October 1929 and this, together with the carriage shed, was demolished. In their place a longer run

Hemyock. In about 1960 the red brick building, with some external timber framing still surviving, stands on the single platform. At its west end is the small wooden signal box, by now operating only as a ground frame, and behind is the lean-to gent's toilet. The scene is dominated by the large dairy factory.

round loop was installed. A further siding on the north side of this loop served a new corrugated iron goods shed, which replaced the earlier shed behind the station. A ground frame was introduced at the far west end of the layout and the signal box on the platform now became Hemyock East ground frame. The layout of the station remained as these 1930s changes until closure.

Passenger numbers at Hemyock were never high. In 1903 4,237 passenger tickets were issued and a similar number were recorded in 1913 (4,341) and 1923 (4,242). The figure almost halved to 2,286 in 1933. In 1930 four men were employed at the station. Passenger services continued until September 1963 but general goods facilities were available for another two years. The link to the milk factory continued for another ten years with the final milk train running on 31st October 1975. Following a brief closure, the factory reopened, again manufacturing dairy products, but it was no longer rail linked, all products being despatched by road. The former station site was, at this stage, used as a car park and storage area for the factory. Today the factory has gone, the site used for housing. When visited in July 2006 signs indicated that the former station site was also to be developed for housing.

Hole. On 22nd February 1965 a single car DMU working the 0855 hrs Torrington to Halwill stands at the down platform, on which no shelter was provided.

HOLE (FOR BLACK TORRINGTON)

OPENED: 27th July 1925 (with the opening of the North Devon & Cornwall Junction Light Railway, Torrington – Halwill).

CLOSED: Passengers – 1st March 1965.
Goods – 7th September 1964.

This was a remote station on a half mile long lane leading south from the A3072 between Hatherleigh and Holsworthy. The main role of the station was to serve the village of Black Torrington about one and a quarter miles away to the north, and hence the name. To use only the name of Black Torrington would have brought confusion with Torrington station serving Great Torrington. Hole referred to an adjacent small group of houses. Other nearby villages served by the station included Highampton to the east and Sheepwash to the north-east.

Hole was one of three stations on the Torrington to Halwill line to have a passing loop. The station had features similar to those at Petrockstow and Hatherleigh, the main stone building standing on the up (towards Torrington) platform. Its wooden platform canopy was a forward extension of the roof. No shelter was provided on the down platform.

Passenger volumes were very low at Hole. In 1928 1,340 passenger tickets were issued and 1,364 collected; by 1936 the figures had fallen greatly to 329 and 428. Though staffed, there was no station master, Hole coming under the supervision of the station master at Hatherleigh.

The limited goods facilities comprised two sidings behind the up platform, one terminating at a cattle dock adjacent to the building. Beside the outer siding were cattle pens. The provision of the dock and the pens illustrated that the principal goods traffic at

Hole related to the movement of cattle. In addition, in about 1942, a large warehouse/depot was constructed by prisoners of war for the War Agriculture Committee; it was served by a siding and thus brought some extra traffic to the station.

The limited freight facilities ceased in September 1964 and Hole closed to passengers at the beginning of March 1965 with the withdrawal of passenger services on the line. Following closure the buildings remained intact within a Devon Trust for Nature conservation area. In 2005 the station, once derelict, was a dwelling. To the east a section of the track bed is used as a footpath to the village of Highampton.

HOLSWORTHY

OPENED: 20th January 1879 (with the opening of the Meldon Junction – Holsworthy section of the Devon & Cornwall Railway).

CLOSED: Passengers – 3rd October 1966.
Goods – 7th September 1964.

South of the centre of this west Devon market town and livestock centre, the station opened as the then western terminus of the Devon & Cornwall Railway (D&CR) in January 1879. An earlier 1865 scheme had proposed a line through Holsworthy to Bude but the powers lapsed. When the scheme was revived the terminus was at Holsworthy with a horse bus link on to the north Cornwall resort. The London & South Western Railway (LSWR), which had operated the D&CR from the beginning and acquired it in 1880, extended the line to Bude, opening on 10th August 1898. Over the previous 19 years the LSWR had subsidised the horse bus service by £2 per week.

The original 1879 terminus station comprised a single stone built platform on the north side of the line. A single track with a run-round loop ran alongside the platform with a turntable siding at the far end. On the platform was a small stone building details of which are not known. At the station was a small ten lever signal box and east of the station, beyond a rail over bridge, was an engine shed.

With the extension to Bude, the station was redeveloped and extended, a brick face platform being added on the now down side. An impressive stone building was erected on the original, now up, platform with accommodation for the station master occupying the majority of the two storey section at the west end. A single storey section with an apex roof at right angles to the platform incorporated the main station facilities but the gent's toilets were in an

annex at the west end of the station house. A wide canopy extended in front of the building whilst, on the road side, a canopy was provided over the main entrance. A good size open front waiting shelter with an apex slate roof served passengers on the down platform; to the east of the shelter was the replacement 1898 20 lever signal box. The link between the platforms was a rail level board crossing at the west end of the platforms.

At the time of rebuilding the turntable was moved to a site in front of the engine shed. The turntable and engine shed remained for a few years but were little used with the main facilities now at Bude. The turntable was abandoned on 1st January 1911 but the shed survived until the 1920s.

A goods yard developed over the years to the west of and behind the up side buildings. A large yard for a branch line, it included a stone goods shed with a road side canopy and a tall chimney. Beside it was a timber goods office. Also in the yard was a slaughter house, a number of stores operated by local agricultural firms and five cattle pens. The pens were beside a loading dock at the west end of the up platform. There was no yard crane but within the goods shed was a two ton capacity crane. A cattle market opened in 1906 to the south of the station; this and the slaughter house generated much freight traffic at Holsworthy.

In 1928 17,542 passenger tickets were issued at Holsworthy and 32,922 collected; by 1936 the figures had halved to 7,990 and 16,325. Passenger services ceased in early October 1966 when the line to Bude closed. Goods facilities had been withdrawn two years earlier in September 1964. After closure the station site was used for some years for commercial purposes by a number of businesses. These included the station building itself being

Holsworthy. Passengers wait on the down platform for a DMU travelling towards Bude in 1965. On this platform is a waiting shelter and 1898 signal box. The station building, originally incorporating two storey accommodation for the station master, stands on the up (towards Halwill) platform.

occupied by a firm distributing fertilizers and feeds, an appropriate use reflecting business in the station yard over many years. By the mid 1990s the building was boarded up and the station site was then redeveloped for use by a supermarket. Station Road remains today as a reminder of the railway era.

HONITON

OPENED: 19th July 1860 (with the opening of the Yeovil Junction – Exeter section of the London & South Western Railway).
CLOSED: Passengers – remains open for services on the London (Waterloo) – Salisbury – Exeter line. Goods – 8th May 1967.

Approximately a half mile south of the centre of Honiton, a town famous for its lace and glove making industries, the station opened in July 1860 with the commencement of services on the last section of the London & South Western Railway (LSWR) from London to Exeter. At this time much of the line was single track but a passing loop was provided at Honiton. Later the whole line was doubled.

A large and impressive William Tite design building on the down (towards Exeter) platform incorporated, at the west end, the station master's house and featured tall chimneys, steeply pitched roofs and an ornate horizontal platform canopy. A large hipped roof waiting shelter served passengers

Honiton. A view in about 1912 of the impressive down (towards Exeter) side William Tite design building, covered footbridge and forecourt.

Honiton. Looking up towards Axminster on 7th September 1963. The main William Tite building with its ornate horizontal canopy stands on the down platform. A hipped roof waiting shelter serves passengers on the up platform.

on the up platform. Both platforms extended to the east on to a road bridge over New Street. A large covered footbridge linked the platforms just to the east of the main buildings and shelter.

The goods yard was sited on the down side behind, and to the west of, the station building. The yard included a small goods shed with a through siding, cattle pens, coal staithes and a number of buildings belonging to local traders. One siding specifically served the premises of George Blay, timber merchants.

The yard was provided with a five ton capacity crane and a 20 ton weighbridge. There were also sidings on the up side west of the platform. An original 1875 signal box stood off the west end of the down platform. This was replaced from 16th June 1957 by a 26 lever box just to the west of the station on the up side between the platform and the sidings.

Freight facilities were withdrawn at Honiton in May 1967. As from 11th June 1967 the line was generally singled but a passing loop was maintained at Honiton, the 1957 signal box continuing to control the loop and one refuge siding, which was retained on the up side west of the station. The down side track was now signalled for bi-directional movements to allow east bound trains to use the down platform when no west bound trains were scheduled. This permitted passengers to use the station facilities that remained on the down side.

It was in these down side facilities that the greatest change came at Honiton with the very unfortunate demolition of the William Tite building and its replacement by a clasp type austere structure, an action described at the time as 'architectural vandalism'. The reason given was that the original building was too expensive to maintain. A similar disaster almost occurred at Axminster but here the building was saved and stands today, recently renovated (see Axminster text). The austere structure at Honiton has been now improved a little by the addition of an apex style roof. On the up side the original attractive shelter was also removed, being replaced by a basic structure which stands today, in a poor condition.

Today the original footbridge remains in place, though now open. On the site of the former up sidings is the station car park, whilst in the former goods yard are the premises of a building supplies firm.

HORRABRIDGE

OPENED: Passengers - 22nd June 1859, Goods – 1st February 1860. (with the opening of the Tavistock & South Devon Railway, Tavistock Junction - Tavistock).

CLOSED: Passengers and Goods – 31st December 1962.

Sited above the village of Horrabridge, the station opened for passengers with the commencement of services on the then broad gauge line from Plymouth to Tavistock in June 1859. Goods facilities became available some six months later. For a short period from August 1883 to May 1885 Horrabridge was also the junction station for the Princetown branch (see Yelverton text).

The main running line was adjacent to the up (towards Yelverton) platform with the passing loop alongside the longer down platform. Both platforms were constructed of earth and rock infill behind stone facing with edges of concrete slabs. The original surfaces were of blue Staffordshire brick but by the 1950s some areas had been replaced by slabs and tarmac with chippings. Along the rear of the up platform was a white paling fence separating it from the station forecourt and approach road; behind the down platform there was no fence, a grass bank rising up from the platform. At both ends of the platforms were water cranes between the tracks, there being ample space because of the early broad gauge tracks. The cranes were fed from a large water tank at the northern approach to the station on the down side.

The principal station building on the up platform was basically constructed of a timber frame and wide lateral wood planks with a gabled slate roof, a tall chimney and a short horizontal canopy on the platform side. The wooden station contrasted with Bickleigh, on the same line, where the building was of stone. Housed in the building were the main waiting, booking and toilet facilities. On the down platform was a small stone open front waiting shelter, in this case similar to that at Bickleigh. The station was lit by gas.

The main access to the station was from the approach road behind the up side building. No footbridge was provided, inter-platform public movements being via a level crossing carrying the Horrabridge to Buckland Monachorum road at the south end of the station. This crossing closed in March 1952. The original crossing gates were said to have the largest single span in the country. In 1903 24,763 passenger tickets were issued at Horrabridge. The figure rose to 26,570 in 1913 but then fell very slightly to 25,715 in 1923 and 24,281 in 1933, a much lower fall over this period than at many Devon stations as it seems the developing bus services were less competitive than in many places.

On the up side, north of the main building, was a small goods yard with a goods loop and a single siding that ran to a loading bay behind the north end of the up platform. The yard included a goods shed and cranes whose capacity varied over the years from 5 tons in 1877 to 3½ tons in 1928. Horrabridge dealt with goods generated over a wide area as no facility was provided at Yelverton station. Movements at Horrabridge were controlled from an original South Devon Railway design signal box on the up platform adjacent to, and north of, the main building. The box had a slate roof, brick chimney and windows along the platform side and at the

Horrabridge. No.3521 class 4-4-0 enters with an up (towards Yelverton) train in about 1910. The wide space between the platforms is a legacy of the broad gauge era. The track is laid on longitudinal sleepers. The signal box is seen above the wooden main building. Behind the train is the goods shed.

ends. A wooden porch and steps were at the northern end. Following closure to both passengers and goods traffic at the end of 1962, the site was sold. In 1979 the buildings were demolished and replaced with a small factory in the early 1980s. When visited in May 2007 the station site had been redeveloped for a housing development 'The Old Station'. Where the station itself stood is a house appropriately named Great Western Lodge with a sign in the form of an engine by the front door.

IDE

OPENED: 1st July 1903 (with the opening of the Exeter Railway, Exeter – Ashton).
CLOSED: Passengers – 9th June 1958.
    Goods – 7th March 1955.

Ide station, on the western edge of the village and on the north side of the line, was a low brick building with a slate roof and two chimneys, which incorporated waiting, booking and toilet facilities. It was a well used station, with villagers travelling to and from Exeter for work and shopping. Passenger numbers were relatively high with 5,276 tickets issued in 1903, 7,782 in 1913, 7,819 in 1923 and 7,149 in 1933. Numbers declined, however, when passengers opted for buses to and from Exeter, which went through the middle of the village.

Ide, which had closed as a war-time measure from 1st January 1917 until 1st May 1919, was reduced to the status of a halt in 1923, with staffing reduced to mornings only. Staffing ceased altogether on 7th March 1955; the building remained, however, used

Ide. The station building on the north side of the line in about 1912.

as a waiting shelter. To the west of the station was a small goods loop with a short spur trailing back to a small loading dock at the west end of the platform. A camping coach was stabled in this spur from 1934 to 1939. No signal box ever operated at Ide. Goods services were withdrawn in March 1955 when staffing ended; passenger services ceased with the withdrawal of trains on the line in June 1958. Today a small estate of bungalows in St Ida's Close occupies the former station site. The Close leads off Station Road which rises from the village centre. The nearby former Railway Inn is now renamed the Poachers Inn.

Ilfracombe. A general view looking north, in about 1915, of the extensive station site. In the centre is the main building and, to its right, the pre 1928 engine shed. At the extreme right is the goods shed. To the left of the station are three carriage sidings, increased to seven in 1929.

ILFRACOMBE

OPENED: 20th July 1874 (with the opening of the Barnstaple & Ilfracombe Railway).
CLOSED: Passengers – 5th October 1970.
  Goods – 7th September 1964.

The topography of this resort dictated that Ilfracombe station was sited about a mile inland from the harbour high above the town at some 250 ft above sea level. The site was modified a number of times over the years to the extent that one commentator describes it as a man-made plateau. It was not really practical for the station to be any closer to the town centre.

The opening in July 1874 prompted much celebration in Ilfracombe. An unusual feature was that the station itself was decorated with flags and banners used previously at Windsor for the reception of the Czar and Czarina of Russia. Banners read 'Welcome VR' (Queen Victoria) and 'Welcome AM' (Alexander and Maria). The platform and roof pillars were turned into Venetian masts, being striped with coloured cloth; the platform roof was decorated with artificial flowers. A triumphal arch over the station approach road read 'United in Bonds of Iron'. Specific activities included a tea in the market for 'aged people and schoolchildren of the town', a public promenade, a ball, illuminations and rural sports. A public dinner was held on 21st July at the Ilfracombe Hotel. Messers Attwood & Co, outfitters in the town, celebrated the opening by having a medal struck.

The 1874 station was basically a single storey

terminal building and north-south island platform. The longest west face (no.2), with a canopy, ran behind the building and the shorter (no.1) terminated adjacent to its south wall. This original layout was planned on the basis of the comparatively short length of trains in that era. By 1892 a large screen had been erected west of the platform no.2 track to protect passengers from the prevailing westerly winds. A bookstall was provided as early as August 1874. In about 1901 the platform was lengthened and an umbrella style canopy added.

In the late 1920s the Southern Railway undertook a major redevelopment programme at Ilfracombe. In 1929 the platform was extended by 277 ft to accommodate the longer excursion trains. It is recorded that prior to this some passengers travelling in the rear of incoming trains had to climb down on to the track on arrival at the station! The opportunity was also taken to raise the level of the old platform; the whole surface being tarmaced. The station building itself was renovated and improved, electric lighting being introduced. An engine run-round loop was also laid alongside platform 2 in 1929. Prior to this 'gravity' shunting of carriages was used on occasions; in February 1925 a carriage ran through the buffers during such a manoeuvre! At busy times number 2 platform was used for arrivals and number 1 for departures, these uses being assisted by the provision of the run-round loop.

Passenger flows were high, particularly during the summer months. Trains such as the Atlantic Coast Express came to the resort. In 1932 69,218 passenger tickets were issued and 151,641 collected. Comparable figures for 1936 were 23,943 and 98,929. Tickets were also sold in ticket offices run by the GWR and LSWR in the town centre. The SR opened an office in 1930 and in 1936 issued 2,263 tickets there. Traffic continued to be high after the Second World War and the mid 1950s saw some of the highest numbers using the station.

A range of other facilities were provided over the years at Ilfracombe. To the south of the station on the up (east) side was the goods yard including a stone goods shed and a ten ton capacity crane. The original engine shed stood between the station building and the goods shed but this was replaced in July 1928 by a concrete single road shed at the far south end of the station site. A 64 ft 10 inch turntable was also provided, superseding an earlier small facility in front of the old shed. An even longer 70 ft turntable was later installed to cope with the large locomotives hauling the expresses to

Ilfracombe. Looking south from the buffers in 1963 showing the west facing platform with, to the right, the long screen erected in 1892 to protect passengers from the prevailing westerly winds.

Ilfracombe. It is alleged that engines on this turntable sometimes turned themselves in the strong winds across the site! The removal of the first engine shed permitted a much needed expansion of the goods yard to the east of the station.

To the west of the station carriage sidings were increased from three to seven in 1929. Material excavated with the development of the goods yard was apparently used to give a level site for these new sidings.

Ilfracombe's original signal box stood opposite the goods shed but this was replaced in 1929 by a larger box with 50 levers further south on the down side near the engine shed. The box closed on 17th December 1967, a small ground frame being installed in the shell of the box.

This was one of a series of closures at Ilfracombe in the mid to late 1960s. All goods facilities were withdrawn in September 1964. The engine shed was also closed in 1964 and all tracks, apart from that alongside platform 2, the run-round loop and one carriage siding, were taken out of use when the Barnstaple to Ilfracombe line was singled from 17th December 1967. The surviving carriage siding was taken out of use from 5th May 1968.

The last through train to London ran on 26th September 1970 and the station closed on 5th October. All station buildings were subsequently demolished and the whole site redeveloped for light industry and warehousing. Station Road is a reminder of the railway era in Ilfracombe.

Ingra Tor Halt. A view of the halt on 26th September 1951. A wooden shelter stands behind the platform. The 'snake' notice is directly in front of the shelter.

INGRA TOR HALT

OPENED: 2nd March 1936 (on the Princetown branch originally opened through this site in 1883).
CLOSED: 5th March 1956.

A stopping place on Dartmoor for walkers, Ingra Tor opened in March 1936 for a lifespan of only twenty years and three days. The wooden platform on the north side of the line stood on wood trestle legs. A wooden shelter stood behind the platform. Its door was in the east end. Two posts on the platform carrying lamp frames provided some illumination. Ingra Tor was famous for the notice displayed for walkers, 'In the interests of game preservation and for their protection against snakes etc dogs should be kept on a lead. By order'. Following closure of the Halt, this notice was preserved at Saltram House. There is now no trace of the halt though a path follows the trackbed.

INSTOW

OPENED: 2nd November 1855 (with the opening of the Bideford Extension Railway, Fremington – Bideford).
CLOSED: Passengers – 4th October 1965.
Goods – 30th April 1962.

At the formal opening of the Bideford Extension Railway from Fremington to Bideford on 29th October 1855 a triumphal arch was erected at Instow. Public services commenced three days later. Serving the small village from which a pedestrian ferry ran to Appledore, the station, on the east bank of the River Torridge estuary, was on a long curve of the railway. On a restricted waterfront site, there were two platforms serving the main line and the passing loop that could accommodate a locomotive and 27 wagons. The main station building, on the up

Instow. Looking north in the early 1960s. The main building, with an unusual rounded canopy, stands on the up (towards Barnstaple) waterfront side. A concrete shelter serves passengers on the down platform beyond which, in the distance, is the signal box controlling the adjacent level crossing. Most of the structures survive today.

waterfront side, with a slate roof and two chimneys, housed the station facilities. An unusual rounded canopy was a later addition by the London & South Western Railway (LSWR). A shelter served passengers on the down platform, originally metal but later concrete.

The only freight facility was a single siding running behind the up platform; unusually it had its own entrance gate, a feature normally only found on private sidings. The goods traffic inwards was mostly coal and out was predominantly sugar beet and pit props. Instow's 1872 signal box (13 levers), sited at the north end of the down platform, was particularly busy controlling an important passing point on the Barnstaple to Torrington line. In 1909 nine trains crossed here per day. The box controlled the adjacent level crossing, which for many years carried the main A39 road from Barnstaple to Bideford and North Devon. Traffic returns indicated strongly that the sands and other seaside attractions were the key generators of passengers at Instow, the number of tickets collected being far higher than the number issued. In 1928 9,041 tickets were issued and 28,177 collected; the figures dropped markedly to 3,280 and 8,756 in 1936 but still showed this marked difference.

The limited goods facilities were withdrawn at the end of April 1962 and passenger services ceased just over three years later in October 1965. Staffing had ceased on 4th January 1965. The line continued to be used until the early 1980s by milk, clay and other traffic generated in the Torrington area (see

Ivybridge. A view in about 1910 of the original Brunel chalet style building behind the east end of the up platform.

IVYBRIDGE

OPENED: 15th June 1848 (on the Totnes – Plymouth Laira Green) section of the South Devon Railway opened through this site 6 weeks earlier on 5th May).
CLOSED: Passengers – 2nd March 1959.
        Goods – 29th November 1965.
RE-OPENED: 15th July 1994 (for local passenger services).

Torrington text). The loop was taken out of use on 3rd November 1968 and the up track was removed in July 1970. The signal box closed on 17th January 1979 and automatic lights came into use, though by that date the main A39 traffic had been diverted. In the early 1980s the Instow Signal Box Group saved the box from demolition and campaigned for its listing. This was achieved in 1984, the first box to be designated Grade II. When the line was lifted in 1984 Devon County Council purchased the site for development of the track bed as a part of the Tarka Trail cycleway. The box was handed over to the Group in 1989 and subsequently renovated, including the 13 lever frame and gate wheel. Further development included the relaying of a section of track alongside the box, linked to surviving rails in the road, and the installation of replica level crossing gates. The down platform was also preserved with a station nameboard. The former main station building, now fenced off and minus its canopy, is used by the North Devon Yacht Club. In January 1992 the Instow Signal Box Group and Bideford Railway Station Group merged to take on responsibility for the two former station sites in co-operation with the owners, Devon County Council. The new Group is the Bideford and Instow Railway Group (BIRG). In 2003 the signal box received a National Railway Heritage Award, the Carillion Award, as indicated on a plaque beside the box.

The first station was located about a half mile north of the village centre. Records indicate that, although services commenced on the single track broad gauge line on 5th May, Ivybridge station did not open until 15th June (see also Brent and Plympton).

The 1848 platform and wooden chalet style building were sited on the up (towards Brent) side of the single track immediately to the west of a large wooden viaduct with stone pillars over the River Erne. The line through the station was doubled from 13th August 1893 and a down platform and waiting shelter added. A year later a new stone viaduct immediately south of, and adjacent to, the old wooden structure came into use, this requiring the re-alignment of the tracks through the station. The up platform was extended and widened and the down platform re-built. The original building on the up side was now at the extreme end of the platform and a brick waiting shelter was added at the centre but closer to the platform edge than the building. A wooden goods shed stood between the building and the shelter. A covered footbridge, with roofs over the span itself and the steps, linked the two platforms

Ivybridge. Looking north-east in 1958 showing the original Brunel chalet building in the distance under the now open footbridge and the two brick shelters on the up (left) and down platforms. A new Ivybridge station was opened a half mile east of this site in 1994.

immediately to the east of the up and down waiting shelters. In later years the footbridge roofs were removed. A rail level board crossing was also provided across the tracks at the west end of the station. In 1903 39,832 passenger tickets were issued at Ivybridge; comparable figures were 1913 (33,263), 1923 (23,340) and 1933 (14,392). Over the period 1900 to 1940 an average of 10 to 12 men were based at the station.

An original goods yard, sited east of the viaduct, remained in use until 1st October 1911. Following the doubling of the track a goods yard was developed west of the station on the down side; facilities included a goods shed, cattle pens and 6 ton capacity crane. At the station end of the yard was a 30 lever signal box in operation from 1895 to 17th December 1973. A dock siding also ran behind the up platform at the west end. Three GWR cottages were sited behind the down platform for use by the station master and signalmen.

The first station closed for passengers in March 1959; goods facilities were withdrawn from November 1965. Major expansion of Ivybridge in the 1980s and early 1990s led to the opening, a half mile east of the original site, of the second Ivybridge station on 15th July 1994 at a cost of £380,000. Waiting shelters stand on the two slightly staggered platforms which can only accommodate four coach trains. One hundred car parking spaces are also provided. There is now no trace of the first station; the old goods shed survives, used by a garage (Victoria Garage).

KENWITH CASTLE

OPENED: 18th May 1901 (with the opening of the Bideford Quay – Northam section of the Bideford, Westward Ho! & Appledore Railway)
CLOSED: 28th March 1917.

Named after an ancient earth works north of the line where it runs east to west to the north-west of Bideford, this was a small request stop principally for the sparse inhabitants of surrounding farms but also visitors to Kenwith Castle. A small wooden platform was provided for passengers. If early plans had come to fruition the site could have been a junction between a main line from Bideford to Clovelly and a branch to Appledore. Abbotsham Road was also another possible site. Kenwith Castle closed after only 16 years (see Bideford Quay text).

KEYHAM

OPENED: 2nd July 1900 (on the Plymouth – Saltash – Truro line originally opened through this site in 1859).
CLOSED: Passengers – remains open for local passenger services on the main line to Cornwall and the Tamar Valley line to Gunnislake.
Goods – 19th July 1965 (except private siding).

On the main GWR Plymouth to Cornwall line between Devonport and the Royal Albert Bridge, Keyham opened following completion of track doubling from the south. Brick buildings with apex style canopies stood on both platforms, the principal facilities being on the down (towards Saltash) side. Additional metal shelters stood on both platforms, that at the north end of the down platform being for

Keyham. Looking north with the main building off to the left and the up building and metal waiting shelter on the up (towards Plymouth) platform (right). The footbridge, shown covered, survives today but without its roof.

parcels and that on the Plymouth end of the up platform serving principally as an additional waiting room. A covered footbridge connected the two platforms; a later extension of the bridge east over the goods yard was uncovered.

Behind the up platform was Keyham goods yard; a short siding was originally laid in 1903 but additional sidings and a goods shed were provided by 1922. Goods facilities were withdrawn from July 1965; the goods shed was demolished in 2000 but loops were retained to assist with the marshalling of trucks from the Dockyard. Keyham signal box, at the north end of the down platform, was in use from 25th June 1900 to 2nd July 1972.

Soon after it opened in 1903 10 staff were based at Keyham; this increased to an average of 14 in the 1930s, it was unstaffed from May 1969. The buildings have been demolished, modern metal shelters now stand on both platforms for passengers on local services. The footbridge and its eastern extension remain, all now uncovered.

KILLINGTON LANE

OPENED: 27th May 2006 (as the then western terminus of the reopened Lynton & Barnstaple line from Woody Bay)

CLOSED: Remains open for services on the reopened Lynton & Barnstaple Railway.

This halt on the northern side of the line opened at the end of May 2006. A small wooden shelter had just been erected when visited in May 2007.

Kingsbridge. Horsedrawn carriages stand in the station approach in about 1910. A Brent bound train stands in the platform. In the distance is the large goods shed which, with the station building, survives today.

Killington Lane. Looking west on 3rd May 2007 with a Lynton & Barnstaple train standing beside the platform and recently erected wooden shelter.

KINGSBRIDGE

OPENED: 19th December 1893 (with the opening of the Kingsbridge & South Devon Railway, Brent – Kingsbridge).

CLOSED: Passenger and Goods – 16th December 1963.

Despite being a busy port with some ship building, and the focus of activity in this part of south Devon, Kingsbridge did not feature in early railway schemes. With the opening of the South Devon Railway in 1848, a horse bus service to Kingsbridge was inaugurated from Wrangaton station (appropriately called Kingsbridge Road from 1849 to 1895). Road links were also provided from Dartmouth after the rail service to Kingswear and Dartmouth commenced in 1864. A local company obtained an Act of Parliament, also in 1864, and limited work on a line to Kingsbridge took place but was abandoned, because of financial problems.

Eventually, in accord with the Kingsbridge & Salcombe Railway Acts of 1882 and 1887, Kingsbridge joined the Devon rail network in

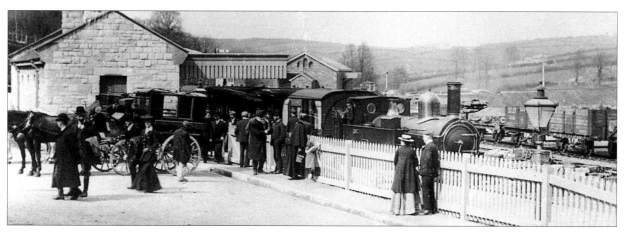

Kingsbridge. A detailed look in the early 1960s at the typical William Clarke style stone building that served stations on the Kingsbridge branch. Note the characteristic three tall chimneys and wide canopy.

December 1893. Salcombe was never reached probably because of the expensive engineering required. Such an extension was considered in the 1920s but again abandoned, it being concluded that the bus service from Kingsbridge, inaugurated by the GWR from 2nd July 1909 and taken over by the Western National on 31st December 1928, was adequate.

The official opening of the station on 19th December 1893 prompted much celebration in the town. The special train was met by local dignitaries and a procession, led by the regimental band of the Kings Own Scottish Borderers, marched through decorated streets to the bandstand on the quay. Speeches were given and lunch taken at the Town Hall and other events included a firework display and a dance at the Kings Arms and even a rugby match between Kingsbridge and Totnes!

Sited to the west of, and above, the town centre, the layout of Kingsbridge station, originally completed at a cost of £180,000, evolved over the years. The final form was a long curved platform with an engine release track and a bay platform, the latter added from 15th August 1915. The platforms were extended to the west in the 1920s. The light grey stone building, in the style of William Clarke (see Avonwick text) was also extended at its western end in the mid 1920s. The original short canopy at the eastern end of the building was also extended at this time. Following this expansion the building included, from west to east on the platform side, a left luggage/parcels office, a gent's toilet, a ladies' room, the booking office and the station master's office.

A spur off the bay platform track led to the engine shed, a stone building with roof lights but no windows. Alongside the shed was a water tank, supplying a water crane at the west end of the platform. Opposite the station building and adjacent to the engine release track was a 1920s carriage shed, a black corrugated iron structure accommodating two carriages. This shed also acted as a waiting shelter for bus passengers to Dartmouth and Salcombe. An original shed stood at the west end of the station but this was demolished when the platform was extended.

The 1920s carriage shed was at the east end of Kingsbridge goods yard, sited north and west of the station. The yard included an impressive large goods shed with an office at the east end, an internal crane and a small canopy on the road side; other yard facilities included a cattle dock, animal food store and crane, together with a number of small huts on concrete blocks. The yard had been extended as early as 1894 with the provision of the cattle facilities. Substantial goods traffic was handled in the goods yard over the years, in particular related to the local horticulture and agriculture. Rail movements at Kingsbridge were controlled from the signal box at the west end of the station; the 1924 version was wooden on a stone base.

Kingsbridge station was also a hive of passenger activity, a specific traffic generator being the annual Kingsbridge Fair held in late July. The Second World War brought much traffic through the station: many children were evacuated to the area and troops were based in the South Hams area. In 1943/1944 the branch was particularly busy being in the time leading up to D Day, as the nearby coast at Slapton was used for training for the Normandy landings. Many special trains ran to the station and visitors included both Field Marshall Montgomery and General Eisenhower. By the end of the war the Kingsbridge station master was supported at times by up to 19 staff.

All traffic ceased at Kingsbridge in September 1963. The former site is now Station Yard Industrial Estate. The main station building, with the canopy enclosed and doors blocked up, is in a semi derelict state within the curtilage of the Devon Boat Centre yard. The former goods shed was, in January 2007, unused but a new structure was being erected at its eastern end. The site of the carriage shed is occupied by a new building and the signal box has gone.

KINGSKERSWELL

OPENED: 1st July 1853 (on the Newton Abbot –
Torquay line originally opened through this site in
1848).
CLOSED: Passengers – 5th October 1964.
Goods – 5th August 1963.

The single broad gauge Newton Abbot – Torre (then
Torquay) section of the South Devon Railway
opened through the station site in 1848 but, despite
petitions in 1849 and 1852, Kingskerswell, then only
a village east of the line, did not get a station until
July 1853. The opening of what was described as a
'neat small station' was the catalyst for much local
celebration including sports on a hill close to the
station and the firing of cannons.

At its opening, Kingskerswell station comprised
only a short wooden platform on the up (west) side;
in mid 1861 a crossing loop and siding were added,
the latter on the up side at the Torquay end. The
down platform and stone shelter were added in
1876, in conjunction with the doubling of the tracks
from Aller Junction (south of Newton Abbot) to
Kingskerswell. The platforms were doubled in length
to 600 ft in July 1911. The extensions at the
southern end were required to cope with the long
holiday trains to Torquay and Paignton which
sometimes stopped at Kingskerswell. A shelter was
also provided on the up platform, at the northern
end of which was the stone two storey main
building. Sited at the western end of a road
overbridge that spanned the line north of the station,
passengers entered the building at first floor level
and, through the booking office and waiting hall,
reached the up platform via two flights of stairs
within the building. The road bridge also served as
the inter-platform link, access to the down platform
being by a long flight of steps.

Although freight traffic was limited and no
significant facilities provided, passenger use was good:
in 1903 41,596 passenger tickets were issued, in 1913
46,429 and in 1923 50,506. The figure fell to 29,050
in 1933. In 1903 six staff were based at the station;
this fell to an average of four between the wars.

The original signal box stood beyond the south
end of the up platform close to the goods siding
points. This was replaced in 1911/1912 by a 13 lever
box on the southern end of the up platform; the box
closed on 28th September 1964. Goods facilities had
been withdrawn in August 1963 and the station
closed finally to passengers in October 1964, the

Kingskerswell. The two storey main building stands at the
north end of the up (towards Newton Abbot) platform in
the 1960s. A long flight of steps connects the down platform
to the road bridge.

Kingskerswell. A close up view of the main station building
with the first storey entrance on the road over bridge.

building being demolished in April 1968.

Today the basic structure of the two platforms can
still be seen though largely covered by vegetation. A
campaign to reopen the station has so far proved
unsuccessful; a service from Kingskerswell would be
of great benefit to commuters and shoppers wishing
to go north to Newton Abbot and Exeter or south to
Torquay and Paignton.

KINGSNYMPTON

OPENED: 1st August 1854 (with the opening of the
North Devon Railway, Crediton – Barnstaple).
CLOSED: Passengers – remains open as a request stop
for a very limited service on the Exeter – Barnstaple
line.
Goods -4th December 1967.

In the valley of the River Taw, and adjacent to the
main Barnstaple road (A377), the station was called
South Molton Road for nearly one hundred years

Kingsnympton. Looking north on 3rd August 1955 at the fine twin gabled station building on the up (towards Exeter) platform. The 1873 signal box is at the south end of the down platform.

from its opening in August 1854 until its renaming as Kingsnympton from 1st March 1951. South Molton, some eight miles away to the north-east, received its own station in 1873, with the opening of the Devon & Somerset Railway between Wiveliscombe and Barnstaple. Even then the London & South Western Railway, for some years, ran a coach service between South Molton Road and the town. The village of Kingsnympton lies some two miles to the north-east of the station.

The station, on a short crossing loop, had two platforms with the main building, a typical substantial twin gabled North Devon Railway station with later additions, on the up (towards Exeter) platform. Within it were the main facilities including the booking office, waiting room, toilets and station master's office. Accommodation for the station master was provided in a two storey section. A further stone building gave extra storage facilities at the Exeter end of the platform. At the centre of the down platform was an arc roofed waiting shelter. An 1873 signal box (16 levers) stood at the Exeter end and beyond it was a water tower. No footbridge was provided, inter-platform movements being via a rail level board crossing at the Exeter end of the platforms.

In 1928 6,245 passenger tickets were issued and 6,779 collected; by 1936 the figures had fallen to 3,645 and 4,209. A census held on 7th May 1963 indicated that on that day 39 passengers joined or left trains at the, by then, Kingsnympton station. Further surveys over a week in the winter of 1976 and the summer of 1977 showed figures of 40 and 72 using the station. At the peak there were five staff

based at the station: the station master, two signalmen, a signalman/porter and a porter.

The goods yard, on the up side at the Exeter end, included a wooden goods shed, through which ran a long siding. The shed incorporated a loading dock, two ton capacity crane and a goods office. The yard also included a short spur serving a loading bay, with a five ton capacity crane, and cattle pens. For many years a monthly cattle auction market, held close to the Fortescue Arms Hotel, a short distance away to the north of the station, generated much traffic for the station and yard.

The public goods facilities closed in December 1967. The line was singled through the station and the down platform taken out of use from 26th July 1970, at which point the signal box closed. The last remaining siding was taken out of use in 1981.

Today Kingsnympton is a request stop for Exeter to Barnstaple services, trains using the former up platform on which stands a small waiting shelter. The former station building is in private residential use. The former down platform survives but derelict. Also surviving, when visited early in 2007 was the former wooden goods shed.

KINGSWEAR

OPENED: Passengers – 16th August 1864, Goods 2nd April 1866 (with the opening of the Brixham Road – Kingswear section of the Torbay & Dartmouth Railway).

CLOSED: Passengers – remains open for services on the Paignton & Dartmouth Railway.
Goods – 14th June 1965.

As the name suggests, the original aim of the Torbay & Dartmouth railway was a rail terminus in Dartmouth itself with the line south from Paignton crossing the River Dart north of Kingswear near Greenway and then running along the west bank of the river into Dartmouth. Because of construction problems and associated costs, this proved impossible and the compromise was the completed broad gauge line down the east bank to a station at Kingswear, built on reclaimed land alongside the river on the north-west side of a headland. From here a ferry crossed the river to Dartmouth (see Dartmouth text).

Ceremonial opening of the line south from Churston (then Brixham Road) took place on 10th August 1864, the special train being hauled by the then famous engine 'Lion'. Following arrival and greetings at the then incomplete Kingswear station, the party crossed to Dartmouth on the steamer 'Newcomin', being received by the mayor and entertained at the Subscription Rooms. Kingswear station opened for public use on 16th August (the station was reported as complete by November); goods facilities were available from April 1866.

The main component of the terminus station was an island platform, both faces of which were used through the years for arrivals and departures. The longer north-west face ran through to the buffers at the south-west end of the building, whilst the shorter south-east bay face terminated against the one storey wooden building, with a road side canopy, that housed the station offices. A 100 ft long wooden train shed covered the platform in front of the station offices, the platform track and a further non-platform track. A section of the island platform beyond the train shed to the north was later provided with an apex style canopy. In 1891, associated with gauge narrowing on the Kingswear line, the platform was extended at the far end; it was again lengthened by 66 ft in the late 1920s beyond a long footbridge that crossed the station site. This footbridge, from Brixham Road to the river bank, had been constructed in 1896/1897 by the GWR, who were very concerned at the number of people using the station site as a thoroughfare between the town and the quayside. Another access to the quay through the Royal Dart Hotel, adjacent to the station, also brought problems through the years. Electric lighting was provided at the station from 1911. In 1903 47,979 passenger tickets were issued; comparable figures for 1913, 1923 and 1933 were 47,094, 50,418 and 51,105. There was a royal visit on 7th March 1902 when King Edward VII laid the foundation stone for the new Royal Naval College at Dartmouth. A staff of 36 were based at Kingswear in

Kingswear. A general view south in the 1960s showing the platform canopy and the wooden train shed. To the right of the train shed is the goods shed.

the 1930s; this figure included clerks at Dartmouth.

Immediately adjacent to the north-west side of the train shed was a goods shed, through which a siding ran to buffers. Beyond the shed was a goods yard adjoining the river bank along which ran four travelling steam cranes used particularly for handling large quantities of coal. These cranes were replaced by two electric cranes in 1932 when quayside redevelopment was undertaken. A coal jetty had been constructed out into the river in 1902. At the south-west end of the quay was the pontoon used by the Dartmouth ferries, still in use today.

A further set of sidings ran north-east from the station; one of these led to an engine shed close to the end of the island platform. Built of timber (70 ft x 20 ft), with a slate roof, it closed on 14th July 1924 and was demolished in 1930/1931. Another siding led to Kingswear turntable, enlarged from its original 25 ft 5 inches to 55 ft 8 inches in 1900 and to 65 ft in 1928. This last enlargement was to accommodate larger engines now able to reach Kingswear over the Hoodown viaduct north of the station, which had been rebuilt from the original wooden into a steel structure. The widened viaduct also provided access to a further three carriage sidings alongside the line from Churston.

Operations at Kingswear were controlled from the 1894 signal box (originally 45 lever; new frame of 38 levers 1960), sited north of the station on the down side of the main line. The box closed on 20th October 1968 and was demolished soon after.

By the time the Dart Valley Railway took over the operation of the Paignton – Kingswear line in November 1972, Kingswear station was in a very run-down condition, with only one line and a loop

King Tor Platform. A view of the last intermediate stopping place on the Princetown branch on 26th September 1951. At the south-east end is a small wooden shelter.

under the train shed. All the sidings had gone, the goods shed had been demolished and the shorter bay line lifted. The wharf closed on 4th May 1964 and all goods facilities were withdrawn in June 1965.

In the new era the station has taken on a new lease of life: the bay line was reinstated in 1976 and the train shed renovated. Today Kingswear is a rare example of a surviving covered terminus and on the platform are the Paignton & Dartmouth Railway booking office and shop. The former quayside sidings have been redeveloped as a car park for Dart Haven Marina. The former sidings area to the north of the station is another car park with a new access road to the Marina. The long footbridge remains.

KING TOR HALT

OPENED: 2nd April 1928 (on the Princetown branch originally opened through this site in 1883).
CLOSED: 5th March 1956.

Classified in the timetable and shown on the Ordnance survey map as a halt, the term Platform was shown on the nameboard. The facility, on the down (towards Princetown) side of the line, opened to serve local quarrymen's cottages and also as a stopping point for walkers on Dartmoor. The platform was an earthfill structure behind a wall formed of old railway sleepers, the surface was topped with gravel. At the south-east end of the platform was a small wooden shelter, on the platform itself was a seat and a large nameboard. Along the rear of the platform were concrete posts and a wire fence. Closure came after twenty eight years with withdrawal of services on the Princetown line.

LAIRA GREEN

OPENED: 5th May 1848 (with the opening of the Totnes – Plymouth (Laira Green) section of the South Devon Railway).
CLOSED: Passengers – 2nd April 1849.
Goods – 1st May 1849.

Laira Green was the temporary western terminus of the South Devon Railway (SDR) when it opened from Totnes. It is recorded that tens of thousands greeted this first train at the two shed wooden building. At 3.0.p.m. a lunch was provided at the Royal Hotel, Plymouth for about 80 guests; 'the health of Mr Brunel was duly honoured'. This temporary facility, with apparently a ban on 'spiritualistic liquor' in the refreshment room, was closed on, or very soon after, the completion of the SDR through to Plymouth Millbay on 2nd April 1849, goods facilities closing a month later. From the temporary terminus special horse buses ran into Plymouth with a single fare of 6d. It is said that the 'superintendent' of Laira Green was paid £100 per year!

LAIRA HALT

OPENED: 1st June 1904 (on the Totnes – Plymouth GWR line originally opened through this site in 1849).
CLOSED: 7th July 1930.

Opening in June 1904 the catalyst for the halt, as with a number in Plymouth, was the introduction of a steam rail motor service between Plympton and

Laira Green. An engraving of the opening of the South Devon Railway, showing the two shed wooden building.

Laira Halt. A view west in about 1910 of the wooden platforms. At the far end the open footbridge connects the two platform tracks and also spans two further tracks behind the down (towards Plymouth) platform (left).

Lapford. Looking south-east with the main building, on the up (towards Crediton) side. Through the middle arch of the road bridge can be seen the shelter standing on the isolated island platform serving down trains towards Barnstaple.

Saltash. Sited on the east-west main line between Laira Junction to the east and Lipson Junction to the west, south of Brandon Road and north of the massive Laira engine shed, Laira Halt comprised two wooden platforms (each 261 ft long) with a pagoda style shelter on the up (north) platform and a wooden shelter on the down. A long open footbridge connecting the two platforms at the west end spanned not only the two platforms and tracks but also two tracks behind the down platform. In its latter years a subway, authorised in July 1926, replaced the footbridge at a cost of £620. The subway also served a public footpath. Closure came in July 1930; today there seems to be some evidence of the old platform on the up side.

LAPFORD

OPENED: 20th September 1855 (on the Crediton –
  Barnstaple line originally opened through this site a
  year earlier in 1854).
CLOSED: Passengers – remains open as a request stop
  for services on the Exeter – Barnstaple line.
  Goods – 4th December 1967 (except private siding).

Serving the village of Lapford, on a hill some half mile to the north-east, the layout of the station was influenced greatly by the three arched North Devon Railway stone bridge which carries the main Barnstaple road (A377) at an angle over the line at this point. Opened in September 1855, just over a year after passenger services commenced through the site, the initial facility was a platform on the up (towards Crediton) side of the single line north of the bridge. On the platform was Lapford's main building. Similar to that at Chapelton but of a

different design to many others on the line, it incorporated the main booking and waiting facilities and also, at the north end, the two storey station master's house. A small goods shed was sited just behind the south end of the platform. It was not rail connected and freight trains called at the platform for transfer of appropriate goods to and from this shed.

When, in 1873, it was decided to introduce a loop and down platform at Lapford, there was insufficient room opposite the original platform and thus the main section of the loop and new platform were built south of the bridge, the platform being between the original line and the loop. The rear of the platform alongside the now up line was fenced off; thus unusually Lapford's two platforms both faced south-west! On the platform was a stone waiting shelter which incorporated a small booking office, which operated only shortly before the departure of down trains. Access to this island down platform was both by steps from the road bridge and by a rail level sleeper crossing from the up. In 1928 6,400 passenger tickets were issued at Lapford and 7,448 collected. Comparable figures for 1936 were 4,566 and 5,389. A census on 7th May 1963 showed that 67½ (1 child= ½ passenger) joined and left trains on that day. Further surveys over a winter week in 1976 and a summer week in 1977 showed that 37 and 46 passengers used Lapford.

Opposite the original up platform were five sidings serving end and side loading docks and cattle pens. There was no crane. The yard was, however, dominated for many years on its south-west side by an Ambrosia factory manufacturing dried milk and tinned cream. Generating much traffic for the railway, it opened in 1928 and closed in 1970. In the

Liddaton Halt. Looking east in the 1960s at the wooden platform and shelter. Note the four lamps, one at each end of the platform, one at the entrance gate and one on the shelter.

1930s an average of 70 were employed at the factory but this rose to some 200 during the Second World War. Following closure the building was used by a fertiliser factory which continued to use the railway, though to a limited extent, until it closed in 1993. In 2007 the principal occupant was a large furniture removal and storage facility but with no use of the railway. General goods facilities had been withdrawn in December 1967 with only private use of the siding to the fertiliser factory continuing. A 13 lever 1873 wood on stone base signal box opposite the north end of the up platform controlled entrance and exit to the goods yard. The box closed on 21st June 1960.

The isolated down platform was taken out of use in about 1970 and demolished in the early 1980s. The main building on the former up platform was sold for residential use which continues today. Lapford is now a request stop for trains on the Exeter to Barnstaple line with passengers served by a small shelter at the south end of the platform.

LIDDATON HALT

OPENED: 4th April 1938 (on the Lydford – Launceston (Cornwall) line originally opened through this site in 1865).

CLOSED: 31st December 1962.

Opening in April 1938, the halt was a very late addition to passenger facilities on the Tavistock to Launceston line. Serving a small number of scattered farmsteads, the halt was as close to the village of Coryton as Coryton station itself. On the north side of the line, the single platform was alongside a minor road, east of a road overbridge. Although, at that time, the normal practice of the GWR was the use of concrete components, in this instance wood was used. The halt's platform of planks was supported upon bulky timber legs cross braced for strength. It was separated from the road by a wooden post and wire fence. A small white gate gave access via a narrow path to the platform on which was a small timber plank shelter. Lighting was by four oil lamps, two at either end of the platform, one at the entrance gate and one on the shelter. Liddaton Halt closed at the end of December 1962 when passenger services were withdrawn on the line. The nearby overbridge survives and the station site is a small holding.

LIFTON

OPENED: Passengers – 1st July 1865; Goods – 21st August 1865 (with the opening of the Launceston & South Devon Railway, Tavistock – Launceston (Cornwall)).

CLOSED: Passengers and Goods– 31st December 1962 (except for private siding to factory).

Sited to the east of the village of Lifton, the station opened for passenger services at the beginning of July and goods services towards the end of August in 1865. The main line was on the down side (towards Launceston) and the loop on the up. The main building on the up platform was a stone structure with a hipped slate roof and two chimneys. Inside were the usual waiting and booking facilities.

On the down platform was a small stone shelter

Lifton. A Launceston bound train stands at the down platform behind which is a small stone shelter. On the up (towards Lydford) platform stands, from right to left, the main station building, the stone goods lock up and a corrugated iron lamp hut.

house, built in 1928. Lifton signal box, a single storey small (15 ft x 7 ft) cabin of lateral wooden planks with 17 levers, controlled the station loop and sidings and also released the manually operated level crossing gates from its site at the east end of the up platform. The box was reduced to a ground frame in September 1964. Passenger and public goods facilities were withdrawn at the end of December 1962. However, the line east from Lifton remained open for the passage of traffic generated by the dairy factory en route to Lydford, Plymouth and the London area via the Southern lines. This continued until 7th September 1964 when the Lifton to Lydford line closed. At this point the Lifton to Launceston section of the line was reopened to handle the factory traffic, this too closed on 28th February 1966. Following this final closure the dairy factory, now served only by road, expanded over the station site.

with a slate roof. Both platforms were constructed with earth fill behind stone facing, the surface being of chippings with slab edges. In front of the main building the surface was paved. The rear of both platforms was originally lined with wooden fencing but this was later replaced by concrete posts and wires. A rail level board crossing at the west end gave inter-platform access. In 1903 12,018 tickets were issued at Lifton, this figure rose to 12,290 in 1913 and 13,086 in 1923 but then nearly halved to 7,333 in 1933.

To the west of the main building on the up platform was the 1870 built stone goods lock up. There were large wooden doors running on steel rails on both the platform and road sides. On the road side was a high platform to assist transfer to and from road transport of small parcels, packages and general merchandise. To the west of the goods shed was a corrugated iron lamp hut.

Lifton goods yard, behind the east end of the up platform, had three sidings, the longest of which served a 40 foot loading dock behind the platform. From 1894 to 1966 a private siding led into a corn mill at the east end of the yard. The yard included cattle pens and a 6 ton capacity crane. In 1917 a large Ambrosia milk factory was developed adjacent to the outer most goods siding in the yard and in 1965 an average of 16 container loads of rice pudding left the factory.

At the west end of the station site was a road level crossing and to the north was the station master's

LIPSON VALE HALT

OPENED: 1st June 1904 (on the Totnes – Plymouth GWR line originally opened through this site in 1849).
CLOSED: 22nd March 1942.

The catalyst for this halt, as with a number in Plymouth, was the introduction of a steam rail motor service between Plympton and Saltash. Serving an area of dense housing, this halt on the main GWR line between Lipson Vale Junction and Mutley station, was sited between Ashford Road to the north and Alexandra Road to the south. Access was

Lipson Vale Halt. A 1922 view west of the halt originally opened to serve an area of dense housing in east Plymouth.

Littleham. Looking east in 1958. A train is departing towards Budleigh Salterton. The main building, with its wide ornate canopy and bay window, incorporates, at the far end, two storey station master's accommodation. This latter survives today, in Jarvis Close.

via a gate in Ashford Lane and also by steps adjoining the road overbridge at the east end of the platforms. The up and down platforms were of wood with a shelter, in the form of a pagoda style hut, only provided on the down. The platforms were shortened in about March 1933 and the halt closed nine years later in March 1942. There is now no trace of the halt.

LITTLEHAM

OPENED: 1st June 1903 (with the opening of the London & South Western Railway, Budleigh Salterton – Exmouth).
CLOSED: Passengers – 6th March 1967.
　　Goods – 27th January 1964.

Sited on a curve in the Budleigh Salterton to Exmouth line the station, a facility required by the local landowners the Rolle Estate, was approximately half a mile west of the village of Littleham. When opened in June 1903, it was on the eastern outskirts of Exmouth but today the site is well within the expanded urban area.

There were two 402 ft long platforms alongside the up through line and the down (towards Exmouth) passing loop. The main station buildings, including a two storey station master's house at the east end, stood on the up side incorporating all the principal facilities. A particular feature of the building was the wide ornate canopy under which a bay window faced on to the platform. On the down platform was a small open timber waiting shelter with a backward facing roof. Inter platform movement was via a rail level board crossing at the east end of the platforms adjacent to a level crossing.

In 1928 14,453 passenger tickets were issued at Littleham and 18,443 collected. By 1936 the figures had fallen drastically to 3,109 and 4,363, the competition of bus operations within the town clearly having a major impact. Many passengers used the station however, travelling to the nearby Sandy Bay Holiday Camp. In the station's early years there was a station master and four staff. From the 1920s there were two signalmen and a porter under the supervision of the Budleigh Salterton station master. In its last years the signalman was also responsible for issuing tickets from a matching wooden extension to the signal box added in May 1961. A sign 'ticket office' was hung on the box.

The goods yard on the down side behind the platform included four sidings serving a cattle dock, coal staithes for the local merchants and a timber goods shed with two small canopies. The shed was, in later years, used as a coal store. The yard included a long siding used, on occasions, for the storage of carriages coming to Exmouth on long excursion trains. In the summer months right up to 1964 two to four camping coaches were based in the yard. A low ground level signal box at the Exmouth end of the down platform controlling rail movements at the station also included a wheel for the operation of the adjacent level crossing gates.

Goods facilities ceased at Littleham at the end of January 1964 but passenger services continued for another three years until March 1967 when services were withdrawn on the Exmouth line. In 1970 the whole station site was purchased by the local Council for housing redevelopment. This subsequently took place, the only survivor being the former station master's house in Jarvis Close, now white rendered. The Close approximately follows the alignment of the trackbed and beyond, to the east, a further section of the alignment is now a footpath.

LODDISWELL

OPENED: 19th December 1893 (with the opening of the Kingsbridge & South Devon Railway, Brent – Kingsbridge).
CLOSED: Passengers – 16th September 1963.
　　Goods – 4th September 1961.

Sited in a valley almost a mile east of, and 200 ft below, the village of Loddiswell, the station opened in December 1893. The platform and main building were on the down (east) side of the slightly curved single line, a siting similar to all three of the line's

Loddiswell. Looking north on 10th June 1921 at the William Clarke design main building on the down (towards Kingsbridge) side. Its features include three tall chimneys, a wide decorative canopy and platform entrance via a gate (foreground). Beyond the building is a stone goods shed.

three intermediate stations between Brent and Kingsbridge. The main building, designed by William Clarke (see Avonwick text), was stone built with three tall chimneys and a wide wooden horizontal canopy. Access to the platform and building (the latter via platform doors) was through a gate at the south end of the building. The building incorporated, from north to south: the gent's toilet, the ladies' waiting room, the booking hall and the station master's office. A house for the station master stood on the hillside behind and above the down platform.

A goods loop, north of the station on the down side, served a small goods yard that included cattle pens and a small crane. A short siding trailed back from the loop behind the north end of platform, terminating close to a stone goods shed that stood behind the platform north of the building. In later years this siding was occupied by a camping coach; this ceased at the end of the summer in 1961.

Loddiswell closed to goods traffic in September 1961 and at the same time became unstaffed. In its latter years a porter had been in charge. Formal down grading to a halt came in 1962 and passenger services ceased in September 1963 with closure of the Kingsbridge line, known in its latter years as the Primrose Line. Following closure the station buildings, including the canopy and goods shed, were restored and converted into a residence.

LONGDOWN

OPENED: 1st July 1903 (with the opening of the Exeter Railway, Exeter – Ashton).
CLOSED: Passengers and Goods – 9th June 1958.

On a curve in woods at the summit of the whole Exeter to Heathfield line, Longdown station opened at the beginning of July 1903. To the west was Culver tunnel and to the east of the station Perridge tunnel. The low brick station building, with slate roof and two chimneys, stood at the west end of the brick platform. On the north side of the line, it incorporated the waiting, booking and toilet facilities. Water for the last was supplied by a nearby well. In 1903 2,789 passenger tickets were issued; for 1913 and 1933 the figures were 5,359 and 1,826.

A short (90 ft) goods loop to the west of the station, with a short spur to the platform end, was in use until 18th November 1956. One of the principal uses of the goods facilities was the supply of coal to, and despatch of timber from, the nearby Culver House. A small (5 lever) ground level signal box was added west of the station in 1916. Associated with the up-grade of the line between Exeter and Newton Abbot as a Second World War expediency, a long (100 ft) loop was added at Longdown from 19th September 1943. This remained in use until 20th July 1954 but was removed in 1957. A new nine lever frame had been added to the signal box in 1943 to control the loop. Following closure to passengers and goods in June 1958, the building and platform were not demolished. Under the conditions governing the sale of land to the railway, a clause was included for the land to be handed back, if the railway closed, to the owner or descendants. When seen in mid 2006, the building was in use as a gamekeeper's store; remnants of the platform were also in place.

Longdown. The low brick built station at the extreme west end of the platform in about 1910. In 2006 the building was in use as a gamekeeper's store.

LOVERS LANE

OPENED: 1st May 1908 (with the opening of the
Northam – Appledore section of the Bideford,
Westward Ho! & Appledore Railway).
CLOSED: 28th March 1917.

This was the penultimate stopping place on the
Bideford, Westward Ho! & Appledore Railway, sited
just above Appledore lifeboat station. A low (1 ft
above rail level) platform was provided but there
was no shelter. Opening in May 1908, it closed after
less than nine years in 1917 (see Bideford Quay text).
No photograph is known.

LUCAS TERRACE HALT

OPENED: October 1905 (on the Plymouth Friary –
Cattewater Junction line).
CLOSED: 10th September 1951.

In the late 1890s and early 1900s there was
considerable housing development in the eastern
suburbs of Plymouth and, responding to the
potential for extra passengers, the London & South
Western Railway opened Lucas Terrace Halt in
October 1905. Sited on the south side of the single
track Cattewater/Turnchapel line, the halt was on an
embankment above the main line into Plymouth
Friary to the north and the Friary engine shed
complex to the south-west. Lucas Terrace opened
some eight years after passenger services commenced
on the Turnchapel branch. Originally comprising a
wooden platform with a corrugated iron pagoda
style shelter, the halt was rebuilt with concrete
components in 1923, the platform being lengthened

Lucas Terrace Halt. A train approaches from the east in
about 1939. The halt had been rebuilt in concrete
components about 16 years earlier. To the left at a lower
level are the main lines serving Plymouth Friary station.

by 125 ft to accommodate longer trains. Its entire
length was now of stone and earth infill with
concrete edging and a loose chipping surface. A small
pre-cast concrete shelter with a tiled roof and
windows at each end stood on the platform. A
winding path, with steps and a wooden handrail, led
down to Lucas Terrace from the east end of the
shelter. Between 3rd November 1941 and 7th
October 1947 Lucas Terrace was also used by trains
on the Yealmpton branch when this reopened (see
Yealmpton text). Passenger services ceased in
September 1951. Forty years later the concrete
platform was still in reasonable condition but when
visited early in 2007 no trace could be seen.

LUSTLEIGH

OPENED: 4th July 1866 (with the opening of the
Moretonhampstead & South Devon Railway,
Newton Abbot – Moretonhampstead).
CLOSED: Passengers – 2nd March 1959
Goods – 6th April 1964.

Sited on the northern edge of the village, Lustleigh
opened in July 1866 with the commencement of
services on the Moretonhampstead & South Devon
Railway between Newton Abbot and
Moretonhampstead. On the down (west) side of the
single track line, south of a road bridge, the station
had a 245 ft long platform constructed of stone and
earth fill, partly faced with brick. The surface was
principally of tarmac and chippings edged with
rounded concrete slabs. A white paling four foot
fence ran along the back of the platform for much of
its length; behind the northern end there was a
hedge. Steps led down to the platform from the west
side of the road bridge.

In the middle of the platform, where the surface
was paved, stood the main building, smaller but an
almost exact replica of that at Bovey. The main
difference was that at Lustleigh there was only one
wing. The neat stone building had an apex slate roof,
arched windows and also two tall chimneys, one at
each end. The only entrance to the building was via
the platform itself, accessed by a gate at the north
end of the building. An unusual feature on the
forecourt side was a narrow projecting stone
extension with a pitched grey slate roof. An open
fronted lean-to wooden bicycle shed was added later
on the south end of this rear extension. There was no
canopy on the platform side. Inside the building was
a waiting room/booking hall, the station office (the

Lustleigh. Passengers wait as a Newton Abbot bound train enters the station in about 1910, hauled by an 0-6-0 saddle tank locomotive. On the platform is the main building, with two tall chimneys, and the former wooden signal box, by this time in use as a store.

station master's office before 1930 when the post was amalgamated with that at Moretonhampstead), the waiting room and ladies' toilet. The gent's toilet was in a flat roof extension at the south end of the building accessed by an arched door from the platform.

A small goods lock up stood adjacent to the south end of the building. Between the gent's toilet and the stop block of the goods siding, it had sliding doors at the front and rear that assisted transfer of goods from trains standing at the platform. In 1903 16,898 passenger tickets were issued at Lustleigh; figures for other years included 1913 (16,986), 1923 (19,710), 1933 (13,458), 1943 (17,943) and 1953 (10,968).

A small goods yard, immediately to the south of the station forecourt and behind the platform, had only one dead end siding and no goods shed, provision for goods being provided only by the platform lock up. From 1934 until the outbreak of the Second World War, a camping coach stood at the buffer end of the siding. A coal store, constructed of stone with a corrugated iron roof, stood at the yard entrance close to the start of the siding. A small oil store/lamp room of corrugated iron was sited just outside the goods yard entrance. From 1893 rail movements at Lustleigh were controlled from a 13 lever wooden signal box on the platform adjacent to the goods lock up. This ceased in 1901 after which

the box was used as a store before being demolished.

A particular feature of Lustleigh was the well tended station garden on the eastern side of the line on land originally earmarked for a possible crossing loop and second platform. In it were buried two station cats, Jemima James and her predecessor Jumbo for whom a small gravestone was provided with an epitaph, 'Beneath this slab and stretched out flat, lies Jumbo, once our station cat'.

Passenger services ceased in March 1959 and goods facilities were withdrawn in April 1964. After a period of dereliction the stone building was restored and extended in the original style to form a house. The former waiting room and booking office became the living room, the ladies' waiting room and toilet the kitchen. The platform also remains at this attractive residence, which is today accessed by a private drive, at the head of which is a rail gatepost. The remains of the footpath down from the west side of the road bridge can still be traced.

OPENED: Passengers – 1st July 1865, Goods 21st
August 1865 (with the opening of the Launceston &
South Devon Railway, Tavistock – Launceston).
CLOSED: Passengers – 31st December 1962.
Goods – 7th September 1964.

LYDFORD (LSWR)

OPENED: 12th October 1874 (with the opening of the
London & South Western Railway, Okehampton –
Lydford).
CLOSED: Passengers – 6th May 1968.
Goods – 7th September 1964.

Lydford station, sited about 1½ miles south-west of
the village at a height of 650 ft above sea level, had
a complicated early history linked to the evolution of
the railway network in this area of mid Devon. The
first station, opened in July (passengers) and August
(goods) 1865 on the broad gauge Launceston &
South Devon Railway from Tavistock to Launceston
(The L&SDR became part of the GWR in 1878).
The standard gauge London & South Western
Railway (LSWR), which had reached Okehampton
in October 1871, opened to an adjoining station at
Lydford on 12th October 1874. At this point
Lydford became an interchange station, as travellers
who wished to travel on to the Plymouth area had to
change to the broad gauge trains via Tavistock and
Marsh Mills. In 1876 the LSWR started using the
Tavistock line on which mixed gauge had been
introduced. The final change came in 1890 with the
opening of the Lydford to Devonport line via the
Tamar Valley line. The connection between the GWR
and LSWR lines at Lydford ceased to be used, but
remained in place, until 1895. Re-connection only

Lydford. A 1939 view south-west of the two stations. From
left to right the main LSWR 1874 building incorporating
two storey accommodation for the station master, the open
footbridge, the wide central platform with 1916 signal box
and L&SDR 1874 building.

came in 1943 as a war-time measure. From about
1890 Lydford became a dual company station, the
GWR and LSWR co-habiting the site but each
operating independently. However, supervision of
the GWR station was handed over to the LSWR as
from 1st March 1914.

It is of no surprise that the building and
architectural style of Lydford station (Lidford until
1897) was a mixture of GWR and LSWR designs.
With the opening of the Launceston & South Devon
Railway, a small building opened on the up (towards
Plymouth) platform with a gable roof, two chimneys
and gothic style windows and door openings. With
the arrival of the LSWR an up (towards
Okehampton) platform was built contiguous to the
original L&SDR up, creating a wide island platform.
The L&SDR buildings were re-orientated, the
original structure on the island being downgraded to
a waiting shelter and a new main brick building,
with cement rendering, being constructed on the
down side. It comprised a central section with brick
chimneys at either end and two lower projecting
wings with apex style roofs. Other features included
eight tall windows all on the platform side and a
short canopy on the platform side of the central
section. The building incorporated the waiting room
and booking office. The platform itself was brick
faced with a slab edged chipping surface. At the
southern end was a goods loading dock and at the
north end, beyond a barrow crossing to the island
platform, was a water tower. The central double
sided island platform was stone faced and brick

Lydford. This view of 1939 shows the initial 1865 L&SDR building with two chimneys on the central island and the large 1916 signal box.

south end of the LSWR down platform were closed at the end of 1916. A new box, manned by the LSWR staff opened on the central island with the levers for the LSWR and GWR services on the appropriate side of the joint box, the GWR frame on the west side and the LSWR on the east.

Passenger services through Lydford on the GWR line were withdrawn at the end of December 1962 but services on the LSWR line continued until May 1968. Goods facilities were withdrawn at the station in September 1964. Following the final closure of Lydford station in 1968 the buildings were demolished, much of the site now being privately owned and overgrown.

LYMPSTONE COMMANDO

OPENED: 3rd May 1976 (on the Exeter – Exmouth line originally opened through this site in 1861).
CLOSED: Passengers – remains open as a request stop for Royal Marines personnel only using services on the Exeter – Exmouth line.

On the Exmouth branch, north of Lympstone Village station, this facility opened at the beginning of May 1976 to serve the large Royal Marines Training Camp east of the line. Although it is in the timetable, the station is for the use only of personnel having business at the Camp and thus is not available for general public use. The inaugural train from Exeter St Davids carried a special headboard with the BR emblem and the Royal Marines insignia.

The 224 ft long concrete platform, on the east side of the single track, has only a bus stop type shelter. There is no booking office but a guards depot stands behind the platform at the Camp entrance. The

Lympstone Commando. A view of the basic platform and shelter opened in 1976. Under the name is a notice stating that only those who have business at the training camp may alight.

edged on the LSWR side and brick faced and slab edged on the other. The surface of the wide platform was a mixture of blue Staffordshire bricks and chippings. On the platform was the original L&DR building incorporating a waiting room and a booking office and also a structure added by the LSWR, a flat roofed brick cement-rendered building, housing toilets. The principal LSWR building on the down (south-east) side of the station was of a similar design to that at other LSWR Devon stations incorporating a two storey station master's house and a single storey section containing the station offices and a waiting shelter. An open footbridge connecting this LSWR down platform and the central island platform stood to the south-west of the buildings.

Lydford station did not have large numbers commencing or completing their journeys, interchange being of equal or more importance. For the GWR services 5,872 passenger tickets were issued in 1903; this figure decreased in subsequent years to 4,823 in 1913, 4,278 in 1923 and 2,417 in 1933. For the Southern Railway services in 1928 4,606 tickets were issued and, in 1936 4,089.

Goods facilities at Lydford were concentrated to the north of the joint station, mainly on a restricted site between the GWR and LSWR lines. At the centre was a large gable roof goods shed. This was, at one time, used as a transfer shed between broad and standard gauge freight trains. Cattle pens were also sited in the yard. Five new sidings were added during the Second World War.

An original GWR signal box at the south end of the GWR down platform and LSWR box at the platform originated as the down platform at Weston Milton Halt in Somerset, which became redundant when the Weston-super-Mare loop line was singled from 31st January 1972. Today Lympstone Commando is a request stop for Exmouth line trains.

LYMPSTONE VILLAGE

OPENED: 1st May 1861 (with the opening of the Exeter & Exmouth Railway).
CLOSED: Passengers – remains open for services on the Exeter - Exmouth line.
Goods – 4th April 1960.

In a cutting on the Exmouth branch, near the centre of the village, the station was in a sheltered position close to the west bank of the River Exe estuary. Its opening, at the beginning of May 1861, was the catalyst of much celebration in the village. Declared a public holiday, a procession led by a brass band marched through the streets, decorated with banners and flags. One banner proclaimed 'Prosperity to the Exeter & Exmouth Railway'. Sports were held and food served.

The 323 ft long platform was constructed on the west side of the line. On it stood the brick station building with the booking office at the south end. A canopy supported by four posts sheltered the platform in front of the building. Adjoining it to the north were two small sheds, both timber built.

In 1928 43,965 passenger tickets were issued and 55,518 collected; by 1936 the figures had fallen to 33,358 and 45,048. In the 1920s there was a station master, a clerk, two signalmen and a porter/signalman based at the station. The level gradually fell until the station became unstaffed as from 28th February 1965.

There were limited goods facilities at Lympstone. A goods loop, with a short stub siding at the north end serving a cattle dock, was sited opposite the platform. The principal goods traffic at Lympstone was the import of coal for local merchants. Shellfish from the estuary were loaded on to trains particularly before the Second World War. Freight facilities were withdrawn in April 1960 and the sidings were removed in September 1962. An original signal box stood opposite the platform; this box was replaced as from 29th September 1929 by a 12 lever frame in the station booking office. This too closed from 16th September 1962.

Decline set in during the 1960s and the station building was boarded up in 1965. The larger of the two sheds remained as a waiting shelter until the demolition of all buildings in December 1976. A metal shelter was provided together with improved lighting. The station was designated a halt from 5th May 1969 but was then renamed Lympstone Village from 13th May 1991, a name by which it is known today.

Lympstone Village. The station, with the River Exe estuary beyond, seen in about 1904. When the main building was boarded up in 1965, the goods shed on the right was converted into a waiting shelter.

LYNTON

OPENED: 16th May 1898 (with the opening of the
  Lynton & Barnstaple Railway).
CLOSED: Passenger and Goods – 30th September 1935.

The coming of the railway to Lynton provoked much
excitement in the hill-top town, illustrated by the
celebrations even at the cutting of the first sod by
Lady Newnes, the wife of the chairman of the
narrow gauge (1 ft 11 ½ inches) Lynton &
Barnstaple Railway, on 17th September 1895. Even
greater rejoicing came on 11th May 1898 at the line's
formal opening. The first train from Barnstaple
stopped just short of the station so that Lady
Newnes could cut the red, white and blue ribbon.
Large crowds and a triumphal arch, 'Success to the
new Railway' greeted the first train. After the arrival
of the second train, the party adjourned to the Valley
of the Rocks Hotel for lunch where the Lynton &
Barnstaple Railway Company entertained the Mayor
and Corporation of Barnstaple and members of the
Lynton Urban District Council and other guests.

The siting of the station about 250 ft above the
town centre and 750 ft above sea level, was the
subject of much debate. At the opening, Sir George
Newnes referred to this issue, noting that there were
engineering difficulties in taking the line closer into
the town and also that the Company was anxious
not to disfigure the beautiful alpine style village.
Other views were that there objections by the land
owners and that the local residents did not want the
railway as it could bring more trippers to the town!

The basic layout of the station was a terminal
building from which a long (306 ft) low level
platform ran north to south. The main track ran
along the west side of the platform and into the
goods yard to the north of the building. A long (360
ft) run-round loop ran parallel to this line. A trailing
siding ran back from this loop through a small
engine shed which was open at both ends and rarely
used. This trailing siding replaced an earlier track
into the shed from the south. On the east side of the
single platform was the bay line terminating close to
the south end wall of the main building. The station
was originally lit by oil lamps but later by electric
lighting.

The main station building was constructed in what
was described as a 'Nuremberg' chalet style, in
keeping with the alpine image of the town. When
opened it included accommodation for the station
master, two bedrooms on the first floor and the

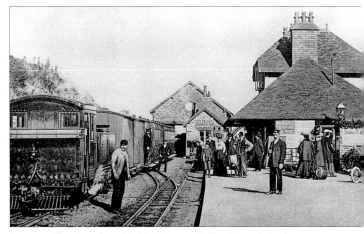

Lynton. The American (Baldwin) 2-4-2T 'Lyn' stands in the
loop in about 1930. Staff and passengers pose in front of the
main Nuremberg style building. In the middle distance is the
goods shed with goods office.

living room (parlour) and kitchen on the ground. In
the remainder of the ground floor were the general
waiting room, refreshment room and a ticket office.
The ladies' toilet was in the main building itself but
the gent's toilets were in a low annex at the south
end. The operation of the toilets was often a problem
due to water supply difficulties at this high level
above the town. (The water problem also posed
difficulties for the water crane on the platform.)
When the Southern Railway took over the operation
of the railway, the station building was altered
internally with station facilities taking over the
station master's accommodation on the ground floor.
A bungalow was built for him on the bank opposite
the station. In the summer the station was normally
staffed by the station master and two porters.

The number of passenger tickets collected was far
higher than the number issued, a pattern typical of a
resort station in Devon. In 1928 11,699 passenger
tickets were issued and 30,981 collected; by 1934 the
numbers had dropped greatly to 5,583 and 19,326.

North of the station the goods yard included a
large stone goods shed (30 ft long) with a through
siding. Two small canopies covered the road side
loading bays and at the southern end was the goods
office and a room for porters and lamp storage. To
the west of the shed a later siding served a coal yard.
Rail traffic at Lynton was controlled from a small (9
ft x 8 ft) box containing an eight lever ground frame
sited at the southern end of the station site on the
east side of the line.

Lynton station closed to passengers and goods at
the end of September 1935, the town band playing

Maddaford Moor Halt. Looking east in 1964 at the basic halt originally opened in 1926 to serve a proposed new health resort at Thorndon Cross. Note that the nameboard states 'for Thorndon Cross'.

Auld Lang Syne as the last train left. Most of the buildings survived and became derelict. The station building itself was withdrawn from auction in 1938 when bidding stopped at £475. It was later sold and is now a fine private house (Station House), its previous history as the railway terminus acknowledged by a plaque on the end wall. The goods shed was converted and extended to form two cottages (1 and 2 Station Cottages) and the former station master's bungalow is also a residence (Four Winds). A house was constructed on the former site of the engine shed with a garage on the track bed.

MADDAFORD MOOR HALT

OPENED: 26th July 1926 (on the Okehampton –
  Holsworthy line originally opened through this site
  in 1879).
CLOSED: 3rd October 1966.

The halt opened in July 1926, its primary purpose being seen to serve a proposed new health resort at nearby Thorndon Cross. Little came of this scheme however, but some local housing, including a terrace of railway cottages, provided some custom.

Built at a height of some 800 ft above sea level on the down (towards Halwill) side of the line, it was on the site of a former passing loop which had operated from 1899 until 21st August 1921. The platform and nameboard were constructed of concrete components manufactured at the Southern Railway works at Exmouth Junction. On the platform was a small wooden shelter with the sign 'waiting shed'. Maddaford Moor Halt closed with the withdrawal of passenger services on the line in October 1966. The site was overgrown in 2005 with no obvious evidence of the halt.

MARSH MILLS

OPENED: Goods – 1st February 1860, Passengers 15th
  March 1861 (on the Plymouth – Tavistock GWR
  line originally opened through this site in 1859).
CLOSED: Passenger – 31st December 1962.
  Goods – 1st June 1964 (except private sidings).

Passenger services on the Tavistock & South Devon Railway began through this site in June 1859 but no facility was then available at Marsh Mills. However, records indicate that goods traffic was accepted from 1st February 1860. It is also recorded that some form of passenger facility was provided from 15th March 1861 so that residents from the Plympton area could travel to Tavistock, principally for the Friday market. A full passenger facility opened on 1st November 1865 on the west side of the single line. The track through Marsh Mills was doubled in 1874 to accommodate London & South Western Railway trains between Lydford and Devonport and an up platform was added. The main buildings at the station date from the 1860s and 1870s.

The up (towards Plymouth) and down platforms were of earth infill with a brick face, the surfaces being of tarmac and chippings with brick end ramps. The edges were of concrete slabs with rounded shoulders. The down platform was slightly longer than the up. The principal building on the down platform was of local stone with granite facings at its corners, windows and door linings. The slate roof with gable ends and plain barge boards was topped with two ornate chimney stacks. The building housed the booking, waiting and toilet facilities. On the up platform the building, of similar construction but with only one chimney, was basically an open front waiting shelter. Both buildings were approximately in the centre of the platform. No footbridge was provided and inter-platform movement was via a rail level board crossing at the south end of the platforms. In 1903 17,320 passenger tickets were issued at Marsh Mills, the figure rose to 19,263 in 1913, fell a little to 14,224 in 1923 and then fell significantly to 5,342 in 1933.

The publicly available goods facilities were limited compared to most stations of this size in Devon, there being no cattle pens, end loading docks, crane yard or goods shed. March Mills was, however, the focus for a number of private sidings and industrial lines, the first of which predated the station by over 20 years. At one time from 1894 a large flour mill stood behind the up platform, whilst to the north

Marsh Mills. A view north in 1958 with the main building on the down (towards Tavistock) platform. On the up platform (right) is a waiting shelter and signal box. To the north of the site is now the focus of activities by the Plym Valley Railway.

was a large china clay works whose sidings were behind the up platform. By 1939 sidings were also developed for the Ministry of Defence on the west side of the line.

Marsh Mills signal box stood on the up platform north of the shelter, the 1894 hipped slate roof box with some 32 levers (from 1919) had a brick base and timber top with large windows along the platform side and at the ends. The box closed on 4th April 1965. Passenger services had ceased on the line at the end of December 1962 and the limited goods facilities were withdrawn in June 1964. Today the former down platform can still be seen alongside a single track. A section of the National Cycle Network (route 27) and the West Devon Way runs along this platform. The site of the former up line and platform is taken by a road.

Marsh Mills has, in recent years, become the focus of activities by the Plym Valley Railway developing what is known as the Woodland Line, the goal being to run trains as far north as the former Plym Bridge Platform, 1½ miles north of Marsh Mills. By early 2007 track had been laid for about a half mile to Langford Bridge. The Railway is intending to erect a building using material from the former station at Billacombe. The former LSWR footbridge from Tavistock North and the refreshment bar from Millbay Docks are also at the site.

MARY TAVY & BLACKDOWN

OPENED: Passengers – 1st July 1865, Goods 21st August 1865 (with the opening of the Launceston & South Devon Railway, Tavistock – Launceston (Cornwall)).
CLOSED: Passengers – 31st December 1962. Goods – 11th August 1941.

Mary Tavy & Blackdown, alongside the east bank of the River Burn, was about a half mile west of Mary Tavy and also a half mile west of Blackdown. The name Blackdown was added to this station as from 1907. It was originally a crossing place with up and down platforms on the Plymouth – Tavistock – Launceston line after it opened to passengers in July

Mary Tavy & Blackdown. A goods train runs through the single platform station from the north (Lydford) in 1939. The down side platform and signal box had been out of use since 1890 when LSWR trains ceased using the line.

1865. Services were particularly frequent between 1876 and 1890 when the London & South Western Railway (LSWR) trains also used the line travelling between Exeter and Devonport. After this traffic ceased the loop was taken out in 1892 and the down platform, on which stood a small shelter, closed.

A small stone rectangular building, with a slate roof and a tall chimney at either end, stood on the up (towards Tavistock) platform incorporating a booking office, waiting room and toilet facilities. The doorways, arched windows and cornices were lined with buff colour bricks. The stone faced up platform was surfaced with blue Staffordshire bricks, edged with slabs and backed by a wooden fence.

As from 11th August 1941 the station became unstaffed and the doorways and windows of the main building were boarded up. The withdrawal of staff was a reflection of the dwindling business at the station: in 1903 9,037 passenger tickets were issued; the total increased to 11,433 in 1913 but fell away in 1923 to 9,098 and then down again to 4,895 in 1933.

The limited goods facility was a single dead end siding on the up side north of the platform; this served a 42 ft loading platform. There was no goods shed nor crane. Goods facilities were withdrawn co-incident with the de-staffing in 1941 and the siding was removed on 14th December 1945. An original South Devon Railway all brick signal box stood on the up platform north of the main building; this became disused after the loop closed in 1892 but remained for many years.

The station house, with a double gable front, stood on the up side to the south of, and behind, the station. Today this house, with extensions, remains a residence, with sections of the former up platform in the garden. The station building itself was demolished after closure to passengers in 1962.

Meeth Halt. A down train towards Halwill, pulled by No.41312, is about to cross the A486, adjacent to the stone platform and shelter, on 25th September 1962.

the only point where the Torrington to Halwill line crossed an A class road. The halt comprised a stone platform on the north (down) side of the single line. A stone shelter stood at the east end of the platform. The halt was south of the section of line that ran adjacent to the Meeth Clay Works but no workmen's service ran to and from it. As a result passenger volumes were very low with few trains stopping at Meeth. A single siding behind the platform was sometimes used for dropping off wagons from the clay works to be collected by other trains.

Meeth siding closed to the public goods traffic in September 1964 but remained in place for private use by the clay company until the line closed south of the Meeth works in 1966. Passenger services were withdrawn on the line at the beginning of March 1965. Subsequently the tracks were removed and the track bed north to the clay works was converted into an access road. The platform and shelter were left and in spring 2007 were in relatively good condition.

MEETH HALT

OPENED: 27th July 1925 (with the opening of the North Devon & Cornwall Junction Light Railway, Torrington – Halwill).

CLOSED: Passengers – 1st March 1965.
Goods – 7th September 1964 (except private sidings).

Meeth Halt, like Dunsbear Halt to the north beyond Petrockstow, opened with the line in late July 1925. About a quarter of a mile south of the village of Meeth, it was sited immediately to the west of an ungated level crossing where the line crosses the A386,

MELDON QUARRY HALT

OPENED: 1920s (on the Okehampton – Lydford line originally opened through this site in 1874). (see text)

CLOSED: 6th May 1968.

REOPENED: 6th July 2002 (see text)

In 1897 the London & South Western Railway (LSWR) acquired Meldon Quarry, west of Okehampton, alongside the line to Lydford and Plymouth. The aim of the LSWR was to use stone from the quarry for engineering work on its lines. Records suggest that some form of facility was provided at an early date adjacent to the quarry both for use by workers travelling to and from the quarry, in particular from Okehampton, and also by quarry workers and their families who lived close to the quarry in the twelve cottages sited there. It is certain however, that in the 1920s a halt, with two platforms constructed of Southern Railway concrete components, was erected. This closed in May 1968.

A temporary platform was erected in May 1997 to celebrate the quarry's centenary and the reopening of Okehampton station. In 2002 the Dartmoor Railway developed a new halt 'Meldon Quarry' as the western terminus of its operations. Opening on 6th July it is to the west of the original halt and close to the east end of Meldon viaduct. A new platform today stands on the north side of the line; on the platform is a replica of the traditional design LSWR wooden shelter. Nearby is an old carriage incorporating a buffet.

Meldon Quarry Halt. West Country 4-6-2 No.34023 Blackmore Vale is hauling an up (towards Okehampton) express through the halt on 19th July 1958.

Morchard Road. Looking north-west in about 1930. The main building, including accommodation for the station master, is on the down (towards Barnstaple) side and a stone waiting shelter serves passengers on the up platform. In the distance on the down side is the wooden goods shed.

MORCHARD ROAD

OPENED: 1st August 1854 (with the opening of the North Devon Railway, Crediton – Barnstaple).
CLOSED: Passengers – remains open as a request stop on the Exeter – Barnstaple line.
Goods – 30th December 1963.

Built to serve the village of Morchard Bishop some 2½ miles to the north-east, Morchard Road was a passing place on a single track section of the North Devon Railway (NDR), Crediton to Barnstaple. It opened at the beginning of August 1854.

The main station building on the down (towards Barnstaple) platform was a good example of the substantial structures developed from the outset by the NDR. Similar to that at five other stations on the line, it incorporated the booking office, waiting room, toilets and station master's office; it also included a two storey station master's house. There was no platform canopy or footbridge. On the up platform was a stone waiting shelter. For much of its life the station was oil lit but electricity was later introduced. In 1928 5,056 passenger tickets were issued and 5,785 collected; comparable figures in 1936 were halved, 2,035 and 2,528. A census on 7th May 1963 indicated that 21½ passengers (1 child = ½ passenger) joined or left the train. Further surveys over a winter week in 1976 and a summer week in 1977 gave the astonishing result that no passengers used Morchard Road in either week!

A small goods yard was sited on the down side at the Barnstaple end. The yard included a goods loop, with short spurs serving side and end loading docks, cattle pens and a wooden goods shed; the siding did not pass through the shed, which was equipped with a two ton capacity crane. A further five ton crane stood in the yard. General goods facilities were withdrawn at the end of December 1963 and the sidings were taken out of use on 6th March 1964. An 1873 12 lever signal box, of wood construction on a brick base, stood beyond the Barnstaple end of the up platform, adjacent to the rail level board crossing. The box closed on 6th March 1964.

Staffing ceased at Morchard Road and it was re-designated as a halt on 12th September 1965. The suffix was, however, dropped four years later on 5th May 1969. Today the station is a request stop for Exeter to Barnstaple services, trains using the former down platform, which has a small waiting shelter at the Crediton end. The up platform has been demolished. The former station building is in private residential use, Station House.

137

Morebath. A view west in about 1960. On the down (towards Barnstaple) platform is the main building (centre) and the 1937 signal box. An open front wooden shelter stands on the up platform.

Morebath Junction Halt. Looking east towards Taunton in 1963. Note the unusual small canopy supported by a single pole and the impressive tall lamps. The concrete block platform face replaced earlier railway sleepers.

MOREBATH

OPENED: 1st November 1873 (with the opening of the Wiveliscombe – Barnstaple section of the Devon & Somerset Railway).
CLOSED: Passengers – 3rd October 1966.
 Goods – 3rd June 1963.

Sited in a remote location some two miles east of the village of Morebath and three miles north-east of Bampton, the station was at one time known as Morebath and Bampton. Morebath Junction Halt, which opened in 1928, was much closer to Morebath.

The original 1873 station was on the down side of a, then single track, section of the Devon & Somerset Railway. A passing loop and up platform were added in 1876. Both platforms were extended in timber at the west end, when the loop was lengthened in June 1937. Lightweight construction was required, as the extensions passed over a road bridge on to an embankment.

The main building, on the original downside, was a single storey stone structure, including a central section with an apex roof at right angles to the line and two wings, with lower roofs, parallel to the line. A number of chimney stacks rose above the roofs. The station booking, waiting and ladies' toilet facilities were within this building. The gent's toilet was at the east end, entered by a door in the east elevation. A small open front wooden shelter, with a backward sloping roof, stood at the centre of the up platform. No footbridge was provided, a rail level board crossing at the west end provided for inter-platform movements.

In 1903 3,208 passenger tickets were issued at

Morebath, by 1933 the figure had more than halved to 1,184. Two staff were based here in 1903; in all subsequent years to 1933 there were three.

The goods yard and stone built goods shed were sited behind, and to the east of, the down platform. The original signal box stood just beyond the west end of the down platform. It was replaced, as from 6th June 1937, by a second box on the west end of the same platform, coincident with the lengthening of the loop and platforms. The box closed on 2nd March 1963 when the station loop was taken out of use. All goods facilities were withdrawn three months later. Following closure of the station, with the withdrawal of passenger services on the line in October 1966, the station building and goods shed were converted into dwellings. In spring 2007 a sign 'Pixies Laughter Cottages 1-4' stood at the former station entrance where the original gate posts and gate survive.

MOREBATH JUNCTION HALT

OPENED: 1st December 1928 (on the Taunton – Barnstaple line originally opened through this site in 1873).
CLOSED: 3rd October 1966.

A late addition to passenger facilities in mid Devon, the halt opened in December 1928 just to the west of the junction between the Taunton to Barnstaple line and the Exe Valley line south to Bampton, Tiverton and Exeter. With most trains on both lines stopping, the halt, on the north side of the single track, had a through service to all the main towns of the area. With this siting it thus enjoyed a superior service to that at Morebath station itself, some two miles to the east. In contrast also, the halt was only a quarter of a mile south of the village. A significant problem, however, was the poor access to the halt, there being no metalled road or proper footpath to it. Passengers used a path across fields which were often muddy. Accounts indicate that, in wet weather, shoppers and schoolchildren would walk there in boots and then change to shoes at the halt, leaving the boots under the seat in the waiting shelter. Apparently none ever went missing!

The halt itself was basic. Originally constructed of infill behind a face of old railway sleepers, the face was later replaced by concrete blocks. On the platform was a small wooden shelter. In later years a small canopy, supported by a single pole, was added, a welcome addition in this exposed location. At each end of the platform were tall lamp standards and at the back of the platform was a concrete post and wire fence. Morebath Junction Halt closed in October 1966 with the withdrawal of services on the Taunton to Barnstaple line, services on the Exe Valley line having ceased three years earlier.

MORETONHAMPSTEAD

OPENED: Passengers – 4th July 1866, Goods 8th
    October 1866 (with the opening of the
    Moretonhampstead & South Devon Railway,
    Newton Abbot – Moretonhampstead).
CLOSED: Passengers – 2nd March 1959.
    Goods – 6th April 1964.

On the south-east edge of the moorland town, Moretonhampstead station was the terminus of the branch line from Newton Abbot, although there were early plans for the line to continue as far as Chagford. The formal opening took place on 26th June, declared a public holiday in the town. Records indicate that the arrival of the first train was greeted by 'three resounding cheers'. The arrival was followed by a celebration lunch at the Smythurst Unitarian schoolroom for over 200 guests. Streets were decorated and afternoon teas were available on Greenhill and in the vicinity of the market. Rural sports were held and the Newton Band performed throughout the celebrations. Passenger services commenced eight days later.

Moretonhampstead, like Ashburton, was a classic GWR terminus, the main station building (59 ft x 17 ft) having granite walls incorporating arched windows and doorways. The low pitched roof with

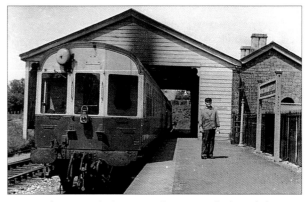

Moretonhampstead. A view in the 1930s of a branch line train standing partly under the Brunel type wooden train shed. The main station building is to the right.

Moretonhampstead. A general view of the classic GWR terminus on 1st August 1955. By that time the slate on the train shed roof had been replaced by heavy duty felt and the glazed skylights taken out and replaced by corrugated iron sheets. The road side entrance canopy on the main building had also gone.

two chimneys was of grey slate. A small horizontal canopy over the double door entrance protected passengers. Inside, the accommodation comprised a booking hall/waiting room, station master's office, parcels office and toilets.

Backing onto the platform side of the building was a typical Brunel type train shed with an arched roof (80 ft x 40 ft) covering the platform, platform line and loop line. The shed was supported by nine vertical posts set in granite plinths on the far side of the loop line. The south wall and gable ends were constructed of lateral wooden planks. On the platform side the rear wall of the building, together with two open arched extensions, supported the roof, the extensions being required as the shed was 21 ft longer than the building. The roof itself was constructed of diagonal wood planks covered by felt and battens. The whole roof structure, originally with some glazing at the top, was reinforced by a network of trusses and tie-bars. The one 300 ft long platform on the north side was surfaced with paving stones under the roof, outside it was of tarmac and

Mortehoe and Woolacombe. A detailed view, looking north-west, of the buildings on the down (towards Ilfracombe) side in the 1930s. From left to right is the original small wooden goods shed, the 1891 wooden signal box and the main building incorporating the station master's accommodation.

chippings, edged with concrete slabs.

Beyond the buffers end of the station were cattle pens served by a short spur and dock from the loop line. The dock was also used for loading and unloading Dartmoor ponies; a small building was the store for hay and sawdust. A trailing siding on the down (south) side led to the engine shed (43 ft x 23 ft), a substantial granite structure with a low pitched slate roof and four large arched windows on either side. At the west end was a large arched entrance sufficient for the passage of early broad gauge locomotives. The shed closed in November 1947 when Moretonhampstead ceased to be a sub-shed for the main shed at Newton Abbot. To the west of the shed was a turntable and water tower. On the northern wall of the engine shed was the very unusual lean-to 15 lever signal box. Added in 1893, it was built of brick and timber with a slate roof and tall brick chimney.

The relatively small goods yard was on the up (north) side and east of the station building, with the stone goods shed with arched windows adjoining the rear of the platform. The yard had two dead end sidings, one originally running through the goods shed terminating close to the station building; this was later cut back to terminate in the shed. The shed incorporated a two ton crane. Outside, between the building and the shed, was a larger six ton crane, sited at an end loading dock.

The level of both passenger and goods traffic was

relatively high at Moretonhampstead: in 1903 30,292 passenger tickets were issued; other figures were: 1913 (47,666), 1923 (28,323), 1933 (12,099), 1943 (18,439) and 1953 (11,899). In March 1929 the GWR bought the 1907 built Manor House at North Bovey, two miles south-west of the station and converted it into a hotel. The hotel generated considerable traffic, its facilities being widely advertised in railway timetables and guides (eg Holiday Haunts). Passenger traffic was also generated by buses running to the station from a number of Dartmoor towns. In April 1906 the GWR had started a service to Chagford. Later, services ran to Princetown and Dartmeet. In relation to both passenger and freight traffic, the monthly cattle market also brought considerable business to the station.

Closure to passengers came in March 1959 and to goods in April 1964. There were early attempts by the South Devon Railway Preservation Society to revive services on the branch but these failed and the Society's attention turned to the eventually successful re-introduction of trains on the Ashburton line. Following a period of short term uses, the station site was taken over in 1976 by a firm of transport hauliers, Thompson & Sons, and this use continues today. Both the goods shed and engine shed (now a listed building) remain in situ but a new office block has been built on the site of the demolished station building.

MORTEHOE AND WOOLACOMBE

OPENED: 20th July 1874 (with the opening of the Barnstaple & Ilfracombe Railway).
CLOSED: Passengers – 5th October 1970.
  Goods – 7th September 1964.

Sited at the highest point on the Barnstaple to Ilfracombe line, at some 600 ft above sea level, the station opened in July 1874. In this position the railway approach to the station was steep from both north and south; from the north a long section from Ilfracombe at 1 in 36 and from the south a section of 1 in 40. The station opened as Morthoe in the timetable but changed to Mortehoe from 13th May 1902. It changed to Mortehoe for Woolacombe and Lee and then, from 5th June 1950, it finally became Mortehoe and Woolacombe. The village of Mortehoe was some two miles to the north-west. Woolacombe and Lee were at a similar distance to the west and north.

When it opened the station was a passing place on the single track Barnstaple to Ilfracombe line. The section from Mortehoe to Ilfracombe was doubled from 1st July 1891. The principal station buildings on the down (towards Ilfracombe) side comprised a two storey station master's house together with a single storey section at the north end containing the waiting and booking facilities. A wide platform canopy was added at a later date. On the south end of the platform was a small goods shed; originally of wood with an apex roof, it was later replaced by a flat roof concrete structure. On the up platform passengers were served by a wooden shelter, the form changing over the years. The station had a bad start to its life with a serious fire on 17th August 1874.

To the south of the station buildings on the down side was the goods yard with five sidings, a 25 cwt crane, a cattle dock and cattle pens. A further two sidings were sited opposite the yard on the up side. The station signal box with 20 levers was on the down platform between the building and the goods shed. Built of wood on a brick base with a slate roof, it operated from the time of track doubling in 1891. Mortehoe and Woolacombe station was particularly busy on summer Saturdays with banking engines arriving from both directions, to be returned to Braunton and Ilfracombe.

Until about 1925 all down trains stopped at the station for tickets to be collected, Ilfracombe being an 'open' station. In 1928 20,806 passenger tickets were issued and 52,145 collected; by 1936 the numbers had almost halved to 11,553 and 29,698.

Goods facilities were withdrawn in September 1964. The Ilfracombe line was singled in December 1967 and the up platform became disused. The signal box closed. Passenger services lasted until October 1970 when the Ilfracombe line closed. For some years the station site was derelict apart from the station master's house used as a residence. From 1987 a children's centre, 'Once upon a Time', was created on the site. A new building was erected on the former up platform and the space between the platforms was covered by a large canopy. Track was laid between the platforms and four Mark 1 carriages were introduced containing various children's activities. Children's play equipment was laid between the platforms beyond the canopy and a miniature railway ran along the former up platform. A visit in early May 2007 revealed however that 'Once upon a Time' had closed. A planning site notice indicated that a planning application had been submitted for redevelopment of the site for seven dwellings, 37 units of holiday accommodation and the conversion of an outbuilding for use as a reception centre. It is anticipated that a number of the old station buildings will be incorporated in the final approved scheme.

MOUNT GOULD AND TOTHILL HALT

OPENED: 1st October 1905 (on the Mount Gould
  Junction to Friary Junction line).
CLOSED: 1st February 1915.

Sited in east Plymouth on the north-south line between Mount Gould Junction to the north and Friary Junction to the south, Mount Gould and Tothill Halt was only open for just over 12 years. With two platforms but no buildings, its entrance was through a swing gate within railings adjacent to the road bridge that carried Lanhydrock Road over the railway. The halt was immediately south of the bridge. The swing gate entry survived until the bridge was renewed during the 1980s. No close up photograph is known of this short lived halt.

MOUNT PLEASANT ROAD HALT

OPENED: 26th January 1906 (on the Honiton – Exeter
  Queen St (Central) line originally opened through
  this site in 1860).
CLOSED: 2nd January 1928.

This small halt, with two wooden platforms but no shelters, opened in January 1906 to serve passengers on the new steam rail-motor service from Exeter to Honiton. Two years later the shuttle service

Mount Pleasant Road Halt. Looking down from Mount Pleasant Road on this short-lived halt in east Exeter.

Mutley. Looking east through the station in about 1910 towards the western portal of Mutley tunnel. The main building is on the up platform (left) with a stone shelter on the down. Note the fine metal lattice footbridge and the flight of steps up to Gordon Terrace (right).

introduced to Topsham, also called. Sited immediately east of the eastern portal of Blackboy tunnel, access was via steeply sloping paths down from Mount Pleasant Road. The halt was not a success and closed after 22 years in January 1928.

MUTLEY

OPENED: 1st August 1871 (on the Totnes – Plymouth GWR line originally opened through this site in 1849).
CLOSED: Passengers – 3rd July 1939.
Goods – no facilities provided.

Built to serve the inner Plymouth suburb of Mutley, the station opened in August 1871 on the GWR line east of Plymouth Millbay and west of Mutley tunnel. Plymouth North Road opened a short distance west of Mutley nearly six years later, in March 1877. Access to Mutley station on the north (up) side was at the junction of Apsley Road, Pentillie Road and Station Road (now Ermington Terrace); to the south access was at the junction of Gordon Terrace and Napier Terrace. East of the station the scene was dominated by the west portal of Mutley tunnel (183 yds) and the twin towers of Mutley Baptist Church.

Standing on the up platform, the principal stone building with a horizontal lineside canopy incorporated the booking office, main waiting

rooms, toilets and other station offices. A typical GWR metal lattice covered footbridge linked the east ends of the platforms; a stone waiting shelter with toilets served passengers on the down platform. Towards the west end of this platform a flight of metal steps led up to Gordon Terrace. A small 8 lever signal box on the up platform, between the building and the footbridge, operated for about 12 years from 1896 to 1908 before it was superseded by levers in the Plymouth North Road East Box.

Although from 1877 very close to Plymouth North Road, Mutley was a very busy station and indeed in 1913 364,395 tickets were issued here compared with 246,245 at North Road. By 1938 ticket sales had dropped to 48,722. Although developed as a GWR station, Mutley was also used by London & South Western Railway (LSWR) trains from 1876 when that company's service began running to Devonport Kings Road from Exeter and Tavistock via Marsh Mills. It also served temporarily as the terminus for some LSWR trains when they approached from the west after the opening, on 1st June 1890, of the new route via Bere Alston and the Tamar Valley. This terminus role ceased on 1st July 1891, with the opening of the main LSWR terminus of Plymouth Friary. For a long period there were separate GWR and LSWR booking offices at Mutley. The station was also served by the steam rail motor services that started in the Plymouth area in 1904. In 1905 it is recorded that 10 westbound services commenced and terminated at Mutley and the station was a stopping place for another 15 through trains running on the Plympton to Saltash service. A staff of 17 were based at Mutley in 1913; these worked solely at the passenger station as no goods facilities were provided.

Despite the continuing volume of business, Mutley closed in July 1939, this linked with the commencement of redevelopment at Plymouth North Road. After closure two sidings were laid on the site of the former up platform, these being extensions of North Road sidings. Today no trace remains of Mutley station; just to the east a large car park has been constructed over the line at the west end of Mutley tunnel, in effect extending the tunnel to 317 yards.

NEWTON ABBOT

OPENED: 31st December 1846 (with the opening of the Teignmouth – Newton Abbot section of the South Devon Railway).

CLOSED: Passengers – remains open for services on the Exeter – Plymouth line and the branch to Torquay and Paignton.

Goods – 1970.

Sited to the east of the town centre, the first station at Newton Abbot opened on New Year's Eve 1846 as the terminus of the latest section of the South Devon Railway (SDR). With the initial name of Newton (Abbot added 1st March 1877), this original station comprised three independent passenger sheds, one for up main line trains, one for down main line trains (both sheds on the west side of the line) and one for trains on the Torquay branch. This last came into use when the branch opened to Torre in 1848. Newton Abbot was the southern terminus of the line that briefly used the atmospheric system in 1847-1848.

In January 1860 the SDR Board authorised the reconstruction of Newton station. A Brunel style structure with brick walls and a 300 ft long wooden train shed was built and opened in 1861 at a cost of some £9,500. Three narrow 400 ft long platforms were sited under the shed: a one face platform on the west side attached to the main single storey station offices, a middle island platform and an eastern island platform. An internal open footbridge connected the platforms. Three lines ran north-south: the up main line between the up and middle island platforms, a line for branch trains to Torquay (south) and Moretonhampstead/Teign Valley (north) between the two island platforms and a down main line alongside the outer face of the eastern island. A relief down line passed outside the main shed roof to the east. A smaller roof covered this line despite there being no platform serving it.

Newton Abbot. The first Newton Station and atmospheric engine house in 1848. The station was the southern limit of the operational atmospheric pumping system 1847-1848.

Newton Abbot. An overall view from the south in about 1910 showing the 1861 structure including the overall wooden train shed. A down express train is in the centre crossing to the down main line.

Again the facilities proved inadequate with summer traffic overwhelming the 1861 SDR station. Plans were drawn up in 1905 but although it was authorised in 1914, a new GWR station was not completed until 1927, the structures of the 1861 station being replaced in a phased rebuilding. The 1927 station incorporated two wide (56 ft up, 42 ft down) long island platforms with generous canopies (570 ft long); there was also a detached dead end bay platform (320 ft) at the north end of the station on the up side for trains on the Moretonhampstead branch and Teign Valley lines. The two island platforms had tracks on either side, all the four platform faces being divided into two for operational purposes by signalling. The outer faces of the up and down islands were provided with scissors cross-over tracks linking to adjacent up and down through lines for non stop trains. Passengers for Moreton-hampstead/Teign Valley line services gained access to the bay platform at the northern end of the main building on the west side, the outstanding feature of this 1927 station. Built of red Somerset bricks and

Newton Abbot. A view in about 1910 of the station approach and road side frontage of the 1861 station. Note the gathering of horse drawn carriages.

with Portland stone dressings, it was three storeys high; the ground floor housed a spacious booking hall and offices and offices for parcels and left luggage. A splendid dining room (66 ft x 19 ft) occupied the second floor whilst the top floor was the headquarters of the South Devon Divisional Locomotive Superintendent. Central heating and electric lighting was installed from the outset. The residents of Newton Abbot presented a clock to the GWR which was (and still is) mounted at the top of the road side frontage. A wide covered pedestrian footbridge ran from this building across the lines giving access to the island platforms. Early in the Second World War, on 20th August, 1940, five bombs exploded at the station wrecking the down main and relief tracks and also, particularly, the first coach of the 7.0 p.m. local train to Plymouth. Fourteen people were killed and a further 29 seriously injured. Traffic was resumed after ten hours.

As from 27th April 1987 the two tracks on the west side between the up main and up island platforms were lifted and the up main platform closed. Thus passengers using trains on the former up island were now able to reach there on the level; the direct access from the pedestrian bridge to the offices at first floor level was also closed to the public. Other land released by the track lifting to the south of the building was converted into a car park.

Today the operations at Newton Abbot remain similar to these that commenced in 1987 with the up and down main line trains using the inner faces of the original island platforms and the Torquay line

trains normally using the outer face of the eastern island. The whole station, including the covered footbridge, is in good condition and a modern glass lounge has been installed on the now up platform. The main building is in office use as 'South Devon House' with the main booking office on the ground floor. The Railway Inn stands adjacent to the north end of the station on the up side.

Over the years extensive goods facilities have been provided at Newton Abbot, the principal action being the replacement, as from 12th June 1911, of the original goods yard north of the station on the up side by an extensive yard (15 acres) and goods station a short distance up the Moretonhampstead branch. This was an essential prelude to the extensive remodelling of the station which did not take place for another 16 years. Also north of the station on the down side was the Hackney marshalling yard. Open from 1911 to 10th January 1971, at its peak it contained two through goods lines and 18 sidings.

Newton Abbot was, through the years, a major centre for locomotive and wagon repairs and servicing with extensive buildings mostly on the down side east of the station. Much of this activity ceased during the 1960s, particularly with the withdrawal of steam locomotives. Servicing of diesels continued however.

After the 1927 rebuilding, operations at Newton Abbot were controlled by two signal boxes; the East box (206 levers) at the fork with the Moretonhampstead branch and the West box (153 levers) at the Torquay/Plymouth end of the up platform. As from 1st May 1987 these boxes were superseded by the Exeter power box.

NEWTON POPPLEFORD

OPENED: 1st June 1899 (on the Tipton St Johns –
Budleigh Salterton line originally opened through
this site in 1897).
CLOSED: Passengers – 6th March 1967.
Goods – 27th January 1964.

Serving the village of Newton Poppleford, just to the west, the station, sited in the valley of the River Otter, was immediately north of a road bridge carrying the A35 (now A3052) road over the Tipton St Johns to Budleigh Salterton line. The station opened in June 1899, two years after services started on that line.

The single storey brick building, with an apex roof

Newton Poppleford. Looking north from the road bridge in 1950. The single storey brick building stands on the down (towards Budleigh Salterton) platform. There appear to be posts supporting the front projection of the roof. Two trucks stand on the one siding serving the small goods yard.

and two chimneys, stood on the 184 ft long platform on the down (east) side of the line. A narrow section of the roof projected over the front of the building providing limited shelter to a platform seat. At the south end of the building was a small annex again with an apex roof but lower in height. A path from the east end of the road bridge led down to the southern end of the platform. In 1928 7,856 passenger tickets were issued and 5,744 collected; in 1936 4,306 and 3919 were the comparable figures. These figures were rather unusual in Devon where the normal pattern was the number of tickets collected being greater than those sold.

The small goods yard, on the west side of the line, was opposite the station and platform. Road access was from a minor road running north from the A35. The link with the platform was via a rail level board crossing at the north end of the yard. The yard was served by just one siding which continued south through and slightly beyond the road bridge. There was no goods shed but the siding served a wooden cattle food store. For a time before the Second World War two camping coaches were based in the siding.

The original staffing comprised a station master and porter. This was reduced, first to only a station master and later to a porter under the supervision initially from the station master at Tipton St Johns and, when this post was abolished, from the station master at Budleigh Salterton. Eventually Newton Poppleford was unstaffed from 16th August 1965 and became a halt. Goods facilities had ceased in January 1964 and the station closed with the withdrawal of passenger services on the line in March 1967. The station was demolished, as was the road bridge. The site became privately owned and

when seen in mid 2006 was undeveloped. The platform had remained intact for some years but had gone by 1990.

NEWTON ST CYRES

OPENED: October 1851 (on the Cowley Bridge – Crediton line opened earlier that year in May).
CLOSED: Passengers – remains open as a request stop for limited services on the Exeter – Barnstaple line. Goods – 12th September 1960.

Sited in the small settlement of Sweetham and about a mile north of the village of Newton St Cyres, records indicate that the station opened in October 1851. Originally named St Cyres (the prefix Newton being added from 1st October 1913), it was the only intermediate station on the line between Exeter and Crediton. The principal wooden building, on the up (towards Exeter) platform incorporated the station master's office, booking office, waiting room and toilets. On the down platform stood a small wooden shelter, replaced from 1959 by a concrete structure. This down platform was offset a little to the east compared with the up; this permitted passage of a short siding, serving a small goods yard with cattle pens behind the platform. This siding closed on 12th September 1960. No footbridge was ever provided, inter-platform movements could take place via the

Newton St Cyres. Looking west on 3rd October 1964. The wooden main building stands on the up (towards Exeter) platform beyond which is the station master's house. A 1959 concrete waiting shelter serves passengers on the down platform.

north-south road bridge to the west of the station, carrying the road to Newton St Cyres.

In 1928 10,385 passenger tickets were issued; the figure nearly halved to 5,608 in 1936. Equivalent figures for tickets collected were 10,987 and 5,683. A later survey showed that in a winter week in 1976 only one passenger used the station. In a summer week of 1977 the figure was six. The signal box at the east end of the up platform was closed as from 17th August 1930, the function being taken on by a 12 lever frame housed in a lean-to extension at the east end of the main building. The booking office building and this extension closed on 31st July 1968 and the building was subsequently demolished. The line through the station was singled as from 16th December 1984. The former up platform, with a bus stop type shelter, remains in use as a request stop for trains on the Exeter to Barnstaple line. The derelict down platform remains but the shelter has gone. The former station master's house beyond the Barnstaple end of the up platform on the north side survives in private residential use, Station House. The nearby Railway Inn has been renamed The Beer Engine, reflecting the fact that a small brewery operates here.

NORTHAM

OPENED: 18th May 1901 (with the opening of the Bideford Quay – Northam section of the Bideford, Westward Ho! & Appledore Railway).
CLOSED: 28th March 1917.

Sited at that time north-west of the village of Northam, the station opened in May 1901 as the terminus of the first section of the Bideford,

Westward Ho! & Appledore Railway. In this role the track layout was a main line to a buffer stop together with a run-round loop from which a short stub siding ran also to a buffer stop. This siding, on the up side (towards Bideford), was primarily used for locomotive coal and other local deliveries. The loop and siding were lifted in 1908 when the line was extended to Appledore. Northam's layout was then reduced to a single line running alongside a 6 inch high, 180 ft long platform on the down (north) side. A small waiting room and toilets stood on the platform. When first opened there was a five lever signal box at the end of the platform and one semaphore signal. Signalling became redundant in 1908 and the box closed. From that date Northam was re-designated as a halt. The station closed early in 1917 when the railway infrastructure was requisitioned by the War Department (see Bideford Quay text). The former station site is now within the expanded Northam urban area. No photograph is known of the station.

NORTH TAWTON

OPENED: 1st November 1865 (with the opening of the Coleford Junction (west of Crediton) – North Tawton section of the Devon & Cornwall Railway).
CLOSED: Passengers – 5th June 1972.
    Goods – 7th September 1964.

The Devon & Cornwall Railway from Coleford Junction, on the Exeter to Barnstaple line, to Okehampton and Holsworthy opened in stages, the first of which opened from the Junction to North Tawton at the beginning of November 1865. This terminus status lasted just over a year until the next stage on to Sampford Courtenay opened in January 1867.

North Tawton village was just over a mile to the north of the station. The substantial local stone building stood on the up (towards Coleford Junction) side of the line. It included a two storey station master's house and a single storey section incorporating the main station facilities. Both the house and the lower section had steeply pitched roofs at right angles to the line. Other features of the building included tall round headed windows in pointed arches, a small platform canopy and a variety of chimneys. On the down platform was a wooden shelter with a canopy. A footbridge, originally covered, connected the platforms at the east end of the station. In 1928 11,421 passenger tickets were issued at North Tawton and 13,731 collected; in 1936 the figures were 7,931 and 10,330.

North Tawton goods yard was on the up side to the west of and behind the main station building. The yard included a stone goods shed and a dock siding which terminated to the west of the main building. Rail movements at North Tawton were controlled from an 18 lever wooden signal box on the west end of the up platform.

Goods facilities were withdrawn in September 1964 and the signal box closed on 24th September 1967. North Tawton remained open to passengers until June 1972 when the local service between Okehampton and Exeter was withdrawn. The through service to Plymouth via Bere Alston had ceased in 1968. The station building was subsequently converted into two houses fenced off from the line on the disused up platform. The rail over bridge to the east of the station was raised to allow the passage of higher road vehicles. As a consequence the track level was raised through North Tawton station to above platform level. The footbridge was removed in 1986 to Ropley on the Mid Hants Railway and in 1994 the former down side shelter was also moved to the Hampshire line. The single track through the station is still used both by freight traffic from Meldon Quarry, west of Okehampton and also by the weekend passenger services run by the Dartmoor Railway between Exeter and Okehampton but which do not call at North Tawton. The adjacent Railway Inn contains a number of photographs of the line in operation.

OKEHAMPTON

OPENED: 3rd October 1871 (with the opening of the Belstone Corner (Sampford Courtenay) – Okehampton section of the Devon & Cornwall Railway).
CLOSED: Passengers – 5th June 1972.
  Goods – 1979.
REOPENED: 24th May 1997 (see text).

The Devon & Cornwall Railway (D&CR) from Coleford Junction, on the Exeter to Barnstaple line, to Okehampton and Holsworthy opened in stages, the third of which was completed from Sampford Courtenay to Okehampton in October 1871, about a year before the D&CR was fully absorbed by the London & South Western Railway (LSWR). Okehampton was a terminus station until October

North Tawton. A detailed view of the magnificent station building on the up platform, now converted into two dwellings.

1874 when the line to Lydford was opened. This was followed by the line to Halwill and Holsworthy in 1879 and that to Launceston in 1886. These two lines were subsequently extended on to Bude and Padstow. Thus Okehampton became a key junction station in mid Devon with carriages on through expresses to and from London being joined or divided here.

The station itself, on the northern edge of Dartmoor at about 750 ft above sea level on the slopes of East Hill, was built about half a mile south of the town centre. The original main station building, on the up (towards Exeter) side of the line, comprised a two storey station master's house and a single storey section with a decorative horizontal canopy and valence. This lower section contained the main station booking, waiting and toilet facilities. A glazed weather shield below the west end of the canopy protected passengers. Also on the up platform was a flat roof refreshment room. The down side building housed a refreshment room and waiting rooms. This building served passengers both on the main down side platform and also on the bay platform behind its west end. This bay was used by local trains on the Bude and Padstow lines. A lattice type footbridge connected the platforms west of the buildings. Originally open, it was later covered.

The buildings on the up side were demolished and then completely rebuilt in 1928. The new brick structure incorporated waiting rooms, ticket office, a refreshment room and toilets. A wide glass canopy covered the platform, the extensive glazing giving

Okehampton. A Plymouth to Exeter train enters in about 1905. On the up side (right) is the original main building, including two storey accommodation for the station master, and a decorative horizontal canopy and valence. The original signal box can be seen above the down side building which, at that time, had no canopy.

good illumination. During this rebuilding a canopy supported by concrete brackets was added to the down side building. Passenger volumes were high at Okehampton between the Wars: in 1928 42,537 tickets were issued and 39,806 collected; by 1936 the number issued had fallen to 28,899 but the number collected had risen to 43,317.

Okehampton's extensive goods yard was on the down side behind the platform. The yard included a large stone goods shed with a through siding. The shed had 14 bays and three road side doors, a reflection of the importance of goods traffic at the station. The engine shed was on the up side east of the station. The original wooden shed, opened in 1894, was doubled in length in 1914. It was, however, destroyed by fire on 7th June 1920 and replaced by a structure of concrete blocks and an asbestos roof. An early 50 ft turntable close to the shed was replaced by a 70 ft facility closer to the station from 12th October 1947. The original signal box was on the down platform between the building and the foot of the bridge steps; the box was in use until 12th May 1935 when it was replaced by a box at the west end of the up platform, a box that was one storey high at the front and two at the back on account of its embankment siting.

A little to the west of the station, close to Okehampton Camp, two long sidings were laid on

the up side in about 1890 (with platforms added in 1909) to serve troop trains and the handling of military equipment using the ranges on Dartmoor. These sidings were, between 1960 and 1964, used for a motor-rail service running to and from Surbiton in Surrey. The sidings were taken out of use in 1982.

General goods facilities were withdrawn at Okehampton in 1979. Okehampton had remained open to passengers until June 1972 when the local service between Exeter and Okehampton was withdrawn. The through service to Plymouth via Bere Alston had ceased in 1968. Special excursion traffic continued however for some years. Following closure the principal station buildings were not demolished and in 1993 the main building was occupied by 'Devon Training for Skills'. As a major tourism initiative involving European funding Okehampton station, following some renovation, was reopened on 24th May 1997 with trains running at weekends and bank holidays from Exeter. Over the following ten years extensive work was undertaken. Passenger trains in the Okehampton area are now run by the Dartmoor Railway (DR). These run from Exeter to Okehampton on Sundays and DR also operates trains from Sampford Courtenay through Okehampton to the new Meldon Quarry Halt at the east end of the former Meldon viaduct.

When visited in 2006 the main station building incorporated a buffet, booking office, shop and toilets. Picnic tables stood on the platform beneath the surviving canopy. At this time the down platform building, reached by the surviving covered footbridge, was undergoing renovation for future use as a craft workshop, retail units and visitor centre.

Oreston. A view up (towards Plymouth) shortly before it closed in 1951. Note the unusual small canopy over the main doorway into the waiting room.

From this down platform steam hauled trips, known as the Dartmoor Pony, which had started on 28th May, were operating to Meldon. The former goods shed is now the YHA Okehampton Adventure Centre. A further survivor is the 1935 signal box. The former site of the engine shed and turntable is used as a car park.

ORESTON

OPENED: 1st January 1897 (with the opening of the London & South Western Railway Turnchapel branch, Plymouth – Tavistock).
CLOSED: Passengers – 10th September 1951
Goods – 2nd October 1961.

Built close to the heart of the village it served, Oreston opened on New Year's Day 1897. The one platform, on the up (west) side of the single line, was constructed of stone and earth infill behind stone facing, with concrete edge slabs and a loose chipping surface. The small station building, built of vertical wooden planks and asbestos sheets, had a small canopy over the doorway into the waiting room. To the south of the room was a small booking office and to the north a goods shed/office. The two rooms each had a window at the ends of the building.

At the northern end of the platform a rail level board crossing over the line linked to a footpath to six railway cottages. A small two lever ground frame controlled access to an 11 wagon capacity siding behind the platform; the siding was for private use only for many years but from 1938 became available for public use. Along with the rest of the branch, Oreston station closed from 15th January to 2nd July 1951 due to the national coal shortage.

Passenger services ceased in September 1951 and the building was demolished. Goods facilities were withdrawn ten years later. The trackbed is now used as a footpath adjacent to Houldsworth Road. There is now no trace of Oreston station but the nearby railway cottages survive.

OTTERY ST MARY

OPENED: 6th July 1874 (with the opening of the Sidmouth Railway, Sidmouth Junction – Sidmouth).
CLOSED: Passengers – 6th March 1967.
Goods – 8th May 1967 (coal depot only from 6th September 1965).

Sited in the Otter valley, about half a mile west of the town centre, Ottery St Mary opened in July 1874. To the north of a level crossing carrying the B3174 west from the town towards Rockbeare and Exeter, the station stood on a passing loop on the otherwise single line Sidmouth Railway. The main through line ran alongside the up (towards Sidmouth Junction) platform and the loop along the down. The loop was extended by about 50 yards at the south end from 22nd November 1936 to accommodate the long excursion trains running to and from Sidmouth.

The opening day was marked by teas being provided for the young and elderly of the town. The main brick building, including a two storey gabled house for the station master, stood on the down platform. A single storey section at the south end of the building housed the principal waiting and booking facilities and the ladies' toilets. A separate

Ottery St Mary. The main brick building, on the down platform, including the station master's accommodation, as seen on 6th October 1964. The building complete with canopy is now in use as 'The Station Youth Centre'.

annex at the north end of the building contained the gent's toilets. The platform canopy, along the front of the single storey section and a part of the station house, had a decorative valence and was supported close to the platform edge by cast iron posts and brackets. A large brick open front shelter with a slate roof and finials stood on the up platform. In 1928 20,190 passenger tickets were issued at Ottery St Mary and 29,027 collected. By 1936 the figures had fallen to 9,601 and 17,360. In its later years the station was well used by students attending King's School at Ottery St Mary.

The goods yard, east of the station building behind the down platform, contained a brick goods shed with a lean-to office at the north end. The yard contained three sidings, one ran through the goods shed and another served a dock at the north end of the platform. A two ton capacity crane operated in the yard. Cattle truck trains were run from the station when Ottery St Mary market operated on alternate Mondays. General goods facilities were withdrawn in September 1965 but coal continued to be handled until the yard closed in May 1967.

A small low 1874 timber signal box, off the south end of the up platform, was replaced from 20th November 1955 by a modern brick box on the opposite side of the line adjacent to the level crossing, where gates were operated by a wheel in the box.

The station closed to passengers when services were withdrawn on the Sidmouth line in March 1967. The main buildings have survived. The station building, with the canopy still there and filled in to platform level, is 'The Station Youth Centre'. To the north of the building an industrial estate covers the track bed.

Paignton. The station forecourt on 9th July 1946. A Western National bus on the Totnes service is waiting to leave. The Western National waiting room is behind the sliding double doors in the small building on the left. Behind the bus is the main up side building and beyond (right) is the old goods shed, now renovated and in use as the station concourse and booking office, following demolition of the main building in 1993.

PAIGNTON

OPENED: 2nd August 1859 (with the opening of the Torre – Paignton section of the Torbay & Dartmouth Railway).

CLOSED: Passengers – remains open for services on the Exeter – Newton Abbot – Paignton line and the Paignton & Dartmouth Railway.
Goods: 4th December 1967.

As at many towns in Devon, great celebrations were held with the arrival of the railway, in this case the Torre – Paignton section of the Torbay & Dartmouth Railway which opened at the beginning of August 1859. Public services commenced on 2nd August after the ceremonial opening on the previous day. An estimated 18,000 people celebrated: flags were flown, houses were bedecked with flowers and trees were planted. Visitors poured into the resort, some coming by steamer from 'remote parts of the coast'. The high point of the celebrations was planned to be the parade and eating by the poor and needy of a massive plum pudding, an event normally held in Paignton every fifty years. The most recent staging was in 1819; though ten years short of the fifty year gap, the arrival of the railway was deemed to be worthy of the special celebration, but things did not work out! The large pudding, weighing some 1½ tons in eight sections, was drawn to the promenade by a team of eight horses but, before the ceremony commenced, rioting broke out; the pudding was demolished and no addresses or speeches took place. This was not an auspicious opening for the station, an omen perhaps for the following chequered history.

The original station had only one platform but by mid 1861 a second platform on a loop had been added. Close to the main shopping area and sea front, it was in an ideal location but the actual site between two main roads was, originally, and continued to be, a serious handicap, restricting the scope for enlargement. The station has only ever had two platforms. Paignton residents were, from an early date, drawing unfavourable comparisons with Torquay where the original inadequate station was replaced by an impressive structure, opened in 1878. Indeed in 1882 a local newspaper referred to Paignton station as 'a primitive little wooden house'.

Over the years a series of improvements took place: 1884 saw an extension of the platforms, the provision of a new waiting room and toilets and the building of an up platform canopy. The up side building was finally completed in the late 1880s and in 1887 a footbridge was erected at the north end of the station on Torquay Road. A covered station footbridge was also provided between the middle of the platforms. Platform extensions were also undertaken in 1890 and 1910, the latter bringing the length to 600 ft, coincident with the doubling of the tracks between Torquay and Paignton. Further major improvements came in 1924 including an enlarged booking office, a new parcels office and additional platform canopies. As an early contribution to Government schemes to reduce unemployment, new facilities were developed in 1930. The line south

from Paignton to Goodrington was doubled and new goods facilities were constructed on the up side close to Goodrington. A new large goods shed (300 ft long), with an office for 20 clerks, was opened on 1st June 1931. An old goods shed, sited behind the southern end of the up platform was, with a southern extension, converted into a parcels and luggage office. New carriage facilities were also laid out and came into use in May 1930 behind the down platform. Both platforms were again lengthened to cope with the ever longer trains. Passenger volumes throughout this whole period were very high: in 1903 232,281 passenger tickets were issued at Paignton. The comparable figure for 1933 was 143,107. In the early 1930s some 40 staff were based at Paignton and an extra eight could be taken on during the peak summer months.

A further major scheme proposed to reduce unemployment involved the complete redevelopment of Paignton station into a five platform facility. To be sited a little to the south of the original, it was designed to extend beyond the Sands Road level crossing which would be eliminated, with pedestrians crossing via a new subway. Approval was given in August 1937 for the scheme costing £138,550. Some site work was completed including a recess for a new signal box but work soon halted with the outbreak of the Second World War. The

Paignton. Looking south from the footbridge adjacent to the level crossing on 8th July 1957. On the up platform (right) is the main building with a horizontal canopy and a small building which contains the station master's office. The former was demolished in 1993 but the latter survives today. On the extreme left carriages stand in the Park sidings, now the site of the Paignton & Dartmouth Railway building.

Parracombe. The original pre 1924 wooden shelter on the Lynton & Barnstaple Railway. It was replaced by a concrete structure, which survives today by the road side.

scheme was not resurrected and Paignton never got its new station!

Following the Second World War, little improvement came for over ten years. In 1956/1957, however, extensions were made to carriage sidings at Goodrington and new refreshment facilities were provided at the station itself. The cramped station continued to serve the heavy summer traffic. Significant action came, however, in the early 1970s. Following extensive negotiations, the then Dart Valley Railway (DVR) took over the services on the line south from Paignton to Kingswear. Much of the trackbed, particularly that south of Goodrington, was sold to the DVR as were the former Park sidings behind the down platform. The eastern pair of these sidings was retained by the DVR for the platform line and a loop, whilst the site released by the removal of the remaining three sidings was used for the construction of the DVR's Paignton Queens Park Station. The DVR and its successor, the Paignton & Dartmouth Railway, took over the former down line, south of the station, for its services whilst the other two tracks were replaced by a single track over Sands Road level crossing, leading south to sidings used by main line stock terminating or departing from Paignton station. To the north of the station, alongside the north of the level crossing, the footbridge was replaced and slightly re-sited in November 1976; at the same time the gates were replaced by lifting barriers. During 1993 the principal up side building was demolished but the old goods shed was retained and redeveloped as the station concourse and booking office. It also incorporates the station signal panel.

This last was the latest step in the evolution of the signalling at Paignton. In 1889 boxes were opened at the north and south ends of the station incorporating wheels for the operation of the Torquay Road and Sands Road level crossing gates, both previously hand operated. The North and South boxes had 13 and 17 levers respectively. The North box, at the end of the up platform, was replaced in 1924 and operational until 26th March 1988 when barrier operation switched to the South box. The second South box was built in 1924, the original frame of 41 levers being later extended to 60. The panel was transferred to the station itself in 1990 when the box became unsafe and was demolished.

Today the station operates broadly in accord with the 1993 changes. The former goods yard to the south of the up building is in use as a car park and base for a car rental firm. The former large 1931 goods yard and shed towards Goodrington has been redeveloped for housing (Great Western Close). The booking office continues to operate in the former goods shed where the high shed roof beams are clearly visible. At the north end of the shed is the Whistle Stop Café, looking out onto Great Western Road. The Paignton & Dartmouth Railway operates south to Kingswear from the adjacent Queens Park Station.

PARRACOMBE

OPENED: July 1899 (on the Lynton & Barnstaple Railway opened through this site in May 1898) (see text).

CLOSED: 30th September 1935.

Sited about 120 ft below the village of Parracombe, the early history of the station was chequered. It first featured in the public timetable in July 1899, though there is some indication that trains called there late in 1898. This was probably only on Fridays relating to market days in Barnstaple. For a period from September 1899 to May 1903 there was no entry in the public timetable; during this time the nameboard at Blackmoor station stated 'Blackmoor for Parracombe'. A further omission from the timetable occurred between June 1917 and July 1924. In the early days of intermittent services it was sometimes the duty of the porter at Blackmoor to walk down the line to issue tickets at Parracombe! Later, as services increased, tickets could be obtained from the village post office.

The short platform on a curve was on the west (down) side of the single line. Initially there was no shelter but a wooden structure was soon provided. This was replaced in 1924 by a concrete shelter which was not demolished when the line closed in September 1935 and survives today by the roadside.

Parracombe water tank beyond the Lynton end of the platform on the up (towards Barnstaple) side had a good supply of water. This was important for the railway as there was no water at Woody Bay and the supply was unreliable at Lynton.

PETROCKSTOW

OPENED: 27th July 1925 (with the opening of the North Devon & Cornwall Junction Light Railway, Torrington – Halwill).
CLOSED: Passengers – 1st March 1965.
　Goods – 7th September 1964.

About half a mile north of the village in a wooded setting, the station was sited at one of only three passing loops on the line between Torrington and Halwill. Opening with the line in July 1925, there were two platforms with the stone built main building standing on the up (towards Torrington) side. A small wooden canopy over the platform was a forward extension of the roof. No shelter was provided on the down platform, which was accessed by a rail level board crossing at the north end close to an ungated level crossing carrying a minor road from Huish to Petrockstow.

Passenger figures were low with the returns for tickets issued, unusually for Devon, being higher than those collected. In 1928 2,692 tickets were issued and 2,580 collected; by 1936 the figures had fallen to 1,417 and 1,229. Although staffed, there was no formal position as station master, the supervision being from the station master at Hatherleigh.

The goods facilities comprised a two siding yard on the up side including a cattle dock terminating behind the south end of the platform adjacent to the building. A store was provided for animal foods but there was no goods shed or crane. There were also cattle pens. The principal inward goods were fertilizers, coal and animal food, whilst timber and cattle were the main exports. On occasions the sidings were used for storing clay wagons.

Goods facilities were withdrawn in September 1964 and Petrockstow closed for passengers at the beginning of March 1965 with the withdrawal of services on the line. The down side passing loop was reduced to a siding from 26th February 1967, the same month in which the station building was demolished. In spring 2007 both platforms could still be seen with the Tarka Trail cycleway running along the former up platform before returning to the track

Petrockstow. A single car DMU stands at the down platform running towards Halwill. The stone built main building with a wooden canopy serves passengers on the up (towards Torrington) platform.

bed south of the station site. The former station forecourt is a car park for Trail users with the goods yard occupied by SWH Civil Highways Maintenance.

PILTON YARD HALT

OPENED: October/November 1898 (on the Lynton & Barnstaple Railway originally opened through this site in May 1898).
CLOSED: May 1904 (closed to public use).

Starting in October or November 1898 the timetable for the Lynton & Barnstaple Railway showed that the first train of the day started from Barnstaple Pilton Yard, sited at the Pilton Road crossing, rather than from Barnstaple Town. The public use probably ceased after May 1904, the date of the last timetable entry. Subsequently the halt was used only be railwaymen. No details of the facility or photograph are known.

PINHOE

OPENED: 30th October 1871 (on the Honiton – Exeter Queen Street (Central) line originally opened through this site in 1860).
CLOSED: Passengers – 7th March 1966.
　Goods – 10th June 1967.
REOPENED: Passengers only - 16th May 1983.

The station, on the southern edge of what, at that time, was the village of Pinhoe, opened in October 1871, eleven years after services commenced between Honiton and Exeter on the last section of

Pinhoe. A detailed look at the up side building. From left to right the station building with notices, 'Gentlemen' and 'Ticket Office', the station master's house (which survives today) and, beyond the level crossing, the 1875 signal box.

the London & South Western Railway (LSWR) between London and Exeter. Being a later station, Pinhoe was one of few on this line in the West Country that did not have a distinctive William Tate design building. A single storey brick building stood at the east end of the up (towards Honiton) platform, incorporating the booking office, waiting room and toilets. A small waiting shelter and open store stood on the down platform. At the east end of the station between the end of the up platform and a level crossing, was the two storey station master's house. The platforms were originally linked by a wooden footbridge. This was later replaced by a concrete structure, reported to be one of the first products of the Southern Railway (SR) works at Exmouth Junction, and the first concrete footbridge erected on the Southern Railway.

Freight facilities were minimal at Pinhoe; a single siding opened on 3rd April 1882, trailed back from the up line east of the level crossing. Coal staithes were served by this siding. West of the station on the up side, sidings served a Government cold store facility, which came into use in 1943. This use continued until 1969. After temporary closure the siding reopened for a private cold store company, finally closing in 1979. An 1875 signal box, originally equipped with an 11 lever frame, was sited beside the up line immediately to the east of the level crossing controlled from the box. The gates were replaced by lifting barriers from 17th March 1963. The signal box frame had been extended to 17 levers in 1943 when the cold store sidings came into use.

The box operated until 13th February 1988 after which it was dismantled and re-located for preservation at Bere Ferrers station.

The station closed to goods traffic from June 1967; for many years the yard continued to be used by a coal merchant, though by 2004 the site was vacant. Despite by now being within the outer eastern suburbs of Exeter and therefore with potential for good commuter movements into the city, Pinhoe station closed to passengers on 7th March 1966 with the withdrawal of local services on the Honiton to Exeter line. The footbridge was removed and the station buildings demolished, apart from the former station master's house which survives today in residential use.

Pinhoe station reopened in May 1983, the second station to reopen on the Honiton to Exeter line after Feniton (Sidmouth Junction), which served passengers again from May 1971. The opening at Pinhoe, initially for a trial period, was conducted by Tony Speller, the M.P. for North Devon, who had introduced an amendment to the Transport Act 1962, which allowed the reopening of stations which, in the event of a failure, could be closed again without any undue formal procedures. Clearly, however, the reopening was a success. Today Pinhoe is at the eastern end of the double track line from Exeter and two platforms, with metal shelters, are in use once again. Initially there was no shelter on the up side, it being considered there was no prospect of large passenger numbers using that platform.

PLYM BRIDGE PLATFORM

OPENED: 1st May 1906 (on the Plymouth – Tavistock GWR line originally opened through this site in 1859).

CLOSED: 31st December 1962.

Plym Bridge Platform, on the east side of the line, took its name from a narrow old granite bridge which spanned the river immediately below the rail embankment at this point. With a length of 360 ft, the original halt, equipped with a booking office, was entirely constructed of timber. Heavy wooden legs carried long lengths of hardwood planks forming the platform. In 1949 Plym Bridge was shortened by 100 ft and reconstructed of concrete slabs and legs. Passengers were provided with a corrugated asbestos shelter, with a small canopy, and two wooden seats with concrete legs on the platform.

Surrounded by beautiful woodlands, the platform

Plym Bridge Platform. Looking north in about 1960 at the post 1949 concrete platform and corrugated asbestos shelter with canopy.

was visited extensively by Plymouth residents who travelled there both by ordinary trains and also by special services on bank holidays. These were sometimes known as Woolworths Specials, so called because the fare from Plymouth was 6d, the same price as any item in the store at that time! In its rebuilt form there was no lighting in its latter days and thus early morning and late evening trains did not call. Plym Bridge closed at the end of December 1962, with the withdrawal of passenger services on the line, and was subsequently demolished. Today some remnants of the concrete foundations of the platform can still be traced on the embankment above the car park. Plym Bridge is the ultimate northern goal of the Plym Valley Railway (see Marsh Mills text).

The following sets out a résumé of the history of the passenger railway network in the Plymouth/Devonport area. This should be read in conjunction with the diagram.

Passenger services came to the Plymouth area in May 1848 with the opening of the section of the South Devon Railway from Totnes to Laira Green, a temporary station on the eastern edge of the city. From here the line was extended in April 1849 to Plymouth's first main station at Millbay, at a site west of today's city centre. Some ten years later, in May 1859, the Cornwall Railway entered the city from the west over the Royal Albert Bridge terminating also at Millbay station. Through trains from Cornwall to Exeter and London had to reverse at Millbay; this manoeuvre was needed for 17 years until, in May 1876, a new west-east chord was opened north of Millbay. From March 1877 trains used the new Plymouth North Road station, sited just to the east of the chord.

To the east of the city an early development was the opening in June 1859 of a branch line north to Tavistock from the main Newton Abbot to Plymouth line at Tavistock Junction. This line was extended north to Lydford and Launceston in July 1865. The section of the branch from Lydford to Tavistock

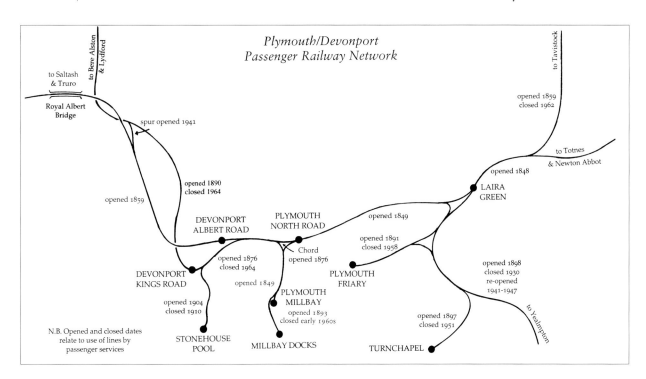

Plymouth Friary. A general view west of the site from the Tothill Road bridge on 5th July 1957, just over a year before the station closed to passengers. The covered footbridge at the east end of the platform has gone. To the left is the large goods shed.

Junction was, from May 1876, used by London & South Western Railway trains running from Exeter via Okehampton to its new terminus at Devonport Kings Road. This arrangement lasted for some 14 years until June 1890 when the Plymouth, Devonport & South Western Junction Railway opened south-west from Lydford to the Tamar Valley entering Plymouth from the west via Bere Alston, running through Devonport Kings Road. Services terminated initially at Plymouth North Road or Mutley and then, from July 1891, at the new Plymouth Friary station sited east of today's city centre.

Other developments in the passenger rail network of the Plymouth/Devonport area included lines to Millbay Docks in 1897 and Devonport Stonehouse Pool in 1904. Services on the former continued until the early 1960s but on the latter they only lasted six years. To the south-east of the city branch lines opened to Turnchapel in 1897 and to Yealmpton in 1898. The former closed in 1951 and the latter initially as early as 1930; however, it reopened from 1941 to 1947. The Tavistock line closed in 1962. The most significant event however was the closure of the Lydford – Tavistock – Bere Alston – Devonport line via the Tamar Valley apart from the section between Bere Alston and St Budeaux in the north-west of the city. Services to Gunnislake using the section of this line in Plymouth transferred to the main Cornwall line linking to the surviving Bere Alston section, in the Tamar Valley, at St Budeaux.

PLYMOUTH FRIARY

OPENED: 1st July 1891 (with the opening of the London & South Western Railway line Lipson Junction – Plymouth Friary).
CLOSED: Passengers – 15th September 1958.
Goods – 5th May 1963.

When the Plymouth, Devonport and South Western Junction Railway opened from Lydford via Tavistock and Bere Alston into the city in 1890, trains terminated for the first 13 months at Plymouth North Road, or occasionally at Mutley. Trains were only able to access the new LSWR Friary station complex following the completion of a chord between Lipson Junction and Mount Gould Junction in the east of the city. Services to the new terminus commenced on the first day of July 1891.

Ideally situated east of, and adjacent to, Plymouth city centre and principal shopping area, the grandeur of the building reflected its status as a main line terminus station. Built in part on the site of an old friary, it was sited in a triangle of land bounded by Beaumont Road and Knighton Road to the north, Friary Gate to the west and Exeter Street/St Judes Road and Desborough Road to the south. The far eastern section of the complex was spanned by a multi-arch stone bridge carrying Tothill Road.

The Plymouth Friary complex basically comprised, in its northern section, an impressive passenger terminus with good facilities for both main and branch line services and, to the south, a large goods yard with a range of facilities and good road/rail access. A half mile to the east, beyond the Tothill Road bridge, a motive power depot opened in 1908; in part this replaced an earlier engine shed sited at the south west end of the goods yard.

The principal station building on the up (north)

side, faced north, with access via two curved approach roads down from Beaumont Street. A long generally single storey structure constructed of rough blue limestone, it incorporated the main booking hall and office, a general waiting room, ladies' waiting room, refreshment room, bookstall and toilets. Access to the facilities was under a glass panelled canopy supported on two ornate cast iron pillars. The station building roof was in three sections covered by Welsh slate. There were four chimney stacks and a central 'spire' topped by a large weather vane. A matching set of buildings stood on the down (south) side, facilities here were principally for station staff.

The up and down platforms were joined at the western end by a short end platform; from the southwest of this platform a set of steps provided a second station access to Exeter Road. A covered lattice steel bridge also linked the platforms at the east end spanning three tracks. Much of the eastern sections of the two platforms were covered by large canopies supported by round cast iron pillars.

Six terminal tracks entered the station site from the east, the up and down main tracks adjacent to the platforms with a central track used both for stabling coaching stock and also for engine release from the two platform tracks. There were also two bay tracks at the east end of the two platforms for use by branch line trains, principally for the Turnchapel branch but also, for the 1941-1947 period, trains to Yealmpton. An additional track north of the branch bay on the up side was what was termed the 'scenery' bay, used by touring companies performing at Plymouth theatres. Peak use of Friary station was during the Second World War but high inter-war use is illustrated by the total number of passenger tickets issued and collected in 1928, 410,205.

South-east of the main station buildings was a large goods shed (300 ft x 100 ft). generally matching the other buildings in stone and with a Welsh slate roof, the apex was glazed laterally giving good interior light. Two sidings ran through the shed with another four on the south side and two to the north. Along the south edge of the goods yard a track led into a tunnel serving Sutton Harbour and North Quay until 1950. Operations both at the passenger station and in the goods yard were controlled by a signal box (demolished 1965) at the east end of the down platform.

The whole station complex generally survived the 1941 blitz with only superficial damage. Plymouth Friary closed for passenger traffic in September 1958. The whole complex was converted into Plymouth's main goods station. The goods shed was demolished in 1965 and a new freight concentration depot opened the following year. The main station building was demolished in March-May 1976. By the early 1990s the tracks had been truncated east of the Tothill Road bridge and the freight depot demolished. The whole station site has now been redeveloped west of the road bridge. On the south side is Friary Park, a complex of large warehouses; to the north is the Friary Court housing development, at the entrance to which, on Beaumont Road, stand two former station gate posts. The stone built former station master's house at the corner of Beaumont Road and Tothill Road has been modernised to become a doctor's surgery. In mid 2006 the land east of the road bridge lay generally derelict with two apparently disused sidings.

PLYMOUTH MILLBAY

OPENED: 2nd April 1849 (with the opening of the
Plymouth (Laira Green) – Plymouth Millbay section
of the South Devon Railway).
CLOSED: Passengers – 24th April 1941.
Goods – 20th June 1966.

Passenger services to Plymouth opened to a
temporary terminus at Laira Green on the eastern
outskirts of the city on 5th May 1848. It was nearly
a year before a double track extension of the
South Devon Railway (SDR) was completed to the
city's first permanent station in the Millbay area,
west of the city centre. Few details are recorded of
this first structure, known simply as Plymouth, but it
has been described by one historian as 'an
unpretentious wooden erection with the usual all-
over roof'. An extension of the line for freight only
opened south to Millbay Docks in 1850.

With the opening of the Royal Albert Bridge over
the River Tamar, the Cornwall Railway (CR) from
Truro came to Millbay station as from 4th May
1859. The extra traffic required extensions that
almost doubled the size of the facilities; completed in
1863 the development was a joint venture of the
SDR and CR. Further traffic into the station had also
been generated by local trains on the SDR Tavistock
branch opened in June 1859. A ticket platform,
north of the station, operated from 1851 to 1896,
the structure coming second hand from Starcross.
Being a terminal station meant that through traffic
between Cornwall, Exeter and London had to
reverse, bringing delays and operational difficulties.
The coming of the London and South Western

Railway (LSWR) to the city prompted the
construction of an east-west chord north of Millbay
linking the previous terminal lines from Exeter and
Cornwall running south into Millbay. This chord
opened on 17th May 1876, the same day as the
commencement of the LSWR service to Devonport.
A further development was the opening in March
1877 of the new Plymouth North Road station on
the SDR line just east of the chord. The new station
was a joint GWR/LSWR venture. At this point, to
avoid confusion, the suffix 'Millbay' was added to
the 1849 terminal station.

In spite of the competition of the new Plymouth
North Road station, extensive services continued to
serve Plymouth Millbay and a spacious new
limestone building was developed in 1899/1900 on a
site enlarged from the original, bordered now by
Adelaide Road and Bath Street. Much of the earlier
structure was demolished including the overall roof.
Three main lines and a shorter bay line were
provided, the two wide platforms being linked at the
buffer ends by a concourse covered by a vaulted roof
supported by lattice girders. Shelter at the outer ends
of the platforms was provided by large canopies and,
from 1907, a footbridge gave an extra link between
them. The two middle platform faces (2 and 3) were
used by main line trains and the outer two, including
the bay platform (1), were used by local trains. Other
early improvements included a new clock (1902) and
improved booking facilities (1906).

The impressive front of the terminus faced onto a
large forecourt available for associated road
transport links. A number of heavy wrought iron
gates with GWR monograms and impressive pillars
topped by tall lamps guarded the main road
entrances/exits. A large apex roofed canopy, or porte
cochère, provided cover outside the booking office
entrance. This canopy was removed in later years.
The station forecourt on Millbay Road was
overlooked by the large Duke of Cornwall Hotel,
built in the 1860s to cater for the new railway
generated passenger traffic, in particular those
transferring to and from transatlantic lines at
Millbay Docks. The scale of traffic at Millbay station
is illustrated by the 1,456,581 passenger tickets
issued in 1913. A figure of some 400,000 was more
usual by the 1930s.

To the north-west of the passenger station beyond
the link line to Millbay Docks, and bordering on
Bath Street, was the goods yard (including a 6 ton
capacity crane) incorporating a large goods shed
with ten 2 ton cranes. Built on the site of dwellings

Plymouth Millbay. The first standard gauge train leaves the
station in 1892 after gauge conversion. The photograph
shows the station as it was from 1859 to 1900, including an
overall train shed.

Plymouth Millbay. A general view of the station buildings in about 1912. Off to the left is the Duke of Cornwall Hotel. Note the tram lines.

in Bath Street, the 1860s shed replaced an earlier shed south of the station whose site was then used for the fish platform. An engine shed and extensive carriage sidings were also provided north of Millbay station towards Cornwall Junction. The engine shed closed in 1931 and was destroyed in a 1941 air raid. The 1914 Millbay signal box with 114 levers, sited north of the station on the down side, closed on 14th December 1969.

Bombing early in the Second World War severely damaged the goods station and the urgent need for alternative facilities led to the closure of Plymouth Millbay from 24th April 1941. The former station platforms were used for loading goods traffic. In 1958/59 the former station was converted into carriage sidings with the platforms removed. Millbay goods facilities closed in June 1966 and all tracks in the station area were taken out of use on 14th December 1969, apart from the link line to the Docks. This too closed as from 30th June 1971, all use of tracks south from Plymouth North Road ceasing on that date.

Today virtually all trace of Plymouth Millbay has gone, the site being occupied by the Pavilions Leisure Complex and associated car parks. Two of the original gate pillars remain as a small reminder of the railway with the Duke of Cornwall Hotel continuing to overlook the site.

PLYMOUTH MILLBAY DOCKS

OPENED: 1893 (with the commencement of passenger trains on the Millbay Docks branch).
CLOSED: Early 1960s (see text).

A rail connection to Millbay Docks was opened in 1850 and, for many years, the GWR unloaded mail from ocean liners at Plymouth for transport by train to Bristol and Paddington. From 1893 passengers were also taken off the boats. Tenders arrived at East Quay, the principal mooring point being in the outer basin of Millbay Docks at the end of Millbay Pier. No platform was provided, passengers entering and leaving the trains by means of portable steps. Passengers landed at this open wharf until 1905

Plymouth Millbay Docks. A view at the Docks station.

Plymouth North Road. A rare view west in about 1900 of the 1877 station before the major redevelopment completed in 1908. Two platform lines and two through lines pass through, the platforms covered by wooden train sheds and connected by a long footbridge. Longitudinal sleepers are still in place.

OPENED: 28th March 1877 (on the Totnes – Plymouth Millbay line originally opened through this site in 1849).

CLOSED: Passengers – remains open for services on the main line London (Paddington) – Exeter – Penzance and the Tamar Valley Gunnislake branch.

Goods: See text.

Plymouth North Road (suffix dropped on 16th September 1958 with the closure of Plymouth Friary), now the only main passenger station serving the city, was a relative latecomer on the railway scene, not opening until 1877. It continued to be subordinate for many years to Plymouth Millbay, opened 28 years earlier in 1849. Although Millbay was more than adequate for passengers whose origin or destination was Plymouth, its terminus layout resulted in through GWR trains between London and Cornwall having to reverse. The completion of an east-west chord in May 1876, eliminated this GWR manoeuvre and also enabled London & South Western (LSWR) trains to proceed direct to the terminus in Devonport.

The GWR thus wanted a station on the now direct route to Cornwall that eliminated the reversal at Millbay and the LSWR desired a station close to the city centre. The solution was the joint provision of the new station, Plymouth North Road, just east of the east-west chord and north of the city centre. Like Millbay, the original North Road station, opened in 1877, was constructed principally of timber.

Four lines passed through the station, two adjoining the platform faces and two through lines. A footbridge crossed the four parallel tracks. By the turn of the century facilities were proving inadequate and major extensions were constructed, completed in 1908. The redeveloped North Road station now comprised four long platforms, one each on the north and south sides and two island. These platforms served four through lines whilst another through line ran through in the centre between the two island platforms. The northernmost and southernmost tracks were served by two platform faces. There were also loading bays at the ends of the two side platforms whose use varied through the years. Two apex style wooden sheds (42 ft wide) sheltered passengers on the platforms, one to the north and one to the south, between these the centre tracks were uncovered spanned by 58 ft long transverse girders linking the two sheds. The

when it was covered. New facilities at this time included a waiting room with booking office. From April 1904 to May 1910 the GWR boat trains to and from Millbay had serious competition from the London & South Western Railway (LSWR) which had developed a station at Devonport Stonehouse Pool to handle boat trains to and from London Waterloo. Following an agreement between the LSWR and GWR these LSWR facilities ceased from 1910 (see Devonport Stonehouse Pool text). In 1930 the GWR Ocean Specials carried some 45,300 passengers. In 1936 improvements to the Docks station included a new reception hall with seats for 170 passengers, a buffet, facilities for the despatch of cables and telegrams and a money exchange. The floor covering incorporated the slogan 'Land at Plymouth and save a day'. In the late 1930s Plymouth dealt with an average of 500 liners per anum.

Goods traffic continued after the Second World War and in 1952 further new accommodation was opened for liner passengers; in 1957 19,203 passengers were carried on the boat trains. Thousands of West Indians landed at Plymouth during the 1950s. Early in the 1960s liners started to withdraw from Plymouth and complete boat trains ceased to operate, although some carriages were added to ordinary service trains at Plymouth North Road.

All rail traffic in the Docks was withdrawn as from 30th June 1971 and the Millbay Docks branch closed.

principal building on the down side, incorporating all the main facilities, was a long wooden structure with five tall chimneys; on the up side was a further wooden structure also with tall chimneys. The east section of the up platform was later provided with a long canopy extending out from the shed. A fine ornate footbridge connected the platforms in the centre of the sheds. A large building was sited to the west of the station on the down side; originally a parcel sorting office, it was converted into the central parcels office for Plymouth in 1928/29. In January 1938 it was moved a little to the east to permit widening of the road bridge; it closed in June 1957.

During the 1930s, as a contribution to the Government's New Works Scheme to relieve unemployment, the GWR drew up plans to completely rebuild the station. Before the onset of the Second World War some work was completed including the provision of a new platform on the northern side (1085 ft long) and a replacement East signal box, opened on 25th June 1939.

It was not until 1956 that British Rail commenced a £1.8 million modernisation scheme; the rebuilt station was opened by Dr Beeching on 26th March 1962. In its new form to cope with larger trains seven long through platform faces were provided with additional bays and docks for local passenger and parcel traffic. All structures were built in a then modern style including extensive glass and concrete canopies. A ten storey office block incorporating the Divisional Manager's office, erected above the booking office area, dominated the scene on the station's south side. The original 1930's scheme had envisaged separate passenger and luggage bridges but the post war work included the provision of subways.

In April 1974 the two through lines on the south

Plymouth North Road. A view from the station forecourt on the down side of the timber built main building with five tall chimneys. Note the transverse girder (left) linking the two apex style train sheds in this photo of the 1908 redeveloped station.

side were truncated in the middle of the station, two sets of two bay lines being created. A new platform filled the gap between the bay lines linking to the first island platform accessible now on the level under a pitched roof. The subway continued to give access to the remaining platforms. The format of the station operations has remained very similar since the 1974 changes, the bay lines being used primarily for parcels traffic. The bay line alongside the former island platform (no 3) is currently the only one regularly in use for passengers being the platform used by Tamar Valley trains to Gunnislake and local trains serving Cornwall. The through lines are signalled for bi-directional working ensuring maximum flexibility of platform use. Over the years no significant provision for goods traffic was provided at North Road station, the principal facilities for the city being at Plymouth Millbay and

Plymouth North Road. Looking west in about 1935. Ex LSWR 0-4-0T No. 232 is leaving the up side with a local passenger train.

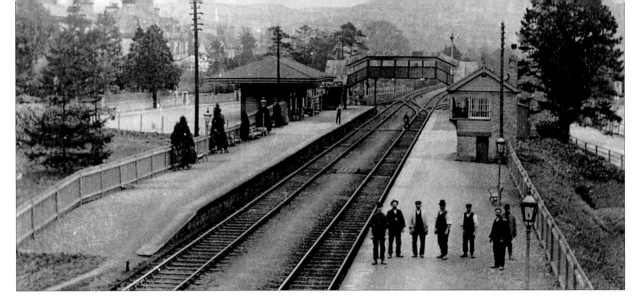

Plympton. Looking east in about 1912 towards the covered footbridge. The original 1848 platform and chalet type building stand on the up (towards Newton Abbot) platform. Staff pose on the down platform.

Plymouth Friary.

Prior to the post-war rebuilding, operations at the station were controlled by Plymouth North Road West signal box opened in 1904 and constructed in timber on a brick base. In January 1938 it was moved northwards in conjunction with the widening of the adjacent road bridge; some 38 ft by 13 ft, it had 59 levers. To the east, control was by the North Road East box originally opened in 1908 but replaced by a new box as from 25th June 1939. During the 1956-1962 modernisation of the station a new power signal box was built and opened on 26th November 1960. It was on the site of the large parcels office which had closed in June 1957.

PLYMPTON

OPENED: 15th June 1848 (on the Totnes – Plymouth (Laira Green) line originally opened through this site 6 weeks earlier on 5th May).
CLOSED: Passenger – 2nd March 1959.
Goods – 1st June 1964.

The station was sited in the centre of the village of Plympton, a settlement now absorbed within the large built up area of Plymouth. Trains began to run on the broad gauge single track line from Totnes to Plymouth on 5th May but records indicate the Plympton station did not open until 15th June (see also Brent and Ivybridge).

The original 1848 platform and chalet style building stood on the up side of the single track.

With the doubling of the track in 1893, a down platform and shelter were added. The canopy of this shelter was later extended to the platform edge. A pagoda style goods shed was also added on the up platform west of the building, as was an open wooden structure with a fretted roof east of the shelter on the down side. A footbridge with roofs over the span itself and the steps linked the eastern ends of the platforms. Unusually the footbridge retained its cover until the station closed. Dock sidings ran behind both platforms from the east. A 33 lever signal box stood on the down platform west of the shelter; this closed on 25th June 1967 and for some time was used by permanent way staff.

Plympton was at its peak in the 1920s with 8 staff based at the station; from 1904 to 1930 a steam rail-motor service ran from Plympton through Plymouth to Saltash. Despite the developing residential area around it, the station closed to passengers in March 1959, freight facilities continuing until June 1964. Today no line side trace remains.

PLYMSTOCK

OPENED: 5th September 1892 (with the opening of London & South Western Railway line, Plymouth Friary – Plymouth)
CLOSED: Passenger -10th September 1951
Goods – 7th October 1963.

Sited about a mile north-west of the centre of Plymstock, the station opened in September 1892 with the commencement of London & South Western Railway (LSWR) services from Plymouth Friary. The LSWR services were extended to Turnchapel from 1st January 1897. Plymstock became a junction station with the opening of the GWR branch to Yealmpton on 17th January 1898. To serve the two single line branches the two platforms at Plymstock formed a V or triangular configuration joining at the west (Plymouth) end.

The station building, with roof and walls constructed of corrugated iron sheeting, incorporated the booking hall and office, the station master's office, a goods/parcels office and a ladies' room. An additional lean to housed the gents' toilet. Wooden fascia boards and tall finials at each apex gave a decorative touch. The GWR platform for the Yealmpton branch featured a shelter with a rather ornate apex style canopy of vertical wood planks with wrought ironwork and also glazed end panels giving some protection from the wind. The LSWR Turnchapel platform had no cover though passengers no doubt used the adjacent GWR canopy! The Turnchapel platform was enhanced by five twisted spiral cast iron lamp standards. At one time Plymstock station enjoyed a service of over 60 trains a day on the two branch lines. This was reflected in the high passenger returns: in 1928 29,589 tickets were issued and 55,950 collected, the 1936 comparable figures were 21,827 and 30,298.

The original signal box, of LSWR design, stood on the up side of the line, just to the west of Plymstock Junction at the junction of the two branch lines. The box closed in July 1935, replaced by a new frame in the station booking office.

In 1941 incendiary bombs destroyed the station buildings, though the platforms survived. In their place were erected what was described by one commentator as 'a motley collection of hutments'. These included a booking office and waiting room and also a goods shed, both constructed of pre-fabricated concrete. A replacement signal box, attached to the concrete booking office, and also small gent's and ladies' toilets were built of lateral wooden planks under asbestos roofs. Also erected were a number of concrete lamp standards.

Passenger services ceased in 1951, a victim of bus competition. General freight facilities were withdrawn in October 1963 and the station buildings were demolished. After closure the station site continued to be used for sidings to a cement siding and a S.W.Gas Board depot. All tracks were lifted in 1994 and there is now no trace of Plymstock station, the area being redeveloped including new roads.

Plymstock. Looking south-east in about 1939. The central building has the Yealmpton branch shelter, with ornate canopy, on the left and the Turnchapel platform to the right, the latter features fine spiral cast iron lamp posts.

Polsloe Bridge Halt. Looking south in 1958 along the concrete down platform towards Exmouth. The earlier shelter is in the foreground and the later in the distance at the centre of the platform. This platform is now disused, trains only using the up platform (right).

POLSLOE BRIDGE HALT

OPENED: 1st June 1908 (on the Exeter – Exmouth line originally opened through this site in 1861).

CLOSED: Remains open for passenger services on the Exeter-Exmouth line.

The impetus for the opening of this halt, sited high on an embankment just south of where the Exmouth branch crosses Pinhoe Road, was the inauguration, in June 1908, of a steam rail-motor service from Exeter to Topsham. The line from Exmouth Junction south to Topsham had been recently doubled. The original wooden platforms, built at a cost of £243, only accommodated three carriages. They were replaced in 1927 by concrete components manufactured at the nearby Southern Railway Exmouth Junction works. These rebuilt platforms were much longer than the originals, the down (towards Exmouth) being 488 ft long and the up 607 ft. Also at this time original wooden steps up each side of the embankment to the platforms were

replaced by concrete steps. A concrete shelter was erected at the north end of the down platform. This was later supplemented by a small concrete shelter at the north end of the up platform at the head of the steps and a second concrete shelter, centrally sited, on the down platform.

The original ticket office at the foot of the steps served the down platform and was some distance from the path leading to the up on the other side of the bridge. Thus on occasions the ticket clerk left the office with a ticket rack to deal with customers for the up trains. In the 1950s a ticket booth was incorporated in the main down platform shelter, a small porch being added. The road side ticket office was generally closed, though it was opened at very busy times. These ticket facilities ceased in the 1960s, though early in that decade some 600 passengers still used the halt daily. The halt became unstaffed on 28th February 1965. The line was singled between Exmouth Junction and Topsham over the period 3rd-5th February 1973, the down track being lifted. Today trains on the Exmouth line use the former up platform, the small shelter at the Exeter end remains. The former down platform survives, some parts covered in vegetation, but the shelters have gone.

PORTSMOUTH ARMS

OPENED: September 1855 (on the Crediton –
    Barnstaple line originally opened through this site in
    1854).
CLOSED: Passengers – remains open as a request stop
    for services on the Exeter – Barnstaple line.
    Goods – 3rd July 1961.

Records indicate that the station opened in September 1855, just over a year after services commenced through the site on the North Devon Railway between Crediton and Barnstaple. In an isolated position beside the main Barnstaple road

Portsmouth Arms. The main station building is on the down (towards Barnstaple) platform in this view west of 1965. The station master's house is off left behind the short lamp post. A stone shelter serves passengers on the up platform.

(A377) in the River Taw valley, the station was named after the nearby public house, itself named after the 4th Earl of Portsmouth, a keen supporter of the railway (see Eggesford text).

Sited on a short crossing loop, there were two platforms, the main building standing on the down (towards Barnstaple) platform. A single storey two gabled brick building, it contained the booking, waiting and toilet facilities. Unusually for this line, it did not incorporate accommodation for the station master, which was provided in a separate substantial stone building at the Exeter end of the down platform, between the station building and the small goods yard. A stone waiting shelter served passengers in the centre of the up platform. Also on this platform, at the Exeter end, was a small stone goods shed. Both up and down goods trains called at this platform to transfer goods to and from this shed. There was no station footbridge.

The goods yard on the down side, at the Exeter end, with cattle pens and a five ton capacity crane had one long (272 yards) siding, which could accommodate some 40 wagons. As at a number of stations along this line, business was boosted at the station itself and yard by a monthly cattle auction that was held nearby for some years. Goods facilities were withdrawn in early July 1961 and the siding lifted at the end of 1963. A ten lever wooden signal box on a stone base, erected in 1873, stood on the Barnstaple end of the down platform. It ceased to operate from 3rd April 1966 when the line through the station was singled, the up platform becoming disused.

In 1928 4,997 passenger tickets were issued at Portsmouth Arms and 5,873 collected; by 1936 the figures had fallen to 3,357 and 4,042. A census held on 7th May 1963 showed that on that day 26½ passengers (1 child = ½ passenger) joined and left trains at Portsmouth Arms. Surveys over a week in the winter of 1976 and summer 1977 indicated that in those weeks 7 and 11 passengers used the station.

Today Portsmouth Arms is a request stop for Exeter to Barnstaple services, trains calling at the former down platform, which lost its main building some years ago. Today a metal and glass shelter serves passengers. The former up platform remains largely intact but is overgrown with weeds and shrubs. The impressive station master's house survives in private residential use. When visited early in 2007 a short stretch of track had been laid behind the down platform at the west end on which stood a carriage covered in polythene sheeting.

PRESTON PLATFORM

OPENED: 24th July 1911 (on the Torquay – Paignton line originally opened through this site in 1859).
CLOSED: 21st September 1914.

Serving nearby residential areas and the beach, and close to Seaway Road between Torquay and Paignton, the platform opened in July 1911. Its opening almost coincided with the withdrawal of the GWR bus service between Torquay and Paignton which had started seven years earlier on 11th July 1904. It is also thought that the halt was aimed to compete with the new tram service between the two resorts that had started a week earlier on 17th July 1911. Preston Platform comprised two 300 ft platforms each 8 ft wide; there was no footbridge. If inter-platform movement was required a road under the line was available. Corrugated iron huts stood on the platforms, one 30 ft by 9 ft, the other 20 ft by 9 ft. Preston was an early casualty of the First World War closing in September 1914. No photograph is known.

PRINCETOWN

OPENED: 11th August 1883 (with the opening of the Princetown Railway, Yelverton – Princetown).
CLOSED: Passenger and Goods – 5th March 1956.

At 1373 ft above sea level, the station, on the south-west edge of this Dartmoor town, was the highest in England. It opened with the start of services on the branch which left the Plymouth to Tavistock line at Yelverton. For the first two years there was no station at Yelverton and trains to and from Princetown used Horrabridge station north of Yelverton.

The layout at Princetown principally comprised a west-to-east platform track with a long parallel loop. Until 1928 there was a corrugated iron carriage shed at the far east end of these tracks. Also at the east end of the 170 ft long platform were cattle pens which were particularly busy at the time of the annual September cattle fair. At the west end of the loop points gave access to two long sidings which ran either side of the goods shed opposite the station. A further outer siding on the south side of the site served the engine shed, water crane and, with a reversal into a short siding, a 23 ft 6 inch turntable.

The station itself was on the north side of the line, the platform being of rock infill behind a granite face with a surface of tarmac and chippings. Along the platform at the west end was a white painted wood fence. Behind the east end similar wooden fencing was later replaced by concrete posts and a chain link fence. The rectangular station building was built of brick rendered with cement. The slate apex roof, topped with Staffordshire blue ridge tiles at one end and zinc plating at the other, was topped with two chimney stacks, one in the centre and one at the east end. Early photographs indicate there were once three stacks. Attached to the front central section of the building was a wide canopy with a vertical plank canopy giving cover right to the platform edge. At both ends were wooden screens across half the platform offering some protection to passengers from the often severe weather conditions. Along the

Princetown. In this view looking west towards Yelverton in about 1905, railway cottages are under construction behind the station building. Note the two wooden screens offering some protection to passengers on the platform.

Pullabrook Halt. Looking down on this small halt on 4th August 1955, about two months after its name was changed from Hawkmoor Halt.

platform side of the building were ten windows and three doors providing light and access to the rooms containing the usual waiting, booking and cloakroom facilities. The entrance to the gent's toilet was at the west end protected by a wooden screen. There were windows in the rear of the building but no doors, access to the platform being via a gate at the east end of the building.

Behind the station building was the station master's house and railway cottages. At the beginning of the twentieth century there were five staff based at the station. In 1903 11,535 passenger tickets were issued, the number increased to 12,679 in 1913 but this fell slightly to 10,665 in 1923 and 10,715 in 1933. The station was mainly used by residents travelling to and from Tavistock and Plymouth and also by visitors to Dartmoor. The inmates of the prison ceased to be conveyed on the branch after about 1930 except during, and soon after, the Second World War. Instead of using the Princetown branch, prisoners were conveyed on the Southern Railway route to Tavistock and then completed the journey by road.

The goods yard, opposite the station, incorporated a goods shed of similar construction to the main building. Large sliding doors under a canopy gave access to a 40 ft granite faced loading platform with ramps at either end. Inside the shed was a 2 ton capacity crane and outside, to the east of the shed, was a larger 5 ton crane. At the west end of the shed was the goods office behind which was the road access door under another small canopy. South of the goods shed was the single road engine shed built again of similar materials. Over its door at the western end was a large water tank supplying the nearby water crane. Movements at the station and in the yard were controlled from an unusual design two storey 14 lever signal box at the far west of the station site. The box was constructed of granite with an apex slate roof, the ridge formed of zinc sheets. Eight timber frame windows gave good visibility.

Both passenger and goods facilities were withdrawn in 1956 and the buildings were demolished during the summer of 1960. The station master's house and railway cottages survived and today continue in residential use. The station site itself remains undeveloped and when seen in May 2007 was in use for animal grazing.

PULLABROOK HALT

OPENED: 1st June 1931 (on the Newton Abbot – Moretonhampstead line originally opened through this site in 1866).

CLOSED: 2nd March 1959.

The halt was opened by the GWR in June 1931, aimed particularly at visitors to Hawkmoor Hospital, a T.B. sanatorium some three quarters of a mile away to the north-east, as the crow flies. It was also hoped to attract walkers on the nearby moorland. A further theory was that the halt was introduced on the line at this late date, some 65 years after the line opened between Newton Abbot and Moretonhampstead, to appease one of the GWR directors who lived at nearby Knowle. At its opening the name was naturally Hawkmoor Halt.

As from 13th June 1955 the name was changed to Pullabrook Halt, deriving from a nearby wood and farm. This change was made following complaints from visitors who found that Hawkmoor Halt was, in fact, some two miles by winding roads from Hawkmoor Sanatorium. Visitors and patients were brought to the halt by rail and some, but not all, were then conveyed by road to the sanatorium. Others were left to walk! Prior to the opening of the halt the nearest station was Bovey. As car travel became more common, arrivals and departures by rail decreased significantly; a further alternative was the bus from Bovey station to Moretonhampstead, which passed the sanatorium gates. It is not surprising that by 1957 an average of only 16 passengers joined or left the train at Pullabrook Halt.

The simple platform (48 ft x 8 ft) on the down (towards Moretonhampstead) side of the single line was earth filled, faced with old wooden sleepers and edged with boards. The platform surface was metalled, a low grassy bank at the rear being topped by a wire fence with wooden posts. At the south end of the platform the bank was cut away to accommodate a basic wooden shelter. Also provided was a wooden bench next to the shelter. The halt closed in March 1959 with the withdrawal of services on the line. Remains of the platform can still be seen.

RICHMOND ROAD HALT

OPENED: 1st May 1908 (with the opening of the Northam – Appledore section of the Bideford, Westward Ho! & Appledore Railway).
CLOSED: 28th March 1917.

A request stop between Northam and Appledore, on the outskirts of Northam, it opened on the second section of the Bideford, Westward Ho! & Appledore Railway at the beginning of May 1908. A short low (1 ft above rail level) platform with a waiting shelter was provided. It closed after less than nine years in 1917 (see Bideford Quay text). No photograph is known.

ROUNDBALL HALT

OPENED: 22nd September 1906 (on the Honiton – Exeter line originally opened through this site in 1860).
CLOSED: See text.

Sited half a mile west of Honiton station, the halt opened in September 1906 for the use by Territorial Army members using the nearby rifle range. No entry ever appeared in a public timetable and its removal was ordered in January 1921. No details of the facilities are known and the exact date of closure is not recorded.

ST BUDEAUX FERRY ROAD

OPENED: 1st June 1904 (on the Plymouth – Saltash – Truro GWR line originally opened through this site in 1859).
CLOSED: Passengers – remains open for very limited services on the Plymouth - Saltash line.

On the GWR Plymouth to Cornwall main line between Keyham and the Royal Albert Bridge over the Tamar, St Budeaux Halt opened at the beginning of June 1904. The trigger, as with many of the halts in the Plymouth area, was the commencement of steam rail motor services through the city from Plympton in the east to Saltash in the west. In 1906, when the name changed to St Budeaux Platform, the platforms were widened and lengthened to about 400 ft. A new booking office and waiting room were

St Budeaux Ferry Road. Looking east over the station in 1962 at the unusual number of huts and shelters on the platforms. Note the covered alcove between the long pagoda hut and toilet building on the up (towards Plymouth) platform.

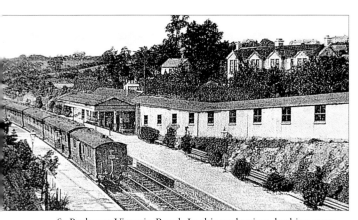

St Budeaux Victoria Road. In this early view, looking west, the main building is on the down (towards Plymouth) platform. The platform is accessed by a long inclined path (right) which, very unusually, is covered throughout.

provided on the up side. Over the years a number of small buildings served passengers on the two platforms including pagoda style huts and small buildings with roof ventilation incorporating toilet facilities. An unusual feature, on the up platform, was a covered alcove with pillars between the long pagoda hut and the toilet building. The suffix 'Ferry Road' was added from 26th September 1949.

Its role in serving a developing residential area is seen in the large increase in annual ticket sales from 88,000 in 1923 to 246,000 in 1938. The number of staff at Ferry Road increased from 4 to 5 over these 15 years.

Today St Budeaux Ferry Road has only a very limited service for local trains on the main line to Cornwall. Trains on the Tamar Valley line to and from Gunnislake call at the adjacent St Budeaux Victoria Road. A metal shelter serves Ferry Road passengers on the former up platform. The disused down platform remains in place.

ST BUDEAUX VICTORIA ROAD

OPENED: 1st June 1890 (with the opening of the Plymouth, Devonport & South Western Junction Railway, Lydford – Devonport).
CLOSED: Passengers – remains open for services on the Tamar Valley line, Plymouth – Gunnislake.
Goods – 11th December 1961 (except private siding).

Opening in June 1890 with the commencement of services on the Lydford to Devonport line via the Tamar Valley, St Budeaux (the suffix Victoria Road was added from 26th September 1949) was sited in

a cutting to the south of the community of St Budeaux in the north-west of Plymouth. At this time the local population was relatively low but residential development was rapid in subsequent years, generating considerable traffic. Just to the south was the GWR St Budeaux station opened fourteen years later in 1904.

The principal building, with an ornate canopy, was on the down[*] side (towards Plymouth); access was via a long inclined path which unusually was originally covered throughout. At the head of the path was the station master's house and booking office. A waiting shelter served passengers on the up side, in this case accessed via an open sloping path. In addition to main line Plymouth to Exeter services, St Budeaux, from 1906, was the northern terminus for steam rail motor serves from Plymouth Friary introduced in an attempt to combat competition from the city's tram service which had been electrified in 1901. In 1928 16,386 passenger tickets were issued and 36,604 collected; in 1936 the equivalent figures were 14,613 and 34,791.

St Budeaux goods yard, with a shed and cattle pens, was sited on the down side, a little to the south-east of the station. The yard closed to general traffic in December 1961. The original signal box, again south-east of the station on the down side beyond the road overbridge, was destroyed in an air raid in March 1941; its replacement closed on 25th July 1965.

The suffix halt was added to St Budeaux Victoria Road from 18th July 1965 when staffing ceased; the suffix was dropped as from 5th May 1969. Today only the former up platform is in use on the now single track Tamar Valley line (single from 7th September 1970); a modern brick shelter with a sloping metal roof provides cover. The down platform remains in place. Trains through St Budeaux on the Gunnislake service use the main GWR line from Devonport crossing to the former Southern Railway (SR) line via a spur just to the south of the station, a spur first introduced as a war time measure in March 1941. The SR route via Devonport Kings Road and Ford (Devon) closed on 7th September 1964.

[*] When the original through line operated from London to Plymouth the down side of the line at the station was for services towards Plymouth; when the line through this station became only a branch from Plymouth to Gunnislake the down side of the line changed to the Gunnislake direction. References in this account to the down and up side relate to the old through route situation.

ST JAMES PARK

OPENED: 26th January 1906 (on the Honiton – Exeter line originally opened through this site in 1860).

CLOSED: Remains open for passenger services on the Exeter – Exmouth line.

Sited on the Exeter to Honiton line between Exeter Central and Blackboy Tunnel, St James Park, when it opened in January 1906, was called Lions Holt Halt. The two platform halt, with a brick shelter on the up (towards Honiton) platform only, was built to serve passengers using the steam rail-motor service introduced on the Exeter – Whimple – Honiton line in 1906 and then the shuttle service to Topsham in 1908. The two platforms were originally both 119 ft long but the down platform was lengthened to 244 ft in May 1928. The name was altered to St James Park Halt on 7th October 1946, which reflected the name of the Exeter City F.C. ground which stands above the cutting on the down side. The suffix halt was dropped in 1969. Today, as St James Park, it is served by trains on the Exmouth branch. Small metal shelters serve passengers on both platforms.

SAMPFORD COURTENAY

OPENED: 8th January 1867 (with the opening of the North Tawton – Okehampton Road (Sampford Courtenay) section of the Devon & Cornwall Railway.

CLOSED: Passengers – 5th June 1972
Goods – 3rd April 1961.

REOPENED: 23rd May 2004 (for services operated by the Dartmoor Railway - see text).

The Devon & Cornwall Railway from Coleford Junction, on the Exeter to Barnstaple line, to Okehampton and Holsworthy opened in stages, the second of which was completed from North Tawton to this station in early 1867. The terminus status lasted over four years until October 1871 when the line on to Okehampton opened. In its initial terminus role it was appropriately called Okehampton Road but was renamed Belstone Corner when the line opened to Okehampton. It became Sampford Courtenay after a village more than a mile to the north, from 1st January 1872.

Despite its initial terminus status, the station was only provided with a modest single storey stone main building on the up (towards North Tawton) side incorporating the booking office and hall, waiting

St James Park. Looking down at the up (towards Honiton) platform brick shelter prior to October 1946 when the name was Lions Holt Halt. The Southern Railway notice to the left advertises a Wednesdays only excursion to Surbiton and London.

room and toilets. Unlike at Bow and North Tawton, no living accommodation was provided at the station though a separate station house was later provided to the east of the down platform. A wooden waiting shelter stood on the down platform. No footbridge was ever installed, inter-platform movements being either via a road overbridge at the north end of the station or via a rail level board crossing at the south end of the platforms. In 1928 2,981 passenger tickets were issued and 3,258 collected; unlike at many other stations in Devon the figures had only fallen slightly by 1936 to 2,755 and 3,152.

The goods yard to the south-west of, and behind, the up platform included five sidings and a large wooden goods shed. The shed had large wooden sliding doors and included a two ton capacity crane. The London & South Western Railway established

Sampford Courtenay. A general view south from a road bridge in 1963, the modest single storey building is on the up side (right). The large wooden goods shed is seen over the building.

an abattoir in the goods yard, one of a number the company erected in Devon. The abattoir came under the control of the Ministry of Food in the First World War and was leased out in about 1920. Sampford Courtenay signal box was on the south end of the up platform.

Goods facilities were withdrawn in April 1961 but the station remained open to passengers until June 1972 when the local service between Okehampton and Exeter was withdrawn. The through service to Plymouth via Bere Alston had ceased in 1968. The station was officially a halt from 12th September 1965 to 5th May 1969. The main building was only demolished in the late 1980s and the down side waiting shelter also survived for some years.

The up side platform was renovated to accommodate up to three carriages and reopened for services run by the Dartmoor Railway on 23rd May 2004. No shelter is provided. The down side platform survives but almost entirely covered in vegetation. The station house remains in residential use.

SAMPFORD PEVERELL

OPENED: 9th July 1928 (on the Taunton – Exeter line originally opened through this site in 1844).
CLOSED: Passengers – 5th October 1964.
 Goods – 9th September 1963.

Freight traffic was handled at this location long before passenger facilities were introduced. A single siding, on the up (towards Taunton) side of the Taunton to Exeter line, was known as Sampford Siding. Local requests for a halt from the village of Sampford Peverell, a mile to the west, were turned down in 1907. However, as a contribution to its programme for generation of extra traffic on the line,

the GWR operated a new halt at the siding site in July 1928. Two wooden platforms and shelters were erected. At the same time the siding was extended, the total cost being £2,130.

Further development came in the early 1930s. As part of the national scheme to relieve unemployment through major engineering work, the GWR undertook track quadrupling of a number of sections of the line between Taunton and Newton Abbot, thus increasing its capacity. At Sampford Peverell two long loops were added, alongside which concrete platforms with shelters were provided. A new signal box beyond the Exeter end of the up platform was erected, replacing an earlier box at the north end, whose site was used by the new down loop. The revised expanded facilities came into use in stages in February and March 1932. The new 50 lever signal box operated from 14th February 1932.

Although regarded as a halt by the surrounding community, it was never described as such in the timetable. This station status was reflected in the fact that staffing was available until 26th September 1955. Sampford Peverell became totally unstaffed, however, as from 3rd October 1960, except for the signalmen.

Freight facilities were withdrawn in September 1963; all sidings were taken out of use on 10th March 1968 and the signal box closed. Passenger services had ceased four years earlier in October 1964. The platforms and buildings were demolished and the site was abandoned for some twenty years until it was redeveloped as Tiverton Parkway station.

Sampford Peverell. This rare photograph looking south shows the 1930s changes in progress. The first signal box is in the foreground with the two original wooden platforms in the centre of the photo. The new concrete platforms, with concrete shelters, are nearing completion behind the old.

SEATON

OPENED: 16th March 1868 (with the opening of the
   Seaton & Beer Railway, Seaton Junction – Seaton).
CLOSED: Passengers – 7th March 1966.
   Goods – 3rd February 1964.
REOPENED: 27th August 1970 (see text).

Seaton. The original 1868 station building as seen in about 1905, including two storey station master's accommodation and the single storey building with two small chimneys. The building was described as 'more in keeping with a farmhouse than a railway terminus'.

Seaton. The art deco style second station at Seaton photographed on 13th March 1965. It is typical of Southern Railway architecture of the 1930s, found more usually at stations of that era in the London suburbs.

Unusually there is no record of public ceremonies to mark the opening of the Seaton branch line in March 1868. The station was sited on the west bank of the River Axe at the far east end of the sea front and shingle beach. Proximity to the beach was an important factor for Seaton, comparing favourably with the stations at Lyme Regis and Sidmouth, which were some distance from the beach and high above the towns. In 1877, to the east of the station, a bridge over the River Axe was constructed by the Seaton & Beer Railway to assist access from settlements east of the river. The less favourable aspect of the station's siting was that it was some way from the town centre, a particular problem when competition from road transport developed.

Initially the station comprised a very short wooden platform with two faces, that facing east used by the branch line trains and the other for storing carriages. In 1870 the platform was extended by 180 ft at a cost of £60. A long wooden shelter with a canopy stood at the south end of the platform facing east. No run round loop was provided at this stage, trains having to reverse out of the station to a short loop north of the platform so that locomotives could change ends. The station buildings, described by one railway historian as 'more in keeping with a farmhouse than a railway terminus', were at the far south end of the site. A two storey section at the east end was the station master's accommodation, whilst the main facilities were within a single storey section with two tall chimneys and a small porch. For many years Seaton was an 'open' station with down trains stopping at a ticket platform north of the station for tickets to be collected. This practice lasted until 1923, the time of railway company grouping.

Seaton's small goods yard, including a small goods shed, was to the west of the station. A five ton capacity crane was added in 1872. For a period up to rebuilding (see below) an overhead crane was installed to deal with stone traffic from nearby Beer but this business failed to come up to expectations. The principal inward traffic handled was coal for the adjacent gas works; goods out included pebbles from the beach. There was, from the early days, a small engine shed, coal stage, water tank, and cattle pens opposite the main platform.

Major redevelopment of Seaton station took place in the mid 1930s. The original station building was demolished and replaced by a new structure constructed mainly in concrete in an art deco style more typical of stations of that era built in the London suburbs. The single platform was retained and lengthened to accommodate up to 12 carriages, the eastern face continuing to be used by the branch trains for which a run round loop was now provided at the station. The original wooden shelter was replaced by a 300 ft long canopy covering part of the platform. The bay line to the west of the platform was again designated for carriage storage. The new run round loop gave access to a new engine shed sited at the terminal end of the station. Also built opposite the buffers end of the main platform face were a new water tower, coal stage and cattle pens. The only original building to survive was the goods

Seaton. Ex LSWR 0-4-0T No.207 stands with a branch train at the east side of the single platform of the original station in the early 1930s. The long wooden shelter is seen behind the engine.

shed, which received a cement rendering and was now more integrated with the rest of the station. Seaton signal box, originally to the north of the station at the entrance to the goods yard, closed on 28th June 1936. It was replaced by a 20 lever box behind the buffers of the bay platform line.

Throughout its life Seaton was busy with passenger excursions to the resort which began as soon as the station opened. On Whit Monday 1909 5,000 passengers arrived including a day excursion from Waterloo. The annual Seaton regatta brought much business to the station. Passenger numbers were boosted in 1935 by the opening of a Warners Holiday Camp adjoining the station to the west. In 1928 25,059 tickets were issued and 65,533 were collected; comparable figures for 1936 were 13,471 and 45,081. In August 1959 3,500 tickets were issued and 12,000 collected. Even in 1964 1,200 passengers used the station on summer Saturdays.

Goods facilities ceased at Seaton in March 1964 and the signal box closed on 2nd May 1965. Despite the continuing good level of traffic, particularly in the summer, passenger services ceased on the Seaton branch on 7th March 1966 and the station closed. The buildings were demolished in 1969, the site subsequently being used by an electronics firm which had closed when seen in 2005.

In 1970 the Seaton & District Tramway Co started to use much of the trackbed of the branch for a 2 ft 9 inch gauge tramway, much of the infrastructure transferring from an operation at Eastbourne. Its depot is at the northern end of the station site; the initial terminus was also there. A half mile extension was constructed and opened in 1975 to a site adjacent to the harbour car park, a little to the west of the old station site. A modern Victorian style terminus is provided for tramway passengers.

SEATON JUNCTION

OPENED: 19th July 1860 (with the opening of the Yeovil Junction – Exeter section of the London & South Western Railway).

CLOSED: Passengers – 7th March 1966.
Goods – 8th May 1967 (coal depot only from 18th April 1966).

Some three miles west of Axminster and south of the village of Shute, the station opened in July 1860 with the commencement of services on the last section of the London & South Western Railway (LSWR) from London to Exeter. Eight years later it became a junction station with the opening of the 4¼ mile Seaton & Beer Railway to the south coast resort. In a similar fashion to Sidmouth Junction, this station had a series of names in its early years, opening as Colyton for Seaton. It was renamed Colyton Junction at the opening of the branch but then soon changed again in 1869 to Seaton Junction, the last change in order to avoid confusion with Colyton on the branch line.

When the station originally opened it was on a passing loop on the otherwise generally single line. Doubling took place in about 1868. The main William Tite design building on the up (towards Axminster) side incorporated the station master's house and featured tall chimneys, steeply pitched roofs and an ornate platform canopy. A large hipped roof waiting shelter served passengers on the down platform. A covered footbridge connected the two platforms at the east end of the platforms. With the opening of the branch line a bay platform was added on the down side, at the west end of the down platform. Unfortunately trains from Seaton needed to run past the station and then reverse into the bay line. Reversal was also of course required for Seaton bound trains. An additional shelter with a canopy was provided at the west end of the platform for Seaton branch passengers.

In 1927/1928 the station was rebuilt to accommodate the widening of the line to four tracks, two through and two loops alongside platforms thus providing the only opportunity between Yeovil and Exeter for trains to overtake. The up platform and canopy were lengthened and the William Tite building was retained. On the down side however, there were major changes. The original platform and footbridge were demolished and a new V shaped structure created comprising a long down main platform and a branch line platform. No longer were

Seaton Junction. A general view looking north-west towards Honiton in 1958. The William Tite main building is on the up platform (right). The station footbridge crosses the now four tracks. On the down platform its base is in front of the 1927/1928 new building which also serves the branch line (centre left).

branch trains required to reverse. At the west head of the V was a new building containing a waiting room and toilets. The platforms were linked by a long concrete footbridge from the west side of the main building to the east side of the new down side waiting room. Another even longer concrete footbridge across the west of the station site carried a footpath from Shute to Lexhayne. In 1928 11,790 passenger tickets were issued and 14,397 collected; in 1936 the equivalent figures were 8,919 and 10,916. With the redevelopment a new 55 lever signal box came into use on 2nd April 1928 at the west end of the new down platform. This replaced an 1875 box at the west end of the bay platform.

The principal goods facilities beyond the west end of the up platform included a goods shed with a 40 cwt internal crane, cattle pens and also a five ton capacity crane. There were also sidings on the down side west of the station. Considerable rail borne traffic was generated by a large dairy, part of which adjoined the up platform at the west end. The goods shed was converted into a cooling shed for milk in April 1934.

Passenger facilities at the station ceased in March 1966, with the withdrawal of services on both the main line and the Seaton branch. General goods facilities were withdrawn from April 1966 but coal was handled until May 1967 and milk a little longer. The main line was singled from 11th June 1967 and the signal box also closed on that day. At the singling the former down through line was retained for use but in August 1972 it was slewed to the site of the former up through line. The former up loop line was retained as a siding until the 1980s.

Today the main station building survives including the metal framework of the former canopy. Over the years it has been occupied by a number of organisations and in June 2005 was used by the

Shaugh Bridge Platform. Looking north in about 1910 at the pagoda shelter standing at that time behind the original wooden platform.

Devon Training Centre. The former down platform also survives though scrub covered. The two footbridges remain in place, the longer one still in use carrying the footpath.

SHAUGH BRIDGE PLATFORM

OPENED: 21st August 1907 (on the Tavistock –
   Plymouth line originally opened through this site in
   1859).
CLOSED: 31st December 1962.

On a curve on the down (east) side of the line north of Bickleigh, Shaugh Bridge Platform served the village of Shaugh Prior, a mile to the east. It was also well used by day trippers from Plymouth, who came to the surrounding woods and to the nearby Dewerstone Rock. Indeed on bank holidays and sometimes in school holidays rail auto-coaches worked from Plymouth only to the Platform, not proceeding on to Yelverton. The 350 ft long platform was originally constructed of wood but was later replaced by an earth fill structure behind brick facing, with concrete slab edges and a chipping surface. The only building was a 20 ft x 8 ft corrugated iron pagoda style shelter incorporating a booking office and waiting room. Along the rear of the platform was a concrete post and wire fence; cast iron posts carried standards for oil lamps. At one time privately owned tea rooms were sited nearby but these closed prior to the Second World War. Shaugh Bridge closed to passengers at the end of December 1962 with the withdrawal of passenger services on the line. Today the platform survives together with a number of concrete fence posts.

SIDMOUTH

OPENED: 6th July 1874 (with the opening of the Sidmouth Railway, Sidmouth Junction – Sidmouth).
CLOSED: Passengers – 6th March 1967.
Goods – 8th May 1967 (coal depot only from 6th September 1965).

Opening in July 1874 as the terminus of the Sidmouth Railway, the station was sited nearly a mile inland in the north-west outskirts of the town at some 300 ft above sea level. Local historians suggest

Sidmouth. The station forecourt in about 1910 with a number of horse drawn carriages. The rear of the 1900 engine shed can be seen in the distance.

that the coming of the railway had less impact than at many resorts, as Sidmouth had been the destination for fashionable visitors for many years. It has also been suggested that the siting of the station some distance away from, and above, the beach was deliberate in order to discourage day trippers from coming to the town! More relevant was that engineering work to take the line further into the town would have been costly. From the outset horse buses and then motor buses provided regular services from the station to the town and beach.

Despite these concerns, the town celebrated the arrival of the railway over four days: 6th-9th July 1874! On the opening day some 800 school children marched up hill from the esplanade behind a band and then saw the 2.45 p.m. train depart to the sound of 'loud and long cheers'. They then moved to a nearby field where teas were served for young and old. Subsequent events included a dinner at the Town Hall on the 7th, special trains on the 8th, Regatta Day, and a public dinner for 400 elderly residents on the 9th. There was also a distribution of half crowns and portions of plum pudding.

The attractive terminus was a red brick built structure comprising a two storey house for the station master at the south end and a single storey northern section containing the main station offices. Over the west facing main station entrance of two arched doorways was a small wooden fretted canopy. Behind this entrance was a south to north island platform with a canopy supported by decorative brackets and cast iron pillars. The canopy was extended at the north end in 1935. The east face of the island platform could accommodate seven carriages and the west five carriages. The longer main platform had an engine release track but the shorter did not.

To the west of the platform was an engine shed and turntable. The original wooden shed was badly damaged by a fire on 7th January 1900. The brick replacement was built on the original foundations and thus the shed did not increase beyond its original one tank engine capacity. The replacement shed, with a roof top ventilator was little used and closed in the mid 1930s. Close to the engine shed was a loading dock and a water tank fed from a nearby reservoir.

To the east of the platform was Sidmouth goods yard, which included a large goods shed with a goods office at the southern end. The shed contained a two ton capacity crane. On the eastern edge of the yard a siding served a number of premises owned by

Sidmouth. The main station buildings in about 1965. The buildings on this elevation are virtually unchanged today, over 40 years later. The station master's house (right) continues in residential use

local businesses. Coal was an important import into the yard but also handled were building materials, agricultural products and general merchandise. The goods shed remained in use until general goods facilities were withdrawn at Sidmouth in September 1965; coal was handled until May 1967.

From 1905 a tall signal box stood at the north end of the station on the east side. With 23 levers, the box controlled movements at the station itself and in the goods yard. This replaced an earlier box close to the engine coaling stage. A siding to the gas works east of the station ran behind the signal box. This was provided in the 1930s. Prior to this, coal for the gas works was unloaded in the goods yard and delivered by horse drawn carts.

Sidmouth had relatively high volumes of passenger traffic. In 1928 30,253 passenger tickets were issued, the total fell to 16,368 in 1932 and 14,916 in 1936. In the same three years the number of tickets collected was 57,432, 35,244 and 37,910. Prior to the First World War the London & South Western Railway operated three or four excursions each week from Waterloo to Sidmouth in addition to the through coaches detached from trains at Sidmouth Junction. A through train from Cleethorpes, introduced in 1960, running via Bath and Templecombe only lasted for three summers. In the mid 1960s up to one hundred passengers used the station on summer weekdays and this could rise to some nine hundred on summer Saturdays. In 1964 a local Hotel & Catering Association survey showed that up to 20% of visitors to the town used the train.

Despite this use the Sidmouth line closed to passengers in March 1967.

Today much of the station survives with buildings in various uses within an industrial estate. The station building is relatively unchanged at the front and part of the platform canopy survives. The station master's house is in private residential use. The goods shed is occupied by a firm of builders merchants.

SIDMOUTH JUNCTION (FENITON)

OPENED: 19th July 1860 (with the opening of the Yeovil Junction – Exeter section of the London & South Western Railway).
CLOSED: Passengers – 6th March 1967.
 Goods – 6th September 1965.
REOPENED: Passengers only - 3rd May 1971.

At that time about a mile west of the village of Feniton, the station opened in July 1860 with the commencement of services on the last section of the London & South Western Railway (LSWR) route from London to Exeter. Fourteen years later it became a junction station with the opening of the branch line to Sidmouth via Ottery St Mary and Tipton St Johns. In 1897 a further line opened from Tipton St Johns to Budleigh Salterton and then on to Exmouth in 1903. All main line LSWR trains stopped at the station, including famous express trains such as the Devon Belle and Atlantic Coast Express. Carriages were also detached here for onward travel to Tipton St Johns, where they were again divided either for Sidmouth or Exmouth.

The station experienced more name changes than any other in Devon, reflecting its varying role. Opened as Feniton in July 1860, it became Ottery & Sidmouth Road from 1st July 1861, Feniton for Ottery St Mary in February 1868, Ottery Road in April 1868 and Sidmouth Junction from 6th July 1874. The last coincided with the opening of the Sidmouth line. When the station reopened in May 1971 (see below) the name reverted to the original Feniton.

The large and impressive brick built William Tite design building, incorporating at the west end the station master's house, and featuring tall chimneys, steeply pitched roofs and an ornate canopy, stood on the down platform. The building housed the main station offices, two waiting rooms (one for ladies) and the booking office. A large hipped roof brick waiting shelter served passengers on the up (towards

Sidmouth Junction. A westward view with the William Tite design main building on the down (towards Exeter) platform. A hipped roof shelter stands on the up platform. A covered footbridge connects the platforms at the west end, close to a level crossing.

Honiton) side. A covered footbridge linked the two platforms at the west end close to the level crossing carrying a minor road from Payhembury to Ottery St Mary. The level crossing gates were worked from a small gate box equipped with five levers sited on the west side of the crossing alongside the down line. This box had originally been on the up side. The gateman could not open the crossing gates until the locking had been released by the signalman in the main signal box. This box, dating from 1875, was sited east of the station alongside the up main line and up side siding, the latter running behind the east end of the up platform. The siding was often used by goods trains awaiting a path to travel up the Honiton bank.

With the introduction of Sidmouth branch line trains, a bay platform was developed at the rear of the east end of the down platform. However no engine release track was provided, trains having to reverse out of the station to a loop where engine run round was possible; this could be accomplished without fouling the main line. With the development of the bay platform the canopy, originally only in front of the building, was extended to the east to also provide shelter for passengers at the buffers end of the bay line. For some years there was a W H Smith bookstall on the platform but no refreshment facilities were provided.

Sidmouth Junction. No.82024 stands at the head of a train in the Sidmouth branch bay platform in 1962. To its left is the goods shed.

Passenger numbers at Sidmouth Junction were never at a very high level with inter-change being of equal or more importance. In 1928 20,015 passenger tickets were issued and 22,489 collected. By 1936 the equivalent figures had fallen to 13,373 and 16,061. At its peak some 20 staff were based at the station.

The goods yard, sited behind and south-east of the main building, included a goods shed with a 30 cwt crane, stores and cattle pens. The track through the goods shed led to a loading dock. A five ton capacity crane was also provided in the yard which handled bricks, coal, stone, timber, lime and agricultural machinery inwards, and milk, potatoes, sugar beet and cider apples outwards. A turntable was at one time sited between the main down line and the branch line; it was little used and was removed in about 1930.

Goods facilities were withdrawn in September 1965 and the station closed entirely in March 1967 when services to Sidmouth and Exmouth via Tipton St Johns were withdrawn. Local services on the main line had ceased earlier on 7th March 1966. The signal box (31 levers) closed on 21st May 1967 after the final freight workings on the branch line stopped. The line through the station was singled from 11th June 1967.

After strong local pressure the station reopened in May 1971 with the original name of Feniton, the first to reopen on the line between Salisbury and Exeter. All trains now used the down platform which was halved in length just before reopening. Until 1974 tickets were issued from the level crossing gate box but in that year an office and shelter were erected on the platform, the fine buildings and goods shed having been previously demolished. In 1992 the platform was reconstructed and lengthened in preparation for the arrival of the new Turbo trains on the line.

Today a green metal office with a 'Sidmouth Junction' nameboard and also a metal and glass shelter stand on the down platform. The former up platform remains but unused with no track alongside. New housing (Signals) covers the former goods yard and site of the old bay line; housing has also been built close to the rear of the up platform. The level crossing west of the station is protected by lifting barriers, installed in 1974, and operated from the platform building. At that time the crossing box was closed.

Silverton. Looking north along the up (towards Taunton) platform in the early 1960s, showing the wooden building with barge boards and attractive gardens. The original signal box still stands beyond the building; its 1928 replacement can be seen on the down side in the far distance.

SILVERTON

OPENED: 1st November 1867 (on the Taunton – Exeter line originally opened through this site in 1844).
CLOSED: Passengers – 5th October 1964.
   Goods – 3rd May 1965.

Sited over one and a half miles south-east of the village, Silverton station opened at the beginning of November 1867, over 23 years after service on the Bristol & Exeter Railway commenced through the site. Up Exe Halt on the Exe Valley line, between Stoke Canon and Tiverton, was much closer to the village but the advantage for Silverton was that it was served by trains on the main Bristol to Exeter line. The station had staggered platforms; the up (towards Taunton) being to the north of a road over bridge that today carries the Silverton to Broadclyst road, and the down to the south. A compact wooden building with attractive bargeboards and finials, but no canopy, stood on the up platform and incorporated the main station facilities, the gent's toilet being at the north end. A small metal hut stood at the south end of the platform close to the bridge. Attractive gardens were a feature of this platform, behind which was the station master's house. Passengers on the down platform were served by a small waiting shelter at the extreme north end, accessed by a flight of steps linked to the road bridge.

Passenger numbers remained relatively steady between 1903 and 1933. In the first, 8,656 passenger tickets were issued; the figure fell to 7,030 in 1913 but recovered to 8,594 in 1923 before falling slightly to 8,098 in 1933.

Snapper Halt. A view of the single platform and shelter looking up (towards Barnstaple) in about 1930. It survives today.

South Molton. Looking down (towards Barnstaple) in the 1920s. On the down platform is the main building, including two storey accommodation for the station master, and the 1901 signal box. Beyond the building is the goods shed.

Silverton goods yard, sited opposite the up platform and served by a goods loop, incorporated a small goods shed at right angles to the loop and a four ton capacity crane. From this yard a half mile long siding led south to a large paper mill. The siding opened on 26th July 1894 and continued in use until 31st August 1967. Records suggest that an even earlier siding had been laid to the mill in 1864 before the station opened.

The original signal box stood on the up platform north of the building. From 21st November 1928 this was superseded by a new box north of the station on the down side. This box was fitted with a 30 lever frame from Dunkerton colliery in Somerset. This second box closed on 12th May 1968.

Passenger services ceased at Silverton in October 1964 and goods facilities were withdrawn less than a year later in May 1965. Today there is no lineside trace of the station, the former goods yard now part of a farmyard. The station master's house survives in residential use.

SNAPPER HALT

OPENED: February 1903/May 1904 (on the Lynton - Barnstaple line originally opened through this site in 1898).
CLOSED: 30th September 1935.

Sources disagree on the opening date of this halt, varying between February 1903 and May 1904. Sited close to the hamlet of Yeotown, the halt was named after a former inn about a quarter of a mile to the north. Snapper Halt was not in the original prospectus of the Lynton & Barnstaple Railway (L&BR) but was constructed at the request of the residents of Goodleigh, half a mile to the east, a village that generated most of the revenue at the halt. Trains only stopped by request (and never after dark) at Snapper, sited on the up (towards Barnstaple) side of the line. The platform surface was of asphalt with the edge defined by bricks. A small rendered brick hut provided limited shelter. Following closure an L&BR carriage was, for some reason, left at the halt. After falling into disrepair, it was eventually burnt. The shelter is still there today.

SOUTH MOLTON

OPENED: 1st November 1873 (with the opening of the Wiveliscombe – Barnstaple section of the Devon & Somerset Railway).
CLOSED: Passengers – 3rd October 1966.
Goods – 3rd August 1964.

Sited about a mile north of the town centre in the River Mole valley, South Molton was one of only three passing places on the whole Devon & Somerset Railway (D&SR) (Taunton to Barnstaple) when the second section of the D&SR opened in November 1873 from Wiveliscombe to Barnstaple. The other two were in Somerset at Wiveliscombe and Dulverton. The opening of the line was a cause of much celebration in South Molton, including a lunch for over 500 guests.

The loop line was extended at the east end in 1907 and again at both ends in 1937, the latter one of many improvements on the line in that year. The initial 464 ft long two platforms were also extended.

On the down (towards Barnstaple) platform a substantial stone building was provided by the D&SR, comprising a central two storey house for the station master and two lower wings, that to the east including an open front waiting area. This main structure incorporated a booking office, waiting room, ladies' room, parcels office and the station master's office. The gent's toilet was in a flat roof annex at the extreme west end of the building. The 1907 improvements included the provision of a new waiting room and screen. On the up platform stood a small wooden waiting shelter with a roof sloping towards the line, the front of which formed a very small canopy. No footbridge was ever provided at South Molton, passengers and trolleys crossing the line by a rail level board crossing at the west end of the platforms. In 1911 a request from the local council for a footbridge was turned down. Lighting at the station was converted from paraffin vapour to gas in 1936. In 1903 24,099 passenger tickets were issued at South Molton; by 1933 the figure had fallen greatly to 8,978. In 1903 12 staff were based at the station, the total fell to nine by 1933.

South Molton goods yard was on the down side behind and west of the platform. The substantial stone goods shed (60 ft long) with a through track and two ton capacity crane, was close to the west end of the platform. The yard included a 140 ft long loading bank to the west of the goods shed, a number of cattle pens at the west end and, initially, a three ton capacity crane. By 1938 the capacity of the crane had risen to five tons. Along the southern side of the yard, sidings served a number of private traders. In 1945 the GWR purchased these private siding facilities. The monthly Great Market and biennial sheep fairs provided much business both for the goods yard and the station itself. Much local produce was carried and, at the peak, some 600-700 wagons were handled per month. From 2nd May 1928 the down platform was signalled also for the passage of up trains; this allowed goods traffic, carried on the passenger trains, to be nearer to the main goods yard where transfer to road vehicles was easier. It also reduced the need for passengers to cross the rail level boards to access trains towards Taunton.

Initially the signal box was an elevated wooden structure at the west end of the down platform, immediately in front of the goods shed. It was replaced, probably in 1901, by a substantial brick box with a slate roof and one chimney, on the down platform east of the main building.

Starcross. Looking up (towards Exeter) in the early 1960s. Note the unusual design shelter on the down side protecting passengers in this exposed position above the sea. The footbridge still has its roof. Passengers for Exmouth use the cross river ferry.

Following closure of the station to goods in August 1964 and to passengers in October 1966, the main station building survived until about 2003. The North Devon Link Road (A361) now passes through the northern edge of the former station site. In spring 2007 the former goods yard, including the shed, was used by South Molton Concrete in the Pathfields Industrial Estate.

STARCROSS

OPENED: 30th May 1846 (with the opening of the Exeter – Teignmouth section of the South Devon Railway).

CLOSED: Passengers – remains open for local services on the Exeter – Newton Abbot line.
Goods – 4th December 1967 (coal depot only from 6th September 1965).

The construction of the South Devon Railway (SDR) along the sea front at Starcross undoubtedly hindered the ambition of the village to develop as a resort. Opening with the line in 1846, the original wooden station on the landward up side of the line was sited on a loop, the main through line being on the sea side on the alignment of the current down line. The second down platform, only five feet wide, was erected on the sea wall in 1848. In the early years, up to 1906, a wooden train shed covered the tracks. The large shelter on the down platform was unusual and unique on the GWR, the design being clearly to provide maximum protection for passengers in this very exposed location. A covered

footbridge was erected in 1895. Though losing its roof, the basic structure stood for over 100 years until replaced by another open bridge in 1999. The up platform was extended by 200 ft in 1931. Until the opening of the Exeter – Exmouth branch in 1861, Starcross provided the rail service for Exmouth, a ferry running across the River Exe. This ferry service continued however for many years after 1861, the nameboard at Starcross bearing the words 'for Exmouth'.

Starcross was the location of one of Brunel's pumping stations, operating his atmospheric system in 1847 and 1848. The pumping station to the south of the station on the down side remains today. A siding was laid to bring coal to operate the pumps; this siding remained in use until 1899. An adjacent public siding came into use in 1851 and remained in use for many years. Following the abandonment of the short lived atmospheric system, the pumping house has had a number of uses: the upper floor was a Methodist chapel from 1869 to 1958 and then a youth club; the ground floor was used by a coal merchant from 1858 to 1981. The building was listed in 1979 and became a Museum of Atmospheric Propulsion. In 1993 it was sold to a sailing club and today it houses the Starcross Fishing and Cruising Club.

The 1874 signal box, south of Starcross station on the down side, was built when the SDR line on to Dawlish was doubled. The 1918 tall replacement box (28 levers) on the same site closed on 16th December 1971. Staffing ceased at the station on 3rd May 1971. General goods facilities were withdrawn in September 1965, a coal depot continued until December 1967.

The original wooden building on the up side was demolished in 1981 replaced by a small open shelter. Today there is no shelter on the down platform. The 1999 footbridge remains. Nearby behind the up platform, the 'Atmospheric Railway Inn' is a clear reminder of the very early days of the SDR line.

STAVERTON

OPENED: 1st May 1872 (with the opening of the Buckfastleigh, Totnes & South Devon Railway, Totnes - Ashburton).
CLOSED: Passengers – 3rd November 1958.
  Goods – 10th September 1962.
REOPENED: 5th April 1969.

Sited in an east-west part of the River Dart valley and about a half mile west of Staverton village, this small station opened at the beginning of May 1872 with the commencement of services on the Totnes to Ashburton branch.

The platform was on the northern side of the single track behind which were the station building and two goods sheds. The small building was brick built with an apex roof of timber planks covered with slates. On the road side was a central doorway approached by a short flight of steps and flanked by two small windows. On the platform side a doorway opened into a central porch, which acted as an additional waiting area. With one chimney at the west end of the roof, the building incorporated the station master's office, a general waiting room, a ladies' waiting room, the booking office and toilets. In 1903 9,994 passenger tickets were issued; equivalent figures were 1913 (9,797), 1923 (10,935) and 1933 (7,298). In the 1920s the station staff were the station master, two porters/signalmen and a junior porter.

The two goods sheds were also built of brick with slate roofs. The first, immediately to the east of, and in line with, the station building, had no windows but had two heavy sliding doors opening out on to the platform in its southern and eastern sides. This shed was used particularly for goods carried on passenger trains. The second goods shed, further east again, was set back from the building line to permit the provision of a siding serving it on its southern side. This second shed, used particularly for goods carried on freight trains, also had two heavy wooden sliding doors, in this case opening out on to a loading bay, one at each end. Two further sliding doors gave access both on the road side and on to the platform. Finally, at the west end of the platform was a small metal lamp hut.

The track layout serving the station and shed was simple with a through line and one siding running west across a level crossing at the east end of the station serving the goods shed. A small spur left this siding in an easterly direction. Immediately west of the level crossing, on the south side, was a small vertical wooden plank signal box with an apex roof, asbestos slates and ridge tiles.

Passenger services ceased with the closure of the line to passenger traffic in November 1958; goods facilities survived until September 1962. The station reopened as Staverton Bridge for services run by the Dart Valley Railway in April 1969 (see Ashburton and Buckfastleigh texts); in the very early years it was the southern terminus of operations. The former station building has been carefully restored; the two goods sheds and metal hut are still there. The signal box has been restored to its place after ten years in a local vicar's garden! The suffix Bridge fell into disuse in the 1980s. Staverton is now flourishing on the now South Devon Railway.

STEER POINT

OPENED: 17th January 1898 (with the opening of the GWR branch, Plymstock – Yealmpton).
CLOSED: Passengers and Goods – 7th July 1930.
REOPENED: 3rd November 1941 (for use by Plymouth residents evacuated during the Second World War).
CLOSED: Passengers – 6th October 1947.
Goods – 29th February 1960.

Sited at a point where the Yealmpton branch turns from a southerly to an easterly direction up the River Yealm estuary towards Yealmpton, Steer Point was one of the busiest stations on the branch both for passenger and goods traffic. One reason for use by passengers was that from a landing place on South Creek adjacent to the station, travellers could transfer to a ferry serving Newton Ferrers and Ness

Steer Point. A steam rail motor on the Yealmpton branch is at the platform in about 1910. Beyond the station is the estuary of the River Yealm.

Mayo, two settlements further down the estuary with poor road links to the Plymouth area.

Opening in January 1898 when services commenced between Plymouth Millbay and Yealmpton, on what was sometimes known as the South Hams Railway, Steer Point was sited on the south side of the single line. There was no loop line at this point. The original wood plank platform with trusses was subsequently replaced by an earth filled structure with large paving stone edging. The station building, of corrugated iron with wood ribbing contained a waiting room, booking office and toilets for ladies and gentlemen. In 1903 12,249 passenger tickets were issued at Steer Point. Comparable figures for 1913 and 1923 were 15,739 and 11,867. Along the rear of the platform were iron railings which bordered the road into the goods yard, located east of the station on the south side of the line.

A small goods shed stood in the yard. A large amount of freight was handled at Steer Point, the greatest amount being various types of brick (including GWR bricks) from the South Hams Brick Works, sited to the south of the station. Coal was imported for use at the brickworks. Trade in oysters from the nearby fishery also generated traffic. Two ground frames controlled movements into and within the yard.

Following closure in 1930, the station building fell into disrepair but, for the reopening of the line between 1941 and 1947 (see Yealmpton text), it was renovated and reused. Unlike Billacombe, Brixton Road and Yealmpton on the branch, the Steer Point building had not been let for residential use after the 1930 closure.

The platform edge survived into the 1990s, as well as the old gates of the goods yard, but today the site is overgrown.

STOKE CANON

FIRST STATION
OPENED: c 9th September 1852 (on the Taunton – Exeter line originally opened through this site in 1844).
CLOSED: 1st July 1894.

SECOND STATION
OPENED: 2nd July 1894.
CLOSED: Passengers – 13th June 1960.
Goods 3rd May 1965.

The first Stoke Canon station was in the centre of the village, straddling a level crossing carrying the minor road from Stoke Canon to Up Exe. The platforms were staggered, the up (towards Taunton) being north of the crossing and the down to the south. The main station building stood on the down platform. To the north of the crossing, also on the down side, was an 1876 18 lever signal box, which controlled the crossing gates with a wheel. A small waiting shelter in an alcove served passengers on the up platform. There was no footbridge. The station opened on the Bristol & Exeter Railway some eight years after services commenced through the site; timetables indicate that for the first ten years the services using the station were intermittent, only on certain days of the week. By the late 1860s, however, mixed gauge had been laid through Stoke Canon allowing the station to be used by both broad and standard gauge trains.

When the Exe Valley line to Tiverton opened in 1885 the junction with the Bristol & Exeter line was a quarter of a mile south of the 1852 station. The GWR thus decided to relocate Stoke Canon station just to the south of the junction so that it could be served by both mainline and Exe Valley line trains. This second station opened in July 1894. The two platforms of this second station were directly

Stoke Canon. Looking north in October 1924 a branch line train from the Exe Valley line approaches the down platform. In the distance (right) is the goods shed and beyond that again is the site of the original 1852 station.

opposite one another, both being some 475 feet long (later reduced to 400 ft). The main station building, with an ornate fretted horizontal canopy and one chimney again stood on the down side. A wooden parcels office was sited to the north of the building behind the platform. A matching, but smaller, waiting room served passengers on the up platform.

In the early 1930s sections of the GWR main line between Taunton and Newton Abbot were quadrupled, one of a number of major schemes on the railways undertaken at that time in response to a Government initiative to relieve unemployment. One such section was through Stoke Canon station which was again rebuilt, this time to accommodate five tracks: up and down main through tracks, up and down main platform tracks and, on the far up side, a track to and from the Exe Valley line. Two long platforms were erected, that on the down side having one face, and an island platform on the up side, having two faces, one for the main line trains and one serving Exe Valley trains. The platform face of the last at the north end was shorter than the main line face. Exe Valley trains joined the main line tracks south of the station. Opened in March 1932, rather austere brick buildings served passengers on the two platforms; the main building again on the down side. A new brick signal box (57 levers) opened on the south end of the up platform, commissioned on 19th July 1931. This replaced an earlier box just north of the junction on the up side of the main line.

In 1903 13,288 passenger tickets were issued at Stoke Canon. Virtually the same number (13,292) were issued in 1913 but subsequently the figure fell greatly to 8,974 in 1923 and 5,131 in 1933. Nine staff were based at the station for most of the 1920s and 1930s.

Throughout all these changes, the goods facilities at Stoke Canon stayed in the same location, just to the south of the first station on the down side. Served by two goods loops, the yard incorporated a goods shed and a six ton capacity crane. An original small engine shed was closed in 1879 and, during the 1890s redevelopments, was converted into a goods shed. This replaced an earlier shed which was demolished.

Being sited from 1894 a little way south of the village which, through the years, enjoyed a good bus service, Stoke Canon station was an early casualty, closing to passengers in June 1960, some three years before passenger trains ceased on the Exe Valley line. Goods facilities continued to operate however, for another five years until May 1965 when the station signal box also closed. The signal box adjacent to the level crossing at the site of the first station remained in operation however until 9th December 1985. The gates had been replaced by lifting barriers on 8th September 1974. This box survives today, though boarded up, and is the last box of Bristol & Exeter origin. The 1930s station building also survives today, behind a fence. Housing has been built on part of the former goods yard.

Stoke Canon. A general view north in about 1933 after reconstruction had been completed alongside the now four track line. The main building is on the down platform.

Swimbridge. A mixed train stands at the down (towards Barnstaple) platform in about 1910. The main building and the first signal box stand on the down side. On the up side is the substantial brick and wooden shelter and the goods shed.

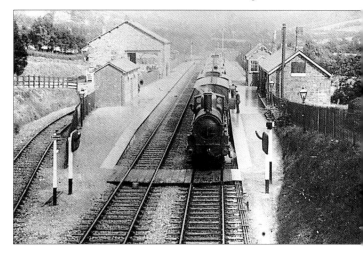

SWIMBRIDGE

OPENED: 1st November 1873 (with the opening of the Wiveliscombe – Barnstaple section of the Devon & Somerset Railway).
CLOSED: Passengers – 3rd October 1966.
Goods – 3rd August 1964.

When Swimbridge station, a short distance north of the village, opened in November 1873, the only facility was the platform and building on the down (towards Barnstaple) side of the line. A space was left, however, for a second running line and this was subsequently used by a loop, opened on 24th February 1904, alongside which a second up platform was constructed.

The design of the original down side building at Swimbridge was different to others on the Taunton to Barnstaple line, being a small stone structure with an apex slate roof and two tall chimneys, one at either end. On the later up platform was a brick and timber waiting shelter, in this case more substantial than other shelters on the line. In 1903 7,572 passenger tickets were issued but by 1933 the total had fallen to 5,574. Over these 30 years three staff were based at the station.

Served by a loop behind the up platform was the goods shed, a larger stone building than either of the station structures. The shed, through which ran the loop, was in operation from the early days before the up platform was added. Swimbridge signal box stood on the down platform east of the building; a large box replacing an earlier box, it opened on 6th April 1937 when an extended loop came into use. The goods yard closed in August 1964. Passenger services ceased with the withdrawal of services on the line in October 1966. Today the whole station site has been taken by the North Devon Link Road (A361) which uses the former track bed in this location.

TAMERTON FOLIOT

OPENED: 22nd December 1897 (on the Lydford –
Devonport line originally opened by the Plymouth,
Devonport & South Western Junction Railway
through this site in 1890).
CLOSED: Passengers – 10th September 1962.
Goods – October 1956.

Tamerton Foliot (Folliott until June 1906) was
located on the southern edge of Warleigh Wood, over
a mile west of the village at the end of a cul-de-sac
(Station Road). It lay on a small headland, just to the
south of the confluence of the Rivers Tamar and
Tavy, between the impressive Tavy viaduct to the
north and Tamerton Bridge to the south. The station
opened in December 1897, seven years after services
commenced on the line between Lydford and
Devonport.

The principal slate hung building, with canopy, on
the east side was of a different design to others on
this line, being erected at a later date.
Accommodation for the station master was
incorporated in the building. A stone waiting shelter
with an apex roof stood on the west side. Inter
platform movement was via the road bridge at the
northern end of the station. Goods traffic, carried on
passenger trains, was handled in a small metal shed,
south of the main building; this traffic ceased to be
handled in October 1956. A small signal box north
of the building was only in use for a short period
after the station opening.

The isolated position of the station was reflected in
the low figures for passenger use, road links from the

Tamerton Foliot. Looking north at the substantial slate hung
building on the east (towards Plymouth) side. To the left can
be seen the stone waiting shelter.

village to Plymouth being superior. In 1928 only 911
tickets were issued and 1243 collected; in 1936 the
figures had dropped to 424 and 482. Tamerton
Foliot became unstaffed and was re-designated a halt
on 5th January 1959 and closed in September 1962.
The line through the station was singled in 1970 and
the remaining track was re-aligned between the
disused platforms. For some years the former station
was derelict but is now a private residence.

TAVISTOCK NORTH

OPENED: 1st June 1890 (with the opening of the
Plymouth, Devonport & South Western Junction
Railway, Lydford – Devonport).
CLOSED: Passengers – 6th May 1968
Goods – 28th February 1966.

From 1876 to 1890 the London & South Western
Railway (LSWR) trains from Exeter to Plymouth
(Devonport) via Okehampton shared the GWR
single line (with mixed gauge) south of Lydford
through Tavistock (GWR) and Marsh Mills. This
was clearly an unsatisfactory arrangement and the
Plymouth, Devonport & South Western Junction
Railway (PD&SWJR) developed a new route south
from Lydford parallel to the GWR line to a separate
new station at Tavistock before continuing around
the west side of Plymouth down the Tamar Valley to
the already opened terminus at Devonport (LSWR
later Kings Road). The suffix North was only added
to the Tavistock station from 26th September 1949.

The PD&SWJR station at Tavistock was built,
following discussion on other locations, on a hillside
site north of the town centre at the east end of a 400
yard long viaduct spanning a tributary of the River
Tavy. Access to the station involved a 150 ft climb up
from the town centre. This hillside location, on a
promontory between two valleys, posed a number of
problems not only for access but also in limiting the
scope for development.

A double track line ran west-east through the
station itself to the goods yard. The main station
building, constructed principally of moorland
granite with a long apex roof parallel to the line, was
on the south (down towards Plymouth) side.
Facilities provided in the building included booking
and parcels offices, general and ladies' waiting
rooms, the gent's toilet, a refreshment room and the
station master's office. On the road forecourt side
were the main entrance doors protected by a small
horizontal canopy, six pairs of windows (two under

the entrance canopy) and one single window. All windows were edged with blue bricks. Other features included three dormer windows protruding from the roof on the road side and two large chimney stacks. At the east end of the building was the matching two storey station master's house with an apex roof at right angles to the building and two tall chimney stacks.

Passengers on the up platform were served by a large waiting room constructed in a similar style to the down side building. On the platform were gent's toilets, at the west end of the waiting room, and also, at one stage, a bookstall. The up (350 ft) and down (375 ft) platforms were also built of local stone with a tarmac surface. Protection was provided over sections of both platforms by wide canopies, that on the down side supported by cast iron columns and brackets attached to the building, that on the up side forming part of the overall apex style roof. The down side canopy had a slate covering on the line side but on the building side there were glass panels giving good illumination on the platform. Additional protection was provided on the up side by wood and glass panel screens at the ends of the waiting room.

Access between the platforms was via an attractive lattice side footbridge with a corrugated iron roof sited at the west end of the station. Station lighting was originally by gas; this had changed to electricity by the 1950s. There were water cranes on both platforms, one on the down side at the west end close to a rail level board crossing and the other on the up side close to the signal box. This 21 lever box, of the PD&SWR design just beyond the end of the up platform had a brick base, timber frame top and grey slate hipped roof. At the west end of the box was a wooden porch and flight of wooden steps linked to the end of the platform. In 1928 29,162 passenger tickets were issued and 54,480 tickets collected; in

Tavistock North. Looking west in 1962 with the main 1890 station building on the down (towards Plymouth) platform, including two storey accommodation for the station master. On the up platform additional protection is provided by screens at the ends of the building.

1936 the figures had increased to 54,480 and 57,868.

The goods yard, on a rather cramped site, was principally to the north and east of the station. Some excavation was needed to achieve a level site for the yard. Included in the track layout was a siding running through a stone goods shed on the up side. Other yard facilities included a 10 ton capacity crane, cattle pens and loading docks at the east end of both platforms. On the northern edge of the yard, a siding served a number of premises belonging to private traders.

Goods facilities were withdrawn in February 1966 and passenger services just over two years later in May 1968 with the withdrawal of services on the Exeter to Plymouth line via Okehampton and Bere Alston. The station master's house, the station building with canopy and a section of the down platform have survived. For a number of years after closure they were the home of the former station master and his wife; it was called 'Beechings Folly'. Today the buildings, now Grade II listed, are in private hands. In the autumn of 2006 it was reported that the three bedroom former station master's house was in residential use with the station building having planning permission and listed building consent to be re-used in a three dwelling development. It was also reported that the house and buildings were on the market for £600,000. When viewed in 2007 the building appeared somewhat neglected.

The former up side platform and building were demolished after closure and the site redeveloped for housing. The former up platform canopy was saved and re-erected at the Launceston Steam Railway. Another housing development has covered the station site west of the footbridge as far as the east end of the viaduct which remains in place carrying a footpath. The former goods yard has been redeveloped for offices of West Devon District Council. The footbridge was dismantled for re-assembly at the Plym Valley Railway at Marsh Mills.

TAVISTOCK SOUTH

OPENED: Passengers – 22nd June 1859, Goods – 1st
December 1860 (with the opening of the Tavistock
& South Devon Railway, Tavistock Junction –
Tavistock).
CLOSED: Passengers – 31st December 1962.
Goods – 7th September 1964.

The formal opening of the Tavistock & South Devon Railway from Plymouth on 21st June 1859 was the cause of much celebration in the town. The first special train from Plymouth Millbay carried directors, company officials, local dignitaries and up to 300 guests in its ten carriages. A second train conveyed the Tavistock Brass Band, the 96th Warwickshire Militia and the Tavistock Fife and Drum Band, who could not be accommodated on the special train itself. After a spectacular reception at the station, a procession wound its way through the town to Bedford Square where the official party and guests, totalling 120, were entertained to a dinner at

the Bedford Hotel. The following day the branch opened for public passenger traffic. The station was a terminus until 1st July 1865 when the line on to Launceston opened for passengers.

Ideally sited on the east bank of the River Tavy, the station was close to, and slightly above, the town centre to the north-west. Tavistock (the suffix South was only added in 1949) was the busiest station on the whole line to Launceston. The original 1859 station was badly damaged by fire in 1887 but was rebuilt in a similar form, this time mainly in stone rather than the original wood. The principal feature of the station was the fine overall timber roof covering two platform tracks and a central track used mainly as a siding.

The main station building on the up (towards Plymouth) side was constructed of limestone, with red brick surrounds to each window and doorway. It had a slate roof with square short chimney stacks capped with one or two chimney pots. The building incorporated the usual facilities including a general waiting room and booking hall, the parcels office, cloakroom and the station master's office. On the road side a canopy gave protection, whilst on the platform side shelter came under the overall roof. This latter rather restricted the light. This problem was eased somewhat by the provision of glass panels in the roof apex although this tended to illuminate the tracks rather than the platforms. The roof on the up side was supported by a series of brackets attached to the platform side of the building. On the down side support came from 14 timber posts rising from the platform. Long lateral planks filled the spaces between the posts, some light being given by windows fitted in every third section. In early days every section had a window. The whole roof was

Tavistock South. Looking north-east, goods trucks stand at the up platform in 1939 under the wooden roof braced with tie bars and vertical rods.

braced with a series of iron tie bars and vertical drop rods.

The two platforms were brick faced with slab edges; the surface was of blue Staffordshire bricks along the entire lengths. An ornate covered footbridge beyond the overall roof, at the northern end, connected the 480 ft up platform to the 320 ft long narrower down platform.

Tavistock was a busy station right from the start, passengers and freight being drawn from the wide surrounding agricultural area for which the town was the focus. The October Goose Fair was a major source of traffic to and from the Plymouth area. During the Second World War many Plymouth residents moved out to the Tavistock area to escape the blitz. Some even came for the night, using both temporary accommodation and tents. A number of camps and depots for the armed forces were sited in the Tavistock area, again bringing extra traffic to the station. Records indicate that in 1903 44,664 passenger tickets were issued at Tavistock, the figure rose greatly to 79,532 in 1913 and then fell to 58,446 in 1923 and 53,591 in 1933.

As noted earlier, Tavistock station was also busy with freight traffic. Much of this was handled in the extensive goods yard on the down side, both behind and to the south of, the station. A large goods shed with a through goods loop and siding stood behind the down platform. Over the years it was much extended and changed. The goods office was at the southern end. Other facilities in the yard included a 10 ton crane, loading docks, a 45 ft turntable and workshops. A short siding behind the south end of the up platform served adjacent cattle pens. Over the years a number of the original goods yard buildings were replaced by prefabricated structures.

The 37 lever signal box, erected in about 1895, was brick based with large timber framed windows at each end and along the platform side. It stood beside the main building at the southern end of the up platform. This replaced a series of earlier boxes. An original box was sited in the centre of the station but this was replaced by two boxes, one at each end of the station and these in turn were replaced by the final 1895 box. The second northern box was demolished but the southern box remained, used as a maintenance hut. The final box closed on 27th July 1964.

For a short period from June 1859 to July 1865, when Tavistock was a terminus, a small (50ft x 20 ft) engine shed stood at the southern end of the station site. It became redundant when the line extended to

Teigngrace Halt. Looking north in about 1960 after the halt closed. In its latter years the building itself had been boarded up but the alcove remained, providing some shelter. The platform remains today, largely covered in vegetation and weeds.

Launceston, the facility moving to the Cornish town. At Tavistock station there were two water cranes, one on the down side near the goods shed and the other on the southern end of the up platform near the signal box.

The station closed to passengers at the end of December 1962 with the withdrawal of services on the line. Goods facilities continued until September 1964. The station buildings were demolished over the period summer 1968 to spring 1969. The site remained largely undeveloped until the early 1980s, although it was sold to Devon County Council soon after track lifting was completed in 1968. A section of the site was soon used for road works but major development came in 1981-1984 with the building of a health centre, fire station, ambulance station and a small factory. Today there is nothing left of the original station.

TEIGNGRACE HALT

OPENED: 16th December 1867 (on the Newton Abbot – Moretonhampstead line originally opened through this site in 1866).
CLOSED: 2nd March 1959.

Opened some 17 months after services commenced on the line between Newton Abbot and Moreton-hampstead, the halt was built at the invitation of the Lord of the Manor at Stover. He had released land for the railway on condition that any train must stop whenever he wished to travel! Sited by the Stover Canal, the original 200 ft stone filled stone faced platform was on the down (west) side of the single line at the end of a tree lined drive that connected to a minor road at the north end of Teigngrace village. There was no crossing loop at the station.

A small brick building, with one chimney at the south end of the grey slate roof, stood at the centre of the platform; it incorporated an open alcove, acting as a waiting area. To the south of the alcove was the ticket office and to the north a toilet block. Behind the waiting area was a small parcels office. The platform was lengthened by 52 ft at the Newton Abbot end at the time of gauge conversion of the line in 1892; this extension was brick faced. At the rear of the platform was a vertical paling fencing which, in some sections, carried metal advertisement panels. The halt's original lighting was by oil lamps in ornamental glass lanterns but these were later replaced by hurricane lamps. Passenger traffic was light at Teigngrace: in 1903 4,808 tickets were issued; in 1913, 1923 and 1933 the figures were 3,519, 3,125 and 1,234. The station closed as a war-time measure from 1st January 1917 to 5th May 1919. Teigngrace had a station master until 1925, from which date it came under the supervision of the station master at Heathfield.

As from 8th May 1939 Teigngrace was reduced to halt status and lost all staff. Most of the station building was abandoned and boarded up but the alcove remained providing shelter. The station garden, an attractive feature when staff were present, deteriorated. Late in its life there was a boost to traffic when, in July 1952, the Royal Devon Show was held on the Stover Estate. A shuttle service was

run between Teigngrace and Newton Abbot.

Aside from the passenger traffic, another justification for a halt at Teigngrace was the presence of ball clay deposits on the Stover Estate. In 1872 a siding was laid at the north end of the station with a short spur back to a loading bay at the end of the platform. In addition to clay other freight, such as coal, milk and general merchandise was handled, in particular for the Stover Estate. The siding closed from 28th May 1962 but the track remained until about 1971. Following closure to passengers, the station building was, for a short while, the headquarters of the South Devon Railway Preservation Society, which sought to restore services to the branch line. These plans did not materialise however (see Moretonhampstead text) and the building was demolished. In March 1983 the remaining platform was cleared of vegetation and gravel was laid when the Prince of Wales arrived for a visit to the Dartmoor National Park Headquarters at Bovey. Today the platform is still there, though largely covered in vegetation and weeds, standing beside the still remaining track.

TEIGNMOUTH

OPENED: 30th May 1846 (with the opening of the Exeter – Teignmouth section of the South Devon Railway).

CLOSED: Passengers – remains open for services on the Exeter – Newton Abbot line.
Goods – 4th December 1967 (coal depot only from 14th June 1965).

In contrast to Dawlish, the station at Teignmouth was not developed immediately alongside the sea. The line veers away from the coast just to the north of the town, heading for the north bank of the Teign estuary en route to Newton Abbot. West of, and close to, the town centre, the original 1846 station comprised a wooden building and platform on the down side, together with a wooden train shed spanning two tracks. A second up platform and shed extension date from 1848, two short platform canopies being added in 1860. An early goods yard and small goods shed were sited north of the main building, access to short sidings being via a wagon turntable.

The original late 1840s wooden buildings became very dilapidated and, in 1894, were replaced on a revised track alignment by a fine ornamental stone building in a similar style to that at the second Torquay station completed in 1878. The principal

Teignmouth. Looking west in the early 1890s at the original 1840s Brunel structures. The down platform (left) and train shed spanning two tracks date from the opening in 1846. The up side platform and shed extension (right) date from 1848. The main building is to the left.

single storey stone building with a long road side canopy was built on the down (towards Newton Abbot) side facing the town centre. From south-west to north-east it incorporated the gent's toilets, porters' room, parcels office, general waiting room, third class ladies' waiting room and toilets, second class ladies' waiting room and toilets, second class waiting room, booking hall and office and station master's office. The matching up side building included the gent's toilets, general waiting room, ladies' waiting room and ladies' toilets. Both platforms were covered by extensive canopies supported on a series of pillars. A covered footbridge at the east end of the buildings connected the two platforms. The down platform was extended at the Dawlish end in 1938 to accommodate 15 coach trains but this extension is no longer used. The up platform was extended in 1980/1981 to accommodate the High Speed Trains. A staff of about 30 was based at the station in the 1930s.

The land behind the up side was originally occupied by a pumping station that operated on the atmospheric railway that ran through the station in 1847 and 1848. The pumping station and its associated sidings were replaced in about 1856 by a permanent way depot and works but these were little used after 1877. The 1890s rebuild brought a considerable re-arrangement of the freight facilities. A new goods yard with a goods shed, through which ran a loop line, was developed behind the up platform. The Myrtle Road bridge, at the east end of the station, was extended to allow access to the new yard. Another siding served a loading platform and workshops were also sited in the area. At the south-west end of the station on the down side, a loading dock and platform provided further freight facilities. Teignmouth signal box, at the Newton Abbot end of the down platform, dated from 1896. With 25 levers, it closed on 14th November 1986.

General goods facilities were withdrawn at Teignmouth in June 1965, the surviving rail coal depot ceasing to operate in December 1967. Today the 1895 station buildings, canopies and covered footbridge continue to serve passengers on both main line and local services. A major renovation took place in 1998. In contrast, the goods yard and shed behind the up platform, the loading dock on the down side and signal box have gone. When visited in summer 2006, the station was being well used and looked attractive with flower baskets over the platform and in the forecourt. The 'Whistle Stop' café was serving customers on the down platform.

Teignmouth. A train comes alongside a very busy up platform at the rebuilt station in about 1910. Note the decorative brackets supporting the large canopy and the substantial covered footbridge.

THORVERTON

OPENED: 1st May 1885 (with the opening of the Exe Valley line Stoke Canon – Tiverton).
CLOSED: Passengers – 7th October 1963.
  Goods – 4th May 1964.

On the west side of the River Exe flood plain, about half a mile east of the village of Thorverton, the station opened at the beginning of May 1885. It was the first passing place on the Exe Valley line north from Stoke Canon. The opening prompted celebrations in the village, including a dinner for pensioners, served under an awning over the street. There were sports and also a tea for children and the elderly.

The two stone faced platforms, some 320 ft long, were connected by a rail level board crossing at the north end, there being no footbridge. The main blue-grey stone building with twin gabled slate roofs, at right angles to the line, stood on the down (towards Stoke Canon) platform. A canopy between the two wings created a sheltered porch. A wooden shelter, with a backward sloping roof, served passengers on the up platform. Thorverton was one of the best used stations on the Exe Valley line; the village was not on the main A396 road to Exeter and, until the station closed, there was no bus service. In 1903 11,633 passenger tickets were issued; this figure rose to 12,025 in 1913, 16,249 in 1923 and 17,958 in 1933. It is also recorded that 100-200 passengers used the station per day in 1938. A peak of 170 was reached in 1953 with the figure falling to 85-90 in the 1960s.

Thorverton. An overall view looking north in about 1963. The main building and signal box stand on the down platform (right) with a wooden shelter on the up platform.

In the 1930s a staff of six were based at the station. The station master's house was north of the station at the end of the main station approach road.

Thorverton was also an important station for goods traffic. In 1925 it was estimated that about 78% of the revenue was from freight and this figure remained fairly constant throughout the years, much of it related to the nearby mill. The goods yard was mostly behind the up side platform, a goods loop running through the stone goods shed, which was immediately behind the waiting shelter. Within the shed was a 30 cwt capacity crane and in the yard itself a five ton version. A siding also led to a loading dock and cattle pens joined to the south end of the goods shed. The annual cattle fair, held in the village, was a particularly good earner for the station in its early days. Camping coaches were based in the yard in the 1936 to 1939 summers. A long siding curved north-east from the line north of the station serving Thorverton Mill, with trains working to Exeter and Avonmouth. Movements at the station and in the yard were controlled from a 20 lever signal box on the down platform, south of the building. The box closed on 6th April 1964.

Passenger facilities ceased with the withdrawal of services on the Exe Valley line in October 1963; goods services continued for a further six months. Today much remains of the former station structures. The main building, considerably extended, is now in residential use (Beeching's Way), the additions being of stone from the demolished goods shed. The station master's house also survives and, in the former goods yard, is a large new house.

TIPTON ST JOHNS

OPENED: 6th July 1874 (with the opening of the
   Sidmouth Railway, Sidmouth Junction – Sidmouth).
CLOSED: Passengers – 6th March 1967.
   Goods – 27th January 1964.

Serving the village of Tipton St Johns just to the east, the station opened in July 1874 with the name of Tipton. The suffix St Johns was added from 2nd January 1881 to avoid confusion with two stations at Tipton in Staffordshire. The station opened as a passing point on the Sidmouth Railway but, from 15th May 1897, it became a junction station with the new Budleigh Salterton Railway branching west from the Sidmouth line just south of a level crossing at the south end of the platforms. The line to Budleigh Salterton was extended to Exmouth in 1903. For some years Tipton St Johns was the point where through express trains from London Waterloo either split or linked sections serving Sidmouth and Exmouth. (For a photograph see the Frontispiece, pages 2 and 3).

The main single storey brick building, with a wide backward sloping canopy, stood on the 250 ft long up platform. A waiting shelter, originally of timber but later brick built, served passengers on the 244 ft down (towards Sidmouth) platform. A covered footbridge, linking the platforms at the south end, came into use in February 1898 replacing a rail level board crossing. It was unusual for a branch line to have a footbridge but it was deemed necessary once Tipton St Johns became a junction station. The footbridge lost its roof in the mid 1950s. In 1928 10,524 passenger tickets were issued at Tipton St Johns and 10,480 collected. The figures for 1936 were much reduced to 5,014 and 6,154.

The main facilities for handling goods were on the up side behind the main building. These included a cattle dock and coal staithes but no goods shed or crane was ever provided. Some expansion of the limited goods facilities came with the junction status. Camping coaches were for some years accommodated on one of three up side sidings. A further long siding was on the down side north of the station.

An original small signal box serving just the Sidmouth line stood south of the level crossing on the up side. This was replaced from March 1897 by a 32 lever brick box at the Sidmouth end of the down platform in readiness for the opening, two months later, of the line to Budleigh Salterton. This new box

contained a wheel for operating the level crossing gates. A four lever ground frame at the north end of the down platform was removed in 1930 when its function was taken over by the main signal box. A large water tank on a brick base stood on the up side south of the level crossing, approximately on the site of the first signal box.

Goods facilities were withdrawn at Tipton St Johns in January 1964 but passenger services continued for another three years until March 1967. The main station building was converted into a private house complete with canopy and a portion of the up platform. The down platform was demolished. A level crossing gate post survives today by the road side and to the south a pub car park and housing covers the former trackbed towards and at the former junction.

TIVERTON

OPENED: 12th June 1848 (with the opening of the Bristol & Exeter Railway Tiverton branch, Tiverton Junction – Tiverton).
CLOSED: Passengers – 5th October 1964.
   Goods – 5th June 1967.

The early history of Tiverton station needs to be seen in the context of the arrival in the town of three lines: the Bristol & Exeter (B&E) branch from Tiverton Junction in June 1848, the Tiverton & North Devon Railway from Morebath Junction on the Taunton – Barnstaple line on 1st August 1884, and the Exe Valley Railway from Stoke Canon on the Taunton – Exeter line on 1st May 1885.

The initial B&E terminus station was built on a

Tiverton. A train arrives from Exeter under the covered footbridge at the west end of the platform. The main entrance arch to the platform can be seen under the notices on the up platform (right).

flat low lying site east of the town centre. Two platforms served passengers, the Tiverton branch trains on the broad gauge track normally using the northern (up) platform. An overall wooden roof covered the platforms and the two broad gauge tracks at the buffers end. Passengers entered the station through a door with a canopy, located on the north side of the train shed. This entrance faced on to the then Station Road. This was renamed Blundells Road when the second station was built (see below), leading off a new Station Road, which name remains today. A wagon turntable was located behind the northern platform, allowing trucks to be shunted individually into one of the short sidings or the goods shed.

When services commenced on the standard gauge line south from Morebath Junction in August 1884, the trains used this first station. The Tiverton Junction branch had been converted from broad to standard gauge on 26th June. The 1848 structure was clearly inadequate and the imminent opening of the Exe Valley line south from Tiverton, and the opportunity for through running from Morebath Junction through the town to Stoke Canon, created the urgent need for a new through station. A new stone built station was constructed, south of the original terminus, which was then used for a short while for freight traffic, before being demolished. The layout of tracks on the old station site was, however, largely retained. This 1885 through station

Tiverton. A view looking east of the main buildings on 19th July 1955. Note the tall towers at each end of the impressive covered footbridge.

was described at its opening as being 'worthy of the most important town in mid-Devon'. It included up and down platforms, each 350 ft long, and a 145 ft bay platform on the up (north) side; this latter was for trains on the Tiverton Junction line. A striking feature was the covered footbridge at the western end of the platforms with two tall towers at each end. The impressive principal building, on the up (north) side featured a three gable roof line and impressive barge boards. From west to east it included a store, gent's toilet, parcels office, station entrance through a fine arch, station master's office, booking office, general waiting room, ladies' waiting room, first class waiting room, porters' room and bookstall. The only facilities in the down side building were a gent's toilet and a general waiting room. Both platforms had attractive wooden platform canopies with etched valences and elaborate glass roofs. In May 1931 further developments took place. These included the lengthening of the platforms and the provision of a down bay at the east end of the down platform. The former up bay became a siding. This change meant that Tiverton Junction trains (known often as the Tivvy Bumpers) no longer needed to cross the through lines as they entered and left Tiverton station.

After 1885, and indeed until shortly before its closure, Tiverton was a very busy passenger station. In 1903 76,374 passenger tickets were issued; the comparative figure in 1933 was 50,741. Peak traffic occurred just before the Second World War and continued to be high in the 1950s. In 1959 52,592 tickets were issued. An important generator of traffic was Blundells School, whose first premises were close to the station; after its transfer out of town,

large numbers of pupils continued however to travel to and from the school by train. It is recalled that on some occasions 400-500 trunks were handled at the beginning or end of terms. To meet the demands of both passenger and freight traffic, staff levels were high for a rural station: 1950 was a peak year with 38 staff based at the station. However, the station master was not provided with a house.

These staff were also involved with the extensive freight traffic, handled in the large goods yard north of the station, adjacent to Blundells Road. The yard included a large goods shed (100 ft long with one ton and 30 cwt capacity cranes), a six ton yard crane, cattle pens and extensive coal facilities. Coal was the principal import, serving a number of coal merchants in the area. Water for the station water cranes was drawn from a tank on a grass bank above the east end of the down platform. This water tank was fed by gravity from the Grand Western Canal 80 ft above on the hillside to the south of the station.

Initially there were two signal boxes controlling passenger and freight traffic: a 25 lever North box beyond the east end of the station and a nine lever South box at the Exeter (west) end of the down platform. Replacing these two early boxes, a new 40 lever box came into use on the down side east of the station on 6th May 1912.

The Exe Valley line from Morebath Junction through Tiverton to Stoke Canon closed on 7th October 1963, followed by the Tiverton Junction line on 5th October 1964, the closure date for passengers. Freight facilities were withdrawn in June 1967; the signal box had closed on 1st March 1965. For some years after closure the station site and buildings were derelict, but all tracks had been lifted by 1968. A new Tiverton relief road appropriately called Great Western Way, was then constructed on the track bed through the station site. Station Road is today a reminder of Tiverton's railway era.

TIVERTON JUNCTION

OPENED: 1st May 1844 (with the opening of the Beam Bridge (south of Wellington, Somerset) – Exeter section of the Bristol & Exeter Railway).
CLOSED: Passengers – 11th May 1986.
Goods – 8th May 1967.

With the start of passenger services on the broad gauge Bristol & Exeter Railway at the beginning of May 1844, a small station known as Tiverton Road opened, acting as a rail head for the Tiverton area

Tiverton Junction. Looking north in the late 1920s. Tiverton branch trains departed from the bay platform (left), covered for half its length by a wooden train shed. The buildings mainly serve the then two through lines. Hemyock branch trains use the outside of the down platform (extreme right).

and the Upper Culm valley. The town of Tiverton was some four miles to the west. This initial station had two platforms and a small goods yard on the down (east) side of the line. With the opening of the branch line to Tiverton on 12th June 1848, the station was renamed Tiverton Junction. A 280 ft long bay platform, with buffers at the north end, was added on the up side, covered for over half its length by an open ended wooden train shed. The main up and down platforms were covered by more conventional canopies, that on the up side being a separate structure and that on the down being an extension of the roof.

The opening of the Culm Valley line to Hemyock on 29th May 1876 brought the conversion of the down platform into an island. At this point three different gauges operated at Tiverton Junction. The main Bristol to Exeter line was by then mixed gauge, the Tiverton branch was still broad gauge, while the Culm Valley line was standard gauge. The change to standard gauge on the Tiverton branch in June 1884, and the abandonment of the mixed gauge on the main line in 1892, allowed more flexible operation at the station.

The principal station building, incorporating all the main facilities, was on the up platform accessed by a covered footbridge at the northern end, linking to the island platform and the main station approach road to the east. A matching smaller structure stood on the down island.

In the early 1930s Tiverton Junction underwent major redevelopment associated with the quadrupling of the GWR line between Taunton and Newton Abbot. The original layout was changed basically to four through main tracks with an up side loop line and two bay lines on the down side. Between the two outer main lines and the loop/bay lines were two island platforms linked by a long footbridge at the northern end, the bridge being initially open but covered from 1946. The two down side bay lines, one entering from the north, and the other from the south, terminated at buffers alongside the centre of the outer face of the down island. Passengers were served by substantial buildings on both platforms. The re-building was completed in the period March to October 1932.

Passenger traffic was relatively high at Tiverton Junction. In 1903 26,690 tickets were issued; the number rose to 29,002 in 1913, fell to 27,331 in 1923 and then rose again to 34,424 in 1933, the last figure relating to the rebuilt station. In the early 1930s 27 staff were based at the station.

Throughout its life, Tiverton Junction was busy with freight traffic. With the opening of the Tiverton branch in 1848 a number of short sidings were laid adjacent to the branch line; an engine shed was also built on the up side south of the station for use by branch line engines. The mid 1890s saw the provision of two new sidings on the down side close to the goods shed, which was south of the station on the down side. Also added was a 34 ft turntable in front of the engine shed. The early twentieth century

Tiverton Junction. Looking south soon after the major reconstruction of the early 1930s. The four through tracks passing between the down (left) and up island platforms are connected at the north end by a long footbridge here open but covered from 1946.

again saw the lengthening of the sidings to accommodate the increased level of traffic being generated in the Tiverton area. A slaughterhouse was built in the area between the engine shed and the branch sidings. The re-building of Tiverton Junction again brought expansion of the freight facilities, a new goods shed being constructed to the east of the station beyond the bay lines. East of this again were a number of sidings. On the up side a local butter factory provided a 'butter' platform to speed up the despatch of products, essential when refrigeration was not readily available. The original engine shed was replaced by a new structure that operated until October 1964. The turntable had been removed in 1908.

Movements were originally controlled at Tiverton Junction by a signal box on the up side of the line south of the station. This was replaced in the early 1930s by a large 120 lever box on the up platform itself, south of the building. The box closed on 1st

March 1986 though it had been little used in its latter years.

The closure of the Culm Valley line to passengers in 1963 and to goods traffic in 1965, and the closure of the Tiverton branch to passengers in 1964 and to goods in 1967, brought a significant loss of traffic at the Junction station, which closed to general goods traffic in May 1967. In May 1984 it was announced that it would close and be replaced by Tiverton Parkway two miles to the north; this closure came on 11th May 1986. The buildings survived until demolition in April 1991. After closure two loop lines and two sidings were left but in recent years some sections of these have been lifted. The up platform can still clearly be seen as can remnants of the down. The former goods shed is used by a repair garage.

TIVERTON PARKWAY

OPENED: 12th May 1986 (replacing Tiverton Junction on the Taunton – Exeter line originally opened through this site in 1844).

CLOSED: Remains open for passenger services on the Bristol – Taunton – Exeter line.

At a strategic location close to the junction of the M5 motorway and the North Devon Link Road (A371), Tiverton Parkway station was developed to replace the less accessible Tiverton Junction station, two miles to the south. The latter no longer acted as a junction following the closure of the branch lines to Tiverton and Hemyock. Opened on 12th May 1986 by the Rt Hon David Mitchell, the Minister of State for Transport, the funding of some £730,000 was jointly provided by Inter City, Devon County Council and Mid Devon District Council. The principal low brick building incorporating waiting, booking and refreshment facilities stands at the centre of the up platform. A section at the north end of the building includes gent's, ladies' and disabled toilets.

On the down platform two metal shelters give protection. The platforms are connected towards the south end by an open footbridge with approach ramps. The main feature of the station is the very large car park provided for passengers using the many trains, both long distance and local, that now stop. In recent years Tiverton Parkway has enjoyed an enhanced service compared to that when it opened some twenty years ago.

Tiverton Parkway. A view south on 26th July 2006 with the main building on the up (towards Taunton) platform.

TOPSHAM

OPENED: 1st May 1861 (with the opening of the
Exeter & Exmouth Railway).
CLOSED: Passengers – remains open for services on the
Exeter-Exmouth line.
Goods – 4th December 1967.

The negotiations regarding the construction of the line between Exeter and Exmouth were protracted but eventually in September 1857 agreement was reached that the Yeovil & Exeter Railway (Y&ER) would construct the line from Exeter to Topsham with the Exeter & Exmouth Railway building the remainder. The completed line was to be worked by the London & South Western Railway (LSWR). It was also agreed that the Y&ER and E&ER would share the cost of the station at Topsham and the branch to the quay. Also agreed was that Sir William Tite, the architect of many LSWR stations (eg Axminster) would be the station architect.

Opening at the beginning of May 1861 Topsham station, close to but above the village centre, included a typical William Tite red brick building on the up (towards Exeter) platform. Its features included two storey station master's accommodation (dated 1860), tall chimneys, steeply pitched roofs, and an ornate horizontal canopy. On the down platform was a wooden shelter with a wide canopy sloping back from the line that covered the whole width of the platform. Both platforms were lengthened in concrete at the south end in 1909.

Topsham station, throughout its life, has had a good level of passenger use on the Exmouth line. For some years after 1908 Topsham was the terminus of a rail steam-motor service from Exeter. In 1928 87,397 passenger tickets were issued and 100,595 collected. By 1936 the numbers had fallen to 51,159 and 63,984. In the 1920s the station master was supported by eight staff.

Topsham. Looking north in 1958 with the William Tite brick building on the up (towards Exeter) platform. On the down platform is a wooden shelter with a very wide canopy.

Topsham goods yard, on the down side behind the platform, was accessed from the Exmouth end. Including a large goods shed, loading docks, cattle pens and a two ton capacity crane, the principal outward traffic from the yard was of local produce such as raspberries, cherries, plums, flowers and fish. The main imports were of timber and coal. Further sidings were sited on the up side south of the station. From these a 700 yard line led to the quay at Topsham. The primary purpose of this line, which opened on 22nd September 1861, was to convey goods to Exeter from ships too large to reach Exeter via the Exeter Canal.

Movements at Topsham were controlled by an 1875 signal box sited on the up platform at the Exeter end, adjacent to a level crossing operated by a wheel in the box. The wheel was last used on 20th May 1973 when crossing barriers came into use, again controlled from the box until operations were transferred to the Exmouth Junction box. Topsham box closed on 30th January 1988 when colour signalling was introduced on the Exmouth line. The track formation in the Topsham area controlled from the box varied over the years. Originally single from Exmouth Junction to Topsham, the line was doubled in 1908; however, from 5th February 1973 it was singled again, though a passing loop was retained at Topsham and remains today. From Topsham south the line has always remained single as far as the approaches to Exmouth.

Over the years the station gardens were well kept and since 1947 an unusual feature has been lettering TOPSHAM in topiary supported by signal and telegraph wires at the north end of the down platform.

Topsham. The up side William Tite building on 2nd July 1957. Evening fares to Exeter (1/1d) and Exmouth (1/3d) are advertised.

Today the original Tite building survives but not in railway use and fenced off by railings from the platform. The canopy has gone. When seen in mid 2006 it was occupied by the Devon Association for the Blind and Blue Ribbon Computers. Shelters and new lighting were installed in 1976 on both platforms. The signal box is Grade II listed and has been in office use but in 2006 appeared to be disused. The goods yard closed from December 1967 though some sidings remained in private use. The former goods shed survived for some twenty years used for light industry and by a builders merchant. The yard has now been developed both as a car park, at the north end, and for housing.

Torquay. Looking north at the 1878 station on 30th May 1921. Behind the south end of the down platform (right) is a short dock siding which was abolished in 1924 when the platform was extended south incorporating the 1910 signal box.

OPENED: 2nd August 1859 (with the opening of the Torre – Paignton section of the Torbay & Dartmouth Railway).

CLOSED: Passengers – remains open for services on the Exeter – Newton Abbot - Paignton line.
Goods – no significant facilities provided, goods for Torquay being handled principally at Torre.

The Torbay & Dartmouth broad gauge line, operated from the outset by the South Devon Railway (SDR), opened from Newton Abbot to Torre in the north-west of Torquay in December 1848 (the station was then named Torquay and only changed to Torre with the opening of Torquay station). Even before the 1848 opening there was pressure to extend the railway further south into Torquay itself and on to Paignton. However, there was also considerable local opposition. A meeting held in the town on 24th September 1852 expressed fears regarding the potential damage to both the physical structure of the town and its character, also 'the hissing and snorting of the engines would . . . in many instances hasten the death of the invalids who resided here'.

Eventually the Torbay & Dartmouth Act was passed and an extension south from Torre through Torquay to Paignton opened, ceremonially on 1st August 1859 and to the public on the following day. The opening was the cue for a day of celebration in the resort. The chosen station site at Livermead, south of the town centre and close to the sea front was, in many ways, a compromise between the local demand for a station and the serious concerns regarding the impact of the railway on the town. Sited approximately where the current station down building stands, the 1859 structure was, from the outset, considered inadequate, described by some as 'a third rate station not worthy of the resort'. Costing some £4,000, it was unfinished at the opening date. In 1860 it was decided to spend a further £1,000 on improvements; in June it was decided to adapt the parcels office into a 'first class refreshment room' in addition to the already opened refreshment room for 'less important travellers'. A small waiting room was also added on the up platform in August 1861.

The continuing serious concerns at the inadequate 1859 structure led to the development of a second station opened on 1st September 1878, though the doubling of the track to Torquay was not complete

Torquay. A view south in 1966. To the right are the two sidings laid in 1911 behind the north end of the up platform. In the 1960s, these were used by touring companies for delivering scenery to the resort's theatres. These sidings have now been redeveloped for housing.

until 1882. The construction was undertaken by Vernon & Evans of Cheltenham who, at this time, were also responsible for major work on the new curved train shed at Bristol Temple Meads. The principal elements of the 1878 station, which largely remain today, included two long platforms on a slight curve behind which were 244 ft long single storey buildings built of black marble with stone dressings. The roofs incorporated four apex dormers topped by cast iron crests. Both platforms were covered by long wooden canopies supported by cast iron cantilevers and columns.

Between the two platforms were three tracks, two along the faces and one central track often used for carriage storage for trains terminating at Torquay. The principal facilities were in the down side building that overlooked the sea front; they included the booking office and hall, waiting rooms, station master's office, refreshment rooms and appropriate cloakrooms and toilets. On the up side there were two waiting rooms, one general and one for ladies. At the opening only the up side platform and building were complete as the 1859 station was still being demolished and replaced by the new down side building and platform. A particular feature of the 1878 station was the covered footbridge with two towers at the southern end of the platforms. The approach roads to both up and down platforms terminated under impressive long canopies that gave shelter along practically the full length of the buildings. Attractive gardens were also a feature.

In 1911 the platforms were extended at the north end from 500 ft to 600 ft at a cost of £796; in 1924 they were again extended, this time at the south end, on the down side over the site of an early dock siding. Facilities for handling freight were always very limited at Torquay, the principal goods yard for the town being at Torre. In addition to the down side dock, two sidings were provided after 1911 behind the north end of the up platform; these replaced three early dock sidings linked to the main line by a wagon turntable. In the 1960s the two sidings were principally used by touring companies playing at theatres in the resort. The centre track and the two sidings behind the up platform were taken out of use in 1970. Two way use of the up platform had ceased five years earlier, having lasted some 40 years.

Throughout the years operations at Torquay were controlled by two signal boxes, both on the down side of the lines. At the south end of the platform the 1878 South box (27 levers) was replaced by the GWR in 1910; prior to 1924 it was south of the dock siding but after the lengthening of the down platform, it was at the south end of the platform itself, closing on 1st November 1984. Torquay North box (1892), a little to the north of the station beyond a road bridge, was converted to a ground frame (14 lever) in 1910 and finally demolished in 1966.

Torquay has always handled large volumes of holidaymakers. In 1903 240,449 passenger tickets were issued but this figure fell to 106,886 by 1933. Demand continued into the 1950s; it is recorded that on 14th June 1958 and the following nine Saturdays, 75,951 passengers arrived at Torquay.

Today Torquay station remains basically in its 1878 form. Some of the rooms are unused and none on the up platform are in railway use. A south extension to the canopy on the down side has been removed and the site of former up sidings at the north end has been redeveloped for housing. The station buildings and remaining South signal box are listed structures.

TORRE

OPENED: Passengers – 18th December 1848 (with the
opening of the South Devon Railway branch,
Newton Abbot – Torre).
Goods – 6th October 1849.

CLOSED: Passengers – remains open for services on the
Exeter – Newton Abbot – Paignton line.
Goods – 4th December 1967.

The 18th December 1848 was a day of celebrations
in Torquay with the opening of the South Devon
Railway south from Newton Abbot to the station
(then called Torquay) in the St Michaels area of the
resort. A procession made its way from the Royal
Hotel Square, at the bottom of Torwood Street, to
the new station. Chapel Hill, above the station, was
thronged with crowds greeting the arrival of the
special train from Newton Abbot. Comprising nine
first class and fifteen second class carriages, its most
distinguished passenger was Isambard Kingdom
Brunel. It was a public holiday in the town with
4,834 lbs of meat, paid for by public subscription,
being distributed to the poor and needy.

The station, on a curve and described at its
opening as 'handsome and commodious', comprised
a wooden building on stone foundations on the
down side, with a wooden train shed covering the
platform and tracks. Its siting, some 100 ft above sea
level and a mile from the town centre and
promenade, was a problem from the start and
prompted calls for an early southern extension of the

Torre. Looking north towards Newton Abbot on 31st
October 1964. The fine covered footbridge dominates the
scene. This bridge (recently renovated), the down side
building and the three storey signal box on the up platform
(left) survive today.

line. Following much discussion (see Torquay text)
the Torbay & Dartmouth Railway opened through
Torquay to Paignton on 2nd August 1859 with a
new Torquay station at Livermead, near the
promenade. At this point the name Torre was
adopted for the 1848 station; at one time the
nameboard stated 'Torre for St Mary Church and
Babbacombe', reflecting tram routes that, until
1934, ran from the station.

With the doubling of the line from Kingskerswell
to Torre on 26th March 1882, an up (towards
Newton Abbot) platform opened together with a
footbridge. The original down side train shed was
demolished, the down platform being extended and
cover provided. In the following year the footbridge
was also roofed and an up side shelter and toilets
provided at a cost of £350. With small extensions the
up platform was 468 ft long and the down 410 ft.
Later plans for development were halted by the
outbreak of the First World War. Passenger levels
were high early in the twentieth century: in 1903
150,661 tickets were issued; in 1913 179,891 and in
1924 158,227.

Torre station opened to goods traffic in October
1849 but even by mid 1850 there was mounting
concern at the inadequacy of freight facilities. In
August 1865 it was decided to erect a large goods
shed in a yard to the north of the station on the
down side. Costing £2,075 this then served as the
principal goods facility for Torquay, the Livermead
station never having any provision for significant
goods traffic. Another goods yard was developed in
1890 on the down side to the south of, and behind,
the down platform, including two loading platforms
under a canopy and a 10 ton capacity crane. Further
sidings were also laid behind the up platform
principally for coal traffic, a coal store being
provided. Prior to the opening of the large goods

depot to the south of Paignton in 1931, the freight handling facilities at Torre were the largest on the entire Newton Abbot – Kingswear line.

The original 1883 signal box (16 levers) was replaced in 1921 by a three storey 42 lever box at the north end of the up platform. The up line was signalled also for down trains as from 24th June 1927 to increase the line capacity. This ceased in November 1964.

The up side station buildings were demolished in the early 1960s and later replaced by the current brick shelter. The goods shed closed in 1965 and all goods facilities were withdrawn in December 1967, all tracks being lifted in the yard by 1969.

Today Torre station is unstaffed but much remains of the old structures. The original principal building on the down side (now Grade II listed) was, in 2006, occupied by 'The Oakloft', 'manufacturers and importers of finest quality oak furniture and sofas'. There is no direct access to the platform from the building, this being via a small passage at the southern end of the building. The goods shed remains with a modern addition, occupied by a joinery firm. Former wooden station buildings, north of the down building, are used by Westwood Meters and Timers. Sadly the signal box was, in October 2006, derelict, though a notice indicated its acquisition by a railway restoration firm. In pleasing contrast the covered footbridge had been recently renovated and painted. The former small goods yard south of the station on the down side was occupied by a Halfords store, with the former coal sidings on the up side used for storage.

TORRINGTON

OPENED: 18th July 1872 (with the opening of the Bideford – Torrington section of the Devon & Cornwall Railway).
CLOSED: Passengers – 4th October 1965.
Goods – 6th September 1965.

The arrival of the first down train on 18th July 1872 was greeted by a large crowd. A well decorated locomotive hauled the first up train back to Bideford. The London & South Western Railway, the operators of the line, chose not to have any special ceremony to mark the opening of the Bideford to Torrington line but Torrington itself held its own celebrations on 24th July. These included triumphal arches, banners and flags over the streets, a procession with several bands, a free dinner for 600

Torrington. A detailed look south in 1945 at the main station building on the up (towards Barnstaple) platform. A wide platform canopy with a decorative valence protects passengers. A train is approaching from the Halwill direction.

men and tea for about 1,600 women and children in the Market House, following sports on the Castle Hill. In the evening a banquet was held in the Town Hall presided over by the Mayor. Torrington had apparently never seen a day like this before! (Nor since?)

Sited deep in the Torridge valley, the station was about one mile north-west of, and 200 ft below, the town centre of Great Torrington. As level a site as possible was used but its restricted nature was, without a doubt, a handicap in the station's development. For some 53 years Torrington was a terminus, though the layout was such that it could easily be converted into a through station. The main station building, constructed of local stone and with a platform canopy, was on the up (towards Barnstaple) side of the line. It included a two storey station master's house at the north end and a single storey section containing the booking and waiting facilities. On the down platform a stone waiting shelter backed on to the large goods shed through which ran one of the three goods yard sidings and in which was a two ton capacity crane. A cattle dock and cattle pens were served by the outer siding. A considerable volume of cattle traffic was handled by the yard, three wagons could be loaded at a time and, on occasions, lengthy cattle specials were run from Torrington. Other traffic through the yard included the import of coal and the export of gloves. A five ton capacity crane operated in this busy yard.

At the north end of the station, behind the up

Torrington. In this view looking north in 1962 a down train towards Halwill is taking on water. Carriages stand at the up platform at the north end of which a milk loading platform was erected in 1975. This replaced the earlier loading facility as seen to the right, south of the goods shed.

platform, Torrington engine shed opened in 1872. A long wooden structure through which ran a single track, it could accommodate two tender locomotives. To the north of the shed was a 48 ft turntable removed in 1930. The shed closed from 2nd November 1959 and was demolished the following year, its functions transferring to Barnstaple Junction. Torrington signal box (30 levers) dating from the opening, was to the north of the station on the up side. A water tank on the down side close to the cattle pens supplied water cranes on both platforms, on the up platform at the north end and on the down at the south.

The down side goods yard was the northern terminus from 1880 of the Torrington and Marland 3 ft gauge mineral railway which ran from the Marland Brick and Clay Works six and a half miles to the south. The narrow gauge line ended in the yard between two standard gauge sidings; this position assisted the transfer of clay for onward transit from Torrington. The mineral line operated until the early 1920s.

In 1925 the North Devon & Cornwall Junction Light Railway opened from Torrington south to Halwill Junction, the line using much of the mineral line's track bed. Thus from this point, Torrington became a through station, though operationally it was more a terminus of two branch lines, the lightly used branch from Halwill to the south and the more heavily used line from Barnstaple and Bideford, the latter carrying some through carriages from London Waterloo. In 1928 54,687 passenger tickets were issued at Torrington and 59,719 collected; by 1936 the figures had fallen to 41,730 and 47,469. In 1962 some 27,000 tickets were issued. In 1925 the station master was supported by 11 station staff. Ten locomotive staff, three guards and three signalmen were also based at Torrington. The LSWR, in addition to the station house, also provided two pairs of semi-detached houses for its staff on a site overlooking the station. By the period 1965-1970, only three staff were left. Passenger services ceased at Torrington in October 1965, general goods facilities had been withdrawn a month earlier. The station briefly reopened on a number of days between the 10th and 22nd January 1968 to relieve traffic problems in North Devon following serious damage to the Bideford road bridge.

Finally a review of Torrington station must refer to the importance of milk traffic. For many years Torrington Creamery generated much business for the station, churns being brought to the station for loading on to passenger trains. In the late 1940s a milk loading depot was erected to the south of the goods shed adjacent to the through shed siding. This operated for some thirty years but the problem was that only three rail milk tankers could be loaded at a time before running through the goods shed. Following closure of the station the opportunity was taken, in 1975, to construct a new covered milk loading facility on the north end of the former up platform; now up to seven tankers could be loaded at a time. The first train was loaded in March 1976 but the facility only operated for two and a half years, closing on 12th October 1978.

In April 1976 the site of the former goods shed, original milk depot and a section of the down platform at the south end was used for the construction of a large ICI fertilizer depot. A rail link to the depot lasted until 11th January 1980 after which road transport was used to and from Avonmouth. From this point the only traffic passing through Torrington station was clay wagon trains from Meeth quarries. This ceased as from September 1982. The last special train for rail enthusiasts came to Torrington from Bristol on 6th November 1982, the track being lifted in 1984. Today the former station building is the Puffing Billy Public House, opened in 1984, with the area under the canopy filled in to platform level. Alongside the former down platform runs the Tarka Trail cycleway. In May 2007 a clay wagon, a brake van and an old carriage were standing on a short section of track alongside the surviving up platform and public house. Cycle hire facilities were available at the south end of the former fertiliser factory. Torridge Transport is based in the former station yard.

TOTNES

OPENED: 20th July 1847 (with the opening of the Newton Abbot – Totnes section of the South Devon Railway).

CLOSED: Passengers – remains open for services on the Exeter – Newton Abbot – Plymouth line.
Goods – 4th December 1967 (coal depot only form 14th June 1965).

Sited in the north-west of the town and half a mile from the town centre, Totnes (Totness until at least December 1866) station opened in July 1847 as the terminus of the latest section of the South Devon Railway (SDR) from Newton Abbot. The opening was a source of much local celebration. The extension of the railway on to Plymouth (Laira Green) came for passengers on 5th May 1848 and

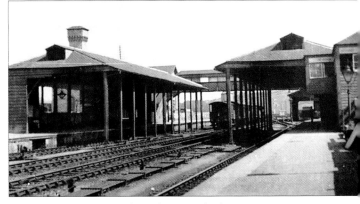

Totnes. An archive view from the 1890s looking east. Wooden sheds supported by thick timber posts cover the platforms and adjacent tracks. On the right is the 1894 timber signal box with a forward extension to improve visibility.

for goods traffic on 13th September that year. This was also a trigger for much celebration. In its early years, the station was dominated by the square tower of the 1840s pumping station which, it was hoped, would operate as part of the atmospheric system on the South Devon Railway. However, after serious problems on the section of the system between Exeter and Newton Abbot, it was abandoned and atmospheric powered trains never reached Totnes. The pumping station building, minus the tower, was subsequently incorporated into a large dairy complex. This generated rail traffic until 1980.

The original station, built for the SDR, comprised timber buildings with timber sheds covering the up and down platform tracks. These early sheds, supported by large one foot thick timber pillars, were later replaced by standard platform canopies supported by iron brackets and decorated with saw tooth valances. A covered iron lattice footbridge, at the Newton Abbot end of the buildings, was erected in December 1887.

Over many years this basic structure of the old 1840s buildings and replacement canopies served passengers at Totnes. Through the station ran four tracks: two central up and down through tracks for non-stop passenger and goods trains and two platform tracks for local services. These latter were used by Ashburton trains from the opening of the branch on 1st May 1872, no bay platform ever being constructed. The platform loops were slightly extended in 1930. A staff of 28 were based at Totnes at this time. The down platform itself received a new roof following an air raid on 21st October 1942, an incident in which two were killed, two injured and a

Totnes. The wooden down side building on 10th July 1956, some six years before it was destroyed in a fire. Temporary structures were used until the current building opened in October 1983.

branch train badly damaged. It is also believed that the footbridge lost its roof in the attack. In 1947 the down platform loop was again extended.

The year 1962 brought a major change when, following a fire on 14th April which destroyed the down side booking office and hall, parcels office and refreshment room, pre-fabricated and unattractive buildings were quickly erected. These remained until the opening of the current attractive stone building on 21st October 1983, built at a cost of £100,000. An original timber building and section of canopy were retained between the new building and the footbridge. Also still in place today are the early wooden buildings and replacement canopies on the up side. The footbridge was damaged by a crane on 18th October 1987 and, following temporary arrangements, replaced by the current open metal bridge.

Throughout much of its life Totnes was important for its freight facilities serving a large rural area of south Devon. A large timber goods shed stood east of the station on the down side. The yard included cattle pens. A loading dock and six ton crane were sited at the west end of the up platform. Following closure of Totnes to general goods facilities in June 1965, the shed was demolished: the coal depot continued to operate until December 1967. The site of the goods shed was subsequently taken over by an extension of the down platform. An early engine shed (demolished in 1904) and turntable (in use until 1909) stood on the down side south-west of the station beyond the road bridge. An 1894 timber signal box, with a forward extension to improve visibility, stood at the Plymouth end of the down

platform building. This was replaced in 1923 by a large brick box with 111 levers, at a mid point on the up platform. Following closure on 9th November 1987, the box was converted into the Signal Box Café, opening in October 1992, with a spur link from the new footbridge. Rail operations in the Totnes area were now controlled from the Exeter Power Box.

Passenger services on the Ashburton branch ceased in 1958 and the line closed in 1962. The line was re-opened by the Dart Valley Railway in April 1969 and, after years of frustration and negotiation, trains began to use the main Totnes station on 5th April 1985. This ceased from 2nd September 1987 because of prohibitive costs. It was only with the opening of Totnes Riverside (later Littlehempston) station, east of the main station, that the now South Devon Railway had a station at Totnes. The former goods yard on the down side is now a car park for both stations. In 2006 both main line and local passenger services continued to call at Totnes. In recent years the station has won a number of awards; for instance in 2006 it received the accolade of best medium station in the west.

TOTNES LITTLEHEMPSTON

OPENED: See text.
CLOSED: Remains open as the southern terminus for services on the South Devon Railway.

From the reopening to passenger services of the line to Buckfastleigh in April 1969, auto-trains ran to a point just north of the main Totnes station (see Ashburton and Buckfastleigh texts). Prior to the reopening, the Dart Valley Railway had endeavoured to reach an agreement with British Railways for its trains to use the main line station but this was unsuccessful. A loop was installed in 1971 and re-positioned further south in the winter of 1976/1977. This allowed the use of non auto-train formations. From these early days there were plans to provide a station at the southern end of the line to be known as Totnes Riverside but this did not happen for some years. In the early 1980s a platform was constructed and the name changed to Littlehempston Riverside to avoid confusion for passengers who believed they would be able to get out of the train and walk into Totnes. From April 1985 the Dart Valley trains used the B.R. Totnes station but this proved very costly and ceased in September 1987. In 1981 members of the Dart Valley Railway Association dismantled piece by piece the station building at Toller on the Bridport branch in Dorset and this was eventually re-assembled on a new platform in June 1986. Other railway buildings were then acquired and re-erected including a goods shed from Bovey and an open shelter from Axbridge in Somerset. A new toilet block was built at the north end of the platform. At long last a footbridge was completed and opened on 30th September 1993 that gave access over the River Dart to the main Totnes station and a limited amount of car parking. The station was renamed again Totnes Littlehempston in March 1994. In 1997 three sidings were laid behind the station, one to form a bay departure line for use at busy times. Today the station is flourishing as the southern terminus of the now South Devon Railway.

Totnes Littlehempston. In this view looking south a South Devon Railway train stands at the platform on 22nd June 2006. In the distance is the re-erected Toller station building and in the foreground is the open shelter from Axbridge. In between is a former goods shed from Bovey.

TOWER HILL

OPENED: 21st July 1886 (with the opening of the
  Halwill Junction – Launceston (Cornwall) section of
  the North Cornwall Railway).
CLOSED: Passengers – 3rd October 1966.
  Goods – 6th January 1964.

Named after a small group of nearby dwellings, and sited on the east bank of the River Carey, Tower Hill was the last station in Devon on the North Cornwall Railway, which opened from Halwill Junction to Launceston in 1886 and on to Padstow in 1899. Of a design almost identical to that at Ashwater, the next station to the north, the main station building, on the up (west) side of the line, was built of dark stone. A two storey section at the south end, incorporating the station master's house, had a steeply pitched roof at right angles to the line. A single storey section with an apex roof, parallel to the line, incorporating the main station facilities, was at the north end. A feature of the building was the tall arched gable windows. On the down side was a small shelter and signal box, the latter controlling the station loop and access to a small goods yard

Tower Hill. Looking south in 1965 at the dark stone building, incorporating accommodation for the station master, on the up (towards Halwill) platform. The signal box extension with glass panels is in front of the single storey section. A small shelter stands on the down platform.

behind the up side building. The yard included a stone goods shed with canopies on both road and rail sides over the loading bays. A row of railway cottages was sited to the rear of the main building. In 1928 4,549 passenger tickets were issued and 4,922 collected; by 1936 the figures had fallen to 2,231 and 2,634.

When originally opened, a crossing loop was laid at Tower Hill but this was taken out of use in 1920; the signal box closed on 15th June and the down platform became disused. In 1943, however, this down loop was restored and the down platform with a Southern Railway concrete shelter brought back into use. The goods yard was expanded to accommodate two extra sidings for war time use associated with nearby U.S.Army ammunition stores. A small signal box was re-established from 28th March 1943 in the booking office with an extension on to the up platform. After the war the loop was retained, being eventually taken out of use, together with the signal box, from 7th November 1965. Goods facilities were withdrawn at Tower Hill in early January 1964 but the station remained open for passengers until October 1966 when services were withdrawn on the Padstow line. It had become unstaffed from 6th December 1965.

Following closure, the station was inexplicably demolished. One account even suggests that this was an error, a contractor sent in to tidy up the site misunderstanding the instructions! The site was laid

Trusham. Trains stand at the staggered platforms in this south facing view on 3rd March 1956. The platform and stone building are from 1882. The concrete shelter on the concrete platform (left distant) dates from 1946, three years after this platform was extended.

out as a paddock and small holding by the owners of the former railway cottages that have been converted into modern houses. A road overbridge to the north of the station survives.

TRUSHAM

OPENED: 9th October 1882 (with the opening of the Teign Valley Railway, Heathfield – Ashton).
CLOSED: Passengers – 9th June 1958.
   Goods – 5th April 1965.

About a mile south-west of the village of Trusham, the low yellow stone station, with a slate roof and two short chimneys, was on the up (west) side of the line, just to the south of a minor road bridge. At the north end of the building was a small lean-to extension. To the south of the building was a metal store room at right angles to the platform. Leaving the line south of the station were two sidings, which ran behind the southern half of the platform. A station master's house was added north of the road bridge in 1912. In 1903 5,111 passenger tickets were issued; the total rose to 9,377 in 1913 and 9,833 in

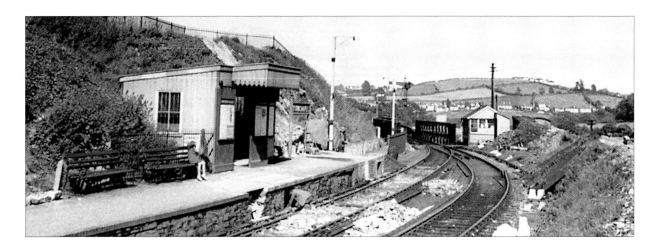

Turnchapel. The original attractive small building in about 1939 with the first timber signal box in the distance on the down side at the west end of the Hooe Lake swing bridge. Both structures were destroyed in November 1940 but later replaced.

1923 before falling to 8,269 in 1933.

In 1911 a goods loop was added opposite the platform. As part of the up-grading of the line as a war-time diversionary route between Exeter and Newton Abbot, this loop was extended to the south in 1943. At this time an earlier short concrete platform on this loop, opposite the south end of the original platform, was extended to 150 ft and, in 1946, a concrete shelter was added.

An original 1882 17 lever signal box stood just beyond the south end of the platform. This was replaced in 1911 by a 25 lever box, a little further to the south, again on the up side. It acted as a ground frame only from June 1958 and closed in 1961. The loop became a siding in June 1958 but was reinstated as a loop in 1960.

Passenger services ceased with the withdrawal of services on the line in 1958, though goods facilities continued to be available until April 1965. The station building and metal store remain today. The nameboard 'The Old Station' was on the gate when seen in summer 2006.

TURNCHAPEL

OPENED: 1st Janaury 1897 (with the opening of the London & South Western Railway Turnchapel branch, Plymstock – Turnchapel).
CLOSED: Passengers – 10th September 1951
Goods – 2nd October 1961

Serving the small village of Turnchapel, the station, opening on New Year's Day 1897, was the terminus for passenger services on the branch line from Plymouth Friary via Plymstock. Beyond the station the line continued for a further 500 yards in a north-west direction to Turnchapel Wharves.

The 1897 station was sited on the north side of the line and immediately to the west of the hand-operated Hooe Lake swing bridge. The layout comprised the platform track and a parallel run-round loop. The 175 ft long platform was constructed of earth and stone fill behind stone facing topped by loose chippings. Along the platform edge was a course of bricks. Access to the platform was by a path and a steep set of steps off the east end linking to Undercliff Road which ran beneath the swing bridge. The station building was basically a wooden plank and asbestos sheeting structure with a small horizontal canopy over the platform entrance. Inside was a small waiting room and booking office. Two lamp standards stood one either side of the building. The original timber signal box was on the down (south) side of the line close to the west end of the bridge. Passenger numbers using Turnchapel were high, some passengers being attracted to the area by nearby beaches. In 1928 39,224 passenger tickets were issued and 54,498 collected and in 1936 comparable figures were higher, 54,498 and 95,610.

The original buildings and signal box were destroyed on 27th November 1940 when an adjacent oil depot was bombed and set alight with blazing oil spilling onto the station. The station reopened on 16th December. The replacement booking office/waiting room and signal box were constructed of lateral wood planking , asbestos sheeting and concrete slabs and were, without doubt, a poor substitute for the original buildings. The replacement

Uffculme. A photograph of about 1910 shows the small station building and also the timber goods shed on the goods loop. The shed was removed in 1926.

signal box, which opened on 8th March 1942 and closed on 30th October 1961 was sited on the up side of the line opposite the site of the original box. The station along with the rest of the branch closed between the 14th January and 2nd July 1951 because of the national coal shortage.

Passenger services ceased in September 1951 but goods facilities continued for another ten years until October 1961. All track was removed in 1963 and subsequently the line was levelled with spoil and rubble and enclosed within the site of an oil storage depot. By the early 1990s only a portion of the platform could be seen through the spoil and undergrowth.

UFFCULME

OPENED: 29th May 1876 (with the opening of the
   Culm Valley Light Railway, Tiverton Junction –
   Hemyock).
CLOSED: 8th May 1967.

South of the village centre, Uffculme station was on a sharp curve in the Culm Valley Light Railway opened in May 1876. The station was sited on the down (towards Hemyock) side of the line. Its red brick building with external timber framing, red roof tiles and a single chimney housed the booking and waiting facilities. The station was gas lit. The 120 ft long brick face platform had well maintained gardens. The engineer to the line, Arthur Pain, a pioneer of light railways, used a similar design of buildings on the Culm Valley line to those on the Swindon & Highworth Railway in Wiltshire and the Southwold Railway in Suffolk, though the former were timber clad. In 1903 8,993 passenger tickets

were issued at Uffculme. The total dropped to 7,786 in 1913 and 6,167 in 1923 but rose again to 7,328 in 1933. In the 1930s an average of four men were based here.

Opposite the station was a goods loop passing through a 29 ft long timber goods shed. A short stub siding close to the west of the loop served cattle pens. Two further sidings ran south of the goods shed leaving the main running track east of the station. The inner siding served a loading dock. In 1926 the goods shed on the loop was removed, thus allowing it to be used for engine run-round movements. The shed was replaced by a corrugated iron lock up, with an apex shaped roof, on the platform east of the building. A sliding door gave access from the platform. At the same time the east end of the platform was slightly raised. The one ton crane that had been in the shed was replaced by a three ton crane in the yard itself. A quarterly cattle market at Uffculme generated traffic for some years. Beyond a level crossing at the west end of the site, a siding served an animal feed mill. New level crossing gates, some 20 ft wide, were installed in 1969 in connection with road widening.

Uffculme closed to passenger traffic in September 1963 with the withdrawal of services on the line. The cattle dock stub was removed at the end of 1963. Goods facilities were available at the station until the beginning of May 1967 but freight traffic continued through the site until late 1975, travelling to and from the dairy factory at Hemyock. All trace of the station has now gone, the site being covered by a cul de sac.

UMBERLEIGH

OPENED: 1st August 1854 (with the opening of the
   North Devon Railway, Crediton – Barnstaple).
CLOSED: Passengers – remains open as a request stop
   for services on the Exeter – Barnstaple line.
   Goods – 4th January 1965.

Sited on the east side of the River Taw valley, close to the junction of the main Barnstaple road (A377), and the B3227, Umberleigh station opened at the beginning of August 1854. Immediately to the north of the station was a picturesque three arch bridge carrying the B3227 to South Molton.

The station was built on a slight curve at the north end of a long largely single track section of the line. Double track ran through the station. The main building, a substantial North Devon Railway (NDR)

Umberleigh. In about 1930 this view looking north towards Barnstaple shows the main building, incorporating two storey station master's accommodation, on the down side (left). A stone waiting shelter and the 1890 signal box are on the up. In the distance is the attractive three arch road bridge.

style structure, incorporating a two storey gabled station master's house, stood on the down (towards Barnstaple) platform. The principal facilities, including the booking office, waiting room and station master's office, were in a single storey section of the building towards the north end of the building. The gent's toilet was in a separate annex at the far north end. A stone waiting shelter served passengers on the up platform.

Umberleigh was one of the best patronised stations on the Barnstaple line. In 1928 9,327 passenger tickets were issued and 10,544 collected; by 1936 the figures, in contrast to others on the line, had only fallen slightly to 8,820 and 10,026. A census held on 7th May 1963 indicated that 26½ passengers (1 child = ½ passenger) used Umberleigh. Surveys carried out over a winter week in 1976 and a summer week in 1977 indicated that 52 and 80 passengers used the station in those weeks.

There were three sets of sidings at Umberleigh on the down side. The first, a little to the south of the station, being the main goods yard incorporating a cattle dock and a siding which, for some years before and after the Second World War, accommodated a camping coach, a very unusual feature in north Devon. The second was a short siding south of the road bridge running behind the Barnstaple end of the down platform which served end and side loading docks and a goods shed, the latter with an internal two ton capacity crane. The third siding was to the north of the road bridge, which in early years had a five ton crane but in later days was used to store cattle trucks and other wagons. An early 1873 signal box south of the waiting shelter on the up platform was replaced from 19th October 1890 by a 31 lever stone base and wood frame box when the tracks were doubled north from Umberleigh.

The goods facilities ceased on 4th January 1965.

The line through Umberleigh was singled and the signal box closed as from 21st May 1971, the former up platform becoming redundant. Umberleigh is now a stopping point for all services between Exeter and Barnstaple, trains using the former down platform on which stands a metal and glass shelter south of the former main building, which appeared to be empty when seen in 2007. The disused up platform remains largely intact but overgrown; the waiting shelter and signal box have gone. The former goods yard is derelict but the former cattle dock could be seen. An old station nameboard stands behind the south end of the down platform.

UP EXE HALT

OPENED: 1st May 1885 (with the opening of the Exe Valley line Stoke Canon – Tiverton).
CLOSED: 7th October 1963.

Built on the east (down) side of the single track Exe Valley line, the station primarily served local farms and cottages. However the GWR clearly considered that it had a wider catchment area as, when it opened, it was called Up Exe and Silverton, the latter being a village some 1¾ miles to the east. In fact, Silverton already had a station on the main GWR Taunton to Exeter line, one mile east of the village. From 1st May 1905 the suffix was dropped but, at that stage, the level of traffic justified its continued status as a station. However, from 1st October 1923,

Up Exe Halt. Looking north-east in about 1930. By that time the building had been converted into a house and a corrugated iron shelter had been erected beyond it.

Watergate Halt. The basic halt comprising a concrete platform but no shelter in this view of 1962 looking north. The platform survives today by the Tarka Trail.

Up Exe was re-designated a halt and staffing ceased.

The blue-grey stone building on the 326 ft long platform was in the form of two wings, with slate gabled roofs at right angles to the line. A canopy between the two wings on the platform side created a sheltered porch area. On the west side of the line, north of the station and adjacent to Up Exe North level crossing, was the stone built station master's house. No goods yard or shed was ever provided at Up Exe. An eight lever wooden signal box, on the east side of the line, adjacent to the level crossing was demoted to a ground frame in 1907.

Following re-designation as a halt, the station building was converted into a house and a small corrugated iron waiting shelter was erected at the north end of the platform. The former station master's house became a house for the level crossing keeper.

Today the station building is a house, Grey Walls, while the former station master's house is South Lawn House. A level crossing gate post survives.

WATERGATE HALT

OPENED: 20th September 1926 (on the Torrington – Halwill Junction line, originally opened through this site in 1925).
CLOSED: Passengers – 1st March 1965.
Goods – 2nd May 1960 (at the siding).

Soon after the opening, in July 1925, of the North Devon & Cornwall Junction Light Railway from Torrington to Halwill Junction, two halts were introduced along the line. At Watergate Bridge, south-west of Torrington, the B2227 from the town

to Holsworthy crossed the line at an ungated crossing. Gates were not required on the line as it was built under a Light Railway Order. All engines were required to whistle continuously for 200 yards when approaching such a crossing and then traverse at only five miles per hour. Some accounts suggest that if gated crossings had been required on the line, the resulting expense could have prevented its construction.

The basic Watergate Halt, opened about 14 months after services commenced on the line, was just to the north of the level crossing on the up (west) side of the line. Constructed of standard Southern Railway concrete components, it comprised a very short platform (only able to accommodate a one carriage train), a nameboard, notice board and lamp posts. There was no shelter. The platform surface was gravel covered along the rear half. Accounts suggest that passengers were very few, the only regulars being about half a dozen workers travelling south to the clay works at Marland. Occasional use was made by workers tending the local woodlands. South of the crossing, also on the up side, was a short siding occasionally occupied by a wagon belonging to a local farmer.

The siding closed in May 1960 and was lifted soon after. Passenger facilities ceased with the withdrawal of services on the line at the beginning of March 1965. The platform survived and in early 2007 could still be seen beside the Tarka Trail which follows the former track bed at this point. Car parking has been provided south of the road for users of the Trail.

WEST EXE HALT

OPENED: 19th March 1928 (on the Stoke Canon –
  Tiverton line originally opened through this site in
  1885).
CLOSED: 7th October 1963.

The halt opened in March 1928 to serve both the growing housing development in the western suburbs of Tiverton and also the town's then main employer Heathcoat's Mill. The original 109 ft long platform, constructed of wooden facing and edging boards, was on the north side of the track, on an embankment just to the west of a bridge carrying the line over Exeter Road. A small wooden shelter with a backward sloping roof stood in the centre of the platform. The access footpath led down to the junction of Exe Vale Terrace and West Exe South.

West Exe Halt became the best patronised halt on the Exe Valley line not only for local movements but also for longer trips down to Exeter and the coast. The heavy use warranted further developments and a pre-cast concrete extension from May 1937 almost doubled the length of the platform at the east (Tiverton) end. The original wooden section was retained. Improved lighting was also installed. At the head of the access path an extra hut was provided for a porter, who, at busy times, was sent from Tiverton to collect, and sometimes sell, tickets. The halt closed in October 1963 with the withdrawal of services on the line and the site is now lost in the large roundabout at the junction of West Exe South and Great Western Way.

West Exe Halt. Looking east in about 1959. In the foreground is the original wooden platform and wooden shelter. In the distance is the 1937 concrete platform extension.

WESTON MILL HALT

OPENED: 1st November 1906 (on the Lydford –
  Devonport line originally opened through this site in
  1890).
CLOSED: 27th June 1921.

Opening with the commencement of LSWR steam road motor services between Plymouth Friary and St Budeaux, Weston Mill Halt was sited a quarter mile south of the latter. The halt's platforms were constructed of wood; no record is available regarding the provision of shelters. The halt closed in June 1921; no trace remains today.

WESTWARD HO!

OPENED: 18th May 1901 (with the opening of the
  Bideford Quay – Northam section of the Bideford,
  Westward Ho! & Appledore Railway).
CLOSED: Passengers and Goods – 28th March 1917.

Close to the sea front, and east of a level crossing adjacent to the Bath Hotel, Westward Ho! was the busiest station on the Bideford, Westward Ho! & Appledore Railway. With the coming of the railway in 1901 the North Devon Journal described the resort as being 'as busy as Weston-super-Mare'!

On a passing loop which enabled three carriage trains to pass, there were two 320 ft long platforms, only 1 ft high. All buildings were on the up (towards Bideford) platform. In the centre was a small substantially built red brick building with one chimney and a slate hipped roof. The windows and doors were slightly arched. Entered through double doors on to the platform, the building incorporated the waiting and ladies' toilet facilities, the gent's urinal being at the west end. Booking facilities were probably also provided. A small refreshment room was an additional facility at the extreme east end of the platform. For a time there was also a bookstall.

In order to stimulate summer holiday traffic the Railway Company, in 1903, built what was called Station Hall at the west end of the up platform. A long single storey stone building, it was used primarily for staging concerts, dances and other entertainment. Combined tickets for the railway and entrance to the hall were sold. The hall also acted both as an extra waiting area in bad weather and as an extra office/storage facility. An eight lever frame signal box with a pointed roof was on the up platform between the main building and the refreshment room. A two lever ground frame stood

at the west end of the down platform adjacent to the level crossing.

Following the very early closure of the line in 1917, the railway's infrastructure being required for war-time purposes (see Bideford Quay text) the station buildings remained largely intact. For some years the station site became a bus terminus; buses ran along the old track bed and passengers used the former up platform for entering and leaving the buses. The station building itself was converted into a bungalow and the signal box became a café and snack bar. The Hall remained in use as a theatre/dance hall. By 1993 the Hall had been incorporated into a restaurant and beer garden with an extension covering part of the former platform. In 2007 this is the Buccaneer Pub. The adjacent station building and signal box have gone, the site now paved.

WHIMPLE

OPENED: 18th July 1860 (with the opening of the Yeovil Junction – Exeter section of the London & South Western Railway).

CLOSED: Passengers - remains open for services on the London (Waterloo) - Salisbury - Exeter line.
Goods – 4th December 1967 (except Whiteways traffic).

Whimple station, to the east of the village centre, opened in July 1860 with the start of services on the last section of the London & South Western Railway (LSWR) route from London to Exeter. The large and impressive William Tite design main building stood

Westward Ho! Looking west with, from left to right, the signal box, the station building and the Station Hall. The last survives today incorporated in a larger structure, the Buccaneer Pub.

on the up (towards Honiton) platform. Its features included two storey station master's accommodation, tall chimneys, steeply pitched roofs and an ornate horizontal platform canopy with a wooden rip saw tooth type valence. The booking, waiting and toilet facilities were contained within this building. A typical LSWR hipped roofed waiting shelter served passengers on the down platform, at the east end of which was an 1875 signal box. The platforms, which were later extended at the west end, were linked by an open metal footbridge towards the east end. A particular feature of Whimple was (and continues to be) the tall monkey puzzle tree behind the east end of the up platform.

The goods yard, east of the station on the up side, contained a goods shed within which was a 40 cwt crane. Outside in the yard was a five ton capacity crane. A feature of Whimple was the traffic generated for many years by the cider factory of Henry Whiteway & Co, established on a site north-west of the station in 1892. Traffic handled included coal, apples, bottles, wooden casks, cider itself and agricultural machinery. At its peak in the 1930s it was estimated that the Whiteways factory generated some 30,000 tons of freight per annum. The factory closed in 1989, production moving to south Bristol.

The main line through the station was singled as from 11th June 1967 and, for a period, passengers had to use the footbridge to access the down

platform used by all trains, the up line only being retained for access to the goods yard. The 1875 signal box closed with the singling of the line and general goods facilities were withdrawn six months later from 4th December 1967, though the goods yard continued to handle Whiteways traffic. The goods shed was demolished in 1991. Staffing ceased at Whimple on 5th October 1970 after which tickets were issued in the mornings only from a small hut at the base of the footbridge steps on the down platform.

Major changes came in the early 1990s. The former down platform, waiting shelter and footbridge were demolished in November 1992 with the single line being slewed to the north alongside the raised, widened, but shortened former up platform. A new passenger shelter and lighting were provided together with some forecourt landscaping. The reconstructed platform was dedicated at a ceremony on 19th February 1993. The total cost of the changes was some £117,000. The former station building was by then used as a house.

Today Whimple station operates in accord with the early 1990s changes. The original gate posts stand to the west of the main building. Housing now covers the former goods yard.

WHIPTON BRIDGE HALT

OPENED: 26th January 1906 (on the Honiton – Exeter line originally opened through this site in 1860).

CLOSED: 1st January 1923.

Sited by the Summer Lane road under bridge crossed

by the Exeter to Honiton line, Whipton Bridge Halt was one of three halts opened by the London & South Western Railway (LSWR) in 1906 with the commencement of steam rail-motor services between Exeter Queen Street and Honiton. No details of the halt are known but it was clearly unsuccessful, closing after only seventeen years. One of its problems, compared with the other two halts, Lions Holt (later St James Park) and Mount Pleasant Road, was that it was east of the junction of the main line and the Exmouth branch and thus not served by trains on the latter. No photograph is known of this halt.

WHITCHURCH DOWN PLATFORM

OPENED: 1st September 1906 (on the Plymouth – Tavistock GWR line originally opened through this site in 1859).

CLOSED: 31st December 1962.

Serving the village of Whitchurch, a mile south of Tavistock, Whitchurch Down Platform was on the east side of the line between Yelverton and Tavistock. The long (351 ft) slightly curved platform was earth filled behind a brick face with slab edges and a chipping surface. The entrance was at the centre of the platform leading on to a paved area on which stood a square corrugated iron shelter. This housed a booking office at which some parcels traffic was also

Whitchurch Down Platform. Looking south towards Yelverton in the early 1960s, shortly before closure. A corrugated iron shelter serves passengers on the east side of the line behind houses in Whitchurch Road.

handled. The back gardens of houses on Whitchurch Road ran up to the rear fence of the platform, a fence constructed of timber posts and horizontal wire. There was a large wooden nameboard with cast iron letters and five gas lamp standards provided illumination. The Platform became unstaffed as from 2nd April 1956. Closure came when passenger services were withdrawn on the line at the end of December 1962.

Whitehall Halt. The very short platform with the wood plank hut behind a level crossing gate in the early 1960s. No train times are indicated on the wooden notice board attached to the hut but a passenger's bike leans against the nameboard.

WHITEHALL HALT

OPENED: 27th February 1933 (on the Tiverton Junction – Hemyock line originally opened through this site in 1876).
CLOSED: 9th September 1963.

In the small settlement of Whitehall between Culmstock and Hemyock, a siding of only three wagon capacity operated from the opening of the Culm Valley Railway in 1876. Despite pleas from the farmer who originally gave land for the siding and also from local residents, a halt was not provided for another 57 years until Whitehall Halt opened at the end of February 1933. The wood sleeper face platform was very short, only accommodating one coach. Shelter was provided in a wood plank hut with a backward sloping roof, sited off the west end of the platform adjacent to a level crossing that carried a north–south minor road. A smaller hut was sited opposite for the crossing keeper but, for many years, the gates were operated by the train guard. Arrangements were very informal at Whitehall. Records indicate that London newspapers were often left in the shelter by the guard for collection by the villagers. The guard also collected payment from a tobacco tin located in the eaves of the shelter! The halt closed in September 1963 with the withdrawal of passenger services on the line. The siding was taken out of use on 28th October 1963. Through goods trains continued to use the line through the halt until late 1975, serving the dairy factory at Hemyock. A grassy platform, with the sleeper face evident, remains today. On the gate at the road side is a name plate 'Whitehall Halt'; nearby is a surviving level crossing gate post.

WHITSTONE AND BRIDGERULE

OPENED: 1st November 1898 (on the Holsworthy – Bude (Cornwall) line originally opened through this site some 10 weeks earlier on 10th August).
CLOSED: Passengers – 3rd October 1966.
Goods – 7th September 1964.

Named after the village of Whitstone, one and a half miles to the south, and Bridgerule, a mile to the north-east, the station was only three quarters of a mile inside the Devon boundary. Sited to the east of the B3254 on a passing loop, the main building was on the down (towards Bude) side of the line. The building included two storey accommodation for the station master at the west end and a single storey

section incorporating the main facilities. In front of the building was a wide apex style canopy. On the up side was a stone shelter with a slate roof and short finials. There was no footbridge and inter-platform movements were via a rail level board crossing at the west end.

The station was not complete when the line opened from Holsworthy to Bude in mid August 1898, its opening being delayed for some ten weeks until the beginning of November. Passenger volumes were generally low. In 1928 7,136 tickets were issued and 7,675 collected; in 1936 the figures had fallen to 4,979 and 5,231.

The goods yard, including a substantial stone goods shed, was on the down side behind the main building. The shed had canopies protecting loading areas on both the road and rail sides. Also in the yard was a cattle pen and a 30 cwt capacity crane. Freight traffic was of reasonable level with coal inwards and agricultural products outwards being the principal traffic. In 1943 a 50 yard section of the down platform at the east end was removed to permit the construction in the yard of two extra sidings to accommodate ammunition trucks for the U.S. Army. A small army camp was also sited here. The platform was restored to its full length in 1947 when the extra sidings were lifted. The restored section was slightly higher than the original platform. The station's signal box, a brick structure with 20 levers, stood to the east of and beside the main building.

Goods facilities ceased in September 1964 but the station remained open for passengers until early October 1966 when services were withdrawn on the Bude line. After closure the station building was converted into a house with the former track bed filled to platform level to form a lawn.

Whitstone and Bridgerule. A Bude bound train stands at the down platform in this view east during 1954. To the right of the main building, that includes two storey accommodation for the station master, is the goods shed.

WINGFIELD VILLAS HALT

OPENED: 1st June 1904 (on the Plymouth – Saltash – Truro GWR line originally opened through this site in 1859).
CLOSED: June 1921.

This small halt, on the GWR main line between Plymouth North Road and Devonport Albert Road, opened with the commencement of steam rail motors using the route between Plympton and Saltash. Comprising two platforms between Wingfield Road to the north and Stuart Road to the south, access was via steps from the road overbridge west of the halt, now Wingfield Way. The name 'Wingfield Villas' derived from a set of large houses on Wingfield Road north west of the halt. Closure came after only 17 years in June 1921. There is now no trace of the old halt and no known photo.

WOODY BAY

OPENED: 16th May 1898 (with the opening of the Lynton & Barnstaple Railway).
CLOSED: Passengers and Goods – 30th September 1935.

Opening as Wooda Bay, but renamed Woody Bay in 1901, the station, on a passing loop of the narrow gauge (1 ft 11½ inches) Lynton & Barnstaple Railway (L&BR), was sited at about 980 ft above sea level. This was close to the summit of the line and

Woody Bay. The station master and three passengers are on the platform in this view east in about 1900. The building, described as being of a 'Nuremberg' design, incorporated the station facilities and accommodation for the station master. It is now the headquarters of the Lynton & Barnstaple Railway Association.

Woody Bay became the highest station on the Southern Railway when it took over the line in the 1920s. The main purpose of the station, sited at Martinhoe Cross, was to support and encourage residential and tourist development around Woody Bay about a mile and a half to the north. An entrepreneur constructed a pier and laid the foundations for some buildings but the scheme failed to develop. Indeed the pier was later swept away in a storm. At one stage the scheme even envisaged a branch line from the L&BR to the coast.

Two low platforms on a passing loop served passengers; that on the down side towards Lynton had no shelter. On the up platform, the chalet type building in what was called a 'Nuremberg' design, was similar to, but smaller than, those at Blackmoor and Lynton, other stations on the L&BR. The building incorporated both the station facilities and accommodation for the station master. As at Lynton and Blackmoor, this accommodation comprised two bedrooms on the first floor with the living room (parlour) and kitchen on the ground. In this case the accommodation also included a scullery. The ground floor also included the station booking hall and office but, unlike Lynton and Blackmoor, no refreshment room. The ladies' toilets were in the main part of the building but the gent's toilets were in a low annex at the west end of the building. As with Blackmoor no significant changes to the building were made during its life. In 1928 2,501 passenger tickets were issued at Woody Bay and 6,497 collected. By 1934 the numbers had fallen to

1,790 and 3,784. Until 1934 down trains stopped for a while at Woody Bay for tickets to be collected, Lynton being an open station. In about 1905 Princess Christian and Princess Victoria came to Woody Bay station during the course of a tour of north Devon beauty spots. To the north-east of the station a large hotel was constructed in solitary isolation. Initially named Station Hotel, it later became the Moorland Hotel and was finally converted into holiday flats.

A short siding behind the west end of the up platform served a small goods yard. A cattle market to the south west of the station generated some traffic in the yard. A small signal box to the west of the main building controlled the passing loop and the goods yard siding. The station closed to passengers and goods at the end of September 1935. At first derelict, the station was sold at auction for £425 in 1938 and converted into a private house. In the late 1990s it was purchased by the Lynton & Barnstaple Railway Association which had been formed in 1995 to reopen sections of the line. The building, now the headquarters of the Association, was officially reopened in May 2003, the 105th anniversary of the line's official opening. By 2005 a half mile of track had been laid west of the station towards Parracombe. On 27th May 2006 the first public train ran on a mile length of line to a new terminus at Killington Lane. The gauge of the revived railway is 2 ft 6 inches. When visiting in early May 2007 the author and his wife were two of only three passengers on the train to Killington Lane and return.

WRAFTON

OPENED: 20th July 1874 (with the opening of the Barnstaple & Ilfracombe Railway).
CLOSED: Passengers – 5th October 1970.
Goods – 7th September 1964.

At the opening of the Ilfracombe line in July 1874, Wrafton was a one platform station on the single track. There was no passing loop but one siding was provided. With the doubling of the track in 1890 a second platform was added. The main station building at the west end of the up (towards Barnstaple) platform incorporated two storey station master's accommodation and a single storey section to the east. Within the building were the booking and waiting facilities and the ladies' toilets. The gent's toilets were in an annex at the east end of the

Wrafton. Looking north-west in 1963 at the main building that incorporated accommodation for the station master in the two storey section. On the down platform (left) is a wooden shelter with the signal box behind, adjacent to the level crossing gates.

building; it was covered by a glass and wood apex roof. Passengers on the down platform were provided with a wooden shelter with a small canopy.

The station was originally built to serve the small village of Wrafton, half a mile to the north-west. Later however, it became important for personnel at the Chivenor RAF Station to the south-east. This role was particularly relevant during the Second World War. In 1928 4,080 passenger tickets were issued at Wrafton and 5,090 collected; in 1936 the figures were 1,353 and 1,380.

Goods facilities were limited at Wrafton. With the doubling of the track two sidings were provided both behind the down platform, access being from the east. For some years one siding was used during the summer season by two six berth camping coaches. In 1955 the rental per week was £5.1s.0d in the low season and £9.in the high. The toilet facilities were in the station building on the other side of the line! The other siding was used on occasions by the RAF. Both sidings were taken out of use from 15th February 1965.

Wrafton signal box stood at the west end of the down platform adjacent to a level crossing carrying a minor road. A wheel in the box controlled the crossing gates. The box was reduced to a ground frame from the 17th December 1967 and was damaged by fire soon after the Ilfracombe line closed in 1970. The gate wheel had been transferred to Tisbury in Wiltshire.

Goods facilities at Wrafton ceased in September 1964 but passenger services continued until

withdrawal of services on the line in October 1970. Much of the station survives today, the former station building being used as a house. A small porch has been added at the front and the former gent's toilet now has a flat roof. The track bed between the platforms has been filled in to form a lawn. The station name board and a signal post remain in place. The track bed from Barnstaple to Braunton through Wrafton has been converted to a cycleway, though it skirts south around the station site.

WRANGATON

OPENED: 5th May 1848 (with the opening of the Totnes – Plymouth (Laira Green) section of the South Devon Railway).

CLOSED: Passengers – 2nd March 1959.
Goods – 9th September 1963.

Located a half mile south east of the small village of Wrangaton, the station opened with the commencement of services in May 1848 on the Totnes to Plymouth (Laira Green) section of the South Devon Railway. Records indicate that, although it opened as Wrangaton, it was re-named in May 1849 as Kingsbridge Road, reflecting its role as the rail head for the south Devon town, which did not join the Devon rail network until 1893. In response to the opening of the Kingsbridge branch, the name Wrangaton was re-introduced from 1st July 1895.

The station's siting in a cutting resulted in a split site. Passengers on the up and down platforms were served by small waiting shelters, each with a short chimney and small canopy. The down (towards

Wrangaton. A view north-east in 1958 of the two platforms with waiting shelters sited in a cutting. The main building stands on the down (towards Plymouth) side on top of the cutting (right) behind the two tall trees.

Yarde Halt. Looking west in 1962 at the single platform on the down (towards Halwill) side of the line. Unusually the small concrete shelter is sited off the east end of the platform.

Plymouth) side principal building, which incorporated the main offices, stood on top of the cutting above the platforms, a canopy giving shelter on the line side. A footbridge led from the building across the two tracks with steps linking to the two platforms. Four staff were based at the station in the 1930s. In 1903 14,699 passenger tickets were issued, comparable figures for 1913, 1923 and 1933 were 11,634, 8,592 and 5,175.

On the down side, a little way beyond the station towards Plymouth, was a small goods yard with a two ton capacity crane but no shed. A 31 lever signal box, also on the down side, between the station and the yard, closed on 16th January 1966 but was not demolished until 1994. A water tank stood on the up side at the Brent end.

To the north of the station was the associated Kingsbridge Road Hotel and, to the west, a row of terraced houses, Station Cottages. Wrangaton closed to passengers in March 1959 but goods facilities continued until September 1963. Today there is no line side trace of the station.

YARDE HALT

OPENED: 19th July 1926 (on the Torrington – Halwill Junction line originally opened through this site in 1925).
CLOSED: 1st March 1965.

When the North Devon & Cornwall Junction Light Railway opened between Torrington and Halwill, the small community of East Yarde was not provided with a halt. There was only an ungated level crossing carrying the road south from Torrington to Peters Marland. The absence of a halt was surprising as a terrace of cottages built by the Marland Clay Company was sited close to the crossing on the up side. When the halt was opened, almost exactly a year after services started on the line, about twenty men used the trains regularly travelling south to the next halt at Dunsbear, close to the clay works. Indeed records indicate that there was more regular traffic at Yarde Halt than at any other station or halt between Torrington and Halwill!

Sited on the down (north) side of the line the halt, like that at Watergate (the other halt added after the line opened), was constructed entirely of Southern Railway concrete components. The rear half of the platform was a gravel surface. Unlike at Watergate, however, a small concrete shelter was provided off the east (down) end of the platform.

After passenger services ceased in 1965 the nameboard and noticeboard were removed but the platform and shelter survived. In spring 2007 the concrete platform was still there but the shelter had gone. A car park is provided for users of the Tarka Trail which uses the former track bed, though it diverts slightly from the alignment through the halt itself. Adjacent to the car park the wooden Yarde Café provides refreshments for Trail users and also the former railway cottages continue in residential use.

YEALMPTON

OPENED: 17th January 1898 (with the opening of the GWR branch, Plymstock – Yealmpton).
CLOSED: Passengers and Goods 7th July 1930.
REOPENED: 3rd November 1941 (for use by Plymouth residents evacuated during the Second World War).
CLOSED: Passengers – 6th October 1947
  Goods – 29th February 1960.

Yealmpton station opened in January 1898 with the commencement of services from Plymouth Millbay on the Yealmpton branch, known in its early days as the South Hams Railway. The ceremonial opening on Saturday 15th January was marked by a lunch in the goods shed which, gaily decorated with flags, bunting and flowers, was transformed into a festive dining room. Opening for public services two days later, the line was originally intended to extend to Modbury; this never materialised but as a consequence Yealmpton was designed and built as a through station. Onward connection to Modbury was provided, from 2nd May 1904, by the first GWR bus service in the Plymouth area. This replaced

Yealmpton. A view in about 1910 of the station building and signal box on the south side of the line. Behind the building a coach stands in a siding in the goods yard.

an earlier privately run service. Bus services also linked to Bigbury on Sea.

The station track layout was simple: a single track alongside the platform together with a long parallel loop which ran some distance east of the station terminating some 70 yards short of the terminal buffers. The single platform and main building were sited on the south side of the line. The platform was constructed of earth infill behind a stone block face; stone slabs formed the platform edge. The stone building, with an apex style canopy over the platform, incorporated the usual waiting, booking and toilet facilities. The station was lit by oil. In 1913 55,798 passenger tickets were issued. Ten years later the total had fallen to 21,909. Alongside the building to the east was the 23 lever Yealmpton signal box constructed of lateral wooden planking on a brick base; this was in use until 23rd January 1931 when it was replaced by three ground frames. Beyond the box was a water crane, providing the only watering facilities along the branch from Plymstock. The crane was supplied from a large square water tank on four girder legs, sited north of the station close to the river from which water was pumped by an oil powered engine. Behind, and south west of, the station was the goods yard containing a large brick goods shed with a through track, three further goods sidings, a 30 cwt capacity hand crane and a number of cattle pens.

The Yealmpton branch was an early casualty of bus competition, passenger services being withdrawn in July 1930. The station building was made available for railway staff accommodation, extra space being created by the addition of a wooden enclosure under the canopy. Early in the Second World War it was decided to reopen the branch for use by Plymouth residents who had moved out to the area to escape the blitz. Yealmpton station reopened for workmen only on 21st July 1941 and for the general public on 3rd November 1941, trains

running to and from Plymouth Friary. With the station building no longer available for railway use, a pagoda style corrugated ticket office was erected at the western end of the platform. A small concrete building was also provided at the eastern end for use as the ladies' and gents' toilet block. Passengers ceased again in October 1947 but goods services continued for a further 13 years until the end of February 1960. In the late 1950s up to three goods trains per week were using the branch.

For some ten years the station site lay derelict until clearance in the winter of 1971/1972. Development, of what is now Riverside Walk, commenced in spring 1972. During the clearance several railway items were 'rescued' by the south-western group of the Great Western Society for the society's depot at Bodmin General. Practically all trace of the former

Yealmpton. Looking west in about 1910. A branch line train stands at the platform whilst behind the fence is a bus to Bigbury-on-Sea. The box on the platform states 'GWR Yealmpton to Plymouth'.

Yelverton. In this view north in about 1905 a class 4-4-0 enters the main up platform with a train from Launceston to Plymouth. On the down platform (left) is the main building and pagoda type shelter. To the right of the train is the five sided waiting room which serves the up platform and the Princetown branch platform (off right).

railway activity at Yealmpton has gone apart from the former right gatepost at the station entrance and the base of a GWR lamp post. On 29th February 1980, the 20th anniversary of the station's final closure, a commemorative plaque recording the former use of the site was erected at the end of Riverside Walk by the Holbeton, Yealmpton & Brixton Society. The plaque remains today.

YELVERTON

OPENED: 1st May 1885 (on the Plymouth – Tavistock GWR line originally opened through the site in 1859).

CLOSED: Passengers – 31st December 1962.
Goods – No facilities provided, service provided at Horrabridge.

When passenger services started in June 1859 on the Tavistock & South Devon Railway between Plymouth and Tavistock, no station was provided at Yelverton. At that time the village was small and an early petition by the residents for a station was rejected on the grounds that the cost of one porter would be more than the traffic could bear! More than twenty years later, on 11th August 1883, there came a significant change in circumstances with the opening of the branch line to Princetown, which joined the Tavistock line at Yelverton and trains

proceeded north as far as Horrabridge. By that time a limited number of sidings had been laid at Yelverton.

Eventually, at the beginning of May 1885, a junction station opened at Yelverton, though the suffix Junction was never used. At 500 ft above sea level, the station was at the summit of the Plymouth to Tavistock line, the village itself was a further 100 ft higher. The coming of the railway was the key to the development of Yelverton, which changed from being a rather remote settlement to an accessible and, many considered, desirable place to live.

Yelverton station had an unusual layout. On the west side were the main line up (towards Plymouth) and down platforms, the latter being staggered further north than the up. A third platform on the east side was the Princetown branch platform. The up main and branch platforms were in a V formation; the two arms pointing south and south-east respectively. A covered footbridge connected the down and up platforms, the base of the steps on the latter being near the head of the V. There were also three rail level board crossings between the main platforms for use by railway staff.

The down platform, constructed of earth and rubble infill behind a brick face, was surfaced with blue Staffordshire bricks and edged by concrete slabs with rounded shoulders. The whole platform was backed by an iron railing fence separating it from the station forecourt and access road. Midway along the platform stood the main station building incorporating booking, waiting and toilet facilities. Constructed of wood planks braced with heavy timbers under a wood frame slate roof with ridge tiles, the building had a wedge shape canopy covering half the platform width. To the south of this building stood a corrugated iron pagoda style shelter with double doors. In its latter years this was used only as a parcels office. Beside it, until 1956, was a large wooden nameboard with cast iron letters 'Yelverton – change for Dousland and Princetown'. Further south again beyond the end of the down platform was the 35 lever brick signal box; like the main building it had a timber apex roof covered with slates and topped with ridge tiles. A small chimney stack protruded from the rear roof. Wooden doors and steps were at the south end and good visibility came through wooden sliding windows along the whole of the line side and across half the ends.

The V shape combined up main and branch platforms were of similar construction as the down main but the surface in this case was paved around the central building and covered with tarmac and chippings. At the head of the V was a five sided waiting room constructed in similar materials to the down side building but in this case centred on a large chimney stack with three chimney pots. Narrow wedge shaped canopies projecting from three of the sides covered the platforms, the exception being the two southernmost sides which overlooked the northern end of a dead end siding which ran alongside the rear of the branch platform. On this siding was a 23 ft 6 inch turntable. The branch platform was shortened in May 1933, this allowed an easing of the branch curve. A nameboard on this platform stated 'Yelverton – change for Tavistock, Launceston and Plymouth'.

Passenger figures were high at Yelverton and at times it was the second busiest station of the entire line to Tavistock and Launceston. At the turn of the 19th/20th centuries the station had its own bookstall and the station forecourt was a scene of great activity. In 1903 42,549 passenger tickets were issued; the figure rose to 48,018 in 1913 but fell to 39,917 in 1923 and 30,418 in 1933. During the Second World War many Plymouth residents moved out to the Yelverton area either permanently or temporarily, creating much business for the railway. The clear up in the city after the blitz included the conveyance of much rubble to a site south of Yelverton station.

Services on the Princetown branch ceased in March 1956. Six years later, at the end of 1962, the station closed with the withdrawal of passenger services on the Tavistock and Launceston line. All buildings were demolished in 1964 and the former station site became part of a private nature reserve.

Yelverton. No 4402 is at the Princetown branch platform in about 1939. The five sided waiting room also serves the up main line. Note the splendid covered footbridge.

YEOFORD

OPENED: July 1857 (on the Crediton – Barnstaple
  line originally opened through this site in 1854).
CLOSED: Passengers – remains open as a request stop
  on the Exeter – Barnstaple line.
  Goods – 10th February 1964.

Sited about a half mile north of the village of Yeoford, the station opened in mid 1857. Historic records indicate that, although the station was due to open on 8th June, there may have been some delay until the beginning of July. Initially only a stop on the Barnstaple line, Yeoford became a junction station from 1865 when the first section of the line to Okehampton and Plymouth (Devonport) opened west from Coleford Junction, north of Yeoford.

From 1865 the station had three platform faces; the up (towards Crediton) side had a single face platform and the down side was an island platform, the outer face of which operated as a bay for trains on the Okehampton line. All the station buildings were basically constructed of wood; those on the up platform incorporated the station master's office, booking office, waiting room, toilets and other facilities. A water column stood at the east end of the platform supplied by a nearby water tower that drew water from the River Troney. The buildings on the down island included waiting facilities and a refreshment room, the last supplying passengers changing trains between the Barnstaple and Okehampton lines. An open iron footbridge connected the two platforms at the west end; this was a later addition as, in the early days, inter-platform connection was via steps and the road bridge at the west end of the platforms. Close to the north end of this bridge was the Railway Hotel, opposite which a cattle auction market generated considerable business for the station. Access to the north side of the station was from this road; on this

Yeoford. Looking south-east from the footbridge in 1965. In the centre is the main station building on the up (towards Crediton) platform.

access was the station master's house behind the west end of the up platform. Rail level board crossings at each end also provided for inter-platform movements. In 1928 12,807 passenger tickets were issued at Yeoford; there was a marked fall to 7,842 in 1936. Comparable figures for tickets collected were 13,262 and 8,640. A census taken on 7th May 1963 indicated 46 passengers joining or leaving trains. In a winter week of 1976 39 passengers used the station, the equivalent figure for a summer week in 1977 was 63.

Yeoford goods yard was on the down side east of the station. Incorporating a cattle loading dock, a five ton crane and sidings with a long loop, it was the focus for transfer of goods between the Okehampton and Barnstaple lines. The number of sidings increased from three to six during the Second World War. The yard closed in February 1964. On the up side there was a siding running behind the east end of the platform.

Yeoford had two signal boxes, West and East. The main West box (35 levers), to the west of the road bridge on the down side, was a tall structure of wood on a high stone base, the height being required to ensure visibility over the bridge. The East box stood to the east of the station on the up side. Both boxes closed on 18th August 1968.

Regular passenger services ceased on the Okehampton line on 5th June 1972; the weekend services introduced in recent years on the Okehampton line do not call at Yeoford, which now only functions as a request stop on the Barnstaple line, trains calling at the former up platform. All the original buildings have gone, a small metal shelter serves passengers on the up side. The down island platform remains unused and derelict. The former station master's house survives in residential use.

YEO MILL HALT

OPENED: 27th June 1932 (on the Taunton – Wiveliscombe – Barnstaple line originally opened through this site in 1873).
CLOSED: 3rd October 1966.

On a single track section of the Taunton to Barnstaple line, this halt was a late addition to passenger facilities when opened in June 1932. The short wooden platform and wooden shelter stood on the up (towards Taunton) side of the track. A wood fence ran along the back of the platform. Serving only a few nearby dwellings, Yeo Mill is described by the author of Great Western Country Stations as a 'nice example of a timber halt with a timber shelter'. There is no record of passenger numbers, figures were included with those of East Anstey, the next station 1½ miles to the east. The halt closed with the withdrawal of passenger services on the line in October 1966 and was subsequently demolished.

Yeo Mill Halt. Looking east at the wooden platform and shelter in about 1960.

FURTHER READING

Anthony G.H., *Tavistock, Launceston & Princetown Railway*, Oakwood Press, 1971

Barber C., *Devon's Railways of Yesteryear*, Obelisk Publications, 2001
Railways on and around Dartmoor, Obelisk Publications, 1997

Bastin C.H., *Great Western Railway Stations of Devon*, CHB Publications, 1990
Southern and Independent Railway Stations of Devon, CHB Publishing, 1993
The Turnchapel and Yealmpton Branch Lines, C.H.Bastin Publishing, 1989

Brown G.A., Prideaux J.D.C. and Radcliff H.G., *Lynton & Barnstaple Railway*, Oakwood Press

Butt R.V.J., *Directory of Railway Stations*, Patrick Stephens, 1995

Catchpole L.T., *Lynton & Barnstaple Railway 1895-1935*, Oakwood Press, 8th Edition, 2005

Cheesman A.J., *The Plymouth, Devonport and South Western Junction Railway*, Oakwood Press, 1967

Clark R.H., *An Historical Survey of Selected Great Western Railway Stations, Layouts and Illustrations*, Oxford Publishing Co. Volume 1 1976, Volume 2 1979, Volume 3 1981

Clinker C.R., *Register of Closed Passenger Stations and Goods Depots 1830-1977*, Avon Anglia, 1978

Dale P., *North Devon's Lost Railways*, Stenlake Publishing, 2001
South Devon's Lost Railways, Stenlake Publishing, 2001

Dart M., *Devon Narrow Gauge*, Middleton Press, 2007

Fricker D., *The St Davids Station Book*, 2005

Gough T., *The Southern – West of Salisbury*, Oxford Publishing Co., 1984
The Tarka Trail Past and Present, Past and Present Publishing Ltd., 1995
The Tamar and Tavy Valleys Past and Present, Past and Present Publishing Ltd., 2001

Gower P., Gray B. and Vinjoe K., *The Lynton and Barnstaple Railway Yesterday and Today*, Oakwood Press, 1999

Gray P.W., *Paignton and Dartmouth Steam Railway Past and Present*, Past and Present Publishing Ltd, 1991.

Harris H., *Devon's Railways*, Bossiney Books, 2001.

Hawkins M., *LSWR West Country Lines, Then and Now*, David and Charles, 1993

Jenkins S.C., *Bideford, Westward Ho! and Appledore Railway*, Oakwood Press, 1993
The Launceston Branch, Oakwood Press, 1997

Jenkins S.C., and Pomroy L.S., *The Moretonhampstead and South Devon Railway*, Oakwood Press, 1989

Kidner R.W., *Southern Railway Halts*, Oakwood Press, 1985

Kingdom A.R., *Tavistock North and South*, ARK Publications (Railways), 2006
The Bombing of Newton Abbot Station, ARK Publications (Railways), 2004
The Plymouth, Tavistock and Launceston Railway, ARK Publications (Railways), 2001
The Plymouth to Turnchapel Railway, ARK Publications (Railways), 1996
The Plymouth to Yealmpton Railway (The South Hams Light Railway), ARK Publications (Railways), 1998
The Totnes to Ashburton Railway, ARK Publications (Railways), 1995
The Turnchapel Branch, Oxford Publishing Co., 1982
The Yealmpton Branch, Oxford Publishing Co., 1974
The Yelverton to Princetown Railway, Forest Publications (in association with ARK Publications), 1991

Kingdom A.R. and Lang M., *The Newton Abbot and Moretonhampstead Railway*, ARK Publications (Railways), 2004

Leigh C., *GWR Country Stations*, Ian Allan, Volume 1 1981/1985, Volume 2 1984.

Madge R., *Railways around Exmoor*, the Exmoor Press, 1975

Maggs C.G., *Branch Lines of Devon: Exeter and South, Central and East Devon*, Alan Sutton, 1995
Branch Lines of Devon: Plymouth, North and West Devon, Alan Sutton, 1995
Rail Centres – Exeter, Ian Allan 1985 and Booklaw Publications 2004
Railways to Exmouth, Oakwood Press, 1980
The Barnstaple and Ilfracombe Railway, Oakwood Press, 1978 and 1988
The Culm Valley Light Railway, Oakwood Press, 2006
The Exeter and Exmouth Railway, Oakwood Press, 1997

The Seaton, Sidmouth and Lyme Regis Branches, Oakwood Press, 1979
The Sidmouth and Budleigh Salterton Branches, Oakwood Press, 1996
The Taunton and Barnstaple Railway, Oakwood Press, 1980

Messenger M., *The Culm Valley Light Railway*, Twelvehead Press, 1993

Mitchell D., *British Railways Past and Present*, Past and Present Publishing
Volume 8, Devon 1991/1994
Volume 52 East Devon, 2005
Volume 53, North and West Devon, 2006

Mitchell V. and Smith K., Middleton Press.
Branch Line to Ashburton, 1997
Branch Line to Bude, 1994
Branch Line to Exmouth, 1992
Branch Line to Ilfracombe, 1993
Branch Line to Kingswear, 1998
Branch Lines to Launceston and Princetown, 1998
Branch Line to Lyme Regis, 1987
Branch Line to Lynton 1992
Branch Line to Moretonhampstead, 1998
Branch Line to Padstow, 1995
Branch Lines around Plymouth, 1997
Branch Lines to Seaton and Sidmouth, 1991
Branch Lines around Tiverton, 2001
Branch Lines to Torrington, 1994
Exeter to Barnstaple, 1993
Exeter to Newton Abbot, 2000
Exeter to Tavistock, 1996
Newton Abbot to Plymouth, 2001
Plymouth to St Austell 2001
Taunton to Barnstaple, 1995
Taunton to Exeter, 2002
Tavistock to Plymouth, 1996
Yeovil to Exeter, 1991

Nicholls J., *The Ilfracombe Line*, Irwell Press, 1998
The North Devon Line, Oxford Publishing Co., 1992
Lines to Torrington, Oxford Publishing Co., 1984

Owen J., *Exe Valley Railway*, Kingfisher 1985
The Moretonhampstead Branch, Waterfront (Kingfisher), 2000

Phillips D. and Pryer G., *Salisbury to Exeter Line*, Oxford Publishing Co., 1997

Phillips D., *Salisbury to Exeter Line - The Branch Lines*, Oxford Publishing Co., 2000

Pomroy L.W., *The Teign Valley Line*, Oxford Publishing Co., 1984

Potts C.R., *The Brixham Branch*, Oakwood Press, 1986
An Historical Survey of Selected Great Western Railway Stations, Layouts and Illustrations, Oxford Publishing Co, Volume 4, 1985
The Newton Abbot to Kingswear Railway 1844-1988, Oakwood Press.

Pryer G. and Bowring G., *An Historical Survey of Selected Southern Stations, Track Layouts and Illustrations*, Volume 1, Oxford Publishing Co., 1980

Quick M.E., *Railway Passenger Stations in England, Scotland and Wales*, RCMS 2nd Edition 2003, Supplement 2005

Robertson K., *Devon and Cornwall Railways in Old Photographs*, Alan Sutton, 1989
Great Western Halts, Volume 1, Irwell Press, 1990., Volume 2, KRB Publications, 2002
Odd Corners of the GWR, Sutton, 1999

Roche T.W.E., *The Withered Arm*, Forge Books, 1977

Sellman R.R., *Illustrations of Devon's History*, Methuen, 1962

Shepherd, E.R., *Branch Line Memories*, ARK Publications (Railways), 2005

Smith M., *The Railways of Devon*, Ian Allan, 1993
Illustrated History of Exmoor's Railways, Irwell Press, 2006

Stuckey D., *Bideford, Westward Ho! and Appledore Railway*, West Country Publications 2nd Edition, 1965

Swift A., *Devon Railway Stations (GWR) on Old Picture Postcards*, Reflections of a By-gone Age, 2001
Devon Railway Stations (SR) on Old Picture Postcards, Reflections of a By-gone Age, 2001

Thomas D. St. J., *Regional History of the Railways of Great Britain*, Volume 1, the West Country, David and Charles, 1981

Thompson V., *Back along the Lines - North Devon's Railways*, Badger Books, 1983

Vaughan A., *Great Western Architecture: A Pictorial Record*, Oxford Publishing Co., 1977

Waters L., *Great Western Railway - Then and Now*, Ian Allan, 1994

Whitmarsh C.F.D. and Stuckey D., *North Devon and Cornwall Junction Light Railway*, Forge Books, 1980

Williams K. and Reymolds D., *The Kingsbridge Branch*, Oxford Publishing Co., 1977

Wroe D., *The Bude Branch*, Kingfisher, 1988

ACKNOWLEDGEMENTS

The author is very grateful for the permission to use photographs from the following collections:

Lens of Sutton (inc. photographs taken by J.L. Smith, the owner of Lens of Sutton); pages 4, 9, 13 (top and bottom), 14, 17 (right), 19, 21 (left and right), 23 (top), 25 (top), 26, 29, 31, 34 (bottom), 35 (top and bottom), 36, 37, 38 (top and middle), 39, 42, 44 (bottom), 46, 47, 49, 52 (top), 54, 57, 59 (top and bottom), 60, 61, 62 (top), 66 (top and middle), 67, 68, 69 (bottom), 70 (left and right), 71 (bottom), 72, 73, 76, 78, 80 (top), 84, 85, 88 (top and bottom), 89, 91 (top and middle), 93 (middle), 95, 96, 97 (bottom), 99, 100 (bottom), 101, 103, 106, 107, 110 (top), 111, 112 (top), 114 (right), 115, 117 (bottom), 118, 119 (top and middle), 120, 121, 123 (left), 124, 127 (top and bottom), 131 (top), 132, 133, 138 (left), 139 (top and middle), 140, 142, 143 (middle), 144, 149 (top), 151, 155, 156, 157, 159 (top), 160, 161 (bottom), 162, 165, 166, 171 (top), 172, 173 (middle), 174, 175, 176 (top), 177, 178 (left and right), 179, 181, 182, 183 (middle), 187, 188, 189, 190, 192, 196 (top and bottom), 201, 202, 206, 209, 210, 212 (top and bottom), 214, 217 (top and bottom), 218, 220 (bottom).

Stations U.K.; pages 2, 3, 12 (bottom), 16, 17 (left), 18 (top), 20, 23 (middle), 25 (bottom), 28, 30, 33, 34 (top), 41 (top), 43, 45, 51, 52 (bottom), 55 (top right), 56, 58, 62 (bottom), 63, 64, 65, 79 (top and middle), 80 (bottom), 81, 82, 83, 87, 97 (top), 98 (top), 102, 109, 112 (bottom), 113 (bottom), 116 (top), 126, 128, 129, 130, 134, 135 (top and bottom), 137 (bottom), 138 (right), 145, 163 (top and middle), 164, 167, 169 (bottom), 173 (top), 176 (bottom), 180, 185, 186, 191, 195, 197, 199, 200, 203 (bottom), 205, 207, 208 (left and right), 211, 213, 215 (top and bottom), 216, 219, 220 (top).

Colin Caddy; pages 44 (top), 48, 71 (top), 92, 110 (middle), 146, 171 (middle), 198.

Norman Simmons; pages 15, 41 (bottom), 204

R.K. Blencowe; pages 108, 123 (right), 125 (top).

E.T. Gill (via R.K. Blencowe); page 153.

J.Moss (via Roger Carpenter); page 18 (bottom).

Colin Maggs Collection; page 24.

Eric R.Shepherd; pages 53, 114 (left), 122 (top).

Hugh Davies; page 137 (top).

David Lawrence; page 154.

The remaining photographs were taken by the author or are from his collection where the copyright owner is unknown or unclear. The author also expresses his appreciation to Brian Cobley who provided much assistance in site visits to a number of locations in south and east Devon.